Mastering Multicamera Techniques

From Preproduction to Editing and Deliverables

Mitch Jacobson

ELSEVIER

AMSTERDAM • BOSTON • HEIDELBERG • LONDON • NEW YORK • OXFORD
PARIS • SAN DIEGO • SAN FRANCISCO • SINGAPORE • SYDNEY • TOKYO
Focal Press is an imprint of Elsevier

Focal Press

Focal Press is an imprint of Elsevier
30 Corporate Drive, Suite 400, Burlington, MA 01803, USA
The Boulevard, Langford Lane, Kidlington, Oxford, OX5 1GB, UK

First edition 2010

Library of Congress Cataloging-in-Publication Data
Jacobson, Mitch.
    Mastering multicamera techniques : from preproduction to editing and deliverables / Mitch Jacobson.
       p. cm.
    Includes bibliographical references and index.
    ISBN 978-0-240-81176-5 (pbk. : alk. paper)
    1. Cinematography—Technique. 2. Video production. 3. Motion pictures—Editing.   I. Title.
    TR850.J32 2010
    778.5'3—dc22   2010005532

British Library Cataloguing-in-Publication Data
A catalogue record for this book is available from the British Library.

ISBN: 978-0-240-81176-5

For information on all Focal Press publications
visit our website at www.elsevierdirect.com

Typeset by MPS Limited, a Macmillan Company, Chennai, India
www.macmillansolutions.com

Printed in China

10 11 12 13 14   5 4 3 2 1

Dedications

To my wife

Jennifer, for her unconditional love, boundless patience, and incredible inspiration. You are my amazing muse.

To my parents

Bennett and Judith, who taught me to work smart and dream big.

To my grandparents

George and Eve Jacobson and Bernard and Helen Greenwald, for their love, encouragement, and early gifts of a guitar and an 8-mm movie camera, which sparked my lifelong passion for music, film, and technology.

To my professional mentors

Guy Bickel, who introduced me to the entertainment production industry as a concert stagehand working on all the big shows.

Ken Cheek and Mike McKown, for two decades of network TV work on live sports broadcasts and for nurturing my growth from production assistant to producer/director.

Mark Haefeli, who gave me the multicamera editing projects of a lifetime: cutting feature-length concert films for the world's greatest musical artists.

Without all of you, this book would not be possible.

CONTENTS

Acknowledgments

Thanks to Future Media Concepts and the Editor's Retreat for providing the forum for my first multicamera presentation and the industry networking that led to this publication: Ben Kozuch, Iva Radivojevic, Joel Bell, and Jeff Greenberg.

Multi-thanks to all the companies who have contributed with their generous support:

Adobe
AJA
All Mobile Video
American Cinema Editors (ACE)
Apple
Avid Technology
Bella Corporation
Carnegie Hall

CBS
Columbia University Graduate School of Journalism
Comedy Central
DuArt Film and Video
Gray Matter Entertainment
Handmade Video, Inc.
Journey

Leonard Bernstein Foundation
MAXX Digital
Motion Picture Editors Guild 700 NYC (MPEG)
San Francisco Symphony
Wizard Entertainment
WNET
Worldwide Pants

Special thanks to my family, friends, and associates who have supported this book and kept me passionate for love and life.

Steve Albany
Ron Amborn
Dan Barnett
John Baruck
Steve Bayes
Dave Bigelow
Lisa Bond
Carmen Borgia
Gary Bradley
Lisa Cohen
Cara Cosentino
Charles Darby
Joe DeAngelus
Anita Engelman
Jerry Foley
Ann Goldenberg
Evan Haiman
Gary Halvorson
David Horn
Maysie Hoy

Steve Hullfish
Patrick Inhofer
Roger and Lisa Jacobson
Madison and Hannah Jacobson
Keith Kieser
Justin Krohn
Marc Laub
Leslie Levin
Janna Levin
Jenni McCormick
Peter Moll
Paul Moore
Tom Ohanian
Dave Olive
Mitch Owgang
Amy Peterson
Tikeshia Pierre
Jermaine Pinnock
Carrie Puckoff

Mark Raudonis
Barry and Nancy Richman
Sean Riordan
Ranfi Rivera
Alan Rosenfeld
Bob Russo
Maurice Schechter
Ted Schiliwitz
Michael Speranza
Jon Thorn
Michael Tilson Thomas
Eli Tishberg
Richard Townhill
Tom Vecchio
John Walker
Anna Weber
John West
Laura Young
My dog and late-night editing buddy, Maizie Mac

In Memory of Michael Vitti, artist, educator and founder of The Moving Pictures Collective of NYC.

Category-5 Publishing Credits

Written by
Mitch Jacobson

Contributing Writers
Oliver Peters, Steve Gibby, Josh Holbreich, Peter Gray, Scott Simmons

Technical Editors
Oliver Peters, Gary Adcock, Bob Zelin, Matt Foglia, CAS, Mark Schubin, Maurice Schechter, Michael Rubin and Tom Ohanian

Copy Editor
Lisa Halliday

Research, Rights, and Clearances
Lilly Morcos

Research Assistant
Andrea Mustaine

Typing Services
After Hours Typing Service
Barbara Thorton

Photography
All photographs courtesy Mitch Jacobson unless otherwise credited and used with permission from the rightful owners.

Cover
Designed by Mitch Jacobson and Patrick Shannon
Journey photographs courtesy Journey, Dan Barnett and Wizard Entertainment. Director: Eli Tishberg.
Photography by Mark Forman, www.screeningroom.com
Keyboard courtesy Bella Corporation

Graphics Production
A7.net

DVD and Authoring
Category-5 Studios at DuArt Film & Video, New York City

Paul McCartney footage courtesy MPL Tours, Inc.
Directed by Mark Haefeli, MHP3
Executive producer: Sir Paul McCartney
For MPL Publishing: Krisstina Hawks

Elton John footage courtesy HST Management, Ltd.
Directed by Peter Moll, Gray Matter Entertainment, Inc.
For Elton John: Keith Bradley, Johnny Barbus, Jon Howard, George Kangis, Clive Banks, and Sanctuary Group, plc.
Music Publishing courtesy Universal Music Publishing Group, Brian Lambert, Sarah Maniquis, Jim Doyle, Responsive Music

XIV CATEGORY-5 PUBLISHING CREDITS

Additional DVD Items

AJA: Timecode Calculator
SequenceLiner: Andreas Kiel, Spherico
Apple: ProRes Decoder
Essentials of Multi-Cam Editing, Steve Martin, Ripple Training
QTChange: Bouke Váhl, VideoToolshed

FOREWORD

While we may take it for granted, something truly magical happens when we open our eyes and view the world. Although we see things in three dimensions, we're limited in that our vision only affords us one angle at a time. And that's why it's always thrilling to see a live action event covered from multiple angles and, by extension, multiple points of view. If you were suddenly faced with the challenge of deciding where to place multiple cameras to cover a live event—be it sports, a musical, a music concert, a live television recording before an audience—what would you do? Where would you put those cameras? What would they focus on? Would you need to switch the cameras live or would everything be recorded for later editing? How would you ensure that you would be able to synchronize all the footage so that everything would be prepared for later postproduction? And, to be sure, the questions go on and on. There are many of them, and a clear, precise workflow must be established when you have any multicamera situation.

I can remember, early in my career, being faced with so many multicamera covered events where no one thought about the hapless editor who had to put the footage together. Where were my sync points? How could I establish sync? Why did they have to turn off the camera? Didn't they realize the life of agony their actions were going to put both the editor and the director through later on? And, surely, we all learn the tricks of the trade. Oh, you don't have any nice sync points? Well wait, that guy over there—he's in all three camera angles. Look, he's just lit a cigarette. That's our sync point! And as absurd as that example sounds, anyone who has done this for a living knows it's completely true!

What you are about to read is a comprehensive and exhaustive explanation of everything you need to consider and know about approaching multicamera-based projects. *Mastering Multicamera Techniques* has been written by a proven expert in the field who has over thirty years of experience and has directed and edited hundreds of multicamera productions. As an inventor of a multicamera system, I wish that this book existed earlier because so many problems could have been avoided if people had the practical and educational information that this book provides in abundance.

Enjoy this book and trust that it provides every angle on what you need to know before those multiple cameras roll and after the audience has departed.

Tom Ohanian
Academy Award® and two-time Emmy® recipient
Avid Media Composer, Film Composer,
and Multicamera systems inventor

INTRODUCTION

Multicamera production is surging. And not just situation comedies but the number of network studio shows, music, sports, feature films and special events employing multiple cameras for maximum coverage is greater than ever.

At another end of the spectrum, boutique event production companies are empowered with a pair of inexpensive digital HDSLR cameras, and teenagers are making their own podcasts and broadcasts, often with more technological savvy than people three times their age. Multicamera techniques are being used everywhere, by virtually everyone interested in the modern moving image—and it seems the trend is growing. Multicamera DVDs and and on-line programs allow everyone to direct and switch their own angles live from their TVs and cell phones! And with multicamera shooting powers come great multicamera editing responsibilites … and opportunities.

Multicamera editing is a specialty and has become a major subcategory of editing. Moreover, these days, all of the top-selling editing platforms support multicam; there is even software that will automatically sync your angles without timecode. But software is no substitute for creativity (at least not yet!), so although the technology is more accessible, the genre itself still needs true human talent.

Because the multicam production and postproduction workspaces are different from those for single-camera production, this book will explore what makes multicam unique, from its advantages to its challenges. The goal is to demystify the multicam universe, allowing anyone with a couple of cameras (or more) to learn the same methods, and perhaps even achieve the same results, as the masters of multicam.

The idea for this book originated while I was directing and editing a multicamera concert in early 2000. I decided to hire an assistant editor with multicam experience. Finding someone qualified, however, proved difficult, because there was no established training track. So I decided to train that person myself. And when I looked for a book or some other resource to supplement my efforts, I came up short. Knowing that I may need to train multiple assistants over time inspired me to take heavy notes on the processes and outline methods learned by way of troubleshooting, improvising and workarounds.

The style throughout is conversational with information rooted in multicamera television technology, history, and culture.

Everybody Has an Angle

Primarily, *Mastering Multicamera Techniques* was written by an editor, for editors. However, it also contains case studies and interviews with more than 100 other editors, producers, directors, engineers, assistants and audio and color post professionals who provide a wealth of insight to anyone seeking a global perspective on multicam techniques, from shooting to preparing deliverable masters. Throughout the book you'll find round table-like discussions with these experts in sections called The Multi-Expert Approach. Whether you're cutting your 50th episode of *Project Runway,* researching techniques for concerts and music video productions, or producing weddings and events, there's something in here for you.

What You'll Learn

This is much more than a book on editing. Because multicamera preproduction directly links the shooting process with post, we'll tie it all together with techniques, tips, tricks, and perspectives. You'll learn camera synchronization, editing sync map secrets, and multicamera math solutions plus strategies for educating others on your team and providing feedback to producers and directors. The book's narrative is meant to resemble the full trajectory of a multicam project. There are six sections, ordered as in a complete production:

1. Preproduction
2. Production
3. Timecode and Sync: calibrating and synchronizing cameras
4. Postproduction: systems, software, and preparing the project
5. Editing: styles and techniques
6. Deliverables: conforming and mastering

Following the chapters on the techniques, we'll explore Multicamera Madness! with colorful case studies, featuring fun projects like a 10-camera RED shoot for the rock band Journey and a mixed-platform 26-camera concert film with Sir Paul McCartney. There's a special feature on history and the important innovations the production team from *I Love Lucy* gave us. Plus, there is a technical report on the film processes for the Rolling Stones movie *Shine a Light* and a look at multicamera HDSLR challenges plus some of my favorite research articles—and more. Due to space limits in the book, mini versions of the case studies are printed here. Fully extended versions can be found on the companion DVD at the back of this book and on-line at www.masteringmulticam.com

Companion DVD

The companion DVD also consists of some very exciting multicamera footage from two of the greatest musical "Sirs": Elton John and Paul McCartney. Both clips are exclusive to this book and have never been released. *Band on the Run* is a "leftover" track from Paul McCartney: The Space Within US concert film that was edited by Zoran Jevromov and myself. Elton's clip is recorded live from his 2009 tour specifically for this book and as part of a technology test for Telestream's Pipeline products. I captured all the clips live on-location concurrently onto one MacPro tower with and an eSata RAID. My Final Cut Pro multicamera line cut of *Love Lies Bleeding* was edited and finished before the capturing was complete. Load them up and cut your own concert clips from more than 20 angles!

For a detailed list see the Companion DVD appendix

1 Multicamera Madness Bonus Chapters

A) Supporting The Director
B) HDSLR and Multicam
C) On-Set Editing
D) No Such Thing as a Firewire Drive
E) How and When to Use Auxiliary Timecode
F) Genlocking And Tri-Level Sync

2 Multicamera Video Clips

Paul McCartney live in concert: *Band on the Run* (2:30). 18 angles. ProRes 422 (Proxy) HD 720/23.98 including: Techno crane, dolly, rail cam, cable cam, jib and handheld camera angles.

Elton John live in concert: *Love Lies Bleeding* (1:00) 5 angles and 1 linecut. ProRes 422 (LT) NTSC 720x480 29.97

3 Video Tutorials

The Essentials of Multicamera Editing: Final Cut Pro Training video clip from RippleTraining.com. Additional video tutorial links are also provided for Avid Media Composer, Sony Vegas and Adobe Premiere Pro

4 Free Applications

AJA DataCalc; SequenceLiner; QT_CHANGE

5 Research Links

Weblinks for blogs, research and equipment websites (html)

The Gist

My goal is to convey a strategic understanding of multicamera production and editing, enabling you to make the most of your multicam productions. The goal is not to teach you how to use and navigate editing programs step by step. That's the domain of basic classes, software manuals, and how-to tutorials. (There are basic multicam tutorials on the companion DVD from each of the major NLE systems.) We will spend a bit of time discussing different software specs, but only enough to establish a foundation for understanding technique and workflows strategically.

My Qualifications

When I was 5 years old, two things happened to determine my fate. My grandfather George and Grandmother Eve gave me their used 8mm home movie camera for my birthday, and I went to a live studio taping of *Bozo the Clown*. I will never forget the feeling of walking into the TV studio and the excitement of the live show. I got the TV bug then, and I've been hooked ever since.

I have been a television professional for the past 30 years and have worked in every capacity of the live multicamera show from cable puller to camera operator, editor, director, and executive producer. I have been fortunate enough to work with the greatest names in the entertainment business and have learned from the best. I am a graduate of the Film Production Technology program from Valencia Community College (curriculum designed by Steven Spielberg), and programs in film producing and directing from New York University (NYU) UCLA. I am a member of the Motion Picture Editors Guild (MPEG Local 700/Hollywood), a certified Avid editor and a Certified Apple Pro in Final Cut. Starting in 1980, I worked my way through all the production departments ending up as a director/cameraman shooting ENG packages and live network sports and music programs. The past 15 years have been devoted to editing and postproducing network multicamera productions for A&E, CBS, MTV, E!, and PBS, several of which have been nominated for prime-time Emmy™ Awards.

Some of my multicam credits include director for Barenaked Ladies, Sugar Ray, and Cheap Trick live in concert; as editor of feature length concert films and documentaries featuring artists such as the Rolling Stones, Aerosmith, Paul McCartney, U2, Keith Urban and Luciano Pavarotti; and as editor for network talk shows such as the *Montel Williams Show,* the *Rachael Ray Show,* and *Isaac Mizrahi.*

Currently, I am the owner of Category-5 Entertainment, Inc. in New York City, a boutique production company that specializes in multicamera productions, editing and color correction for network television, music and entertainment industry projects.

In between projects, I teach classes and present live workshops and seminars at conventions and trade group conferences.

I loved writing this book and hope it helps you achieve your multicamera goals. I would also love to receive your feedback. Please report any praise, errors or omissions for future revised editions to info@masteringmulticam.com. To contact me or to learn more about my work, visit www.masteringmulticam.com and subscribe to my blog: "Cutting it Close".

Enjoy!

—Mitch Jacobson

The Icons Used in this Book

 Gear Up—Recommendations for gear that makes the job easier or adds quality to the final production.

 Further Reading—Recommended books or resources that let you explore a topic in greater depth.

 To Watch—Recommend video sources that will aid in your understanding of podcasting.

 Web Link—External websites that offer additional resources or information.

 Noteworthy—Learn important "gotchas" or pitfalls that can put your production at risk.

 Technical Tips—How-to's or important advice on how to get the job done.

PREPRODUCTION

PREPRODUCTION

Whether you are a producer, director or editor working on a multicamera project, the first place to start is in preproduction.

The edit process starts in preproduction. We'll talk an editor through what I'm planning to do, what angles I've got, and how many nights I'm shooting.

Hamish Hamilton, director*

Preproduction is the foundation of a multicam shoot—it's when many decisions that will directly affect postproduction editing are made. Furthermore, knowledge is power: the more a multicam editor knows about each production phase, the more influence that editor will have when talking to producers and directors about the edit itself. Additionally, there are more opportunities for editors on the set than ever before—not only as a preproduction consultant but as an editor in the field, in the truck, and on the go—but only if you have a measurable knowledge base, an appreciation for your colleagues' roles, and a dedication to organized planning. Know what you want and plan for it. This is the preproduction mantra.

Preproduction planning is critical to a shoot's successful edit. A poorly planned shoot can wreak havoc on the editing phase, especially when multiple cameras are involved. You can waste hours hand-syncing shots, trying to make up for a missing time-code, sorting through cameras that don't roll concurrently, and so on. Multicam shoots are by nature more complex, and not just because there are more tapes in post! Every aspect of a multi-cam shoot is multiplied: disks, drive space, crew, gear—and it all needs to be organized at the outset. Savvy directors will consult their editors *ahead* of time, and ask technical questions about how to use timecode, the best method for tape numbering, which way to set up a project, and what types of codecs should be used in shooting or in formatting edits and deliverables. Smart direc-tors will also ask about high-definition video formats, drive space requirements, and backup solutions. Why? Because they know

* Hamish Hamilton, director, Done and Dusted. Credits: Victoria's Secret Fashion Show, Academy Awards, Super Bowl Halftime Show and many concert films for great artists like Madonna and U2.

Doi: 10.1016/B978-0-240-81176-5.00001-0

that a well-planned shoot will save precious time and probably also money in postproduction. In other words, preproduction can make the difference between a project that goes smoothly and the gig from hell.

Organization

To prepare for multicam editing, you must have an understanding of the actual needs of a multicam shoot. As in any type of production, organization is key, but for multicam it is paramount—and not just for big jobs. All multicam jobs benefit from organization.

Organization is the key to creativity.

Mark Raudonis

Mark Raudonis is the vice president of postproduction at Bunim-Murray Productions, which effectively invented reality TV in the early 1990s when it came out with *The Real World* for MTV. Today, Bunim-Murray Productions, generates almost 4,000 hours of videotape per show each season. Some scenes may use up to 12 or more cameras, so without the proper preparation, a shoot can easily dissolve into chaos. And it's not just the shoot itself that can fall apart. Raudonis says, "The entire post process is at risk." If you're wasting time searching for footage," Raudonis says, "you're not being creative. Less time searching equals more time editing. More editing means being able to try several different options in a given time period. This is why organization is the key to creativity."

Tim Leavitt is an assistant editor on *The Apprentice*:

We had over 3,000 takes, so obviously you've got to keep that super organized to be able to find anything at any time, exactly when you or the editor needs it. So we create separate projects for each episode, and we give the editors the media they need for that episode.

The power of an organized workflow is a value that successful producers of all genres share. Meredith Lerner is a multiple Emmy Award–winning producer who has worked on productions ranging from the Olympics and *The Rachael Ray Show* to the HGTV show *Destination Design*. To make the entire process a smooth one, Meredith Lerner says it's vital to have a clear plan before you go on location or even pick up a camera:

So many things come up in the field, and when you're not prepared it can completely put you behind schedule. It can really cause problems once you're back in the edit room with your footage and you realize there aren't shots that you need. When you're organized, then everyone on the crew will know what you need to achieve.

Figure 1.1a Multiple ENG cameras used for U2 Concert EPK. (Courtesy Mark Haefeli Productions/www.mhp3.com.)

Figure 1.1b Preproduction meeting with director Mark Haefeli. (Courtesy Mark Haefeli Productions/ www.mhp3.com.)

Chris Halasz, workflow supervisor at Livecut in Vienna (www. livecut.at), specializes in unique multicamera workflows and software solutions. Halasz says, "It's best for me to get involved at the preproduction phase." If you're an editor and you're on your game, your knowledge of the technology involved and how it's changing can help everyone avoid nasty surprises in the editing suite.

The Editor's Role in Preproduction

Some of the important preproduction elements an editor should consider to maximize the cost-effectiveness of editing

Aerosmith: You Gotta Move
Multi-Cam Notes

Tape Naming
For loading the concert performance tapes, will use the standard MHP3 naming convention with the following suffix added for the multicam shows:

Ft. Lauderdale show suffix=
FTL100A for part one tapes
and FTL100B for part 2 tapes

Orlando show suffix=
ORL200A for part 1
And ORL200B for part 2

Example=
MHP3Name_ORL200B

Clip Naming
For clips, log individual songs in their entirety. Use handles big enough to include the last few notes of the previous song and next song. Do not skip anything. If there is a "rap" between songs, treat the rap like a song, logged individually with appropriate handles.

Grouped Source Monitor

Cam 1	Cam 2	Cam 3
Cam 4	Cam 5	Cam 6
Cam 7	Cam 8	Line Cut

Figure 1.2 Tape numbering system used for Aerosmith's *You Gotta Move.*

are *type of show, equipment testing, prelabeling and numbering media,* and the *formation of a timecode plan.*

On Different Types of Shows

Concerts are different from reality shows and reality shows are different from sitcoms. A dramatic or comedic production like a sitcom is organized so you can stop, back up, and try a second, third, or fourth take. The director has blocked it all out and knows exactly where everyone needs to be, down to a specific line of dialogue and which camera will be on that actor at any given time. You're still on the high wire, but you're performing over a net. Reality shows, however, are part run-and-gun and part studio. And concerts tend to run the gamut from scripted to more fluid, in a sense directed by the music. When dealing with a live show, which can be an unpredictable circus from start to finish, you don't get a second shot. You need to be thinking about how to cover all of your bases from square one.

Preproduction for remote truck shows needs to be even more detailed. Eric Duke, owner of All Mobile Video, asks all the questions one would expect from the nation's best remote TV truck company: "How many cameras and tape machines do we need? Do we have sufficient crew?" And once he has the answers to those questions, he asks, "How do we cost out the job based on our requirements? How many days will it take? What format (high definition [HD] or standard definition [SD])? Will it require additional formats, too—ones we don't typically use, like a DVCPro HD?"

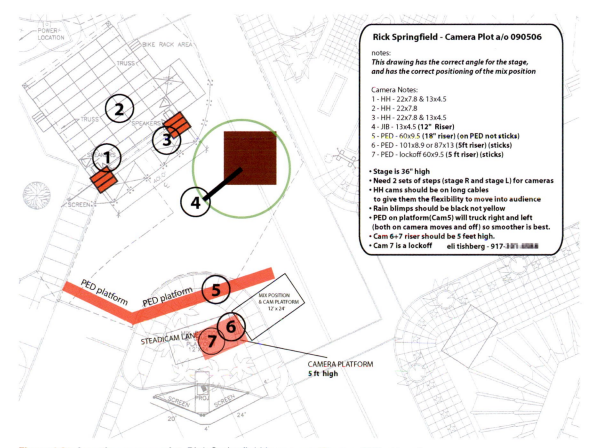

Figure 1.3a Location camera plot. Rick Springfield in concert. (Courtesy Eli Tischberg.)

JOURNEY – WIZARD PRODUCTION SCHEDULE

Saturday 3/14

Time	Event
10:3O AM	Lobby Call: Barnett, Waxman, Noles
11:00 AM	RSVP HD Crew and Cameras arrive
1:00 PM	Lobby Call: Hilmer, S Gibby, Barton, P Gibby, Lisa Goodwin, Tishberg, Mollner, Ravitz, Quinn
2:30 PM	ALL RSVP CREW (23) on site
3:00 PM	Full Crew Meeting/Full Rehearsal
4:00	Lobby Call Blair/Goodwin
6:00 PM	Gates Open
8:00 PM	Show call
8:30 PM	JOURNEY CONCERT
10:00 AM	Strike Pack
1:00 AM	Cargo Pickup

Figure 1.3b Schedule for shoot day. Journey in Manila. (Courtesy Wizard Entertainment/ Dan Barnett.)

Hamish Hamilton brings his editors on early in the preproduction phase:

Organization, preparation, and careful thought are all cornerstones and the absolute key to the success of multicamera directing, no question. It is of massive, massive, massive importance. I think it's a combination of many, many things, like surrounding yourself with people who know their craft and are organized.

Figure 1.3c Hamish Hamilton conducting a camera briefing in Washington, DC. (Courtesy www.doneanddusted.com.)

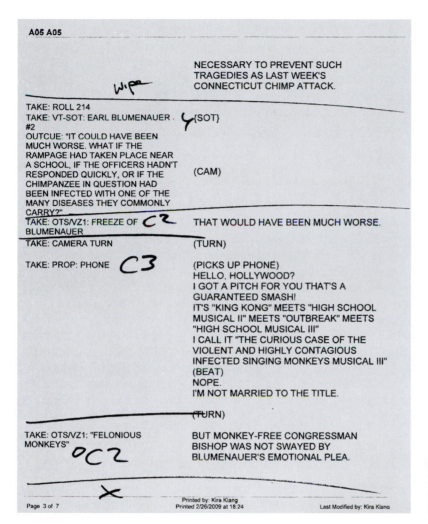

A05 A05

NECESSARY TO PREVENT SUCH
TRAGEDIES AS LAST WEEK'S
CONNECTICUT CHIMP ATTACK.

Wipe

TAKE: ROLL 214
TAKE: VT-SOT: EARL BLUMENAUER   {SOT}
#2
OUTCUE: "IT COULD HAVE BEEN
MUCH WORSE. WHAT IF THE
RAMPAGE HAD TAKEN PLACE NEAR
A SCHOOL, IF THE OFFICERS HADN'T
RESPONDED QUICKLY, OR IF THE   (CAM)
CHIMPANZEE IN QUESTION HAD
BEEN INFECTED WITH ONE OF THE
MANY DISEASES THEY COMMONLY
CARRY?"
TAKE: OTS/VZ1: FREEZE OF *C2*   THAT WOULD HAVE BEEN MUCH WORSE.
BLUMENAUER
TAKE: CAMERA TURN   (TURN)

TAKE: PROP: PHONE *C3*   (PICKS UP PHONE)
                                   HELLO, HOLLYWOOD?
                                   I GOT A PITCH FOR YOU THAT'S A
                                   GUARANTEED SMASH!
                                   IT'S "KING KONG" MEETS "HIGH SCHOOL
                                   MUSICAL II" MEETS "OUTBREAK" MEETS
                                   "HIGH SCHOOL MUSICAL III"
                                   I CALL IT "THE CURIOUS CASE OF THE
                                   VIOLENT AND HIGHLY CONTAGIOUS
                                   INFECTED SINGING MONKEYS MUSICAL III"
                                   (BEAT)
                                   NOPE.
                                   I'M NOT MARRIED TO THE TITLE.

                                   (TURN)

TAKE: OTS/VZ1: "FELONIOUS   BUT MONKEY-FREE CONGRESSMAN
MONKEYS"   BISHOP WAS NOT SWAYED BY
   OC2   BLUMENAUER'S EMOTIONAL PLEA.

   X

Page 3 of 7   Printed by: Kira Klang
                           Printed 2/26/2009 at 18:24   Last Modified by: Kira Klang

Figure 1.4 Director's script from *The Daily Show* with Jon Stewart. (Courtesy Chuck O'Neil/Comedy Central.)

Oliver Peters, an independent film and video editor-colorist, and owner of Oliver Peters Post Production Services, LLC, almost always finds himself involved in the preproduction phase. Sometimes plays the role of assistant director or coordinator on set by helping to sort through camera setups, tape numbering, and isolated camera (ISO) coordination for timecode and labeling.

Figure 1.5 Oliver Peters.

Peters says there are different ways to approach it:

It depends on the nature of the production. The industry used to be one of big trucks, big studios, and big post facilities, and that's become a lot more streamlined these days with ad hoc editing facilities and ad hoc productions out of fly packs. So I think in those kind of cases, editors are more involved in the front end, just because producers, hopefully … ask before they start shooting.

On Prelabeling and Numbering Media and Establishing a Clear Timecode Plan

With multicam shoots, keeping your media straight and getting timecode sync right in the field with a timecode generator or lock-it box (or the old-style slate method) means massive savings at the editing phase. It will save you days or even weeks of trying to get organized after the fact and even more days or weeks of trying to sync everything by hand. It makes sense to rent or buy the proper equipment for the shoot (like a lock-it box or timecode generator) to save the money in post. The same goes for planning the edit for postproduction: learn about proper storage and hard drives with the adequate speeds for multicam playback, or you'll have a frustrating editorial experience because of choppy or stagnated playback of your clips. (See chapter 8: Hardware, Bandwidth and Speed).

Fix It Before Post (for a Change)

Increasingly, multiple cameras start and stop at different times on location, and this causes many sync problems and tape capturing issues that might be avoidable. Dealing with tapeless formats makes a strong case for having postproduction meetings up front because of the massive amount of media generated.

For instance, if you are shooting an event, using time-of-day timecode with continuous recording during the event, all of your cameras will be in sync to themselves via timecode, and they will capture seamlessly. However, if you are shooting ENG-style B-Roll scenes with the camera turning on and off in a B-roll fashion, use record run timecode. Time-of-day timecode will be nightmarish for capturing B-Roll footage and syncing. Lack of preroll will confuse the decks with time-of-day timecode as the timecode breaks every time the camera stops.

But even with editors' input on the front end, decisions may be made that require a lot of fixing in post. And with tapeless cameras like RED, XDCAM, and P2, post will be even more complicated. Reconciling different time bases, like frame rates,

Tip

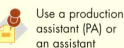 Use a production assistant (PA) or an assistant cameraperson to take timecode notes in the field. These notes will be valuable when you log and capture your media in the post process.

standards, and formats, will eat into time that could otherwise be spent improving the production's quality.

Acquisition Formats

Indeed, there are arguably too many choices for shooting formats. But the choices become clearer when you hone in on your budget, your genre, your editorial preferences, and what deliverables you'll need. If you work backward from the final product, then you'll know which brand of camera to choose and which format performs best for your workflow.

John Walker is a longtime producer at New York City's Thirteen/WNET, the flagship PBS station. With Mitch Owgang, he co-produces many nationally syndicated programs including the Emmy Award–winning *Great Performances.*

"I don't decide what formant to shoot," Mitch Owgang says. "PBS would like us to shoot every one of our shows in HD 5.1 surround sound if we can, so we try to. *Great Performances* has been shooting most of its shows in HDCAM for the last three or four years."

Let's look at the most common shooting formats being used in HD and SD multicamera productions.

Generally, for remote and studio broadcast television, videotape is used more than tapeless systems because of its proven reliability, cost-effectiveness, and archivability. ENG-style types of multicamera production such as reality are refining tapeless methods.

Most directors are shooting HD with either the Sony HDCAM and HDCAM SR with 4:4:4 color space and RGB RAW or the Panasonic DVCPro HD VARI Cam. Sony's HDCAM decks and the F-900 camera format is ubiquitous in the market.

With the introduction of new formats, including tapeless, come new requests for various machines on the truck—like XDCAM HD. But it's impossible to have every format on every truck. Each client's editorial process is usually what drives the format requests.

Richard Wirth (who in addition to winning an Emmy for his work as technical director [TD] on *The Rachael Ray Show* also served as TD on the movie *Tootsie*) says that *The Rachael Ray Show* is currently shot in a 4×3 format Digital BetaCam (29.97) for the live-to-tape show, recorded in multiple formats, and ISOd on Digi-beta—though he hopes to take the show to HD next season (2010). The show is recorded in 29.97, but its crew also works with mixed formats. "Our field pieces are 24P," Wirth says. "It's 23.98 and gets pulled down to 29.97 and has a film look to it. But it's not letter-boxed. It's still 4×3. What we're trying to do is give our field pieces a little bit of a different feel, more cinemagraphic or cinema verite … rather than standard, live-looking television."

Tip

Plan backward from deliverable master requirements.

HD Formats	
NTSC Compatible	
1080i-60	Has high-resolution frames, is able to capture fast movement, and has reduced Vertical resolution due to interlacing. Easily downconverts to NTSC.
1080p-30	Has high-resolution frames. Movement is less smooth but resolution is higher than interlaced formats in areas of movement.
720p-60	Captures fast-action movement with clarity. However, still frames have lower resolution than 1080-line still frames. Ideal for videography and commercial television. Easily downconverts to NTSC.
720p-30	A variant of 720p-60 with a lower frame rate.
PAL Compatible	
1080i-50	Has high-resolution frames, is able to capture fast movement, and has reduced vertical resolution due to interlacing. Easily downconverts to PAL.
1080p-25	Has high-resolution frames, is able to capture fast movement, and has reduced vertical resolution due to interlacing. Easily downconverts to PAL.
720p-50	Captures fast-action movement with clarity. However, still frames have lower resolution than 1080-line still frames. Ideal for sports videography and commerical television. Easily downconverts to PAL.
720p-25	Is a variant of 720p-50 with a lower data rate. Can be slowed down to 24 fps for film transfers or downconverted to PAL.
FILM Compatible	
1080p-24	Has resolution, scanning method, frame rate and aspect ratio closest to film.
720p-24	Same as 1080p-24 but with lower resolution. Ideal for a "file transferred to video" look.

Figure 1.6 HD format chart.

DV Formats				
Digital Format	**Maker**	**Color sample ratio**	**Compression ratio**	**Recorded bit rate**
DV (25)	multiple manufacturers	4:1:1 4:2:0 (PAL)	5:1	25 Mbps
DVCAM	Sony	4:1:1 4:2:0 (PAL)	5:1	25 Mbps
DVCPRO (D-7)	Panasonic	4:1:1 (NTSC and PAL)	5:1	25 Mbps
DVCPRO 50	Panasonic	4:2:2	3.3:1	50 Mbps
DVCPRO HD	Panasonic	4:2:2	6.7:1	100 Mbps

Figure 1.7 DV format chart.

Match Everything

Match is the key word. Match cameras to each other, use only one media format, and pick a matching editing codec. By the time you get to post, you'll be glad you did. It's all about maintaining consistency.

This is the *ideal* situation. The *reality*, however, is often that you end up with mixed formats. Then the question becomes how and why to convert, to unify the footage. In cases like these, there needs to be a budget for conversions, and time must be added to the post-schedule, too. Arranging for footage to be transferred or compressed is going to take some time, either in your edit suite or when you're waiting for the post vendor's work to be completed. The whole schedule could be held up if you're waiting on footage that needs to be grouped with footage that doesn't need to be converted.

Aspect Ratios

Then there's the question of frame size: 4×3 SD? Or 16×9 HD? Anamorphic? Letterbox? Pillar box? Both? Some smaller markets still don't accept tapes with mixed aspect ratios. They claim it confuses their audiences. Increasingly, however, people are understanding it and developing ways to adapt.

It is a good idea to ask these questions up front. Once you know your deliverables, you can work backward from there. In other words, know your market and your deliverables. This may mean mastering in 16×9 and doing a downconvert for certain markets if they don't accept the 16×9 image.

Noteworthy

Sony Vegas allows mixed formats and codecs in the same multiclip; however, most nonlinear editing systems will not work in multicam mode with mixed codecs.

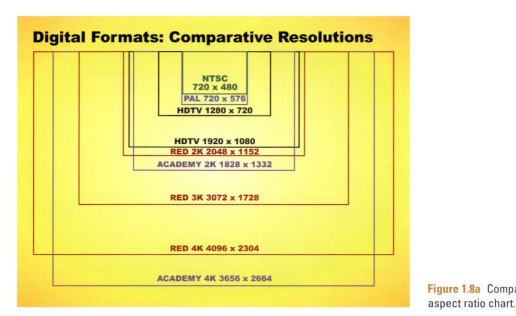

Figure 1.8a Comparatives aspect ratio chart.

Video Frame Sizes

Format	Bytes per Frame	or
NTSC DV25 (compressed)	120,000	117.2 KB
PAL DV25	144,000	140.6 KB
NTSC DV50	240,000	234.4 KB
PAL DV50	288,000	281.2 KB
SD 720x486 8-bit	699,840	683.0 KB
SD 720x486 10-bit	933,120	911.3 KB
SD 720x576 8-bit	829,440	810.0 KB
SD 720x576 10-bit	1,105,920	1.05 MB*
HD 1280x720 8-bit	1,843,200	1.76 MB*
HD 1280x720 10-bit	2,488,320	2.37 MB
DVCProHD 720p-60	240,000	234.4 KB
HD 1920x1080 8-bit	4,147,200	3.96 MB
HD 1920x1080 10-bit	5,529,600	5.27 MB*
DVCProHD 1080i-50	576,000	562.5 KB
DVCProHD 1080i-60	480,000	468.8 KB
HD 1920x1080 10-bit RGB	8,294,400	7.91 MB*
2K 2048x1556 10-bit RGB	12,747,000	12.45 MB*

* denotes a frame size that is an integer multiple of 4 KB.

Figure 1.8b Video frame sizes by format.

Compressed HD Formats

Format	Maker	Color sample ratio	Bit depth	Recorded bit rate
D-5 HD	Panasonic	4:2:2	8-bit 10-bit	235 Mbps
D-6	Philips, Toshiba	4:2:2	10-bit	1.2 Gbps
HDCAM	Sony	3:1:1	8-bit (internal) 10-bit (in/out)	143 Mbps
HDCAM SR	Sony	4:2:2 4:4:4	10-bit log 10-bit linear	440 Mbps (SQ) 800 Mbps (HQ)
DVCPRO HD	Panasonic	4:2:2	8-bit	100 Mbps
XDCAM HD	Sony	4:2:2	8-bit	35 Mbps (LP) 25 Mbps (SP) 18 Mbps (HQ)
HDV	Sony, JVC, Canon	4:2:0	8-bit	19 Mbps (720) 25 Mbps (1080)
RGB Video • 1080p-30 • 720p-60	n/a (computer graphics)	4:4:4	8-bit per color channel	1.39 Gbps 1.24 Gbps

Figure 1.9 Comparison of compressed HD formats for acquisition.

Frame Rates

With HD becoming the broadcast deliverable for all television stations, a whole new family of formats has come barreling out of technology's gates. Always avoid mixing frame rates with any project—especially multicamera projects. Most editing software can't handle it.

Tapeless

Although most productions are still on tape for archival and reliability reasons, it's difficult for producers to resist the lure of new tapeless formats. Tapeless systems are used in multicam from lower budget, run-and-gun–type shoots to high-end, reality shows, features, or commercial work. Inexpensive cameras like Panasonic HVX-200 mean working with the P2 cards for doing capture, and that has migrated to a format that Panasonic has come out with called AVC Intra and AVCHD. AVC-Intra is a compression format that may be recorded on P2 cards. Sony has its version of this, which is called XDCAM, a family of camcorders, some of which (EX) use solid-state SxS cards or an optical format, which is being recorded on BluRay disks, called Sony XDCAM HD; it is different from the EX, which uses the cards. Although XDCAM uses a blue-laser disk, it is not Blu-ray.

Then, of course, are the higher-end products like Panavision Genesis and Thomson Viper or Red, which use the RED flash cards. The data on these cards needs to be immediately transferred onto a disk drive or these cards need to be imported into the software for Final Cut Pro, Adobe Premiere, or Avid.

When working with tapeless files in multicam, the workflow is easily adapted in post. However, when it comes to preparing and organizing the media, tapeless becomes a much bigger job on set and before the edit session. For one thing, there is a massive number of data files that get captured and usually backed up twice.

Alexis Van Hurkman is a writer, director, and colorist based in New York City. He has authored many books including the *Encyclopedia of Color Correction* and many technical articles including "RED Final Cut Studio 2 Whitepaper." According to Van Hurkman:

You don't want to change the name of the source media (as it is acquired in the original hierarchy of files and folders in the field). Typically, all you ever want to do with tapeless source media is archive it somewhere safe and leave it alone. Because you don't want to inadvertently ruin your ability to reconform, because you renamed something inappropriately or you changed a reel number in appropriately or whatever.

Noteworthy

In the tapeless workflow, it is not a good idea to rename the file, because if your NLE crashes and you have to go back to the camera files, you'll have no cross reference to the name the camera has assigned the file.

Universal Unique ID Numbers (UUID)

You can change the name of the clips in your browser, no problem, because the Universal Unique ID (UUID) number is what's used to draw the correspondence. So while you're logging or after you've ingested, you can freely change the name of the clip and you're still going to be able to reconform that source because of the internal UUID number (see Chapter 2: Tapeless Clip Nomenclature).

Bob Zelin is a systems integrator, which means he builds television facilities and postproduction systems. He is known

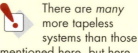
worldwide as a technical guru and consultant and can be found in online forums and as a leader on the CreativeCow.com:

What you're doing is taking the individual cameras, no different than you would be taking the individual tapes from a multicamera shoot, and you would now import all of that footage. You're doing this one at a time. There's no miracle where everything just comes in instantly all at once.

Archivable Deliverables

If you shoot on tape, you have a built-in archive. When you shoot in tapeless formats, on P2 or RED cameras, for example, you need to take extra steps to protect and archive your media reliably. XDCAM uses a Blu-ray DVD in a case and is treated more like tape and it's actually archivable.

On insured production shoots, you may have to get what's called a completion bond. A completion bond may require you to have some archived format at the end of shooting every day. In a tapeless environment, you have a P2, Red, Infinity-type situation where you're not recording anything to tape and all you're handling is data files. Then you have to deal with archiving them on set and making sure there are backups and backups of the backups. One approved method uses linear tape open (LTO) tape and is a tried-and-tested archival system that is also used globally by banks and the financial industry.

Figure 1.10 Tape backup system for the Mac. (Courtesy HP.)

LTO4 is the newest flavor of LTO, and its benefits are considerable:

- A single $50 LTO4 tape can store 800 GB of uncompressed video—that's 26 whopping hours of 720/24p video from a Panasonic P2 camera, 38 hours of 1080/24p footage from a Sony EX3, or nearly 8 hours of 4 K footage from a RED camera.
- An LTO4 tape lasts about 30 years in normal storage conditions (i.e., don't leave it in your trunk indefinitely).
- Some LTO4 drives can read/write data up to 120 Mbps—that is, much faster than reading/writing to a conventional SATA hard drive—so incremental backups go in a hurry.

Gary Adcock, president of Studio 37 out of Chicago and a designer of high-end rigs for multicam and tapeless formats like RED, suggests that "as long as all the cameras are shooting the same format, it can actually expedite the post process, and you can expect to have a more consistent postprocess with all of that media, all of that data, all of those camera tapes, all the same type."

Looking Ahead Toward Postproduction

To save even more time in post, the PBS *Great Performances**
team holds multiple meetings even before the show itself. They
discuss set lists and rundowns, whether the performance in question is a variety show or just a straight concert. It's all laid out.
What the scores are to the director, the rundown is to the editor.
Every anticipated event is detailed in the rundown, which is also
useful for audio and video in preproduction, as well as during
production and post to preserve continuity. Great Performances,
Coordinating Producer, Cara Cosentino says:

*Depending on what turnaround is like, you have to figure out just how
long you have in the edit room to complete the show. And the less time you
have in post, the more time you better prepare in preproduction, which
means probably more rehearsals, and more scripting, and more camera
conferences.*

Other preproduction questions that should be on the producers' minds include these: How much videotape stock should we
buy? How much drive space or cards for tapeless cameras do we
need? How are we going to track and back up our media? How
many ISO decks can we afford? Should we roll on all cameras, or
roll on a few and switch ISOs to a limited number of VTRs? How
much loading and digitizing time is there going to be?

Testing Saves Money and Time

One half day of testing can save countless hours of problem
solving on location and in the edit suite. Often your vendors will
provide you with a no-cost setup at their facility to troubleshoot
your rig. Certainly this is the case when renting cameras from a
reliable rental house. If you're renting a 5- or 10-camera package, it will include the setup, space to calibrate all your tools, and
instructions.

According to Gary Adcock:

*It's imperative for the producers who think, "Oh, we need to save money
because we really don't need the prep," to realize that one day of prep can
save 10% of their postbudget. And if something goes wrong on the shoot
that could have been avoided, then it can save a lot more than that.*

You're going to try to sync hundreds of hours of footage in post.
You cannot afford to have faulty timecode. If you have five cameras
on a 3-hour shoot, that's 15 hours of content to sift through.

*Emmy Award winning Great Performances, (PBS) is one of the longest running
performing arts anthologies on television,since 1972. The show is produced by WNET
in New York City.

the DAILY show February 23rd – February 26th 2009

ACT 1		SHOW OPEN (Obama Charms At Fiscal Summit)		SHOW OPEN (Fox Misspells Criticizing Biden's Gaffe)
	HEADLINES (Oscar Recaps w/John Oliver (& Aasif) Stand-up)	HEADLINES (Obama Visits Canada)	HEADLINES (Obama Addresses Congress/Jindal's Response)	HEADLINES (Hillary Visits Asia)
	STUDIO BUMPER	STUDIO BUMPER	STUDIO BUMPER	STUDIO BUMPER
ACT 2	STUDIO BUMPER	STUDIO BUMPER	STUDIO BUMPER	STUDIO BUMPER
	OTHER NEWS (Republicans Oppose The Stimulus Bill)	OBAMA: GOD OR DEVIL (Jason not in studio) (Producer: Lindsay)	THIRD PARTY STAND-UP (Wyatt)	OTHER NEWS (Interstate Chimp Transport Bill)
	STUDIO BUMPER	STUDIO BUMPER	STUDIO BUMPER	STUDIO BUMPER
ACT 3	DAILY SHOW BUMPER	DAILY SHOW BUMPER	DAILY SHOW BUMPER	DAILY SHOW BUMPER
	JEFF BEZOS (CEO, Amazon.com)	RICKY GERVAIS ("Ricky Gervais: Out of England")	TOM SELLECK ("Jesse Stone: Thin Ice")	BRIAN WILLIAMS (NBC Nightly News)
	STUDIO BUMPER	STUDIO BUMPER	STUDIO BUMPER	STUDIO BUMPER
ACT 4	TEASE TOMORROW	JON/STEPHEN TOSS TEASE TOMORROW	TEASE TOMORROW	TEASE TOMORROW
	MOMENT OF ZEN (Hugh Jackman "seducing" Barbara Walters)	MOMENT OF ZEN (Anderson Cooper & Reporter)	MOMENT OF ZEN (MSNBC ragging on Jindal)	MOMENT OF ZEN
	CREDITS (Boby jindal)	CREDITS (Obama: God Or Devil)	CREDITS (Obama Meet & Greet)	CREDITS
PRE-TAPES AVAIL CORR			**6:45pm:** Tape Global Wraparounds	
	Jason, John Oliver, Samantha, Aasif & Wyatt	Jason, John Oliver, Samantha, Aasif & Wyatt	Jason, John Oliver, Samantha, Aasif & Wyatt	Jason, John Oliver, Samantha, Aasif & Wyatt

Figure 1.11 Rundown. (Courtesy Daily Show, Comedy Central.)

Figure 1.12 Setup day at Rental House. (Courtesy Liman Video Rental, www.lvrusa.com.)

Figure 1.13 Mark Schubin at the Early TV Museum. (Courtesy Mark Schubin.)

With a properly tested setup, you can produce footage that will sync up in minutes. But without it, you could be trapped in hand-sync hell for hours, even days on end. For just one day of prep, you've got to pay the Assistant Cameraperson (AC), the Director of Photography (DP), and maybe a Production Assistant (PA) to be there. That's not a big cost, especially if it's saving an entire day of color correction, or two or three days in an online session, or, in terms of concert footage, audio syncing.

Mark Schubin is a broadcast engineer and SMPTE fellow (Society of Motion Picture and Television Engineers). He is also Engineer in Charge (EIC) for the live global theatrical transmissions for the Metropolitan Opera's HD series: "The Met: Live in HD": says, "My job should be almost 100% preproduction. I'm only involved in the postproduction if we've done something wrong. There's a saying in my end of the business that if I'm working, you're in trouble."

Looking ahead to postproduction during preproduction is crucial. You must always be able to view your project in its entirety—from preproduction to deliverable masters—with an eye on the end result.

2

TAPE LABELING AND SCENE NUMBERING SYSTEMS

An unlabeled tape is a lost tape.

Author unknown

In this chapter, we'll look at some common ways of organizing multicam projects, from shooting formats and editing codecs to labeling and managing systems for tapes and digital media.

All editors, producers, and directors have their own methods for labeling tapes. Some call them by *camera 1, camera 2, camera 3,* or *camera A, camera B, camera C*—it doesn't matter how you do it but simply that it's done. Do not take labeling lightly—it's the backbone of an organized show. And never forget the old expression, "An unlabeled tape is a lost tape."

Figure 2.1 Prelabeled tape set. (Courtesty Christof Halasz, www.livecut.at.)

Prelabeled Tapes

It's smart to *pre*label tapes for the field. Some shows send out sticker labels preprinted so that the location crew cannot vary from the plan—crewmembers just affix the labels and get right to work, saving the editor or an assistant lots of time otherwise spent trying to identify and organize poorly labeled media. Although printing labels for regular-sized tapes is not a problem, it's a challenge with tiny solid-state media (try labeling an SxS card, let alone a MicroSD card). There was a great paper at the Hollywood Post Alliance (HPA; www.hpaonline.com) about intentionally using labels that were so big that they did not allow the media to fit into the players, forcing the tech to remove the label and replace it with a new one each time.

Typically some sort of a numbering convention—along with abbreviations or alpha indicators—makes it easy to organize the material for editing. If the labeling is done in a clear and consistent way, the editor should be able to take one look at a tape and say,

Tip

Here is a nice tip from Cheri Tanimura, co-producer of *Rules of Engagement:* Avid only shows the first eight characters of a reel name in the EDL. This is another reason we designate out tapes 101A1 as opposed to "101reel A1." This would be truncated in an EDL as "101reel A."

"Okay, that's camera 1's second load from the first show." Or, in the case of a reality show, "That tape has an interview with reality contestant X from season 21, episode 9."

When it comes to organizing tapes and media, the tape operator is the key position, and Alan Falkner is one of the best tape ops in the business. He says:

One way that works is to name tapes based on camera angle or number. The assistant producers or production assistants will always send their proposed tape-labeling scheme. It really just needs to make some sense. You like to have some mnemonic scheme rather than just completely arbitrary tape numbers.

Reel Naming Systems

Concerts and Performances

If you're working on a concert and it has seven acts, and you've got a different tape load for every act, the first act or performance might be a 100-series numbering, the second performance might be a 200-series numbering, and so on. The line cut might be 100, camera A might be 101, camera B might be 102, and so on. It really doesn't matter which system you establish as long as it's a system that works for you, your show type, and your crew. Some additional sample methods are described in more detail next.

Aerosmith: You Gotta Move *By Show*

Label by show. Example: 206C (Show/Camera Angle/load)
- 200 for second night's show
- 06 for camera angle 6
- C for that camera's third reel of the night

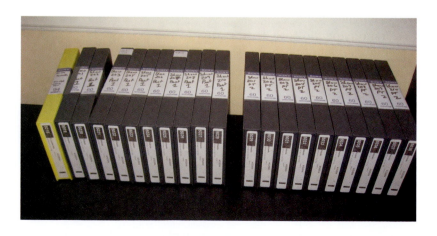

Figure 2.2 Tape set for Aerosmith's *You Gotta Move.* Line cuts and ISO reels over two shows.

PBS Great Performances: *Numbering by Load*

Great Performances is a series, but the shows are original productions and have to be highly organized individually. The crew chooses to label by camera load or reel first, followed by camera angle. Like many nine-camera operations, the team typically uses a numbering system of one through nine, as follows:

Example: *18* corresponds to load one of camera eight, while *312* refers to the third load of camera 12, and so on (load/camera).

"We take care of tape labeling beforehand," says Cara Cosentino, coordinating producer:

Figure 2.3 Close-up showing handwritten labels for ISO cams.

We think about every load that's going to happen and assign numbers that way. And that's something we share with editors and audio, so we're all on the same page. I print what's called tape configuration, which details all of the tape labeling, what we're shooting, what the timecode is going to be, and whether it's going to be time-of-day or 24-hour—just to make it easier later on in the process.

Metropolitan Opera: By Performance

The Metropolitan Opera stages some of the most sophisticated productions in the world, yet its tape-numbering system is basic and clutter-free.

Example: *Reel 64K* means performance 6, act 4, camera K (performance/act/camera).

Figure 2.4 Preprinted tapes from *Carnegie Hall Opening Night.* (Courtesy www.wnet.org and Great Performances.)

The code starts with A and B for the line cut and backup, which are clean feeds (without graphics). Then it goes to C and D for subtitles and titles. Then the ISOs start with E, F, G, and keep on going through S. The Met usually has 16 to 18 cameras with as many as 22 for opening night covering the house, backstage, and remote locations in Times Square and Lincoln Center Plaza. Although not all of these cameras are active at one time, they are all labeled.

Reality Shows

By Episode

Network reality shows like *The Real World* require more information and tend to have a rather elaborate alpha-numeric scheme. Tape numbering in the field often calls for a unique numbering system.

Noteworthy

Here are the main elements to track for reel labels:

1. Season
2. Performance or show
3. Episode
4. Acts or segments
5. Reel or camera load
6. Date
7. Subject

HDNet Concerts: By Artist

For the past 30 years, Ray Volkema of HDNet Concerts has been a director of live television and a postproduction editor of sports, news, and entertainment programs, including several Olympics broadcasts and more than 50 concerts. He uses 9 to 11 clips in a group and just names his tapes with the exact artist—for example: Paul Simon, camera 9, tape 5, or line cut, tape 3 (camera/tape).

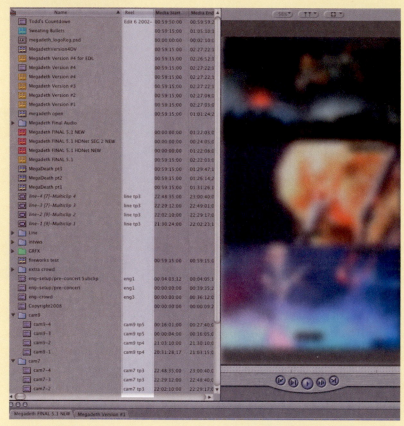

Figure 2.5 Tape set for HDNet concert featuring Megadeath, Editor Ray Volkema. (Courtesy Dave Mustaine, Megadeath, and HDNet.)

Example: *RW21-10-08-A5* (Show/season/date/camera/load). While shooting, crewmembers have no way to know which episode they are working on. *RW* stands for "Real World," *21* is the season number, *10-08* means October 8, *A* is for camera A, and *5* is for load 5.

Anyone who knows and understands the system can look at a shelf full of tapes and immediately identify interview tapes versus production tapes versus B roll. And that's important when it comes to prioritizing your approach to an edit.

Talk Shows

By Season

Because talk shows primarily work in terms of seasons, episodes, and segments, their line cut tapes tend to be numbered in groups by show—for example: 10101 (season/show/segment). In this case, 10000 refers to season 1, 20000 to season 2, and so on. Show 1 of season 1 starts out as 10100, and then the first segment of the show may be 01 after that, giving you 10101. Segment 2 of the first show would then be 10102.

Sitcoms

By Episode

In sitcoms, although it varies a little from show to show, the systems are generally based on three-, four-, and sometimes five-camera studio shows shot on film or, more recently, digitally in 24p but in the film style.

Cheri Tanimura, who is currently co-producer on *Rules of Engagement,* notes:

When we shoot, we typically shoot with four cameras. We have an A, B, C, and X camera. Occasionally we might throw in a jib, which would be a Y camera. It's sort of a throwback to naming with film. For us, with each episode, each episode is a number. For instance, generally a season 1/episode 1 show might be 101, 102; and when you move on to season 2 you're 201, 202, et cetera.

For example, a tape label for *Friends* might read: 322A3 (season/episode/camera/reel).

The episode number is usually the first part of the tape name, so the first digits would represent episode 100, or 111, or, as in the preceding example, episode 322. The letter that follows refers to the camera (A) and the reel (3).

As Cheri Tanimura explains:

When we shoot season 2, episode 2, 202A1 would be the first reel for the A camera. We have a B1, C1, and X1. When we digitize the show into the Avid, the reel numbers would be 202A1, et cetera, so that each reel has a unique number.

> **Tip**
>
>
>
> Use only eight characters for reel names with respect to CMX-style specs for EDLs. Final Cut Pro exports only EDLs with truncated reel names showing only eight characters and adds a comment to warn the user.

By Type

Some sitcoms use a system called tens, twenties, and thirties to label tapes by the type of shoot. Jeff Bass is veteran multicam editor who has worked on shows like *Home Improvement* and helped to develop the multicamera component within the Avid. He says:

Production would shoot a dress rehearsal and put the loads on the tape machine. They call them: ten for program, eleven would be ISO one, twelve would be ISO two, thirteen ISO three, and fourteen ISO four. And the next load of tapes would be called twenties. 20, 21, 22, 23, 24, et cetera. Timecode would be time of day.

Figure 2.6 Editor David Helfand, A.C.E. (Courtesy David Helfand, A.C.E.)

The shots are always slated because, on a film show, although everything has timecode, one must insert the picture over the sound bed of every one of the tapes and sync the dailies.

David Helfand, whose editing career spans seminal comedies from HBO's *Dream On* through *Friends*, *That 70's Show*, and *Weeds*, and who has received multiple awards and Emmy nominations for his work in both television and features says, "You don't need the clapper stick for sync anymore. It's really more about the rolling timecode in the smart slate. And that's what the telecine operator uses to sync up each film clip with the proper sound on the master tapes."

Tapeless Clip Nomenclature

Organizing RED, like most tapeless formats, is backing up from remote data cards to hard drives on location and then backing them up again, ideally in some sort of archival format. The RED camera has an internal nomenclature for naming files. Says Gary Adcock:

With REDs, you can go through the whole alphabet and set the reel numbers on it, and that's about all you can do. So I tend to prefer to change the camera number every day. Day 1, it's camera A; day 2, the same camera is camera B; on day 3, camera C. I know that seems confusing, but it's actually an easier way for the post guy to identify files—because we're not talking about tapes, we're talking about raw files. He can look at it and he knows that everything that's marked as B is day 2 and everything marked as C is day 3.

According to Alexis Van Hurkman:

Tapeless media is managed via the UUID [universal unique ID number]. Some unique ID number components of the original tapeless media [are] snatched up by Final Cut Pro's ingest mechanism and placed into a UUID variable, or container, inside of the metadata for a particular QuickTime clip. Now, it's different for every type of tapeless media, because every type of tapeless media implements [its] unique ID number in a different way.

Slates, Scenes, and Takes

During a scripted production, every shot is labeled with a slate number. This number is the lifeline between the set and the edit room. There are various methods for numbering scenes and takes. The systems vary from continent to continent, producers, directors, and DPs, so it is best to prearrange your preferred methods beforehand with the script supervisors or producers, especially when it comes to continuity and logging in post.

Noteworthy

So be aware: All types of tapeless media that are supported for direct ingest in Final Cut Pro have some sort of UUID correspondence such that a particular QuickTime clip can always be matched with the source media, assuming the following:

1. The UUID has been unmolested and it's an internal number. Ordinarily you have no way of even seeing what it is, it's just there. So it's not like you can change it or lose it on your own. You'd have to do something to the clip somehow to lose that.
2. The timecode is intact and correct. So if you change the timecode of a clip, then you just shot yourself in the foot.

Slating Systems

There are two basic methods for slate numbering:

1. Script scene numbers (this is most common)
2. Consecutive numbers or numerical slating

The U.S. production teams primarily use scene numbers, based on script order. Teams in the Uunited Kingdom use primarily a slate number, based on the number of shots in the production, in production order.

Slating Multiple Cameras

When shooting with more than one camera, a prominent letter is attached to the outside of each camera, identifying it as the A camera, B camera, and so on. Slates are likewise marked A, B, C, and so forth. Sometimes the slates are a different color plastic to further differentiate between them. These individual slates are used without sound to identify each camera's take. For sync sound, all the cameras should roll on a common slate with a marker.

Tip

Draw a simple diagram of a three-walled space with configurations for camera positions, and include it in the notes for the editor.

Further Reading

Various methods are outlined in the book *Script Supervising and Film Continuity* by Pat P. Miller (published by Focal Press). This book goes over the methodology behind scene numbering and organization in excruciating detail.

Common Slates

When shooting with multiple cameras that are positioned more closely together, on a stage or set, for example, or for shooting with sync sound, a more efficient way of slating is called *common markers*. Each camera will grab its own slate as indicated earlier, but for the marker, one single smart slate with timecode (or just a clapboard) will be displayed for all the cameras to shoot concurrently. The assistant cameraperson calls for a common marker and claps for all cameras at once.

Pat Miller, script supervisor and author of *Script Supervising and Film Continuity,* observes:

Always note [on] which side of the A camera the other cameras are positioned. This will preclude any mishap with regard to directions or progression when filming coverage for the sequence. Often when staging a scene, a character will walk out of range of the B camera into the range of the A camera.

Marc Wielage, expert colorist and owner of Cinesound/LA, says, "American multicamera shows sometimes add the camera letter (A/B/C/X) as a suffix to the take number ("29-2A"), but not always. It boils down to preference. In terms of the post facility and/or digital dailies, I think the best course is to ask them what they want."

Scene Designations

The scene designations are taken from the script, so that when footage is digitized, the assistant editor can organize it for each act in a labeled bin.

Filmmakers use numeric scenes followed by a letter for shots within the scene. TV sitcoms use letters to name scenes.

According to Darryl Bates of A.C.E, longtime sitcom editor:

In sitcoms, the scenes are A through ZZZ, basically. So they're letter based. So instead of take 1, 1A take 1, 1B take 1 on a single camera show, you'd have A1, A2, A3. And then in Avid we would actually put the camera number after that. So we would have A-1A, A-1B, A-1C.

Every script supervisor kind of has a different way of labeling and numbering. Part of the

Figure 2.7 The audio department is jamming time-of-day timecode to a smart slate. Films use numbered scenes with letters to ID coverage within the scene. *Wall Street 2,* scene 106A, take 3.

editor's job when working on a multicamera series, if it matters to you, is to sit down with the script supervisor and say, "How do you like to organize it? How do you like to name it? Here's what I would like you to do."

Some editors will use the ScriptSync function in an Avid, in which case the assistant editor would then import a copy of the script and mark where each line is for each of the takes (see Chapter 12: Cutting Techniques and Styles).

PRODUCTION

3

TYPES OF MULTICAMERA PRODUCTIONS

Studio Systems

The studio system for multicam television goes back to the original live broadcast in 1928 of *The Queen's Messenger* (see Chapter 22: History of Multicamera Technology). The lighting director would light for all angles simultaneously with stands on the floor. It was 1951 when Desi Arnaz and his team took this system to the next level. He won a battle with the network to shoot film with multiple cameras for the *I Love Lucy Show* but also wanted to shoot live, in front of a studio audience. Arnaz's team was the first to do it, and his innovation was to add the live audience and modify the set by hanging all of its lights so the cameras could move easily around on the floor during the shooting and between sets. Of course, this is slightly easier in a studio than on a remote shoot, since most of the gear in a studio does not have far to travel.

I Love Lucy's staging and camera plan is still the same setup that we use today on sitcoms and variety shows except now there are more cameras and more sophisticated lighting. As Richard Wirth, technical director of *The Rachael Ray Show*, says:

We have nine cameras available to us, all of different varieties. They would include three studio pedestal cameras, one Steadicam, one handheld camera, one jib, one rail cam, one robotic camera over the cooking service, and a fridge cam, which is a lipstick camera that's inside the refrigerator.

Wirth's team overshoots the segments and then pulls them up with the live audience cutaways to tighten up the show. So even though it's shot multicam with recorded ISOs, the show is switched live to a line cut and the editing is then done to cut the line cut down to time. The ISOs are used to cover the cuts or make Band-Aid-type fixes to the new master.

For news, talk, and game shows, multicam studios reign supreme. Some reality shows also use studio segments in combination with run-and-gun ENG-style remotes. This is the case with *America's Next Top Model*, whose judging scene is shot on

Doi: 10.1016/B978-0-240-81176-5.00003-4

Figure 3.1 (1951) A rare shot of original set for *I Love Lucy* with the bandstand scene. Notice Lucy peeking through on the left and the three cameras on crab dollys, hanging studio lights, and a live audience—all Deslilu innovations. (Courtesy CBS/Getty Images.)

Figure 3.2 (2009) *The Late Show with David Letterman* stage at the Ed Sullivan Theater. (Courtesy CBS.)

a soundstage with 20-plus cameras under controlled conditions on tripods with tethered cameras—which is about as unlike run-and-gun as you can get. The conference table scene where Donald Trump fires someone on *The Apprentice* is shot with 22 cameras in order to cover each contestant, The Donald, his associates, and groups of two and four people.

For *Top Chef* and *Iron Chef America,* a studio is used to shoot the kitchen competitions. Programs like *Rachael Ray, Late Night with David Letterman, Martha Stewart Living, The Daily Show with Jon Stewart,* and most nightly news programs all stay put in the studio, where a safe, tried-and-tested system gets put to use every day.

These studios are wired for multicam recording and audio, with house sync locking it all together, and most are recorded live to tape. Little editing is needed for the studio show; just quick fixes, censoring of profanities, or small last-minute cuts are made. Some shows are live on the air and require no editing at all. But the producers still record ISOs, like other multicam shows, and

Figure 3.3 *Martha Stewart Show* studio photo. (Courtesy Mark Forman, screeningroom.com.)

Figure 3.4 Director Jerry Foley gathers his notes in the studio control room at the Ed Sullivan Theater before taping *The Late Show with David Letterman.* (Courtesy CBS.)

even feed signals directly to editing rooms usually located in the studio or on a nearby floor in the same building.

No Edit, No Cry: *The Daily Show with Jon Stewart*

For studio programs, the director is the ultimate editor, calling the shots live to tape or over the air. For *The Daily Show with Jon Stewart*, director Chuck O'Neil cuts the show live like a news show with tape roll-ins that are fairly quick and succinct. He adds over-the-shoulder graphics, keys, mats—all the things that you have in a regular news show. O'Neil elaborates:

You have to be a little more aware of where you're going and what you're doing than with the single camera. I visualize where all of the cameras are going. My style, and the style that I've always incorporated, is that I try to put myself in the position of a viewer who is sitting at home and I'm trying to give them the shots that they would be thinking in their minds that they want to see.

The whole point is to try to keep it as seamless and as live as possible so that you don't have to edit. But editors, have no fear. There are still several cutters and three edit suites employed for the show. They'll cut all the packages and do little fixes after the live show—like add a graphics, little tweaks on angles, and cut content to time—but for the most part they just fly right through the show.

Chuck O'Neil: *Sometimes we have to cut the interview down because Jon goes a little long, he finds the guest interesting and he will realize that he's going long and he'll do it on purpose and he'll know in his mind where he wants the edit to take place. He's very intelligent, very creative, one of the most amazing people I've ever worked with. When he delivers something, even in rehearsal, he's thinking of the words and the mechanics and he knows if it works, if it doesn't work, or how he wants to rearrange it immediately. He's a brilliant editor on the fly.*

Mobile Television Systems

Let's consider the general show sizes and requirements for multicamera production. The main categories are *ENG/film-style shoots, fly-pack systems,* and *remote truck shows* with large-scale mobile TV vehicles. The basic remote system comes in road cases or in racks inside a truck. There are separate components for inputting all the signals, monitoring, switching, correcting, and recording the signals. The systems come in all shapes and sizes and can be configured into custom packages based on your budget and needs.

Figure 3.5 All Mobile Video's remote truck Resolution.

Figure 3.6 Bexel Hercules fly pack. (Courtesy Bexel Video.)

Let's break them down starting with the least expensive system—the studio in a box.

Studio in a Box

The NewTek TriCaster is literally a complete studio system that could fit in a few small cases. It's the perfect solution for the super-low-budget remotes, classroom programs, or even

Noteworthy

Remote multicam production, also known as outside broadcasting (OB), can be divided into four basic categories:

    Studios in a Box
    ENG-style shoots
    Fly-pack systems
    Remotes (Truck Shoots)

streaming shows for the Web. TriCaster offers a few different models that can all be upgraded to its gold standard in portable live production, the model TriCaster TCXD300™. There are many other products in this category, from such companies as Rushworks, Broadcast Pix, J-Lab, and even Grass Valley.

The system can be set up solo or with a small team to create, broadcast, and live-stream just about any event—anywhere. It has a digital suite of studio tools like a multicamera switcher, virtual digital disc recorders, title generator, video transitions, keyer, audio mixer, and virtual live sets. Oh yeah, it's HD.

Figure 3.7 TriCaster TCXD300™ studio in a box. (Courtesy NewTek.)

Figure 3.8a TriCaster used for a high school news show. (Courtesy Debbie Rein/Osceola Fundamental High School.)

Figure 3.8b TriCaster at Diggnation. (Courtesy NewTek.)

Figure 3.9 TriCaster studio demo with Kiki. Note the digital switcher. (Courtesy NewTek.)

Otto Cedeno is the head of production at Live Stream, which is a Web broadcasting company that produces live multicamera or single-camera event coverage, conference coverage, and live music. NewTek Tricaster is his main tool.

Otto Cedeno: *The good thing about TriCaster is it's literally a portable TV solution in a box. It deals with the camera routing, it deals with the audio routing, in and out, and then it's got the interface. You do everything there, you don't need a separate machine to do graphics. You don't need a separate machine to ingest a projector feed if you're working on news or a corporate conference kind of thing. It's like one box and a monitor and keyboard, and then the rest of production doesn't change. You still need your cameras and tripods, but as far as putting it all together, it's quite amazing.*

ENG-Style Multicam Shoot

The ENG-style multicam production can be the lowest budget professional package and usually consists of two to four (or more) ENG-type cameras shooting independently. One of the main advantages of this type of shoot is its overall flexibility with respect to scenes and locations. The crewmembers move quickly on their feet with very little equipment; thus they can fit into tight spaces.

Figure 3.10 Otto Cedeno on location at NYC Fashion Week with Livestream's Livepack, which uses cell phone towers to send a live signal to the Web. It's like a satellite truck in a backpack. (Courtesy http://livestream.com/platform/livepack.)

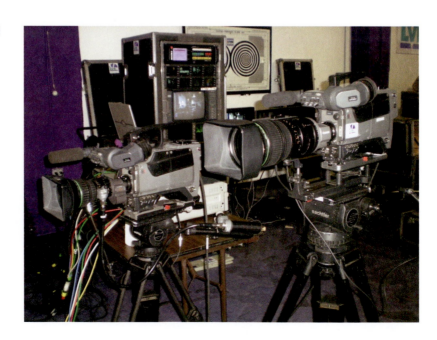

Figure 3.11a ENG cameras being prepared for location at Liman Video Rental. (Courtesy lvrusa.com.)

Figure 3.11b Fly-pack system being tested for the field. (Courtesy lvrusa.com.)

The Reality of Run and Gun: Communicating and Monitoring

On *The Real World* (and many other reality shows), typically three cameras are rolling simultaneously, but not necessarily on the same action. They follow three or more groups of people who separate, come together, separate again, and so on. At the same time, you could have two different cameras running in the same room but following two different stories. So although multiple cameras are rolling, they needn't necessarily be grouped in post-production or even treated as multicams when divided up.

ENG multicam productions are rarely directed live or monitored in the customary way. Rather, planning consists of preproduction meetings with the camera operator to review assigned areas and direction. If the technology is available and the budgets will allow it, some productions go with portable monitor bridges that receive wireless video.

Figure 3.12 Three-way director's remote monitor bridge.

Figure 3.13 Eight-screen color location monitor bridge.

Effective communication among handheld, run-and-gun camera operators requires wireless headset systems or radio mics, which do not work well, or tethered cables, which are cumbersome and limit camera mobility. Cables also require cable pullers, adding to the budget.

Some crews need to use hand signals to communicate what they're shooting. Randy Baker of Randy Baker Productions in Orlando, Florida, shoots and produces for reality shows like *Hogan Knows Best* on MTV. His crewmembers used hand signals when they worked without director's monitors.

Randy Baker: *If you're going to be directing something like that, you should be watching a monitor. And as a director watching monitors, you need to be giving your camera people some kind of direction. It doesn't have to be a lot. But when you're shooting low end, HDV, and DV stuff, when you don't have that luxury of having a camera return or monitors, then you need to know what other people are shooting. If you held up one finger, that meant you were shooting a single shot of the person you were shooting. If you held up two, that meant you were shooting two. Three fingers: three-shot. If you had a wide shot, you'd hold your fist up like in a ball.*

"Toy" Cameras

Some multicam shoots involve "toy" cameras, or what many members of the trade lovingly refer to as LPS cameras: "little pieces of s#%t". Even on mini-multicam shoots, try to keep it consistent. And if you absolutely must use LPSs, use all the same LPSs.

Sync Issues for ENG Cameras

Sync takes a back seat to the story. Ninety-nine percent of the run-and-gun stuff we do [on The Real World*] has an invalid matching timecode—and that becomes a hand effort, where you sync by in point.*

Mark Raudonis, Bunim-Murray Productions

Figure 3.14 LPS cameras on set.

Later in the book, we'll discuss sync and timecode in more detail, but at this point in our coverage of ENG multicam systems, I must mention the importance of getting sync in the field. If you're an editor, you will inevitably come across bad sync in post—probably more often than not. Why? Producers and camera operators are sharp people, and the run-and-gun equipment they use is capable of syncing media, so what's the problem? This: Even if you start out by jam-syncing all your cameras to a common timecode, *the timecode needs to be reset in the field every time a battery goes down or power is lost or a camera simply loses its sync over time.* As Mark Raudonis explains:

In the heat of a run-and-gun production, no cameraman I've ever met is going to stop to re-jam-sync his timecode when there's a story in front of us. Get the shots first, figure out the code later. So sync takes a backseat to the story, and then, of course, post is stuck with trying to make the shots work. So 99% of the run-and-gun stuff we do on The Real World *has an invalid matching timecode—and that becomes a hand effort, where you sync by in point. But that takes 10, 15, 20, or 30 seconds per clip to do … sometimes even longer if you can't figure out where it started. So to me the number one warning to anyone trying to do this is get it right in the field. Because you're going to spend too much time in post trying to fix what could be done easily by spending a little bit of money for a Lockit box or hardwire cameras for sync.*

In other words: *the story is king*—not timecode or sync.

Fly-Pack Systems

Fly-pack systems are portable studios custom-designed to fit in various road case packages and usually also on an airplane, per flight regulations—thus the term "*fly* pack." Fly packs range in size from a lightweight, all-in-one-box to groups of cases that connect together to form major control centers, enabling directors to monitor, switch, and communicate with their camera operators.

Fly Packs Versus Remote Trucks

Video switching, audio mixing, sync generation, and intercom communications are the backbone of any good multicam shoot, and the fly-pack system allows all of this technology. Sometimes it's a good bet if you need a truck-style shoot but cannot get an actual truck into

Figure 3.15 Mini fly-pack system. (Courtesy David Thaler Films.)

Figure 3.16 Fly-packing for the Dalai Lama, with director Todd Gillespie. (Courtesy Todd Gillespie.)

Figure 3.17 U2 video fly-pack system (www.u2.com).

the location. Shooting in hotel ballrooms, remote locations, or in a city when you do not have a truck permit all tend to call for a fly pack. Liman Video Rentals (LVR) supplies them; there's also the All Mobile Video (AMV) Matrix and Bexel's Hercules, which is basically a truck in a (large) box. These systems can cost as much or more than a remote truck because they're usually custom-configured with VTRs and cameras for your needs, whereas a basic remote truck is already retrofitted with a fixed number of decks and cameras. Also, it takes more time to prep a fly-pack system because it has to be wired with every move.

And, of course, nothing beats the ability of fly packs to get close to the event. You can get right up onstage or backstage or just around the corner to the action, which means shorter cable runs and less time running them. With a remote truck, you may end up setting up down the street or a block away, and you'll therefore need an extra day just to run cables.

Eric Duke of All Mobile Video says:

There's a perception by clients that the fly pack is actually cheaper than the truck, for some reason. In reality, it winds up being more. With the fly pack, you actually have to carry your audio boards and tape machines in and build them on location, which means troubleshooting intercom and cabling issues, as well. It's not as neat and easy as just showing up with a truck. But sometimes, there's just no way around using a fly pack.

Figure 3.18a PortaCast™ fly-pack system set up near the studio broadcasting the U.S. House of Representatives. (Courtesy www.MobileStudios. com.)

Figure 13.18b Director's station in a PortaCast™ remote case. (Courtesy www.MobileStudios.com.)

Evan Haiman is the executive producer of Music and Entertainment for HDNet. From beginning to end, he oversees hundreds of concert productions and entertainment programs a year featuring the biggest names in the music business.

I would rather use a truck. The only reasons I haven't used trucks, in specific situations, is because either the truck was too big for the location, or

I couldn't get a truck. Fly packs have to be tweaked. It's separate equipment, and it all has to be put together at the venue, whereas a truck comes together and expands out. We're able to bring a lot more to the table because our trucks have a lot of equipment on [them].

And there are advantages to fly packs, too. They allow almost everyone to be on an intercom or mic, and your cameras are all tethered and locked, which leads to a more consistent workflow of footage in post.

Environmental Issues

Remote productions contend with environmental issues all the time, from setting up in the hot sun of midday to working in the back of a semitrailer in 110-degree weather. One good thing about a mega-remote truck is that it's dry and *cold!* The air conditioners are always on (except in already-cold locations)—some crewmembers even wear winter coats or bundle up. With a fly pack, on the other hand, you're at the mercy of the location's natural climate.

Figure 3.18c HDNet remote truck. (Courtesy HDNet.)

Figure 3.18d Interior of HDNet truck. (Courtesy HDNet.)

Figure 3.19a Fly-pack system. (Courtesy Bexel.)

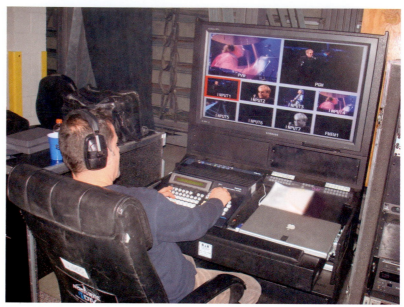

Figure 3.19b Director Peter Moll cuts a live Elton John performance. (Fly-pack system from Nocturne Video.)

"Heat and rain kill us", says Peter Moll, the rock-and-roll director who's toured with Van Halen, Guns 'n' Roses, and Elton John. Obviously, everything has to be wrapped—but heat kills our equipment and our system a lot. Gear shuts down—thermal issues or overheating or there's condensation in the lens, which takes all day to dry out."

The Remote TV Truck

The remote TV truck is the ultimate in production technology, with vehicles specifically designed for professional production. Trucks come in various sizes and are equipped as portable studios complete with everything needed to record a multicam program. Some trucks are small and economical, whereas others can be enormous, triple-wide trailers designed by engineers and architects for maximum productivity and comfort. And they come in NTSC and PAL plus any "flavor" of video format: HD or SD.

Typically, remote TV trucks are divided into four or five rooms. The biggest is where the director, TD, AD, and producers watch the monitors and call the show. Other rooms are designed to house audio, tape decks, and camera control. Some trucks also

Figure 3.20 Remote truck parked outside venue in France. (Courtesy EVS.)

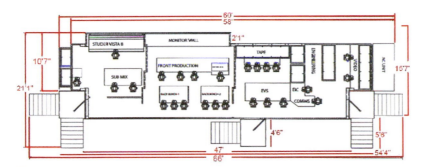

Figure 3.21 Titan remote truck interior layout. (Courtesy AMV.)

have transmission monitoring to send signals via microwave or satellite and to other trucks.

All Mobile Video (AMV) is one of the leading remote video providers in the world. The company offers the industry's leading selection of mobile production solutions used in cutting-edge productions like the Super Bowl, the Grammy Awards, and the MTV Video Music Awards. They supply a wide range of options, from large trucks offering the most advanced capabilities and equipment to smaller, more budget-oriented solutions for venues where space and parking come at a premium. Their biggest and best truck is also one of the most luxurious TV vehicles on the planet, the Titan.

Figure 3.22 ESPN monitor wall. (Courtesy ESPN.)

The Monitor Wall

Every remote truck has a monitor wall that can be programmed to suit an individual show's needs. The director sits in front, watches everything, and decides where each monitor will be placed. The engineer in charge (EIC) sets them up according to a detailed layout designed by the director and TD.

Common elements of the wall include different camera views, playback and record decks, direct-to-hard-drive recorders, and the indispensable Preview and Program functions. Many jumbo productions entail huge walls made up of individual monitors and LED screens programmable to any size or configuration. Some combine views from several locations, including satellite feeds and microwave uplinks.

Some directors choose to set up their monitors in a traditional numbering sequence (say, in two rows and numbered sequentially), whereas others recreate the shooting location of the cameras in a gridlike fashion. Others set up blocks of complementary or opposing angles in rows. Whatever format makes the director's job easiest is best, because in the heat of the live switch, speed is key.

Director Mark Haefeli, a maverick producer/director who specializes in high-end legacy-type artists' (Paul McCartney, Aerosmith, U2, Billy Joel, The Police and Beyonce) music TV and DVD projects, sets up his monitor walls like a checkerboard, with complementary angles above and below. Then he works from left to right, starting as far downstage as possible, with camera 1. Just as a good camera operator works with one eye through the lens and the other taking in everything else, Haefeli can see both the primary shot and the counterparts and choose the most

Figure 3.23 Programmable monitor wall. (Courtesy Oli Laperal-Journey.)

complementary angles. He can look at 16 cameras quickly and know that the ones on top will cut together nicely with the ones on the bottom.

Gary Halvorson is a world-renowned director who has mastered three of the top multicam categories: music (*The Met: Live in HD*, Great Performances), sitcoms *(Friends)*, and live events (Macy's Thanksgiving Day Parade).

Gary Halvorson: *If we do 20 cameras, I can watch, and I live in the bank. When you improvise, you live in your prep cameras, you live down what the next shot is. Once you take that shot, you're not watching that shot anymore. You better be watching what the next shot is because you don't know what it is. You have to be telling your story and anticipating what is going to happen, or not.*

Eli Tishberg is a veteran New York director-editor with notable credits that include the MTV Video Music Awards; VH1 Storytellers with Bruce Springsteen, Jay-Z, and 70 other artists; and live concerts and documentaries featuring the Ramones, Sheryl Crow, Phish, and Bon Jovi. Tishberg tends to set up his monitor wall to be four on top and four on bottom: numbered *1234* and *5678*. If there are handhelds on the stage (almost always), he arranges 1, 2, 3, and 4 clockwise—and makes the jib camera 5, the dolly 6, and the hard cameras in the back (getting the wide and tight shots) 7 and 8.

If you're working in a really big truck, you can have as many as 150 monitors on the wall. As Eli Tishberg says, "When I am directing a straight-ahead concert, all I need to see are my cameras, the line, and the preview. That's all I really need out of life in the truck."

Figure 3.24 Monitor wall diagram on TD switching console for *Carnegie Hall Opening Night*.

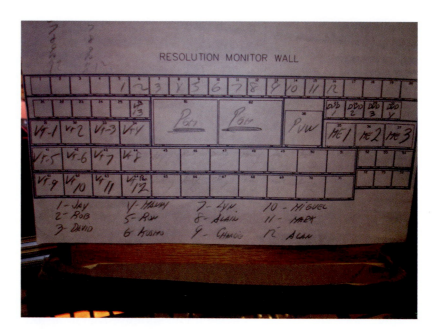

Figure 3.25 **Monitor diagram.** Close-up, *Carnegie Hall Opening Night*.

Film Production

Big studio movies have been using multicamera production since the early 1920s with movies like *Noah's Ark* (from Warner Brothers) and many others. However, its use is not like typical multicam shoots for TV sitcoms or multicam shoots with remote trucks.

PRO*file*

Director Akira Kurosawa liked using multiple cameras, which allowed him to shoot an action scene from different angles. The multiple-camera technique also prevented Kurosawa's actors from "figuring out which one is shooting him [and invariably turning] one-third to halfway in its direction."*

Craig McKay, the editor on *Silence of the Lambs*, remembers that *The Last Samurai* was a brilliant example of the use of multicam:

Kurosawa's probably one of the first directors that I was aware of using multiple cameras. He used it so exquisitely. He would very often shoot with six cameras going on all at once for a fight scene, and it orchestrated quite beautifully. He continued to use it all through his career and used it more effectively than most of us.

*Kurosawa, Akira. (1983). *Something Like an Autobiography*. Vintage Books, p. 195.

Feature films still conform to the single-camera style of shooting; they just use multiple cameras. The major expression is an "A-B camera" shoot for two cameras. Sometimes more than two cameras are used. For explosions, chase scenes, or anything that cannot be recreated, many cameras are employed—as much as the budget will allow. More and more multicamera dialogue scenes are employed, and multicam is becoming more of a staple in features.

But not everyone in filmmaking is a fan of multicam. Directors of photography are well known for going against the decision to use more than one camera. It is simply harder to light for more than one camera, and more times than not, the overall look of the master shot has to be compromised. This can be the difference between a believable, dramatic look and something closer to a talk show or sitcom.

Dan Lebental, A.C.E., is a Hollywood editor who started in music videos and now cuts blockbuster action films such as *Iron Man*:

Lighting for Multiple Cameras

MULTI-EXPERT APPROACH

It's becoming a new art to be able to light for multicam. The old classic DPs would say, I can only light for one set up at a time, one angle…. But now with much more people, the photographers are expected to be able to light for that, which allows … the actors to overlap each other in dialogue and not put you in a complete dilemma, because what are you going to do if they've overlapped on somebody's single and you have nowhere to go? You have to have that matching piece, or it's useless.

Alan Heim, A.C.E., vice president of the American Cinema Editors and vice president of the Motion Pictures Editor's Guild, says:

It's not something we do a lot. If you had talked to me about shooting a scene with a multicamera setup, and it's just not done that much because there's always a sacrifice made in the lighting quality. Also, a director has to kind of split himself if he has to watch both actors at the same time. It's not as easy as watching one actor.

Figure 3.26 Jeff Ravitz at the Super Bowl. (Courtesy Jeff Ravitz/www.visualterrain.net.)

Jeff Ravitz, LD, is the chief executive officer and principal lighting designer of Visual Terrain, Inc.

Jeff Ravitz: *Well, the problem is that there are so many compromises that you have to make in order to make things look good from multiple angles, unless you are completely comfortable with something looking really ideal from one camera angle and completely contrary on another camera angle. If you are trying to achieve some interesting shadowing on somebody but if the camera is shooting on the same side as the light, your result is a flat one, exactly the opposite of what you're going for, but that camera is basically wrapping around your subject from every conceivable angle and something's got to be compromised.*

Says Troy Takaki, A.C.E.:

The director I'm working with right now shoots a lot of multicamera and what he does, which is unusual, is he actually will shoot from both directions at the same time. Usually, because of lighting, with multicam you'll be like medium close-up wide or medium close-up from the same angle. He will often choose from the other sides in order to keep everything going, so I have more options of being able to, like, keep stuff, especially with the improv scenes.

Regardless of the lighting compromises, more and more multicam filmmaking means more and more multicamera editing, and with these types of lighting issues, it also means more work in color correction.

Marc Wielage, digital colorist:

The biggest issue we have with multicamera, aside from exposure, is lighting angles. Somebody's face might appear to be very bright when you view them from the left, and then you view them from the right, especially with a different focal length, and they might appear to be very dark, or vice versa. It all depends on the quality of the original photography, the lighting, the exposure, the dailies, and so on, and how good or bad those look.

Cutting A-B Cameras

Feature editors are sometimes faced with multicam footage shot from the same angle using a single camera lighting set up (the two-sided single). They have multiple cameras, but they treat the cut as if the footage were shot separately—that is, by not grouping, but instead cutting single-cam style and adding B-camera coverage as necessary.

Tim Squyres is a feature film editor who has cut some of the more adventurous multicamera features like Ang Lee's *Taking Woodstock* and Jonathan Demme's *Rachel Getting Married*. According to Tim, there are several reasons why feature directors use multicam: *Sometimes a director shoots with a lot of cameras because he has a specific vision of what will look good. Other times, he'll shoot with multiple cameras because he doesn't know what will look good and is just looking for coverage. Usually he'll use multiple cameras to cover some action he doesn't want to repeat, like a couple hundred guys on horseback charging into a cavalry and shooting, in a Western. You don't want to do that too many times, for lots of reasons.*

Dan Lebental, A.C.E.: *Multicam is only helping to do wonderful work quickly. The big difference between the TV and feature film workflow is that in features I'll do a cut, and then we'll go in deeper and deeper and really dig out the possibilities. I can decide or I can switch up. I can say, well, at first I was playing this 20 seconds all in the two-shot, but now I realize I'm going to play the first five seconds in the two-shot, then I'm going to cut to the two singles. And they're already laid out for me, in my timeline, in my sequence; I don't have to go back and find those. They're ready to go.*

Lebental, A.C.E. still likes to cut on the fly a little. It comes from his past days as a music video editor.

Dan Lebental, A.C.E.: *It's usually a little more carefully thought out. I'm looking for this or that. And then, if I find the moments I want, say in the two-shot or whatever, I know I have the multicams of the actor singles to go to.*

The Two-Sided Single

There seems to be a trend toward using more A-B cam shoots for dialogue scenes. Especially when time is a serious consideration, and provided you have the budget, you can get more camera setups in one day if you don't have to shoot scenes twice, from two directions. For a single shot, there's a single and a two-shot and then the scene is turned around to shoot a single and a two-shot on the other side. What used to be uncommon is now done all the time with dialogue scenes. But more angles does not mean more material.

Figure 3.27 An A-B camera configuration used to shoot two shots from the same the angle.

Directors may shoot from the same angle with two cameras for lighting continuity and then turn the scene around and shoot the reverse—the other actor with two cameras and a similar angle.

Craig McKay has edited more than 50 films, including *The Manchurian Candidate*, *Philadelphia*, and *Silence of the Lambs*.

Craig: *I'm getting more of the same material instead of more material. But it's not necessarily extra performance pieces, because two of them are identically the same—it's just that one's closer and one's wider.*

Tim Squyres observes:

The nice thing about shooting the same action with two cameras is you can cut from the wide to the tight and it's a perfect match. You see more of those kinds of edits now, because you can do it without it looking bad. If the angles are reasonable, if either they're punched straight in or offset enough, you can A-punch straight in, with continuous action from the wide into the tight; the match has to be perfect. Audiences are getting quite used to that now.

Indeed, it's become more and more common—and it does give you a few extra choices as you cut back and forth.

4

THE MULTICAMERA SHOOT DAY

Truck Park and Power

It takes a lot of vehicles to shoot a TV or film production, and parking them all is no small feat. The typical multicam shoot begins with a remote truck pulling up to park and power. This is where the director works, in the control room.

Before pulling up to a venue, however, your production company will have to secure the applicable permit and, during the preproduction phase, anticipate location-related problems. You cannot just pull up in an 18-wheel truck or superwide double expando and park anywhere. You'll need to determine in advance which side of the street your truck should be on, taking into account its doors—and most cities have rules and side-specific parking conditions. You'll also need to determine how you'll secure power: from the venue itself, or from a generator, which means more parking on the street.

Evan Haiman, HDNet: *Power and parking makes me roll my eyes, because, I would say that 50% of the shows I work on, there's always a power issue or a parking issue, no matter how many times you go and you scout a venue. There have even been generators that have caught on fire…. It's amazing.*

Figure 4.1a Power configuration at the Metropolitan Opera, New York City.

Figure 4.1b Film parking permit from the mayor's office of film and television, New York City. Posted on the Lower East Side for *Wall Street 2* production trucks.

Crew Positions

Let's compare a multicam shoot with a traditional single-camera operation. At a single camera shoot, you typically have a three-person crew: a camera operator, an audio operator, and maybe an assistant. If it's a more elaborate production, throw in a lighting director, a gaffer, and maybe an extra audio person.

Inside the truck, each crewmember has his or her designated position. In the main section, the people in the front row include the director; the assistant director (AD), who sits next to the director and calls shot numbers and setups out to the camera operators; and the technical director (TD), who also sits next to the director and cuts the show. A score reader, in the case of classical music shows, is also in the front cabin. Behind these people are the producers, who watch and take notes. Then there may be the lighting director (LD), who would sit in the back to ensure that each cue is hit. (Sometimes, and more often than not, the LD works instead in the house, where he or she can see the stage lighting and the TV lighting via a monitor feed.)

The other cabin in a typical remote shoot is more of a technical room for the engineer, tape operators, camera shaders, and other technical crewmembers. There is also an audio room and

Figure 4.2 Assistant director checking monitor configuration inside All Mobile Video's Resolution remote truck.

sometimes a separate room or even a B-unit truck specifically for graphics. Outside the truck you have your stage crew: camera operators, cable pullers, utilities, assistant audio techs, the stage manager, and everyone's PAs. The engineer in charge (EIC) is the leader of the equipment provider's crew and oversees the capabilities and implementation of the truck or fly-pack equipment. The technical supervisor or technical manager is more commonly in charge of the production crew. Every crew varies. They run the gamut from small productions with only two crewmembers (to set up and shoot with six cameras) to extra-large shows with more than 100 people on set.

Now add in specialty equipment like jibs, dollies, robotic cameras, and their various specialists and you can easily see how the multicam shoot involves much more of everything. You'll definitely need PAs for every department. You'll also need PAs who can pull cable, in cases where everything is cabled back to the trucks. Depending on your lighting situation, you'll need grips. With so many people on set, a lot of thought has to go into choosing the right team.

The *Great Performances, Carnegie Hall Opening Night 2008: A Celebration of Leonard Bernstein*, featuring a tribute to Leonard Bernstein, involved 12 cameras. It had 11 camera operators, three cameras that were operated robotically, and there were two 20-foot vertical towers installed in the hall as well as a dolly hoisted on a sophisticated piece of robotic track. Choosing the right crew for this show was a major part of preproduction. There is a significant difference between a camera handler who is accustomed to shooting symphony orchestras, or even musicians in general, and one who typically shoots sports, or dance, or a talk show. Each kind of camera operator has his or her own nuances and specialties. This means that to match the right crew to the right program is a talent critical to the process itself.

Additionally, the key crew personnel for *Great Performances* must know how to read music as the script for the concert is written into the music score. (See Chapter 13, Cutting Music: The Symphonic Cut.)

Figure 4.3a Handheld and robotic cameras on stage at Carnegie Hall.

Figure 4.3b Robotic camera operators from Atlantic Cine Equipment, Inc.

Brief Crew Definitions

Let's take a quick look at a list of the multicamera crew positions and their relationship to the editing and post process:

- Producer and director: Main contacts for final decisions
- Assistant director: Sometimes calls rundowns. Handles scripts and TC notes
- Associate producer: May deal directly with editors in relation to tracking and supplying elements
- Production manager: Handles call sheets, crew, and equipment details; sometimes called a line producer
- Production coordinator: Also wrangles elements and location details
- Production assistant (PA): May be responsible for timecode notes if camera assistants do not exist or delegate to them
- Camera operator
- Camera utility
- Audio engineer (A1): Usually responsible for timecode generation, jam sync, and slating camera reels if an engineer is not on staff
- Assistant audio tech (A2): Lays out all the audio cables, mics and stands for the mixer. Also responsible for helping to build announcer's booth for sports remotes. Slates scenes physically with clapboard or smart slate
- Technical director (also called vision mixer and smasher): Switches the shots to the tape, kind of like a live editor
- Graphics operator: Builds and manages graphics, lower third titles.
- EVS operator: A combination of a tape operator and editor who handles slow motion instant replay and quick turnaround edited packages. Usually works on live shows, mostly sports
- Tape operator: Programs TC to the VTRs and does the tape labels among other organizational tasks.
- Engineer in charge (EIC): Responsible for all things technical on the set
- Camera shader: Adjusts the lighting and chroma levels for each camera, like a live colorist in a way

The technical director (TD), or vision mixer in Europe, is like an editor for a live show in the sense that this person is cutting cameras on the fly using a switcher console. The TD creates a line cut based on the shots that the director calls.

Richard Wirth, technical director of *The Rachael Ray Show*, says:

We may go to different locations on the studio floor; we go to different sets in the studio. Everybody needs to know that these things are coming up, and we have to make sure that these cameras are ready and color corrected and matching, and everything that needs to be is ready to go.

Merging Crews

In some cases of recording an existing stage show, like a touring concert, a road crew is already in place. The crew that travels

RS Video & Film Productions RSVP Film Studios Philippine Staff & Crew List. "JOURNEY" Concert.		
Title	**Name**	**Contact Number**
Philippine Production Manager	Oli Laperal Jr.	
Equipment Coordinator	Ariel Riel	
SR Prod. Asst.	Awel Galang	
SR Technician DIT	Ading Bagasona	
Admin. Contact	Marites Marin	
T.D. Switcher (1)	Rafael Guerrero	
T.D. Switcher (2)	Arvin Alvarez	
Cameraman (1)	Manny Pelayo	
Cameraman (2)	Leony De Jesus	
Cameraman (3)	Rands Roldan	
Cameraman (4)	Willy Castillo	
Cameraman (5)	Reiner Magbitang	
Cameraman (6)	Ralp Subebe	
Cameraman (7)	Jojo Calonge	
Cameraman (8)	Fred Escosio	
Technician	Hector Javillonar	
Jimmy Jib Technician	Mike Joson	
Jimmy Jib Grip	Carlos Guevarra	
Battery Hot Swapper/HD Drive Runner	Arnel Libari	
Cableman/Utility 1	Erwin Piga	
Cableman/Utility 2	Jhe Encinas	
Cableman/Utility 3	Travis Samonte	
Cableman/Utility 4	Joel Ramirez	
Cableman/Utility 5	Jojit Cabaza	
Thoma Head Technician	Rhum Ocular	
Thoma Head Assistant	Chriz Soriano	
Pegasus Crane Operator	Rocky Guston	
Pegasus Crane Grip (1)	GV venturina	
Panther Dolly Optr.	Dondon Daymon	
Panther Dolly Grip	Rimby Gonzales	
Driver (1) Van # 1	Ferdie Nacion	
Driver (2) Mini Van # 2	JR Albes	
Driver (3) FB (AUV) # 1	Buboy Bepinosa	
Driver (4) Truck	Monching Dades	
Driver (5) Camry	Raffy Gonzales	
Genet Operator	Cesar Calonge	
Genet Operator (Back-up)	Lhoy Santos	
Make-Up Artist	Leila Baun	

Figure 4.4 Crew Call Sheet. Journey concert shot ENG style with RED cameras. Note that no camera shaders were used. (Courtesy Oli Laperal, Jr. RS Video and Film Productions, RSVP Film Studios.)

with the band on a regular basis usually consists of people who have an intimate knowledge of the songs, the performers, how they act and move, and all of the show's cues and nuances. Using or merging with an existing crew for a special one-time production can be greatly advantageous and should not be a hastily dismissed option in favor of replacing the already seasoned crew with your own.

Peter Moll, director: *You're as good as your best camera people. I've got my pick of the best music shooters and crew in the business, including Al Larson, Brian Bateman, Rick Trimmer, Kevin Paul, and Michael Gomez. These guys do this day in, day out. These guys are music guys. They get it. And these guys can make me look great—or sink my ship. These guys are usually the best guys for the job.*

Figure 4.5a *Late Show with David Letterman* TD sets up a triple mix effect on the switcher. (Courtesy CBS.)

Figure 4.5b Switching console. (Courtesy Grass Valley.)

The best scenario involves mixing the house crew with the crew choices of the production company. It's the best of both worlds.

Evan Haiman, HDNet: *The truth is they've been with the band for the last 40 days and then you're bringing in some hot shot guy to shoot in the same position. So why not complement what you're doing by using them? I think the way to do it is you're probably going to get some good stuff from him or her. We've used a few, especially in the pits. They know where everything is going, and it only helps to make the show better.*

Figure 4.6 Camera operator Kevin Paul shooting an Elton John concert.

Over-Under Cable Wrapping

Load-in is when the precable and utility crews unpack the camera equipment cases and lay miles of cable from the trucks or fly packs to the site where the staging is built. It's traditional for these crewmembers to start as apprentice cable pullers and work their way up. Pulling cables is a dirty job, but a utility crewmember who is ambitious and listens carefully can learn a lot and be recognized by a senior member as someone potentially useful in an advanced department, like camera, audio, or engineering.

One of the first things an apprentice learns while working on a remote shoot is how to deal with cables. These are triaxial cables for standard definition video and fiber cables for HD video. The apprentice learns to wrap them in a fashion called *over-under*, which allows the cable to be rolled up and pulled out without tangles. Firefighters originally developed the over-under method to wrap and pull hoses quickly off their trucks.

(Interestingly, many Japanese crews supply boxes of white gloves for all crewmembers to wear while wrapping cables—to protect hands and keep the cables clean. When one pair of gloves becomes dirty, they're thrown out and replaced with another pair!)

Usually the video crew is the last team to load in after staging, lights, audio, and effects. Their cables go on top of all the others, which means they are also the first ones to pack up and wrap out.

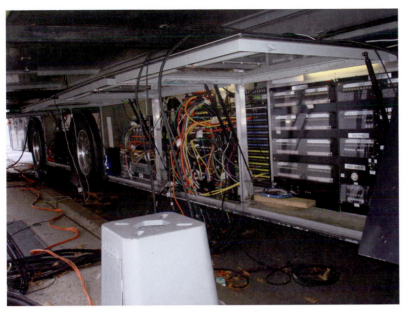

Figure 4.7a Cabling connecting to truck patch panels.

Figure 4.7b Male ends of camera triaxial cable connected to the truck patch bay.

Noteworthy

F*#k the Truck

Methods are passed down through the generations. It is standard that the cables are run backward from the set to the truck. Among insiders, the preferred practice is referred to as *f*#k the truck*. The expression reminds crew to take the "male" cable ends back to the truck. Cables for video, audio, and intercom are fed backward from the camera position to the truck with the male ends of the cables plugged into the patch bay. The lone exception is power cables; they are always run with the "female" ends back to the truck. If you don't lead with the male ends, you'll have to rewrap the cable, flip it around, and reroute it correctly, which could cost several hours if not days of valuable setup time. So always F*#k the truck.

Meet Me at the Butt Farm

On many touring shows, there's a systematic approach to cabling. One method is to make a pit stop halfway between the truck and the cameras to plug into a intermediate cable junction box known as the Butt Farm or Butt World.

Instead of trying to reach the full distance with one cable, known as home run cabling, a primary group of bundled cables is snaked out to a point closer to the stage or camera stages. It is usually a much shorter reach from the staging area back to the truck. The area near the stage where the cables are dropped is called Butt World or the Butt Farm, as in where the "butt end" of each cable is strung out first. With the shorter run to the stage you are essentially making two camera runs.

"I challenge the crew to streamline every day," says Peter Moll. "We pull out a Butt World cable with a married triax mult with co-ax, triax, fiber, whatever you need, and it all goes to upstage center or downstage center and under stage. That's where everything plugs in and spreads out. Rather than have home run cabling into everything, you get everything onto the stage with the Butt World cable and then fan out from there."

Figure 4.8a The Butt Farm. Midpoint connection from stage to truck.

Figure 4.8b Close-up of Butt Farm patch panels with camera feeds from the stage.

Figure 4.8c Butt Farm patch configuration to truck.

Building and Matching Cameras

Once cables are laid in, the EIC assigns crew to build cameras based on preassigned positions that the director has marked on the camera map. Tripods are set up; camera bodies and lenses are married to one another; and jibs, dollies, and other utilities are configured. The LD and the video shader work together closely to prep the cameras on the morning before the production day begins.

Next, the cameras are matched up.

The Art and Science of Camera Matching

There are two components to adjusting cameras: the first is the science of *alignment,* and the second is the art of *painting and shading.*

Alignment is done with charts and scopes. Painting refers to adjusting the color, and shading means adjusting the brightness and contrast. The goal is to conform these qualities in all of the camera shots to achieve a consistent, specific look envisioned by the director.

Figure 4.9a Camera matching at Guitar Hero Aerosmith event.

Figure 4.9b Matching cameras to a chip chart.

Billy Steinberg, a video engineer and operator for music programs ranging from the *Metropolitan Opera Live in HD* to *Sheryl Crow: Rockin' the Globe Live*, says:

While you have test scopes and charts to help make sure everything is aligned the same, painting is done by looking at the picture and knowing what you want it to look like and then knowing how to adjust the camera to make it look that way. You need to understand both the art direction and lighting crafts and what makes something look like it does to the eye. Then you have to understand how to adjust a camera to make it look the way you want.

Ideally, you would start with the same brand and model camera on a truck or fly-pack system. As for how to control the look, there's no objective solution to matching cameras; it's an art. The scientific part begins with the *remote control panel* (RCP) connected to a *camera control unit* (CCU). Multiple cameras can share a master control unit (MCU).

Figure 4.10a Camera remote control panel (CCU).

Remote Control Panels (RCPs)

Each camera has its own remote control panel that allows you to adjust pretty much anything in the camera. The most common adjustments are right at your fingertips, whereas the less common ones are buried in menus. There's also a master control unit that controls all of the cameras, allowing a little more flexibility.

Chip Charts and Color Charts

Good finishing and continuity and making clips look like they belong with each other in a multi-camera shoot start on the set by calibrating those cameras. Generally, cameras are set up with black-and-white chip charts to adjust gamma (which might be construed as contrast); its primary function is for color. Unless the cameras show black and white the same, they will never match with color.

MacBeth charts are color charts for hue and saturation and are rarely used in multicamera. Their only purpose would be if there's a particular shade that someone wants set up specifically. Even then, they'd be rarely used. They're more common in film.

A test chart is put somewhere onstage under the show lights to align the cameras so they'll look the same on all sets and under the proper color temperature.

Sometimes shaders don't have the luxury of charting and have to do their job entirely by eye, which is a little more difficult. But if you're good at what you do, it is possible—especially if you also have experience working with the same trucks and cameras, which would give you a good sense of what to expect.

Figure 4.10b Individual camera remote control unit (CCU).

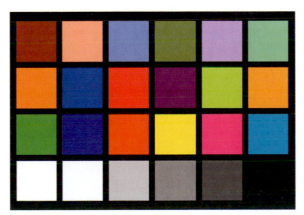

Figure 4.11a MacBeth chart. (Courtesy X-Rite Color Checker.)

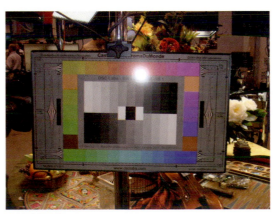

Figure 4.11b Dual Color/chip chart. (Courtesy www.dsclabs.com.)

Notes Robbie Carman, colorist and co-owner of Amigo Media, LLC:

One thing that frustrates me as I work in colors day to day is that people do not pay enough attention to color and contrast calibrating cameras on set. It's one of those things that everybody knows they should do, but they seldom do it.

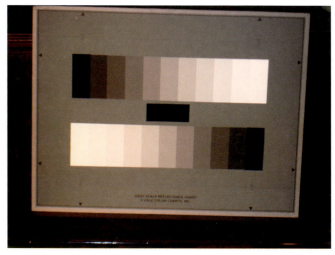

Figure 4.12a Chip chart.

Figure 4.12b Chip chart on drum riser.

White Balancing

White balancing is another way to align cameras for color temperature. In principle, it works by "showing" the camera what "pure white" is supposed to look like on a white card. This helps the camera adjust the rest of its colors to match the same color temperature.

White balancing should be done on scenes where the lighting color temperature changes just as indoor or outdoor lighting changes. Sometimes you might find yourself matching for mixed temperatures, such as a 5600° Kelvin spotlight combined with 3200° Kelvin stage lighting.

Says Peter Moll:

On most tours we do a white balance and match all our cameras every day with lighting and house spots. There's a little more leeway than in

Figure 4.12c Engineer Gary Templeton adjusts camera control units with a chip chart and waveform monitor.

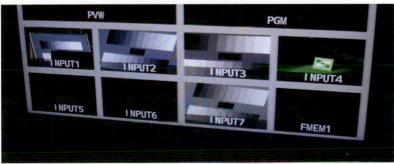

Figure 4.12d Chip charts from all cameras on the director's monitor.

broadcast, because in rock-and-roll, if there's a blue light on the guy, his face is going to be blue. So there isn't so much of chasing flesh tones. One song, it's a red light on him, another song, it's blue—and I'm of the belief that if it's a rock show and there's a red light on him, he should look red. That's rock and roll.

Shading

Shading is about matching cameras and comes from the expression "pulling down the shades." Notes Mark Schubin, broadcast engineer:

"Pulling down the shades" has nothing to do with set light levels. In the old days of iconoscope tubes, they were surrounded (inside the camera) with a ring of lights to bias the sensor to make a nice flat picture. The shades surrounded the side of the tube and shaded the sensor from these bias lights.

Every shader has a router in front of him or her, which allows shaders to switch from camera to camera within the shoot as well as to their own monitoring stations with a large color monitor and test scopes. The shader listens to the AD, and when it's nearly time for a particular shot the shader sees it on the monitor and

Figure 4.13 Master Control Unit (MCU)

adjusts it as necessary before the director takes it. The work done on location by a good shader/colorist gives the editor clips that are nicely color timed and ISO matched.

Legal Limits

As a matter of routine, the shader will also ensure that the signals are all "legal." Shaders do this by consulting waveform monitors and oscilloscopes to check whether "clipping" is taking place, so that the whites don't go to 150 and the colors are set (i.e., not illegally saturated).

Setting up the Tape Room

While the cameras are being set up and matched, another engineer known as the tape operator is prepping all of the recording decks and devices. The tape operator's job is to ensure that all decks are recording video properly, along with the multiple audio and timecode channels. During the show, the tape operator may (along with an additional tape op) provide instant replays—although on bigger shows that work is done on hard drives like an EVS system (see Bonus Chapter on DVD: On-Set Editing). The tape operator's job may involve editing quick fixes as well.

Tech Specs and Routing

Prep begins with a set of requirements delivered by the producers. These requirements are called tech specs, which prescribe how many cameras and tape machines are needed. They also specify which decks are designated for line cuts and protection masters, what cameras are being ISOed to which deck, and what the multiple tracks of audio assignments are. Once these requirements are met, the tape op will start to route and assign signals to the machines. Some tape ops will use a little RAM card to automate the metadata and deck setup. This enables them to accomplish the job in seconds, rather than going through each of the menus and manually duplicating the settings in each VTR. Automation can save an hour or two of prep time.

Sometimes ISOs are switched to a VTR. Routing switchers with salvos (or quick multiple setups) are configured for switching the different sets of ISOs.

The Flip/Flop Master

The flip/flop master is an alternative or opposite to the line cut. An operational mode allows the program/preview mode (PGM/PST) on the switcher to reverse outputs. It flip/flops the

		Second Half of San Jose Show Chart					
	Show A				Show B		
Tape #	Camera #	Position	Tape #	Camera #	Position		TAPE DECK
4050	1	HH-House Left	4070	1	HH Stage-House Right		VTR A
4051	2	HH Aud-House Right	4071	2	HH Aud-House Left		VTR B
4052	3	Techno Jib	4072	3	Techno jib		VTR C
4053	4	House Dolly-Long Lens	4073	4	House Dolly-Longer Lens		VTR D
4054	5	House Left-Wide	4074	5	House Center-Wide		VTR E
4055	6	Fixed Center	4080	6	Fixed Center		VTR F
4056	7	House Jib	4081	7	House Jib		VTR H
4057	8	Cable Cam-Left To Right	4082	8	Cable Cam-Right to Left		VTR I
4060	9	Fixed Left-Tight	4083	9	Fixed Left Tight		VTR J
4061	10	Fixed Right-Wide	4084	10	Fixed Right Wide		VTR K
4062	11	Rail Cam-Pit	4085	11	Rail Cam-Pit		VTR L
4063	12	House Right Long (Piano)	4086	12	House Right Long (Piano)		VTR M
4064	13	HH Stage Center	4087	13	HH Stage Center		VTR N
4059	14	Line Cut MHP	4088	14	Line Cut MHP		VTR O
4058	15	Line Cut MHP	4089	15	Line Cut MHP		VTR P

Figure 4.14 VTR plan/map for Paul McCartney concert. (Courtesy Mark Haefeli Productions.)

Figure 4.15 Tape op Alan Falkner prepping tapes for a show.

Prelabeling Media

A tape op must be conscientious and, like a librarian, keep track of everything. A properly labeled set of media makes a tape op the editing team's best friend. As tape op Alan Falkner puts it, "For a tape op, labeling is half the job."

Figure 4.16 Tape operator station with VTR and videotapes.

Figure 4.17 Preprinted tape labels on tapes ready for recording.

program and preview button output bus with preset handles to a VTR or hard disk. So whatever's being recorded to the line cut, the opposite or preview is recorded to the flip/flop master. Preview is now program and vice versa. It doesn't work with dissolves and requires switching on the same field. The timecode matches, so this tape serves as an excellent way to make quick edit fixes to a show with only two tapes: the line cut and its flip/flop master. No ISOs are needed.

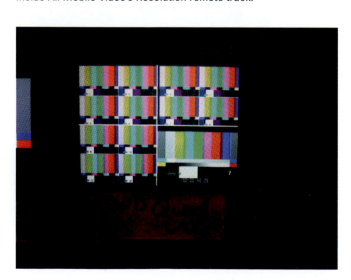

Figure 4.18 Double program monitors and preview monitor (on second row right) inside All Mobile Video's *Resolution* remote truck.

Noteworthy

Multicamera DVD Preview Master

A multicam preview master DVD is a screening copy of the show that has been burned in real time and has all ISOs and line cuts visible on a split screen master with timecode. Producers and assistants use preview masters to make notes or quickly view alternative shots at a given timecode. This is a fast way to see all the camera options available for editing, especially if you do not have access to all the individual reels or multiclips.

Figure 4.19 Split ISO view DVD monitor.

Monitoring

Monitor walls, portable monitor bridges, and split-field plasmas are a few of the most common tools for monitoring multicam signals. The monitor wall is used in megatrucks and smaller versions are rack mounted for fly packs. For portability in an ENG situation, nothing beats a handheld monitor bridge. The latest gimmick is using a large-screen LED or LCD multiviewer monitor and controlling your onscreen viewing configuration with software. You can make one display show 16 monitors, or 4 monitors, or whatever you want. These monitors are very popular because they enable the creation of giant walls of programmable monitors out of a few screens instead of carrying a separate monitor for each view.

Audio Considerations

Audio on a multicam shoot can be complicated. For example, on a reality show using multicam crews that follow contestants, everybody gets a wireless mic. There are also booms and plant mics, all of which have to be recorded to multitrack with matching timecode and to camera inputs for a mix.

Figure 4.20 Monitor wall featuring preview, program, and individual camera views. (Courtesy All Mobile Video.)

Figure 4.21 Portable programmable LCD monitor wall.

Figure 4.22a Audio mixer Tod Maitland on the set of *Wall Street 2*.

Figure 4.22b Location sound equipment featuring a Zaxcom Deva 5.8 10-track hard disk audio recorder with built-in timecode reader/generator.

The important thing to consider in advance of editing is your ability to find and group all of those tracks when building your multi-clips. Mostly you will have these tracks loaded with your cameras, but if they are shot using dual system audio, you will need to sync that to the camera like syncing dailies on a film production.

ESU: Equipment Setup

ESU is short for, you guessed it, equipment setup. The engineers set up and review everything on the truck to ensure all signals are going from the cameras to the proper tape machines and in the proper format; they also check that all monitors are set, that the intercom is working and firing properly, and that the camera operators experience no problems with the specialty lenses or custom gear.

FAX Check

FAX is short for facilities. The facilities include every tool available to a production. Checking them requires that everyone is on a headset to take a first look at the show. Each operator checks his or her own gear and intercom, and then everyone performs a trial run to tally lights, zoom, pan, tilt, focus, and so on. Audio and lighting have FAX checks too.

Once the ESU is complete and the engineers satisfied, then truck operations are turned over to the show's director, who meets with the camera crew and begins to rehearse and shoot the show. From this point on, both on location and in the editing room, it's about the director's vision.

FAX may also be used as a verb for checking something out.

In the Moment: *The Late Show with David Letterman*

As 450 audience members are filing into the historic Ed Sullivan Theater, director Jerry Foley reflects on the value of a good team. He is surrounded by the same core group of people every afternoon to tape the live six-act event known as *Late Show with David Letterman.*

Jerry Foley: *There's not a single contributor to the production who isn't essential. The people running scripts are just as vital as the guy operating camera 2, which is Letterman's primary camera. Disturb one single element and the broadcast becomes infinitely more complicated and less entertaining.*

It's the original reality television show. Letterman goes out with little more than a few observations or experiences he wants to share. He has options, but basically he stands up there, gets a feel for the audience, and uncorks a show right in front of you. It's beyond improvisational comedy. It's more like impulsive comedy. Any given show can morph into something completely unexpected. It's often discovered in the moment, and the energy that comes from performing in front of a live audience cannot be rec-reated on a redo or a retake. You have to nail it live and, as with any great live show, it requires very little editing because Foley and his camera people and crew are always in the moment.

Figure 4.23 *Late Show* director Jerry Foley on set with stage manager Biff Henderson.

Figure 4.24 *Late Show* set with Letterman's desk and Paul Shaffer's bandstand.

As Foley explains:

The camera people are essential to the process. They know Letterman's sensibilities and the probability of what a moment's going to be, and they cover it. They know how to anticipate. When one of these moments transpires and one of these things evolves, they know what to do, they are preediting their own shots as they go along every minute they're behind that viewfinder.

As Jerry Foley calls the live show, each camera operator is in position to capture it. Letterman can stand up at that desk and go in any direction, and if those camera operators don't understand where he may go, if the audio guys don't know what may happen next, if the lighting people don't have contingencies for these moments, then it doesn't work.

Adds Foley:

It starts off, as most of these things do, with a basic understanding of zone coverage. You have contingencies for certain moments—if he goes right, if he goes left, if he goes center—but then you get into the nuances of what the conversation was leading up to this moment, where the reaction shots are going to be. If I have to explain to a camera person what they need to do, the moment has passed.

Figure 4.25 Reverse angle from Letterman's point of view: program monitor, clock and camera 2, Letterman's primary camera.

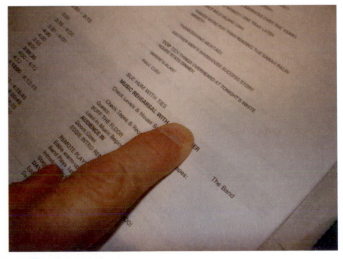

Figure 4.26 The show rundown.

Figure 4.27 *Late Show* editor Mark Spada and director Jerry Foley cut a show down to time.

Figure 4.28 Avid Nitris monitor with multicam angles stacked on a timeline.

After the show is over, the work is essentially done except for a few edits here and there to keep censors and the clock watchers happy. The deliverable show is turned over to the network for same-day broadcasts while Jerry Foley and the crew prepare for the next day's big moments.

TIMECODE AND SYNC

5

TIMECODE BASICS

We live and die by timecode.

Ray Volkema, editor, HDNet Concerts

If cameras, switchers, recording decks, and monitors are the skeleton of a multicam shoot, then timecode and sync are the central nervous system. Timecode is a sequence of binary coded decimals generated at regular intervals and used to label individual frames of video or film with a unique address consisting of the hour, minute, second, and frame number. It's a form of metadata defined by the Society of Motion Picture and Television Engineers (SMPTE) as a master clock that enables the synchronization of editing and camera switching equipment.[1] Timecode numbers are also used for identifying the locations of scenes and shots while logging footage.

Figure 5.1 A typical timecode display.

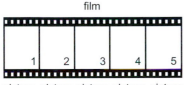

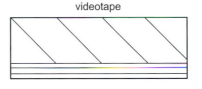

Figure 5.2 Film and video frames. (Courtesy www.alpermann-velte.com/proj_e/tc_intro/tcintro.html#history.)

Additionally, a blackburst or genlock signal connects cameras, tape decks, and other equipment together in unison or sync. This signal can be an SD analog signal or a tri-level signal for HD projects. There are several practices for syncing HD or SD formats.

Doi: 10.1016/B978-0-240-81176-5.00005-8

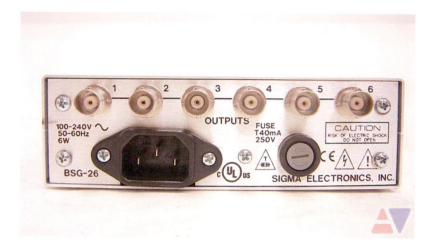

Figure 5.3 Back of Black Burst Generator with six outputs. (Courtesy Sigma Electronics and www.theinventorysolution.com.)

As with any multicam production, genlocking, sync and proper timecode are of utmost importance. On remote trucks, the engineer-in-charge is responsible for wiring the equipment and syncing all cameras to the truck, whereas in the field the sound department is primarily accountable for timecode and sync, using practices that all stem from syncing single-camera productions with dual system audio.

Many producers claim various reasons for not having proper sync on location. They blame budgets, lack of knowledge, ignorance, time, and so on. But the bottom line is that a few extra minutes in the field will save you *hours* in postproduction. *Somebody* needs to take responsibility for timecode. Oftentimes it ends up in the hands of the sound department.

Multi-Expert Approach: Audio Department Handles Sync

The interesting thing that camera people never understand is that timecode is usually generated from the guy doing the audio. Audio always has the clock on. And more often than not in a multicam environment where there's a sound recordist on set, the sound recordist is the one who's actually generating timecode for all of the cameras.

Gary Adcock

It's a collaboration between the sound and picture departments. It's both the lead tech person who usually comes from the rental house that supplies the equipment and the audio mixer who'll usually be running the common timecode generator and be responsible for getting valid locked and synced code to all cameras and audio devices. Audio guys seem to get it because they come from a dual-system paradigm.

Mark Raudonis, Bunim-Murray Productions

Timecode has traditionally been part of the audio world. So let's assume, for example, that sound is the master timecode source. Now, we could simply jam each camera from the sound recorder.

Peter Gray, DP and digital image tech

The Timecode Generator

Timecode is critically important on the job, probably more so than half of the other stuff. It all boils down to timecode.

Alan Falkner, freelance tape operator

The signal is compatible with various cable types including audio, serial digital (SDI), triax, fiber, and 422 control cables. Cameras and decks can have built-in TCGs or generators can be standalone equipment. The timecode is generated in user-programmable ways that include choices of frame rates and various modes including record run, free-run time of day, and drop or nondrop frame counting. One can also refine the process by using operator-defined data called user bits.

Noteworthy

HOURS:MINUTES:SECONDS:FRAMES = 00:00:00:00

SMPTE timecode generator (TCG) systems use *hours: minutes: seconds: frames* to assign each video frame with a unique number (00:00:00:00) for each frame on the tape. Such systems also have the capacity to share this signal with other pieces of electronic equipment in a broadcast studio or remote system.

Figure 5.4 Timecode generators in rack before production.

User Bits

User bits offer a handy way to be even more specific in defining a project, but they are not used often. In addition to timecode,

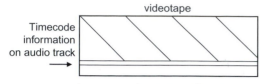

| "time" e.g. date | 10:00:00:00 | 10:00:00:01 | 10:00:00:02 |
| in userbits | 04.11.2009 | 04.11.2009 | 04.11.2009 |

Figure 5.5 Timecode on an audio track. (Courtesy www.alpermann-velte.com/proj_e/tc_intro/tcintro.html#history.)

user bits allow you to track additional production information. Eight additional digits recorded within every frame, user bits could refer to a date, a production number, a secret code to unlock the universe! Anything. They come in handy at the archiving stage of your asset.

Drop and Nondrop Frame

Generally, we use drop frame (DF) and nondrop frame (NDF) when mastering programs for broadcast. DF is recommended for any long-form recording. Both DF and NDF are 29.97 frames per second instead of 30 fps. The term "drop frame" refers to the changes in the counting sequence and not the speed change of 29.97 versus 30.

Drop frame timecode is simply a different way of counting frames: a mathematical way to adjust for a timing error in broadcasting color signals.

Oliver Peters: *DF was used so that shows could be properly timed for broadcast formatting. NDF TC is 108 frames too long over an hour. If you're timing a show based on NDF TC, then your one-hour duration based on NDF numbers will be 108 frames too long compared to one hour measured on a clock. DF TC was developed so that the numbers jived for the purpose of calculating durations for broadcast based on the TC read-out. In fact, you can record camera tapes and masters in either NDF or DF. Most NLE don't care and can easily mix; timelines can be changed after the fact anyway.*

The dirty little secret behind drop frame timecode is that frames are not really "dropped" or "skipped," as the name implies. It's really just an adjustment in the way the frames are counted, so that one hour of timecode generated equals one hour on an actual wall clock. The counter "drops" or omits 18 frames each 10 minutes—or two frames per minute except for the tenth minute. This new counting of 29.97 frames per second comes out almost exactly the same as on the wall clock.[2] No more broadcast mistakes and 1.5 minutes more billable time per day! Brilliant.

You can tell the difference on the generated timecode by looking for a semicolon (;) between the numbers for drop frame and a colon (:) for nondrop frame. I like to remember it by thinking that the colon looks like it's dropping something.

Frame Rates

Pulldown and Frame Rate Differences

Timecode generators work with different frame rates for use in film, 4k, HD, and SD, as well as PAL and SECAM. All of the common rates are there, including (but not limited to) 24, 23.98, 25, 29.97, 30, and 59.94 (and 60) frames per second. But what happens when your frame rates don't match, or your format changes to a different rate that needs converting? You'll need to sync the mechanical film motion of 24 with the electronic video signal 29.97.

The pulldown method has been designed for 24-fps film projects but also applies to any digital video shot at 24 frames per second.

Film is generally shot and projected at 24 frames per second (fps); however, to align itself with TV, it plays back at 23.96 fps. Therefore, when film frames are converted to NTSC video, the rate must be modified to play at 29.97 fps.

During the telecine process, 12 fields are added to each 24 frames of film (12 fields=6 frames), so the same images that made up 24 frames of film then make up 30 frames of video. Video plays at a speed of 29.97 fps, so the film actually runs at 23.976 fps when transferred to video.

I know. This telecine pulldown business can make your head swim. My uber-basic way of explaining it to clients is to say that their 24-frame project doesn't fill the post bucket. Video editing needs 30 frames, so we just need to add six frames a second. Boom. They get it.

According to Alan Stewart, freelance editor and postproduction consultant, "each field scan takes 1/60th of a second; therefore, a whole frame is scanned each 1/30th of a second—which amounts to 29.97 frames per second."

So now it comes down to where we add the six frames into the 24 frames every second. The frames are not added together at the beginning or the end of the 24 frames but rather are woven into the frame with a cadence. The two basic cadences are 2:2 and 3:2 (which is also called 2:3).

3:2 Pulldown

In the United States or anywhere using NTSC-systems with 29.97 fps, the telecine is accurate when using either 2:3 pulldown or 3:2 pulldown. After slowing the film down to 23.97 or starting with 23.98 video, four frames of film are stretched into five frames of video. The interlacing smooths it out between fields.[3]

The Avid Film Composer assumes a 2:3 pulldown. That means that the first frame of film is represented by two fields of video; the second frame is represented by three fields of video (1.5 frames); the third again by two, the fourth by three, and so on. In the end, what was running at 23.976 fps is running at 29.97 fps.

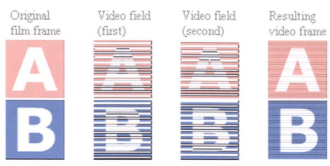

Figure 5.6 Pulldown. (Courtesy Eric Lee and Wikipedia.)

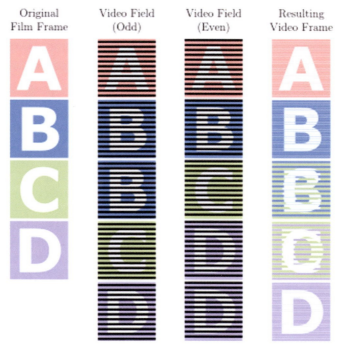

Figure 5.7 Shows how four frames of film become five frames of video; repeat that process six times and 24 frames of film become 30 frames of video (www.zerocut.com).

Modern telecines use 2:3:2:3 cadence for NTCS; therefore, AA BB BC CD DD. If the telecine is set for 3:2, you'll get BB BC CD DD AA, which would require you to change the default pull-in before digitizing the clips, because the clips' head frames would be "B" rather than "A."[4]

There is also 2:3:3:2, referred to as 24pA (advanced). It allows the two superfluous fields to be in the same frame, so that frame can be easily dropped.

Reverse Pulldown

The Avid digitizes (records) and plays the film at 24 fps in a film project, so the video has to be stripped of the fields that were added in the tape transfer process. This is the extraction of the pulldown from tape to digital and can also be accomplished shooting digitally at 24Pa (advance pulldown). Some cameras use this format to capture 23.976 progressive-scan imagery using standard DV tapes at 29.97. With 24Pa, the digital camera recording to tape will flag the original 24 frames in advance so the computer can remove the extra frames and load only the original 24.

So 24p uses the same 2:3 or 3:2 pulldown cadence used to transfer 24 fps film to NTSC video; 24p Advanced uses a syncopated 2:3:3:2 pulldown cadence to stuff 24 frames into 60 fields.[1] The difference is subtle but can be seen on smooth pans or on regular in-frame motion. But 24p Advanced isn't intended for making the 60i video look like film; it's designed to allow the best possible recovery of the original 24 frames.

Record Run Timecode

There are two basic types of timecode reader/generator modes: free run and record run. Free run/record run refers to how the VTR/camera is set. Free run is better for most multicam shoots, and record run is better for single-cam or anything shot that needs continuous timecode.

Philip Hodgetts is the author of *The HD Handbook* and also works as a renowned technical consultant:

SMPTE timecode can be written in two ways. With record run, the timecode counts up whenever the tape is recording. Time-of-day, or free run timecode, runs continuously and what is written to the tape is the time of day or whatever point the free run timecode has counted to when recording starts.

The record run method is good for single-camera shooting because the timecode is continuous for the length of the tape and good for logging. This method is *not* good for multicam, however, because your cameras will each have a different timecode each time they're reset. Accordingly, free run time of day is the preferred method for multicam shoots, enabling us to synchronize all cameras to a timecode that is constant and continuous.

Free Run/Time-of-Day Timecode

The free run (or continuous) mode is timecode that will run continuously until reset. It can be set to start at any user-designated

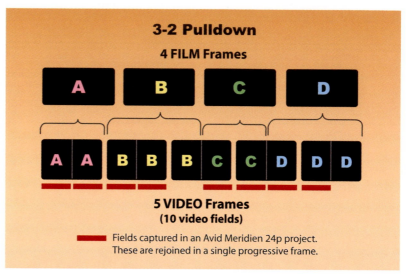

Figure 5.8 Close-up of the Free Run/Record Run switch on camera.

predetermined number. A common use for free run in multicam is to set it for the current time of day (TOD timecode). It is much easier to sync multiple cameras that start and stop with time-of-day timecode.

TOD is used in the studio environment and remote multicam shoots as the house sync. There is no need to use a slate or markers to sync up scenes, because everything is running in harmony with house sync. The timecode will continue running whether the camera is recording or not recording. When you resume recording, there will be a jump in time to match the current TOD, but all cameras jammed to that time will jump to the same timecode no matter when they are turned on or off.

Phillip Hodgetts: *With either type of timecode, ensure there are 5 to 10 seconds of unbroken timecode before any picture that will be used. This preroll time is necessary so the playback deck can accurately locate the desired timecode. A break during the preroll period can confuse equipment later during editing modes.*

Jam-Syncing Timecode

The practice of matching all cameras and VTRs to the same free-running timecode is called jam-syncing. It's our best choice for keeping camera timecode matching, but it's not perfect because the generated signal tends to drift out of sync over time and needs to be corrected.

Not to be confused with blackburst or tri-level synchronization, which we'll discuss later in this chapter, jam-sync is an optional mode on many timecode reader/generators to allow synchronization using SMPTE timecode for multiple cameras, recording machines, and dual system audio configurations.

It works with a master clock that feeds timecode to many slave devices such as cameras, tape decks, and audio recorders. It allows such slave devices to supply their own matching timecode after the master generator is removed. There is also the practice called continuous jam-sync, which works with a continuous matching timecode stream constantly regenerated to the slave unit.

Oliver Peters: *It's important to point out that you have to have genlock in order for jam-sync TC to work properly. If the cameras are genlocked, then the master TC generator also needs to be genlocked from the same sync generator. I personally don't believe that slaving the device and then removing the master source is reliable in the field—especially in a situation where the cameras might be powered down inadvertently.*

During camera setup, a tech will configure the master TC generator with the SMPTE time-of-day set to free run and take the output cable around to each camera's TC input. The camera is also set to time-of-day free run. The camera will slave to the incoming timecode from the master and "jam" or accept the incoming TC as its own. The received or "jammed" TC will be identical to the master TC. The process continues to each camera and device in the production until everything in the chain matches.

Compensating for TC Drifts: Portable Timecode and Sync Boxes

So what if your cameras drift? What does that matter? Well that depends on how close you want to have sync to the field. If you need rock-solid sync to the frame, use a Denecke Syncbox model SB-T or Ambient tri-level Lockit Boxes (ACL 202CT) and you're actually going to get sync to the field. Take the Lockit box around and lock the cameras and audio gear to that, so everything's locking to a third-party unit that syncs everything.

Peter Schneider of Gotham Sound and Communications, Inc., in New York and former location soundman on shows including *The Sopranos* says:

Mechanically, you set up your timecode on your recorder and then you jam a Lockit box and then you take that Lockit box and jam all the other Lockit boxes. When you're done jamming the last camera, you turn that

Lockit box around and feed your audio recorder. You're jamming the value of the timecode into that unit. It's almost like forcing; in fact, I've seen it referred to as force-jam.

It's all based on drift. Resyncing is only a safety measure. Can you do without it? Arguably, every two hours is safe, every four hours is probably necessary, and every eight hours, you're going to see some drift. If you're doing a show that only lasts one hour, then you're probably pretty good with one jam and you're out. But if you're run and gunning all day long in (say you are working on a reality show), then you should have breaks every two hours to rejam everything.

Peter Schneider: *Resyncing does not change the original timecode. It adjusts it. The Lockit boxes continue with time of day and you're just letting the timecode catch up to compensate for a slight frame drift. What you're doing is resyncing all the crystals together. The point in time when you jam becomes the new point where they'll start to drift again, so you'd better rejam two hours after that.*

Many of these types of units are available; some of the more popular ones include the Lockit box and Clockit box. These have user-programmable start times and allow for syncing to source

Noteworthy

NLEs do not actually load the timecode; an NLE normally takes a stamp of the timecode in the first frame and then it interpolates.

Noteworthy

Portable sync boxes generally hold to about one frame per day without rejamming. However, some cameras can drift as much as 10 frames in three hours.

Figure 5.9 Lockit box on ENG camera. (Courtesy Ambient.)

Figure 5.10 Tri-level Syncbox model SB-T. (Courtesy Deneke.)

feeds generated from studio master clocks or remote TC generators using time of day as a stable sync.

Now that we have discussed the timecode types, sync, and remote HD solutions, let's take a quick look at the top ways of recording the timecode signal onto tape and disk. After all, the signal has to live somewhere!

Recording Timecode Tracks

Technology progresses at an unbelievably fast pace. In the same way film editing has stepped aside to digital nonlinear editing, videotape is being phased out by portable hard drives, SxS, and CompactFlash cards. But tape is still in the game for now, so let's take a quick look at the various ways it records.

Figure 5.11 64-GB P2 card. (Courtesy Panasonic.)

Figure 5.12 SxS SD cards. (Courtesy AbelCine.com.)

Figure 5.13 CompactFlash cards. (Courtesy SanDisk.)

Once we generate the timecode, it is fed to the rest of the system: cameras, decks, VTRs, and now hard drives and media cards. The signal is read by the internal or external timecode reader and recorded onto the tape or disk in a variety of tracks as set by SMPTE. These tracks are known as vertical interval TC (VITC) and longitudinal TC (LTC).

The usual array of P2, SxS, and Compact-Flash cards use a metadata file to link to timecode, as well as to link other information about the shot directly to the digital frame.

Figure 5.15 Sonnet Qio Card reader. (Courtesy Sonnet.)

Figure 5.14 The REDFLASH (CF) MODULE does not actually store data. Instead it adds an interface into which CompactFlash media cards can be inserted. Offering the equivalent of a 400-foot film reel per 8-GB card, this "necessity" also provides the solution for a speedy and reliable firmware upgrade path. (Courtesy RED.)

Longitudinal TC

Linear (or longitudinal) timecode (LTC) encodes SMPTE timecode data as an audio signal (at 2400 Hz). This memorable sound signal is commonly recorded onto a VTR audio track or other storage media. Each frame is terminated by a "sync word" that has a special, predefined sync relationship with any video

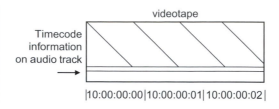

videotape

Timecode information on audio track

|10:00:00:00|10:00:00:01|10:00:00:02|

Figure 5.16 User bits as dates. (Courtesy www .alpermann-velte.com/proj_e/ tc_intro/tcintro.html#history.)

or film content. (In the industry, "LTC" is pronounced "Lit-See"—except in the United Kingdom where it's pronounced "Ell-Tee-See.")[5]

LTC is making a big comeback with many editing tools using Aux TC tracks recorded with LTC. It is being used to automate the synchronization of multicam setups. (See Chapter 6, Sync Methods, and Chapter 13, Cutting Music, and the appendix also has a great article about Aux TC.)

The LTC signal can be distributed by standard audio wiring, connectors, distribution amplifiers, and patch bays. It can also can be ground-isolated with audio transformers and distributed via 75-ohm video cable and video-distribution amplifiers.

Oliver Peters: *Longitudinal SMPTE timecode is generally recorded at 0 VU or 2–3 VU on an analog meter, but sometimes there are other specs. Some decks don't show a level at all (Beta-SP, D2, Digibeta, etc.). If you are recording an analog multitrack, TC should be on track 24 with track 23 left clean as a guard band.*

Vertical Interval TC

In digital, pulses set the timing of the start and end of the video signal, in a spot before the frame information, in what used to be called vertical interval.[6] Vertical interval timecode (VITC, pronounced "Vit-See") is a form of SMPTE timecode embedded as a pair of black-and-white bars in a video signal.

On some older sets, the white bars look as though they are dancing back and forth at the top of the TV picture. These lines are typically inserted into the vertical blanking interval of the video signal, between the frames. There can be more than one VITC pair in a single frame of video—and this can be used to encode extra data that will not fit in a standard timecode frame.[7] The vertical interval is also visible on pro-monitors with under-scan mode.

A video frame may contain more than one VITC code if necessary, recorded on different line pairs. This is often used in production, where different entities may want to encode different sets of timecode metadata on the same tape.

As a practical matter, VITC can be more "frame accurate" than LTC, particularly at very slow tape speeds on analog formats.

Phillip Hodgetts: *Longitudinal TC is very useful because you can still read timecode at low and fast speeds, whereas longitudinal timecode is basically an audio tape with audio tracks and, as you speed it up, of course, it goes higher and higher in pitch, and as you slow it down it goes lower and lower in pitch. Eventually, it can't be read by the reader, at which point usually VITC timecode takes over.*

Timecode Management and Troubleshooting

Establishing the proper timecode and time-base relationship for all the cameras and audio recorders is probably the single most important decision to nail down in preproduction. A few basic tech setups on location or in preproduction will save a huge amount of time and money in post.

Peter Schneider: *What I always do is work backwards from the requirements of editorial. I always look for somebody in postproduction who's going to take responsibility for this. I ask, what do you need to put all these pieces together in the editing room? Do you need exact matching timecode on every camera? Do you need the timecode to be just "in the ballpark"? What's your ideal scenario?*

When we talk about syncing multiple sources with timecode, we're always talking about free run time-of-day timecode as opposed to record run timecode, which is used primarily for single-camera efp-style shoots. Record run TC increments the timecode only when something's recording; it starts and stops.

In multicam, each camera would start and stop on its own and none of the timecode would ever match. Certainly, with one camera and one sound recorder, you could figure out a way to sync them up with record run timecode. But as soon as you get into more than two sources, they're all going to be going independently, and it just doesn't work. So we sync multiple cameras with free run time-of-day timecode to make it easier and save time.

Noteworthy

Use of Timecode

For most nondocumentary use, setting your own 12-hour alternating free-run timecode works best (i.e., on even-numbered days, use 1 to 12 hours; on odd days, use 13 to 24 hours). It's less confusing when shooting for days at a time.

When setting your deck to a 12-hour "day," set your initial timecode to 00:59:00:00 (or 12:59:00:00 on "odd" days), and use the last minute of hour zero to record your 1-khz tone or other normalizing sound. At 01:00:00:00, set your timecode to free run.

TOD isn't a given. The VTR operators at Nickelodeon Studios in Orlando actually used a different system. The line master tape was recorded in assembly: jam-syncing to internal, rec-run code. The line master started at 1;00;00;00 and had contiguous, ascending TC. A house generator was slaved to the master recorder and regenerated this code, which was fed to the external TC inputs of the ISO VTRs. These were all set to crash-record. The reason for doing this was so that the producers could keep a good running total of time in the production. At the end of the recording, they would know exactly how long or short the show was. This gave them the best of both worlds: a line master with uninterrupted TC as well as matching TC on the ISOs.

Oliver Peters

Tip

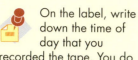

On the label, write down the time of day that you recorded the tape. You do this because on time-of-day timecode, you can tell immediately if somebody makes a mistake on the timecode or the label. For instance, if this is tape 3, but it ended at noon instead of 4 o'clock, you would know there's a problem. Tape 3 starts at 03:00:00:00 and should end with 04:00:00:00, not 12:00:00:00.

Savvy postproduction supervisors know exactly what they need and how to ask for it, no more and no less. So they can determine what equipment they would need to bring as specified by the job.

Time-of-Day Timecode and 24-Hour Clocks

As discussed, free run time-of-day timecode is best for multi-cam. The next decision is which type of clock will you use—a 24-hour clock (military time) or 12-hour clock? When using the 12-hour clock in a time-of-day environment, the clock will reset to hour 00 every 12 hours. If you use a 24-hour clock, you get continuous incremental timecode for 24 hours.

You need very long lead times when you start to record with TOD before the subject matter starts. This is for prerolling and capturing tapes in post. Most decks will drop to about a second preroll, but it's recommended that you have at least 5 to 10 seconds to ensure a hassle-free session.

The Midnight Effect

When a 12-hour clock crosses the midnight hour, the clock will reset to 00:00:00:00 and cause your timecode on those clips to have a number that's lower than those on the clips shot before midnight. This process will also confuse the NLE in capture mode.

Accordingly, it may be a good idea to start your time-of-day timecode a few hours earlier, to offset clips that cross the midnight hour.

Another trick is to use 24-hour clocks for nighttime shows and scroll the clock back by 12 hours. In other words, a show starting at 8 p.m. would begin at 08:00 hours on the clock, rather than at the 20:00 hour mark. This gives you a full 24 hours of continuous incremental time-of-day timecode, and yet there is still some logic to the numbers. Voilà!

Tip

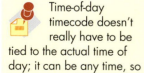

Time-of-day timecode doesn't really have to be tied to the actual time of day; it can be any time, so long as everything matches.

Preshoots and Shooting over Two Nights or Two Days

There are several uses for varying the two types of clocks. If you're doing a show over two nights or doing a preshoot or dress rehearsal shot at the same time on different nights, alternate your timecode: one night, use the 24-hour clock; the next, use the 12-hour clock. That way, the editor can clearly distinguish between the two.

- 8 p.m. on night 1 = 08:00:00:00
- 8 p.m. on night 2 = 20:00:00:00.

Please see the companion DVD for a Bonus Chapter on in-depth information about blackburst, genocking and bi and and tri-level sync.

References

1. Wikipedia
2. http://en.wikipedia.org/wiki/Drop_frame_timecode
3. Courtesy http://en.wikipedia.org/wiki/Telecine#cite_note_filmtopal-3
4. http://en.wikiaudio.org/SMPTE_time_code
5. http://en.wikipedia.org/wiki/CTL_timecode
6. http://en.wikipedia.org/wiki/Vertical_interval
7. http://en.wikipedia.org/wiki/Vertical_interval_timecode

SYNC METHODS

If you don't jam-sync your cameras in the field, it takes hours of work for the editors to try to sync up that material. It's almost pointless that you had a multicamera shoot when you are on a quick turnaround and you spend half your edit session syncing cameras.

Meredith Lerner, producer

Traditional Sync Methods

Jam Sync

The best way to sync multiple cameras is to generate time-of-day timecode to each of the cameras in the system.

Figure 6.1a A timecode generator feed sends matching timecode to each camera. (Courtesy rippletraining.com.)

Even if your cameras do not use timecode or don't have a common source, they can still be synchronized with the following methods.

Doi: 10.1016/B978-0-240-81176-5.00006-X

Clapboard Slate

The clapboard slate has been the standard sync system for filmmakers since the 1920s, when filmmaking with sound began. It's a very basic device, but it works so well. In single-camera film-style shooting or scenes with multiple cameras, every take gets slated with the scene information. A simple clap stick is attached to the top of the slate. When the camera assistant (also known as the clapper/loader) slates the shot, he or she simply claps the sticks together so that each camera can see the clap. The audio team records that clap. Then, when the assistant editor syncs the dailies, this becomes the sync point for each camera and audio recording.

Figure 6.1b Standard clapboard slate.

Figure 6.2 Clapboard used for *Band of Brothers'* director David Nutter. (Courtesy Ben Taylor Lighting and Effects.)

Figure 6.3 Bloop light.
The LED flashes on the first frame after a sync pulse from the camera shutter. This is used in order to provide a frame-accurate visual cue at the beginning of the camera move when used with computerized motion control camera. (Courtesy Mo-Systems.)

Bloop Light or Bloop Slate

A bloop light is a combination of a light source and a sound synchronized for matching a camera with an audio recording device. The light is flashed at the camera at the same time an audio tone is recorded to a dual sound system whenever the button is pressed. The tone sounds like the word "bloop." During the beginning of sync sound, a bloop was used, but often it was found to be inaccurate because of an offset at the telecine phase, causing the film editors to sync by hand. Filmmakers eventually went back to the clapboard slates.

Peter Schneider, Gotham Sound and Communications, Inc.: *The first one that I used was homemade out of a Boy Scouts flashlight. Every time the cameraman turned over, they would pan over to me and I would push the little metal button on the side of the flashlight and it would light the light and it would trigger the oscillator in my recorder.*

Recently, the bloop light has been improved with LED lights, lasers, and wireless technology and is often used in motion-control systems to mark and sync the beginning of a camera's move to motion-control metadata. It can also be used with a speaker to cue actors.

Smart Slate

A Smart Slate is like a clapboard that works with timecode. You can jam-sync the slate to match a timecode generator or sound recording deck. These devices work in free run and record run and most common frame rates. Some newer slates automatically read the frame rate of the timecode.

Usually, an assistant cameraperson or clapper will set the sticks for the marker. Ideally, he or she remembers to roll early and get at least 10 to 15 seconds of preroll for digitizing.

Figure 6.4 Wireless bloop light controller. (Courtesy www.higbie.com.)

Figure 6.5a Denecke TS-3 Smart Slate. (Courtesy Denecke.)

Figure 6.5b Assistant cameraperson preps a pair of Panavision Genesis cameras on the set of *Law & Order* in Manhattan.

Figure 6.5c Close-up of Panavision Genesis camera body featuring a Solid State Recorder SSR-1 mounted on back.

Figure 6.6 Denecke large concert slate with 6 1/2" variable intensity LED readout. (Courtesy Denecke.)

Figure 6.5d *Law & Order* Smart Slate to sync Panavision Genesis cameras.

Sometimes, however, it may be best to use the TC readout another way. Instead of doing the actual clap, you can alternatively set the slate open and put it off in a corner, where it's handy enough to be shot by cameras at the beginning or end of each take. A good way to "cheat," especially on a film-style production, is to put an LED clock or timecode generator up on a wall somewhere offstage, where all the cameras can shoot the show and also track timecode clearly. This system is generally used in concert productions with a concert slate.

Oliver Peters: *Make sure that every cameraman, when he starts to record, goes over and shoots the clock first thing in that clip. Then the editor has a way of syncing it up. This is not just concert stuff. It could be a comedian doing a live show in the round or standup.*

Handclap Sync

The handclap is a cheap, down-and-dirty alterative for getting a sync point. If you don't have a clapboard slate, you just do a simple handclap for all cameras to see and any recording devices to hear. Use the boom mic if you have one.

Meredith Lerner: *In a situation where you can't jam-sync the cameras and it's just not possible to stop the action, we have each camera run their own time-of-day timecode as a loose reference, and then we also have a sync point from the beginning of each scene—whether it's someone literally just clapping her hands for each camera to see or a clapboard or slate, to give the editors a sync point.*

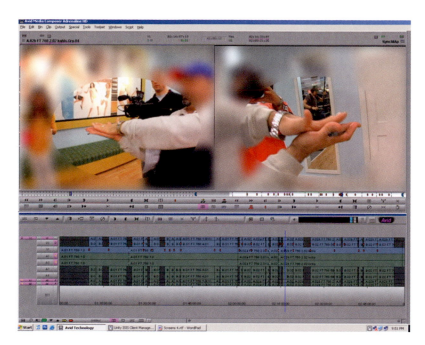

Figure 6.7 Handclap slate for two cameras on-location. Sync map shows V2 where each camera stopped and restarted.

Figure 6.8 Producer Mark Lieberman executes a handclap sync point for *Live from Artist's Den*. (Courtesy Artist's Den Entertainment.)

Flash Sync

Flash sync is another way of syncing cameras. It involves the use of a flashlight or a quick-shot camera with a flash. A visible flash from an audience member's camera could also be used to get a sync point.

Figure 6.9 A visible flash from an audience member's camera makes an excellent sync point. (Courtesy rippletraining.com.)

To actively perform a flash, simply stand where you would normally to slate the cameras. Ensure all the cameras can see the same mark. Roll cameras, and flash the camera or pop the flashlight on and off. This is a simple, fast, and cheap way to sync the cameras. The downside is the same as for using a slate: if even one of the cameras stops recording, then all the cameras have to resync just like clapboard slates for each scene.

This method is popular with wedding and events editors who have built-in flashes, generously donated by audience members and their snappy cams.

Auxiliary LTC Timecode

LTC is the oldest version of timecode, and it's currently making a big comeback among developers using it for sync.

Sometimes cameras may be incapable of accepting a timecode signal—but you still require matching timecode, in which case, recording LTC audio timecode may be a great option. One method for HD cameras is to generate an audio timecode signal directly to the camera via a mini tri-level sync generator.

For standard-definition cameras, a Lockit box will also do the trick. This audio timecode signal is fed to an audio track on the camera. It can also feed an external input for timecode if your camera has that capability. Later, in post, the edit system can read the audio timecode and convert it to an alternate timecode track for sync. Avid has the capacity to do this as part of its standard feature set. It will put an auxiliary track on your master clip and transpose the audio signal to SMPTE timecode. Final Cut Pro can use a third-party solution made by Video Toolshed called FCP auxTC reader (http://www.videotoolshed.com/products), which will decode LTC if present on one of the audio channels.

Bouke Váhl of Video Toolshed in the Netherlands: *If you do a multi-camera shoot and you want to sync up the different reels fast, you normally lock the timecode of all the cameras. Two problems: [One,] you cannot easily batch-digitize the tapes, as there are huge TC jumps wherever there was a pause in the recording. Two, cheap cameras do not have this option. What you can do is broadcast an LTC signal and record it on one of the audio tracks. In post, choose FCPauxTC for display, and you know exactly what goes where.*

Figure 6.10 FCPauxTC Reader will read the LTC timecode off an audio track and convert it to regular TC in FCP. (Courtesy Video ToolShed.)

Tip

44.1K/48K Sampling Rates

Always record digital audio at 48K. If you're dealing with a soundtrack that was recorded— whether it's a CD cut or some sort of external audio recorder—at any other sample rate than 48K, you want to convert it to 48K before you ever bring it into the NLE.

Double-System Audio

There are various examples of syncing using double-system sound production. You have an audio recorder that is its own source. It has to be synchronized with the picture.

Maurice Schechter, chief engineer, DuArt Film and Video, New York City: *It's no different in the HD world than it was in the SD world. A camera has a crystal inside and two cameras have two crystals, and two cameras and a sound recorder have three crystals. They each have a crystal and they're not exactly always the exact frequency and time. So over a longer take, things start to drift. So what did people do in the film world? You have crystal lock in your camera, in your motor. And for the most part that worked fine because the takes are short. But people start shooting one-hour or two-hour takes; that can be a problem. But even that degree, even then the drift seems to be fairly small.*

Sometimes you may have a situation where you'll want to isolate all of the microphones in an interview. You may have more people talking than you have available tracks on the camcorders that you're shooting with. There again, you may have some type of hard disk audio recorder that's recording, let's say, eight tracks of audio as discrete channels. That's going to have to be synchronized.

Reality shows and many other productions run separate multitrack audio recorders with sometimes more than 24 tracks of individual mics. These systems also get simultaneous timecode and sync and record individual tracks as broadcast wave files so they can be matched to the multicam clips in post.

Another example wherein auxiliary timecode becomes very important is when you shoot a music video or a prerecorded show track that has timecode and you want to maintain that as the auxiliary timecode independent of the recording. With playback audio (lip-syncing) on CD or a secondary audio system, you may go through five takes of the same thing but not want the camera timecode to be constantly overlapping. (More on this in Bonus Chapter 7 on the website – How and When to use Aux TC)

iPhone Digital Clapper Boards

A digital slate on your iPhone or iPod. How cool is that? And it gets cooler! Models from Video Toolshed and Movie ☆ Slate have a digital slate that can accept external timecode, but—here's the best part—it can play back user-selectable soundtracks while generating LTC to separate channels. This feature makes it easy to sync clips

LTC and Two Sets of TC

What if you're shooting single-camera film style—with multiple cameras running at 23.98 and a separate multichannel system recording audio at 29.97? Why would you want AuxTC? It's almost like a pair of mismatched gears trying to turn into each other.

You could run both: with an auxiliary LTC track going to the audio channel and another TC through VITC.

Mark Doering-Powell, a Los Angeles–based DP: *Cameras use their own unbroken 24fps Rec/Run TC—for some reason some NLEs cannot cope with simply ascending TC, but require it unbroken as well—and this is one advantage of Master TC on audio channel.*

Gary Adcock, president, Studio 37: *This is really important so that you're matching the time base with the content that's being shot. It's also important for mixed editing environments. Say you're cutting on an Avid and your crew is shooting at 24 frame. The sound recordist can actually set the timecode to have a multiple sync signal so that it shows 23.98 and 29.97 timecode on the audio tracks, which are traditionally used as the master timecode source.*

Mark Doering-Powell: *But it's true: once you start putting TC onto the VITC, you do have to at least consider tri-leveling as well. Don't forget there's that little LED decimal point that tells you what field you're on. The camera and slate may be out of phase by a fraction of that frame, but still in-sync. Rejamming prevents drift. And while the TC roulette may find you 180 degrees out of phase on rare occasions, we've synced sound with a clapper, getting it close enough for editors for more than 70 years.*

Oliver Peters: *One example is a music video. You might want the tape to have its own different, unique timecode, but you still want the cross reference of the timecode that existed on the playback tracks. If you look at this auxiliary timecode from the playback on take 1, 2, or 3, you can find the exact same place in the show track that matches across any of these takes. ...There's also another technical issue that has crept in here in the last few years with the newer forms of cameras. Originally, when everything was NTSC television, it was all a frame rate of 29.97 and everybody knew how to deal with it. Now you have the ability to do video-friendly speeds, like 23.976 for 24 frame recordings and 29.97 for 30 frame, but you can also do the true native speed, like a true 24 frame or a true 30 frame. A lot of people don't understand that, and they start shooting with their cameras set incorrectly and suddenly it no longer syncs up to the audio source, if that's a separate file or recording.*

MULTI-EXPERT APPROACH

shot for a music video, but it also works nicely for more traditional slate applications.

With single-camera videos shot music-video style and an iPhone or iPod digital clapboard, you can do playback and slate the cameras with the same device. The matching cameras can be grouped together as easily as a multiclip and played back as if shot in multicam.

Movie ☆ Slate is a digital slate, clapper board, shot log, and shot notepad all in one, designed for use with film, television, documentaries, interviews, and home movies.

It provides an incredibly easy way to log footage and take notes as you shoot—saving time later, when you capture and edit the footage on your computer. Your notes can be imported into FCP and an XML file to save even more time logging and loading footage.

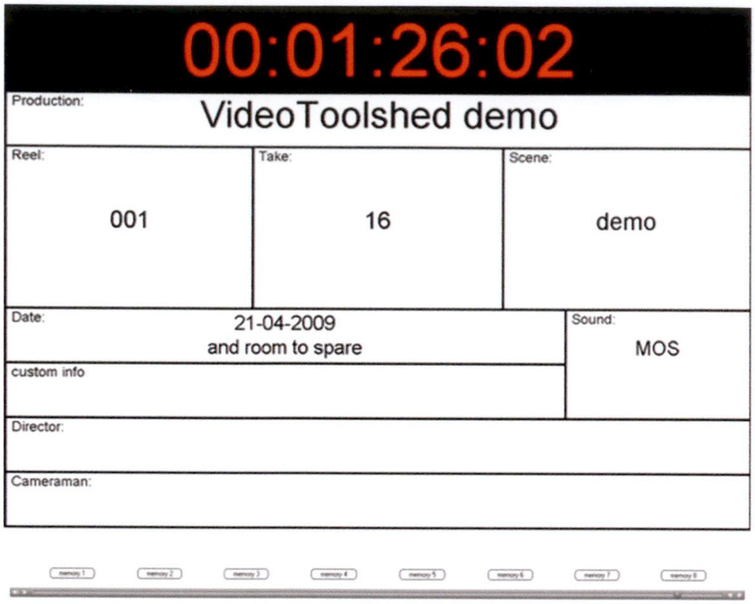

Figure 6.11 Digital clapper board also plays back audio tracks for music video sync. (Courtesy www.videotoolshed.com)

Furthermore, two iPhones can be jammed together for multi-camera shoots.

There are many ways to sync cameras: easy to fast, expensive to free—so there's no reason *not* to do it. If you haven't got a big budget, just get a clapboard—or clap your hands. And discipline your camera crew! Sometimes it's better for them just to keep rolling, even if they're shooting the floor while moving from one

Figure 6.12 Movie ☆ Slate is a digital slate, clapper board, shot log, and shot notepad for your iPod or iPhone. (Courtesy PureBlend Software Design Group.)

Figure 6.13 Shot log software for notes on the take, sound, and picture. (Courtesy PureBlend Software Design Group.)

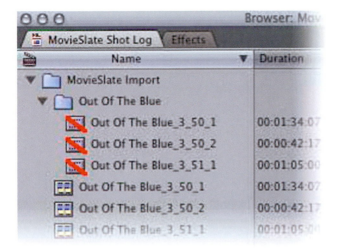

Figure 6.14 Movie Slate Shot log XML as imported into Final Cut Pro. (Courtesy PureBlend Software Design Group.)

Figure 6.15 Syncing two iPhones for multicamera marks is easy with Movie ☆ Slate. (Courtesy PureBlend Software Design Group.)

setup to the next, than it is for them to stop and start their cameras. Tape and storage are relatively cheap these days too, so compared to the cost of syncing in post, getting it right in the early stages will save you a lot of hassle and expense.

Web link

 If you are really into the iPhone, check out the Handheld Hollywood website. It has a great article on all the slates available for the iPhone (www.handheldhollywood. com/).

7

SYNCING THE NONSYNCHRONOUS

On a truck shoot, or any shoot with cameras that use time-code, you don't have to worry about sync. They're rolling tapes on jam-synced decks or there's a generator for wild cameras and sync really isn't an issue.

But what about the rest of us? A lot of people shoot with inexpensive, nonsynchronous cameras. Oh come on! They're so cheap, anyone can buy two cameras to shoot multicam for about the same price as owning *one* camera last year. Sure, some qualities are compromised in a cheaper camera, but there's something to be said for the producer who can fill his or her shoot with four or five cameras that the producer would never have been able to afford if they were all Sony F900s or similarly high-end models.

The problem with these less expensive cameras is that while technology has gotten better at the bottom end of the spectrum, the compromise is fewer bells and whistles and special control functions, such as balanced audio inputs. And, most important to multicam, the majority of these cheaper models do not provide for timecode or sync.

Frustrated editors far and wide ask the same questions, time and again: Can't you jam-sync your stinking cameras? Why am I stuck with a sync nightmare? For the most part, the footage generated from these cameras must be loaded and synced by hand. And unfortunately, it usually falls to the editor to make it work.

In a concert environment, there are a lot of ways to sync manually if you have to—from light changes to the way the talent moves or touches the instrument.

As we've learned, it's not hard to jam-sync cameras that are designed to work with timecode. But what happens when producers start to mix and match B-level cameras with questionable sync abilities to no timecode features at all? More producers are doing more with less money, and the trend continues. This is why you see cheap cameras everywhere. It all comes down to budget. And let's face it, everybody has to sync things by hand sooner or later.

Doi: 10.1016/B978-0-240-81176-5.00007-1

113

Let's start by looking at a few of the nonsynchronous cameras making a mark in multicam and various solutions to get them in sync.

Concert Slate or Open Clapboard Display

One of the easiest ways to get a sync point—particularly on minishoots, when everybody's got his or her own camera—is to use the open clapper method. If you're using these small, mini-DV cameras—HDV, P2, or other nonsynchronous cameras for concerts or other live events with timecode-generated sound—have the sound recordist put a Smart Slate or a concert slate on either side of the stage and just let it run. And at the end of every song, tell the camera operators to make sure—before *and* after every song—to swing over while the camera's rolling and just shoot the slate. Shoot the slate, let it run, and grab some visible timecode; then allow the recordist, editor, and assistant editor (and everyone else who needs it) to see something with a timecode reference on it. It doesn't get much easier than that.

FireWire Sync

There are many cameras that have timecode features but still end up in the nonsynchronous category because of their lack of functionality or actual ability to perform professional, "hassle-free" sync. The best advice is, of course, to employ a simple idea: test before you shoot.

For many cameras like a P2 HVX-200, a FireWire cable is used for jam-syncing to other HVXs, but that FireWire signal is not compatible with (or cannot convert to signals for) most other equipment, like audio recorders. Another point to keep in mind is that the only type of timecode this works with is the timecode embedded in the 1394 cable's signal.

It's also tricky to keep all the cameras in sync. And it's not super-accurate. Basically, you'll need to use one of the cameras as a sender and the rest as receivers in VTR mode. After syncing all of the receivers, the receiver cameras will need to be switched from VTR to camera mode—and with that switch, you'll lose a few frames of sync!

Barry Green, Emmy-winning producer and resident tech guru at dvxuser.com:

This is a frustrating reality of the HVX timecode sync system: every time you toggle between CAMERA and VCR/MCR mode, the timecode will

Further Reading

Portions of this section were written by video pro Barry Green and originally published at www.dvxuser.com. It is republished here by permission of the author. You can find the full article by Barry at www.dvxuser. com/articles/sync/ and buy his books and DVDs at the dvxuser.com shop.

jump or skip a few frames. And it's unavoidable: since the "sender" must be in camera mode and the "receivers" must be in VCR mode, you have to toggle the receivers back to camera mode, and that means losing some frames of sync. There's no way to avoid it. With the 1394 sync method, your timecode will always be a little bit off.

Figure 7.1 TC selection on HVX 200. (Courtesy dvxuser.com.)

There's a workaround for that too.

Just shoot the sender menu with each receiver to get the difference.

Point the "receiver" at the flip-out LCD on the "sender" and record a few seconds.

By shooting the sender camera, you have an exact reference to how far "off" the timecode is. In this example, the "sender" is at 2:50:10 and the "receiver" is at 2:50:17.

The timecode sync feature isn't perfect, but it gets us closer than other cameras in this price range can do. Learn the function's idiosyncrasies, and it can be a valuable tool.

Figure 7.2 Verifying the offset between two cameras by shooting the sender camera's screen. (Courtesy dvxuser.com.)

Remote Control Timecode

Yet another method is to preset a time setting that starts all the cameras with one remote.

You can also get close to matching timecode by triggering free run timecode in sync from a remote control. Line 'em all up and set the same time on each camera—one click and boom! All of your cameras start together—jamming, sort of.

Barry Green: *If you set both cameras to FREE RUN timecode, and PRESET (not REGEN), they will stay in sync throughout the day, so long as you don't turn either camera off. Turning one off (to change a battery, for example) seems to cause the timecode to lose a few frames of sync. And even if you don't turn one off, they may drift a little during a long day. Set them both to the same setting (DF or NDF, FREE RUN, and PRE-SET).*

Set both to the exact same timecode preset, but don't confirm the preset using the menus; instead, use a remote control and put both cameras side by side. That way they'll both respond to the remote control's signal at the same time. Start them off the same and they should stay the same, regardless of when you start or stop recording.

Manually Syncing with Audio Waves

Finally, for one more down-and-dirty approach to syncing nonsynchronous cameras, you could line up the sound waves manually, camera by camera, and get a common point for a grouped clip. This works; it's proven and it is used more frequently than not.

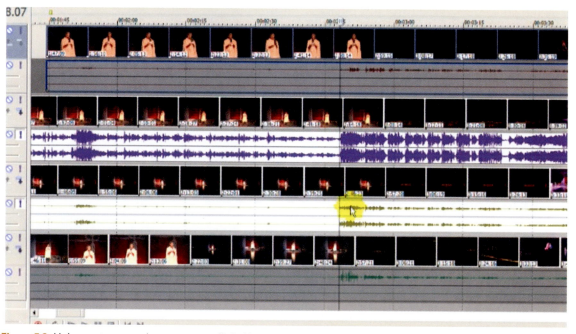

Figure 7.3 Lining up two sound waves manually in Vegas. (Courtesy Gary Kleiner, www.VegasTrainingAndTools.com.)

Auto-Syncing Software

PluralEyes

PluralEyes was one of the most talked about developments at NAB 2009, when it was introduced. Licensed by Singular Systems, this software analyzes the audio tracks from multiple clips and then syncs them together automatically by their sound waveforms. No timecode necessary, just good clean audio. You can even sync up clips downloaded from the Web.

Figure 7.4a Bruce Sharpe, president (on right), and David Kaufman of Singular Systems introduce PluralEyes at NAB 2009.

Bruce Sharp, Singular Software, Inc.: *What PluralEyes does is automatic synchronization without timecode, so if you're doing a multicamera shoot and you're not jam-syncing the cameras or using a clapboard, but you need to get them all synced up for editing, PluralEyes will do it for you, with just a single press of a button.*

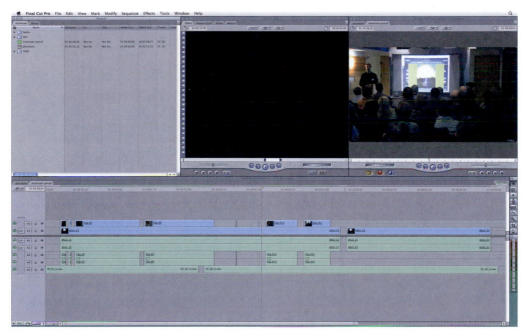

Figure 7.4b PluralEyes automatically created this sync map for Final Cut Pro multiclips. (Courtesy Singular Systems.)

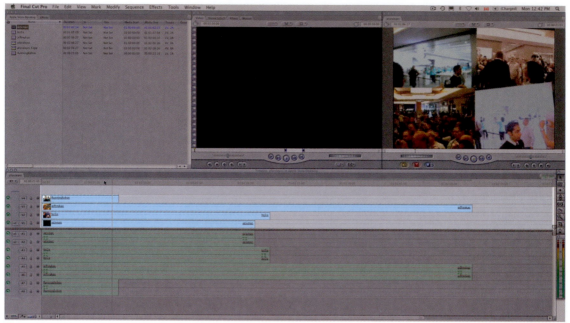

Figure 7.4c Example of multiple camera angles arbitrarily lined up on their first frames—before running PluralEyes. (Courtesy Singular Systems.)

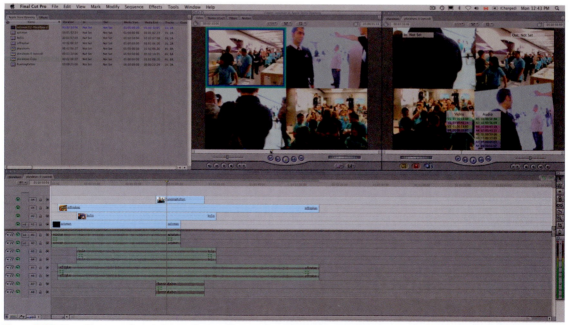

Figure 7.4d PluralEyes analyzed the audio to align each angle and create this syncmap. (Courtesy Singular Systems.)

PluralEyes looks at the audio signature and the audio information that goes along with the video and matches it up—the same way as if you're going to match things up manually, you might look at the waveform for a particular feature that you can find in all the tracks. PluralEyes looks at all of the information available and does a much more accurate job, completely automatically.

Bruce Sharpe: *Our goal is to bring the realm of multicamera editing to many more users. We're really targeted at the independent video producer, the boutique shop, and so on—people who are very capable and who can afford the equipment but who are a little bit put off by the complexity, or the perceived complexity, of issues like timecode. Now they don't have to worry about it.*

PluralEyes or Final Cut Pro is technically not a plug-in. It is a separate application that works in conjunction with FCP. If you have both FCP and PluralEyes open, then PluralEyes looks for any open FCP sequence labeled "pluraleyes" and works its magic on that.

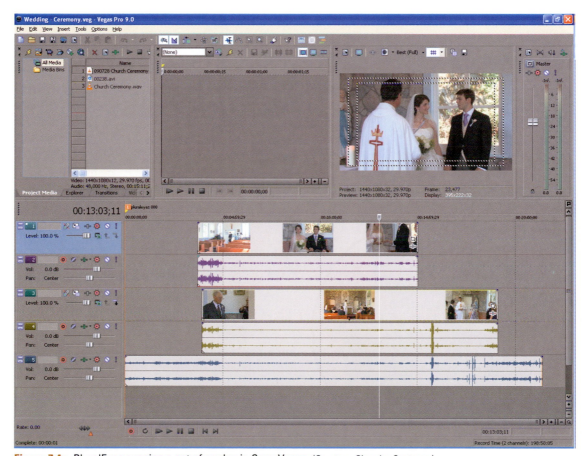

Figure 7.4e PluralEyes syncing a set of angles in Sony Vegas. (Courtesy Singular Systems.)

All you do is you take your clips from your multiple cameras, throw them into a sequence, give that sequence a special name, and start the PluralEyes application: press the SYNC button and wait a minute or two. It analyzes the clips and determines the lineup in a new sequence. It also creates a multiclip so that you can do a multicamera display for editing.

LTC TC Makes a Comeback

LTC timecode, recorded on an audio track, is one of the first systems of TC used professionally. Since then, more sophisticated and complicated methods like recording to VITC have been implemented. Recently there has been a revival of sorts for LTC and syncing the nonsynchronous. Most of the lower-end cameras do not support TC in and out or jam-syncing, but fortunately for LTC, almost all cameras, even consumer DSLR and point-and-shoot types, have audio. New programs and plug-ins that take full advantage of LTC are being developed to take syncing the nonsynchronous to the next level.

LTC can be transmitted wirelessly to receivers on cameras that feed to audio tracks. This is a simple way to get TC on all the cameras. Reading the TC is not a problem in post. (AuxTCReader www.videotoolshed.com)

ALL601, LANC Logger and AuxApp

The newest product out there is called ALL601 Universal TC Interface and LANC Logger by Ambient Recording and software developer Andreas Kiel. It's a universal TC interface box that creates professional EDLs for pro cameras and consumer cameras.

Yes, All601 Lanc Logger works well with pro cameras but its biggest gift is to allow consumer cameras with zero TC capabilities to record highly accurate quartz timecode.

Andreas Kiel: *Bridging between SMPTE, LANC, and MIDI timecode formats, it allows the complete integration of equipment without native TC capabilities into a professional, timecode-based production workflow. It attaches unobtrusively onto the smallest consumer-grade cameras and*

Figure 7.5a The Ambient ALL601 LANC Logger attached to a camera. (Courtesy Ambient.)

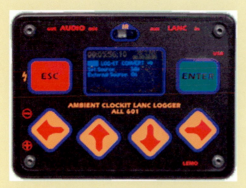

Figure 7.5b The ALL601 LANC Logger control panel. (Courtesy Ambient.)

converts the LANC to LTC through its LANC input/output connection (Sony and Canon), allowing jam-sync TC to get recorded. Panasonic cameras that do not have LANC can use the audio in to get LTC TC right out of the box.

Figure 7.5c PluralEyes syncing a set of angles in Sony Vegas. (Courtesy Ambient.)

In post, you can take a log file to a USB drive and create an EDL log file referring LANC or record run TC to time of day.

With the new AuxApp application, Final Cut Pro users can automatize batch processing by importing a log file into a batch list and exporting an XML to automatically create LTC to the Aux TC track of all the clips. Ready to sync, sir!

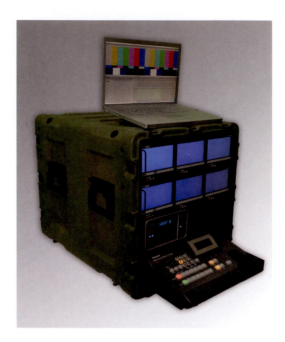

Figure 7.6 Thaler Films fly pack. (Courtesy www.thalerfilms.com)

Figure 7.7 LTC converts to RS-422 with AEC-uBox. (Courtesy Adrielec.com.)

Capture Linecuts with Matching TC

David Thaler, a DP/engineer at Thaler Films, an Emmy Award–winning production company, uses his mini fly-pack rig to switch eight cameras live to a linecut. The switcher feeds the i/o card to Capture Now in Final Cut Pro with matching TC. The trick is in helping Final Cut to "think" that it is recording the output of a deck that it's controlling. AEC-uBox from Adrienne Electronics Corporation is just the box for the job. It makes Final Cut seem like a digital VCR. LTC TC is generated to the AEC box, where it gets converted to the serial nine-pin connection into the AJA ioHD (or any capture card that supports RS-422 deck control—just like deck control from any input). This also works with cameras direct to any SDI input hardware.

POSTPRODUCTION

8

COMPUTERS, BANDWIDTH, AND SPEED

It's not just about codec choice; data rates ripple through the entire architecture of a system. The first good step is understanding how to equip your editing system for the most bandwidth. Prep your hardware to deliver your dreams.

Bruce Nazarian, "the digital guy," MPSE, DVD producer, consultant, author and president of the DVD Association

In this section, we'll focus in more detail on technical tools of the trade and the workflows used to set up multicam projects. Post is where it all comes together—and pulling it alltogether begins on your computer.

Speed is king. You want fast computers, fast hard drives, fast connection. Successful grouped-clip playback requires a combination of drive speed, connection, and codecs processing. If you're planning to group clips in higher resolutions, you're going to need plenty of bandwidth and fast, modern disk drives. Laptops and some older computers just won't cut it. The more bandwidth, the merrier: the more bandwidth you have, the faster your drive array speeds and the more video streams you can handle.

Choking the System

It's easy to choke your system. This is a good reason to think through your project requirements in advance: figure out what's involved and consult the charts. A choking system means lots of frustration and downtime; sometimes it can even bring your entire project to a screeching halt.

For example, try grouping three or four high-res clips on a Mac while editing on a FireWire drive. First you'll hear the stutter of the drive as it hesitates, seeking out each clip independently while trying to play them. Eventually, the sequence will stop and you'll be alerted to a system error during playback. In other words, a slower operating system + slow hard drives + multiple files = *choke*.

Doi: 10.1016/B978-0-240-81176-5.00008-3

In Final Cut Pro, the error you'll see more frequently is something called a *drop frame error*, which means the drives you're using can't keep apace in playing back the chosen material at the speed you want.

In Avid, you'll get errors like *video underrun* or *audio underrun*, which effectively mean the same thing: your disk drives can't keep up.

Just a couple of layers of low bandwidth in your timeline and that FireWire800 drive of yours will lose all reason. In FCP, you could adjust the RT menu to dynamic settings to ease the pain, but chances are you need more bandwidth.

There's no way around it, really: working in multicam requires maximum bandwidth and a CPU powerful enough to handle real-time decompression of your material.

Bandwidth and Data Rates

Several measures of bandwidth are part of the multicam formula. These are computer processing and connectivity, hard drive speed, and the editing codec. Data rates (also called *bit rates*) are the speed of the flow of the bits within the digital chain. They vary between HD and SD frame sizes as much as frame sizes vary from codec to codec. Compressed codecs like ProRes and DNXHD offer high-quality HD content at lower bandwidth than uncompressed SD does. If your system is designed to process uncompressed HD, it can often handle four to six times as much content as when working with compressed codecs.

HD content in Apple's ProRes or Avid's DNXHD is nearly equivalent in file size to what one would find when using 10-bit uncompressed to capture SD content. That data rate is about 30 megabytes per second, so that compressed DVCPro720p is 6 MB/second faster than NTSC 8-bit. A system that can handle uncompressed HD can easily handle four or six channels of ProRes.

HD or SD—it really doesn't matter what format you're using; what matters are the bandwidth and data speed (bit rate).

Bob Zelin, systems integrator/consultant

Definitions

In computer networking, *digital bandwidth, network bandwidth,* or just *bandwidth* is a measure of available or consumed data-communication resources expressed in bit/s or multiples of bits (kbit, Mbit, etc.).

Bitrate (sometimes written *bit rate* or *data rate*) is the number of bits conveyed or processed per unit of time. The bit rate is quantified using the bits per second (bit/s or bps) unit, such as kilo- (kbit/s or kbps), mega- (Mbit/s, Mbps, or Mb/s), giga- (Gbit/s, Gbps, or Gb/s), or tera- (Tbit/s, Tbps, or Tb/s).

Note that Mb/s = megabits per second, and MB/s = megabytes per second.

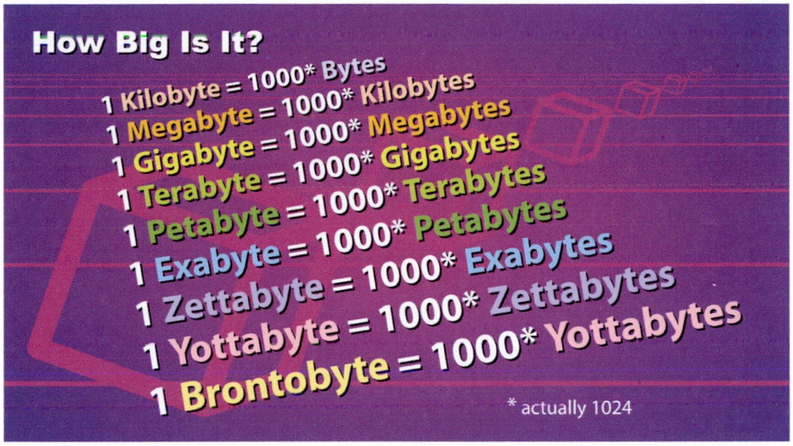

How Big Is It?

1 Kilobyte = 1000* Bytes
1 Megabyte = 1000* Kilobytes
1 Gigabyte = 1000* Megabytes
1 Terabyte = 1000* Gigabytes
1 Petabyte = 1000* Terabytes
1 Exabyte = 1000* Petabytes
1 Zettabyte = 1000* Exabytes
1 Yottabyte = 1000* Zettabytes
1 Brontobyte = 1000* Yottabytes

* actually 1024

Figure 8.1a How big is it? Conversion table.

Editing Codecs

Finishing in uncompressed codecs yields the best quality you can get working digitally, but the idea of working with uncompressed HD for a multicam project is usually unrealistic. Because of these bandwidth limitations, and because of how much storage space is required for multicam's mass of media, it's often desirable to work at lower resolutions or higher compression rates.

Each NLE system "qualifies" certain editing codecs for best practice use with its software. With Avid it's DNX, and with Final Cut it's ProRes. Your choice to use a codec starts with your project's workflow. Ask yourself, *Am I going to be in an offline/online workflow and work in low resolution and later finish in high resolution? Or will I start the project in HD and deliver from there? Am I sharing media? Is my system capable?* For HD, compressed codecs like Apple ProRes HQ and Panasonic's DVCPro HD and the two popular Avid codecs, DNXHD 145 and DNXHD 220, certainly hold up as deliverables and have small enough file sizes and bit rates to edit with single streams. However, in multicam, even compressed formats can choke most systems easily, so in addition to a deliverable codec, you may want to use a transcode to format with a small bit rate.

In multicam, you're also limited by available drive space. With so much footage to be handled, even with large drive arrays, vast amounts of media will have to be captured or transferred—and, with limited storage space, there's only so much media you can store. So to cut with more streams that use less drive space, create a complete set of "down-rezzed" clips.

With this offline/online workflow, you are now planning for two file sets with different codecs: the deliverable masters and the group clips' transcoded format.

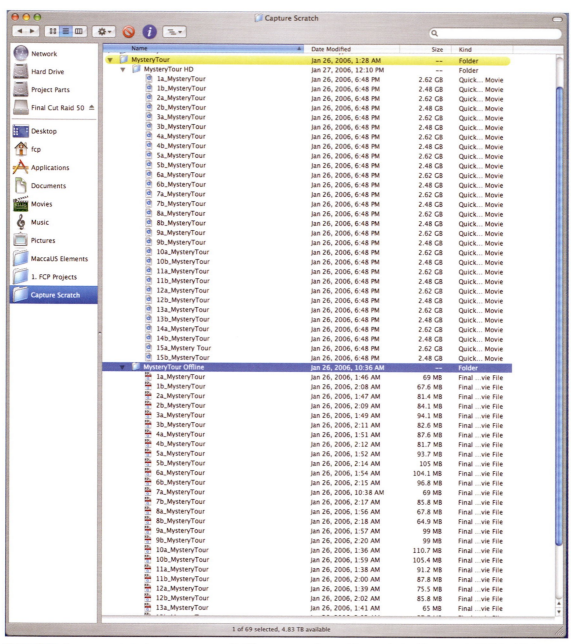

Figure 8.1b Screen capture shows one song with 26 camera angles and four switched line cuts in DVCProHD (about 2.5 GB each) with a complete set of RTOfflineHD (about 75 MB each) transcoded media for use on a laptop.

You might as well start at the top, with uncompressed data rates for SD and HD. The single stream data rates start at around 20 MB/s for SD 8-bit and climb to 237 MB/s for uncompressed 10-bit HD.

Uncompressed Video Storage and Data Rates[1]

What's the data rate for uncompressed video, and how much space is needed? (Data rates are rounded up.)

525 NTSC Uncompressed

8 bit @ 720 × 486 @ 29.97 fps = 20 MB/s, or 77 GB/hr.

10 bit @ 720 × 486 @ 29.97 fps = 27 MB/s, or 101 GB/hr.

625 PAL Uncompressed

8 bit @ 720 × 576 @ 25 fps = 20 MB/s, or 76 GB/hr.

10 bit @ 720 × 576 @ 25 fps = 26 MB/s, or 101 GB/hr.

720p HDTV Uncompressed

8 bit @ 1280 × 720 @ 59.94 fps = 105 MB/s, or 399 GB/hr.

10 bit @ 1280 × 720 @ 59.94 fps = 140 MB/s, or 531 GB/hr.

1080i and 1080p HDTV Uncompressed

8 bit @ 1920 × 1080 @ 23.98 fps = 95 MB/s, or 359 GB/hr.

10 bit @ 1920 × 1080 @ 23.98 fps = 127 MB/s, or 478 GB/hr.

8 bit @ 1920 × 1080 @ 25 fps = 99 MB/s, or 374 GB/hr.

10 bit @ 1920 × 1080 @ 25 fps = 132 MB/s, or 498 GB/hr.

8 bit @ 1920 × 1080 @ 29.97 fps = 119 MB/s, or 449 GB/hr.

10 bit @ 1920 × 1080 @ 29.97 fps = 158 MB/s, or 598 GB/hr.

1080i and 1080p HDTV RGB (4:4:4) Uncompressed

10 bit @ 1920 × 1080 @ 24 PsF = 190 MB/s, or 718 GB/hr.

10 bit @ 1920 × 1080 @ 25 PsF = 198 MB/s, or 748 GB/hr.

10 bit @ 1920 × 1080 @ 60 i = 237 MB/s, or 1,790 GB/hr.

Popular Compressed Video Formats

1. Sony XDCAM and XDCAM EX Formats

Sony's tapeless formats are based on long-GOP compressed MPEG for captures and are designed to offer high quality during recording. The first two generations, XDCAM and XDCAM HD, use a disc similar to Blu-ray and hold either 23 GB of data or 50 GB of recorded media. The third-generation EX format uses solid-state express card media "S×S" cards instead. Content is recorded as MPEG 50 Mbps as 4:2:2 I-frame or in 20, 25, and 35 Mbps long-GOP compression. Only the 35 and 50 Mbps versions of this codec use full raster formats. All others utilize "thin raster" frames, where the content is scaled during capture and playback to allow for higher levels of compression while losing some color.

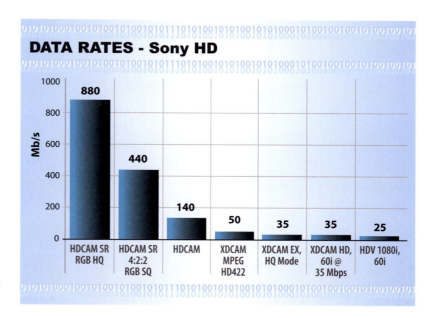

Figure 8.1c Data rates for Sony HD formats.

2. Panasonic's AVC-Intra

Panasonic's replacement for the venerable DVCProHD codec is now available in both 50 and 100 Mbps versions. The AVC-intra codec is based on H.264 compression schemes and uses I-frame compression. Thin raster and long-GOP formats or H.264 are *not* recommended editing formats, so consider transcoding these.

3. Avid DNxHD

Avid's answer to compressed HD files that are indistinguishable from uncompressed HD is the DNxHD family of codecs. One cool thing about DNxHD is that it is a multiprocessor codec, so the more cores you throw at it, the better it performs.

For highest quality, try the DNxHD 220x for full 1920 × 1080/30i file in 10-bit color or Avid DNxHD 220 (without the "x") for 8-bit color sources.

For productions shooting HDCAM or DVCPRO HD, Avid DNxHD 145 (145 Mbps) may be the ticket. It is an 8-bit editing and mastering codec that maintains full frame 1920 × 1080 at 30 fps.

Avid DN×HD family of mastering resolutions

Avid DN×HD is avilable in multiple HD encoding choices per resolution/frame rate combination, each identified by bandwidth (megabits/second) and bit depth, as show below.

Project Format	Resolution	Frame Size	Bits	FPS		min/GB
1080l/59.94	Avid DN×HD 220×	1920 × 1080	10	29.97	220	0.651
1080l/59.94	Avid DN×HD 220	1920 × 1080	8	29.97	220	0.651
1080l/59.94	Avid DN×HD 145	1920 × 1080	8	29.97	145	0.985
1080/50	Avid DN×HD 185×	1920 × 1080	10	25	184	0.780
1080/50	Avid DN×HD 185	1920 × 1080	8	25	184	0.780
1080/50	Avid DN×HD 120	1920 × 1080	8	25	121	1.181
1080p/25	Avid DN×HD 185×	1920 × 1080	10	25	184	0.780
1080p/25	Avid DN×HD 185	1920 × 1080	8	25	184	0.780
1080p/25	Avid DN×HD 120	1920 × 1080	8	25	121	1.181
1080p/25		1920 × 1080	8	25	36	3.98
1080p/24	Avid DN×HD 175×	1920 × 1080	10	24	176	0.814
1080p/24	Avid DN×HD 175	1920 × 1080	8	24	176	0.814
1080p/24	Avid DN×HD 115	1920 × 1080	8	24	116	1.231
1080p/24	Avid DN×HD 36	1920 × 1080	8	24	36	3.98
1080p/23.976	Avid DN×HD 175×	1920 × 1080	10	23.976	176	0.814
1080p/23.976	Avid DN×HD 175	1920 × 1080	8	23.976	176	0.814
1080p/23.976	Avid DN×HD 115	1920 × 1080	8	23.976	116	1.231
1080p/23.976	Avid DN×HD 36	1920 × 1080	8	23.976	36	3.98
1080p/29.97	Avid DN×HD 220×	1920 × 1080	10	29.97	220	0.651
1080p/29.97	Avid DN×HD 220	1920 × 1080	8	29.97	220	0.651
1080p/29.97	Avid DN×HD 145	1920 × 1080	8	29.97	145	0.985
1080p/29.97	Avid DN×HD 45	1920 × 1080	8	29.97	45	3.18
720p/59.94	Avid DN×HD 220×	1280 × 720	10	59.94	220	0.651
720p/59.94	Avid DN×HD 220	1280 × 720	8	59.94	220	0.651
720p/59.94	Avid DN×HD 145	1280 × 720	8	59.94	145	0.985
720p/50	Avid DN×HD 175×	1280 × 720	10	50	175	.818
720p/50	Avid DN×HD 175	1280 × 720	8	50	175	.818
720p/50	Avid DN×HD 115	1280 × 720	8	50	175	1.244
720p/29.97	Avid DN×HD 110×	1280 × 720	10	29.97	110	1.30
720p/29.97	Avid DN×HD 110	1280 × 720	8	29.97	110	1.30
720p/29.97	Avid DN×HD 75	1280 × 720	8	29.97	72	2.05
720p/25	Avid DN×HD 90×	1280 × 720	10	25	92	1.59
720p/25	Avid DN×HD 90	1280 × 720	8	25	92	1.59
720p/25	Avid DN×HD 60	1280 × 720	8	25	60	2.39
720p/23.976	Avid DN×HD 90×	1280 × 720	10	23.976	88	1.566
720p/23.976	Avid DN×HD 90	1280 × 720	8	23.976	88	1.566
720p/23.976	Avid DN×HD 60	1280 × 720	8	23.976	58	2.381

Figure 8.1d Avid DNxHD family of mastering resolutions. (Courtesy Avid.)

Michael Phillips, principal product designer for Avid Technology, Inc.: *You can certainly encode HDCAM in DNxHD 220, but you are not gaining a whole lot except for a more robust color space. The full raster of DNxHD 145 provides a horizontal resolution that is 33% sharper. In addition, it makes the files smaller than the typical 176 Mbps of SD while preserving HD quality.*

DNxHD 36 (36 Mbps) is an offline HD progressive source codec and a great bit rate for multicam. The file sizes are only 1.5× larger than DV25, making it a good choice as a group clip file.

Avid's DNxHD can output a QuickTime file compatible with both Mac OS and Windows platforms.

4. DVCPRO HD

Panasonic's original offering, DVCPRO HD, is still popular because of its small file sizes and excellent quality. It works with an anamorphic frame that is naturally 1440 × 1920 at 100 Mbps. It expands upon playback to full frame. Commonly used as a P2 codec, DVCProHD is broadcast quality and supports RT Extreme effects.

5. Apple ProRes 422

ProRes has been around since 2007 and has been improved and expanded recently with FCP 7. The original codecs are ProRes 422 (HQ) and ProRes 422.

ProRes 422 is the next-generation postproduction format from Apple and uses a full 1920 × 1080 raster in a 10-bit, 4:2:2 color space. It is designed to give you the exact same visual quality as uncompressed HD at SD file sizes. MacBook Pro laptops can use ProRes 422 to play back full-quality HD in real time.

Three new versions of the Apple ProRes codec join ProRes 422 and ProRes 422 (HQ):

- *ProRes 422 (Proxy).* For craft editing or offline editing on a MacBook or MacBook Pro.
- *ProRes 422 (LT).* For projects such as news, sports, and multi-cam events that require reduced file sizes at broadcast quality.
- *ProRes 4444.* For compositing and digital workflows that require the highest possible image fidelity.

All five versions of the ProRes codec share the same fundamental attributes. ProRes uses variable bit rate (VBR) encoding to minimize file sizes for storage efficiency. It also optimizes decoding to offer multistream, real-time editing performance and preserves the original frame width of SD, HD, and 2 K source video, so you won't have to reposition or resize graphics in a finishing workflow.[2]

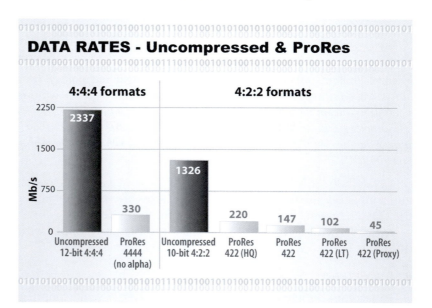

Figure 8.2a Chart shows the comparison of Apple ProRes and uncompressed data rates.

TARGET DATA RATES - Apple ProRes

Dimensions	Frame Rate	ProRes 422 (Proxy)		ProRes 422 (LT)		ProRes 422		ProRes 422 (HQ)		ProRes 4444 (excl. alpha)	
		MB/s	GB/hr	MB/s	GB/hr	MB/s	GB/hr	MB/s	GB/hr	MB/s	GB/hr
720x480	24p	10	4	23	10	34	15	50	23	75	34
	60i, 30p	12	5	29	13	42	19	63	28	94	42
720x486	24p	10	4	23	10	34	15	50	23	75	34
	60i, 30p	12	5	29	14	42	19	63	28	94	42
720x576	50i, 25p	12	6	28	14	41	18	61	28	92	41
960x720	24p	15	7	35	16	50	23	75	34	113	51
	25p	16	7	36	16	52	24	79	35	118	53
	30p	19	9	44	20	63	28	94	42	141	64
	50p	32	14	73	33	105	47	157	71	236	106
	60p	38	17	87	39	126	57	189	85	283	127
1280x720	24p	18	8	41	18	59	26	88	40	132	59
	25p	19	9	42	19	61	28	92	41	138	62
	30p	23	10	51	23	73	33	110	49	165	74
	50p	38	17	84	38	122	55	184	83	275	124
	60p	45	20	101	46	147	66	220	99	330	148
1280x1080	24p	31	14	70	31	101	45	151	68	226	102
	60i, 30p	38	17	87	39	126	57	189	85	283	127
1440x1080	24p	31	14	70	31	101	45	151	68	226	102
	50i, 25p	32	14	73	33	105	47	157	71	236	106
	60i, 30p	38	17	87	39	126	57	189	85	283	127
1920x1080	24p	36	16	82	37	117	53	176	79	264	119
	50i, 25p	38	17	85	38	122	55	184	83	275	124
	60i, 30p	45	20	102	46	147	66	220	99	330	148
	50p	76	34	170	77	245	110	367	165	551	248
	60p	91	41	204	92	293	132	440	198	660	297
2048x1024	24p	41	19	93	42	134	60	201	91	302	136
	25p	43	19	97	44	140	63	210	94	315	142
	30p	52	23	116	52	168	75	251	113	377	170
	50p	86	39	194	87	280	126	419	189	629	283
	60p	103	46	232	104	335	151	503	226	754	339
2048x1080*	24p	41	19	93	42	134	60	201	91	302	136
2048x1152	24p	41	19	93	42	134	60	201	91	302	136
	25p	43	19	97	44	140	63	210	94	315	142
	30p	52	23	116	52	168	75	251	113	377	170
	50p	86	39	194	87	280	126	419	189	629	283
	60p	103	46	232	104	335	151	503	226	754	339
2048x1556*	24p	63	28	142	64	203	91	306	138	458	206

*The 2048x1080 and 2048x1556 frame sizes are enabled for real-time effects in Final Cut Pro for Apple ProRes 4444 only.

Figure 8.2b Target data rates of Apple ProRes by frame size.

Transcoding

Transcoded Files Reduce Bandwidth and Storage Needs

Using an offline editing codec as a temporary substitute to your deliverable media will solve most bandwidth problems. For the price of one uncompressed stream, a system can handle multiples of transcoded down-rezzed size files. Deciding which codec to use for offline should be based on striking a balance between the highest possible resolution with the lowest bandwidth and least amount of storage needs. It's also good to use actual editing codecs if possible; some of the lower resolution codes just don't hold up that well.

You could work as high as compressed HD down to motion JPEG resolutions. Some editors prefer to work in DV anamorphic. Just check the charts in this chapter against your system to see how many streams you can handle at your desired codec.

Common Transcoding Codecs

- JPEG ("PhotoJPEG"): PhotoJPEG has a variable bit rate but is typically lower than DV. Quality is set to "High" or 75% quality. PhotoJPEG (at the default 75% quality) looks better than DV or DV50, although some people would say it looks a little "soft." This is broadcast-video quality, but RT Extreme effects are not supported at NTSC and PAL resolutions.
- DV25 ("DV") = 25 Mb/s. This is consumer video quality and supports RT Extreme effects.
- DV50 ("DVCPRO") = 50 Mb/s. This is professional video quality and supports RT Extreme effects.
- Avid DNX HD 36.
- 14 to 1 s.
- 4 to 1 s.
- ProRes 422 (LT) and (Proxy).
- DVCProHD.

Tip

Transcode file sets with matching frame sizes to avoid having to reset sequence or project settings. This will also allow you to do some resizing, repositioning, or picture-in-picture FX in the offline mode without having to redo them in the online mode.

Creating Sets of Transcoded Files

To make a down-rezzed set of your master clips with matching timecode, you don't have to load your show twice. Load first in the highest resolution for finishing, then use that file set to create a new one. In FCP, you can either batch export or media manage an offline quality file set. In Avid, consolidate or transcode. This works well, and it's fast because the resulting files are small. In Avid, you can use AMA to consolidate/transcode file-based media to a new set of files and switch back and forth to reconnect to either set of media.

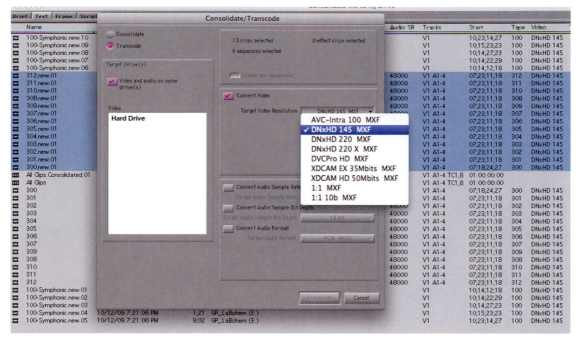

Figure 8.3 Screen capture of Avid's Consolidate/Transcode feature.

Hard Drive Technology

As frequently as every few months, there are dramatic changes in hard drive technology, which seems limitless. When Avid first came out, it was equipped with a heavy drawer-size RAID of a whopping 9 gigs and cost $5,000. This evolved to four 73-gig drives for about a half a terabyte of storage, which was considered enormous. Now, a terabyte drive costs just under $100 and you can get an 8-gig thumb drive for about $20.

Bob Zelin, systems integrator: *There are lots of good brands on the market. Most of the internal drives, the actual disk drives themselves, are made either by Hitachi, SeaGate, or Western Digital—and those are the actual disk drives, the ones spinning around, used in all these boxes. Products from companies like Maxx Digital or CalDigit or Sonnet are actually put together for you; the manufacturers are taking responsibility for them working and taking care of any problems customers have.*

Storage Capacity

Until recently, if you were to buy an 8-drive bay RAID, with eight 1-terabyte drives all striped together, you would get 6.5 terabytes

Figure 8.4 Digital Heaven offers a free video storage calculator. It doesn't do data rates, but it does provide storage for length of video: www.digital-heaven .co.uk/videospace. (Courtesy: Digital Heaven.)

after you created a RAID 5 group—and those drives were fast enough to go beyond HD to handle 2 K files. Now the 2-terabyte drives have come out, so that exact same thing that used to be 8 terabytes is now 16 terabytes, simply because Seagate and Hitachi have come out with larger disk drives.

Bob Zelin: *There are new chassis styles out, allowing you to expand the individual drive chassis. When you need more storage, you just run a little jumper cable that daisy chains one to another, and now instead of 12 terabytes you have 24.*

Figure 8.5 Dulce Systems chart, www.dulcesystems .com/html/video_space.html. (Courtesy: Dulce Systems.)

Video Storage

Video Resolutions	Data Rate (MB/sec)	Storage Capacity (in hours)					
		1 TB	2 TB	4 TB	8 TB	16 TB	32 TB
DV/DV25	3.7	75.1	150.2	300.3	600.6	1201.2	2402.4
DV50	7.4	37.5	75.1	150.2	300.3	600.6	1201.2
HDV 1080i-60	3.2	86.8	173.6	347.2	694.4	1388.9	2777.8
DVCPRO HD 720p-24	5.7	48.7	97.5	194.9	389.9	779.7	1559.5
DVCPRO HD 1080i-60	13.9	20.0	40.0	79.9	159.9	319.7	639.5
ProRes 422 1920x1080 29.97	18.4	15.1	30.2	60.4	120.8	241.5	483.1
ProRes 422 HQ 1920x1080 29.97	27.5	10.1	20.2	40.4	80.8	161.6	323.2
ProRes 4444 1920x1080 29.97	41.3	6.7	13.5	26.9	53.9	107.7	215.5
Redcode RAW	228.0	9.9	19.8	39.7	79.4	158.7	317.5
Redcode RAW	36.0	7.7	15.4	30.9	61.7	123.5	246.9
SD 8 bit	20.2	13.8	27.5	55.0	110.0	220.0	440.0
SD 10 bit	26.9	10.3	20.7	41.3	82.6	165.2	330.4
HD 1080i-29.97 8 bit	118.7	2.3	4.7	9.4	18.7	37.4	74.9
HD 1080i 10 bit	157.2	1.8	3.5	7.1	14.1	28.2	56.5
HD 720p-60 8 bit	105.7	2.6	5.3	10.5	21.0	42.0	84.1
HD 720p 10 bit	138.0	2.0	4.0	8.1	16.1	32.2	64.4
AJA 1920x1080 psf 24 10bit RGB	188.6	1.5	2.9	5.9	11.8	23.6	47.1
AJA 2048x1556 psf 23.98 10bit RGB	291.7	1.0	1.9	3.8	7.6	15.2	30.5
2k DPX full ap 24fps	292.8	0.9	1.9	3.8	7.6	15.2	30.4
4k DPX full ap 24fps	1166.4	0.2	0.5	1.0	1.9	3.8	7.6
4k DPS academy 24fps	892.8	0.3	0.6	1.2	2.5	5.0	10.0

Hard Drive Bandwidth

The data rate of the multiclip will determine the minimal bandwidth of the hard drives and connection. Be sure to add headroom to your calculations. If you have a combined bit rate of 200 MB/s for your grouped clip, you would want to have a hard drive array capable of at least 200 MB/s—but that probably would not be enough to sustain the performance and if the drive has media on it, it will run slower as it fills up. I usually double the bandwidth estimate to be safe. A drive that transfers 350 MB/s should do the trick nicely.

Larry Jordan of Larry Jordan & Associates, Inc., is a producer, director, editor, consultant, and trainer with more than 25 years, video production and postproduction experience (www.larryjordan .biz):

If you're attaching a FireWire 400 device, the FireWire 400 hard disk is generally going to feed data around 20 to 25 MB/sec; FireWire 800 gives us about 50 to 55 MB/s. If you're trying to do a five-camera P2 stream and your hard disk only goes at 20 to 25 MB/s but the streams require 75, it's not going to work. FireWire 800 is around 50 to 55 MB/sec: still no good. You may be able to get there with eSATA, which goes 75 to 90 MB/s. Now is the time, if you're going to do a lot of multicam work: you need to step out of single hard drives and step up to RAIDs, because you just can't get the performance off your hard disk.

This is about throughput, not capacity. Just because your drive holds 500 MB doesn't mean it transfers 500 MB/s. Those are two totally different animals. A FireWire drive may hold 500 GB, but it doesn't transfer the data faster than 55 MB/sec.

Bruce Nazarian: *Throughput is the measure of the real-world performance of the system, the entire drive system. Bandwidth is perhaps the theoretical spec of what it might do. The reality is not what the spec says; the reality is: if you benchmark that particular hard drive system you've set up, how much sustained throughput can you get from drive to CPU?*

In essence, what does your computer's operating system have to do to find the file being requested and deliver it seamlessly, without a dropout? Now, if you have more drives—individual drives, not RAIDs—with the speed capability to deliver content within your requirements, it's actually easier for the CPU to source fewer files per drive across a larger number of drives.

Bruce Nazarian: *Even RAIDs bottleneck at a certain point. Especially in a multiclip environment, if your system requests too many clips of high codec data at high resolution it will bottleneck. The important question is, can you set your system up intelligently to provide you with the most trouble-free environment for sourcing the content you need in order to be working multiclip?*

Sustained Performance

Sustained performance should be the qualifier for hard drive bandwidth. Sustained performance will tell you how fast the computer will operate over time without dropping frames.

Several free programs are available to test your drive speed.

Free System Tests and Data Rate Calculators

- You don't even need to own the AJA hardware to be able to test the speed of your hard drives: www.aja.com
- Black Magic Speed Test: www.blackmagic.com
- Steel Bytes HD Test; Avid recommended, easy for PCs: www.steelbytes.com/?mid=20
- The AJA Data Rate Calculator free application (www.aja.com) is awesome; a must-have download

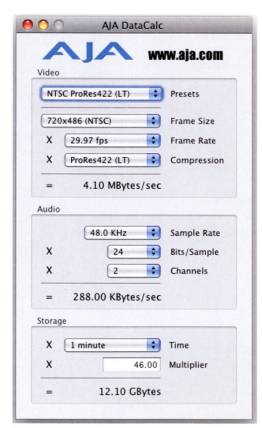

Figure 8.6 AJA DataCalc.
(Courtesy AJA.)

RAIDs

For multicam and multistream, obviously you want a faster format. You can get much faster speeds by having more drives striped together to build an array of disks. Striped disks store higher data rates than a single disk can handle. You can then create a striped RAID from these disks using software such as Disk Utility (in MacOS X) or the Computer Management control panel (in Windows XP Pro). These disks will then appear on your system as a single disk. You can then select this as the capture location in your video capture software.

If you were to get a modern disk drive, with four or five of these drives together with something called an SAS controller (Serial Attached SCSI), you'll be able to do about 300 MB/s. With eight drives (8 to 16 terabytes), you can do about 550 to 600 megabytes per second: double the bandwidth and more drive space.

You can get all kinds of disks, and they vary in speed. You can get a simple disk box and place a few hard disks in it, or you can even put the disks in the computer internally, if space is available. The types of disk arrays where disks are connected are commonly called JBOD (i.e., "Just a Bunch of Disks") arrays.

Throughput: Types of Arrays

- Fibre Channel
- PCI Express

- Dual SCSI
- IDE/ATA/SATA
- eSATA

The new MacPros, including the inexpensive models, all have an internal boot drive, which is one single drive that comes with the computer. Three additional empty slots are available for people to pop drives into easily: they just slide right in. All of the hardware is provided for you. So you can take three raw internal drives and—because 2-terabyte drives are available—you can have 6 terabytes available inside your computer, all striped together, and this has got nothing to do with the internal boot drive of the computer.

Multicamera Math

Here's a common question: How many angles (streams) using DV (codec) can my system (drive) handle (bandwidth)?

To understand the equation, let's break it down:

1. Individual angle's data rate
2. Multiclip aggregate data rate (i.e., total angles in group)
3. Hard drive bandwidth
4. Throughput: connectivity speed
5. Computer processing

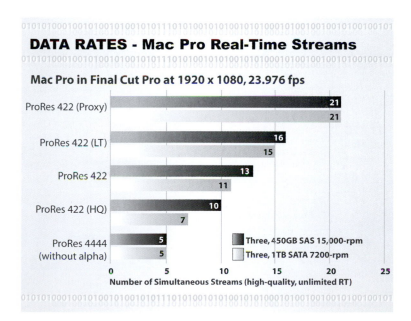

Figure 8.7a Comparison of real-time simultaneous streams of Apple ProRes on a MacPro.

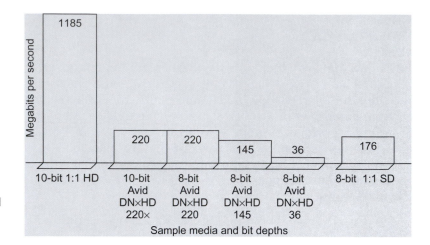

Figure 8.7b Sample media and bit depths for Avid DNxHD. (Courtesy Avid.)

Calculating Data Rates for Multiple Clips

To find out how much drive speed you'll need, first you'll have to calculate the data rate for the codec used. Then get the aggregate data rate for all the cameras in the group by multiplying the codec data rate times the number of camera angles in the group. That's the multiclip data rate: a much higher bit rate for real-time playback of grouped camera clips.

This is not an exact science; there are a few other things to consider. There may be some background "data rate magic" applied to the software code for playing back multiple clips in the

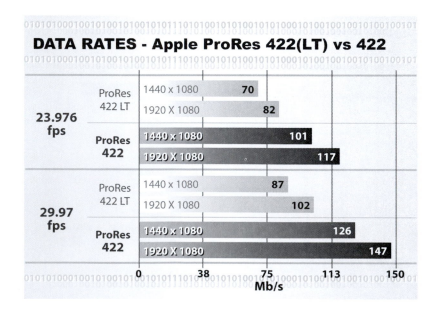

Figure 8.7c Apple ProRes 422 versus LT data rates.

multicam environment. In FCP, for instance, you can group 128 cameras, but the most you can see is 16. So it's entirely possible that the unseen cameras are not actually playing back in real time, or even requesting any bandwidth.

Bob Zelin, systems integrator: *If you're doing a project with 10 cameras and your average data rate is about 30 MB/s and you want to group 10 cameras together, that's about 300 MB/s of bandwidth that you need, minimum. It really doesn't matter what format you're using (HD or SD); what matters are the bandwidth and data speed.*

The Secret to Calculating Real Speed

Benchmark testing of hard drives tends to be under ideal conditions—and we don't usually work in ideal conditions. Factors like latency, variable bit rates, threading, and sustained bandwidth can have a dramatic effect on actual drive speeds. So it's not your computer speed, it's not the RAM, it's not the storage—it's how fast your hard disk *transfers* data to your computer and back again that's important.

Let's say I know I'm doing nine streams of ProRes HQ at 30 MB/s each. Our aggregate bit rate is 270 MB/s. In a perfect world, I'd get a drive rated at 400 MB/s or more and go to town. This should work—especially in a nonshared environment, wherein you have a lot more latitude. But it's not just one 270 MB/s stream coming off the RAID, sequentially. It's *nine* different streams from nine different places on the RAID—nine file pointers. The real question is how fast can a megabyte get through the system?

To approach a more realistic calculation of speed, we'll need to figure out the throughput by milliseconds per MB. Then you can tell whether the actual sustained speed of the drive is capable of moving your media fast enough.

Steve Modica is CTO of Small Tree Systems. He and his team all came from SGI, so they're experts with multithreading, multiprocessing, and dealing with supercomputers and large jobs for NASA.

Steve Modica: *If you know you're moving 30 MB/s, that allows you to figure out how many milliseconds each MB requires. You can invert 30 and come up with 1/30, and that's going to tell you how many milliseconds you have per MB. It isn't a bandwidth calculation; I need to prove to myself that each one of those streams never sees an IO that goes higher than 30 milliseconds per MB.*

Let's say the drive can do 270 MB/s with my nine Angles (threads of execution). The next question is, can the drive sustain low latencies the entire time, or does the RAID have to do housekeeping? Will it run out of internal resources and have to reallocate or free them? Or will it have to do anything internally that might make it glitch momentarily and drop a frame?

Steve Modica: *When you've got one guy trying to read nine threads into a client from a server, you've got nine threads coming in and the RAIDs forced to bounce among all nine clips, all nine angles, reducing its performance. So even though it may have sustained 270 MB/s on a nice, clean benchmark, when you start hitting it with all those angles, it might do 200 MB/s.*

Converting Megabits to Megabytes

Throughput, bit rate, and data transfer rate (or data rate) all relate to the speed at which you can get data from your hard disk to your computer or from your computer to your hard disk. It's measured in what are called bits per second (bps). The Internet is also measured in bps. Bits per second is the measure of the speed that digital data transfers from one point to another.

The problem is that when we deal with bits per second—for instance, with FireWire 400, wherein the 400 refers to the speed of the bus, which is 400 million megabits per second (mbps)—we're used to thinking in terms of storage, which is measured in *bytes*, as opposed to data transfer rate, which is measured in *bits*.

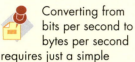

Tip

Converting from bits per second to bytes per second requires just a simple formula: divide the bits per second by eight. Eight bits per second (8/bps) = 1 megabyte per second (1 MB/s).

You need 27.5 MB/s to be able to do a single stream of ProRes 422 HQ, which is a 220-megabit per second data rate; 220 mb/s divided by 8 equals 27.5 MB/s.

Technique: Understanding Video Data Rates
By Larry Jordan

(This article was first published in the November 2008 issue of Larry Jordan's Final Cut Pro Newsletter. It was updated in July 2009 and is reprinted in part here with permission by the author. To subscribe to Larry Jordan's newsletter or read the entire article, go to www.larryjordan.biz/nxlttrs.html.)

Here's the *key concept:* hard disks are not infinite in speed or unlimited in storage. The *corollary* to this rule is that dropped frame errors are most often caused by a hard disk that can't keep up with your video format.

Hard Drive Speeds

While hard drive speed is impacted by how fast it rotates, a much greater controlling factor is how the hard drive attaches to your computer. We call this a drive's "data transfer rate."

Here are several things to keep in mind:

1. All FireWire drives are hubbed. This means that when both fast and slow devices are connected to the built-in ports of your computer, the slower devices (cameras and decks) slow down faster devices (hard drives).
2. FireWire does not operate at its rated speed. While a FireWire 400 drive has the potential to transfer data at up to 50 MB/s, it doesn't. This is due to how the hard drive processes data internally using a FireWire bridge chip.

3. The more FireWire devices you add to your system, especially when you have more than five, the slower the data transfer rate is.

4. The more data you store on a hard drive, the slower it goes. A drive is fastest when it is empty. When a drive is totally full, it neither plays back nor records. It is generally a good idea to keep about 20% free space on your drive. While individual drives vary, I've found that connection speeds generally group into the following speeds.

Connection	Data Transfer Speed
USB 1.0 or 2.0	Not fast enough for video editing
FireWire 400	20-25 MB/s
FireWire 800	40-50 MB/s
eSATA (single drive)	75-100 MB/s
RAIDs	100-600+MB/s

Figure 8.8 Data transfer rates by hard drive connection type. (Courtesy Larry Jordan /www.larryjordan.biz.)

Here's how the theories apply to video editing.

Video Format Data Transfer Requirements

Here's how you read the following table.

Format indicates the video format as indicated by Easy Setup.

Store one hour indicates how much hard disk space it takes to store an hour of material in a particular format. This allows you to estimate your total storage needs, based on the amount of material shot. Remember to add 20% for general storage overhead and free space.

Comp indicates how the codec compresses the video. GOP compression compresses pictures in groups; I-frame compression compresses individual images. GOP compression requires an additional conforming process before output, which increases the time it takes to output your sequence.

Dupe indicates those video formats that Final Cut duplicates the media from its source format (i.e., P2 or AVCHD) into its transcoded format (i.e., QuickTime or ProRes 422). As a general rule of thumb, double all storage requirements for these formats. While not totally accurate (for instance, if you don't transfer the footage into Final Cut Pro, no duplication occurs), it's as reasonable a way to estimate file storage size as anything else.

Transfer rate indicates how much data, on average per second, is required by that format. (The speed is measured in megabytes per second: MB/s.)

Keep in mind that a real-time dissolve doubles each of these transfer rates because during the dissolve two streams of video are playing. A four-camera multiclip increases each rate by four times because four streams of video are playing.

Here's the key point: Assuming your hard drives are healthy, a dropped frame error means that you are trying to read or write more data than your hard drive will support. This table helps you to match the data rate of your video format with the speed of your hard drive, indicated in the preceding table.

Note: HD-CAM and HD-CAM SR create massively big files, and the exact file sizes vary widely by frame rate and image size. In all cases, these formats should be edited using a RAID with a data transfer rate in excess of 200 MB/s. Faster is absolutely better.

Format	Store 1 Hour	Dupe	Comp	Tranfer Rate
SD				
DV NTSC/PAL	13 GB	No	I-frame	3.75 MB/s
DVCPRO-50	27 GB	No	I-frame	7.5 MB/s
Uncompressed 8-bit	72 GB	No	I-frame	20.2 MB/s
Uncompressed 10-bit	96 GB	No	I-frame	26.7 MB/s
ProRes 422 (NTSC or PAL)	19.5 GB	No	I-frame	5.25 MB/s
ProRes 422 HQ	28.1 GB	No	I-frame	7.8 MB/s
HD				
HDV (25 mbps) 60i	13 GB	No	GOP	3.75 MB/s
AVCHD (varies)*	Up to 10.8 GB	Yes	I-frame	1.5-3.0 MB/s
AVC-Intra (Panasonic)*	Up to 10.8 GB	Yes	I-frame	1.5-3.0 MB/s
AVCCAM (Sony & Pana.)*	Up to 10.8 GB	Yes	I-frame	1.5-3.0 MB/s
XDCAM HD (50 mbps)	28 GB	Yes	GOP	7.75 MB/s
XDCAM HD (35 mbps)	19 GB	Yes	GOP	5.2 MB/s
XDCAM EX	19 GB	Yes	GOP	5.2 MB/s
DVCPROHD	54 GB	Yes	I-frame	15 MB/s
ProRes 422 (Proxy)*	20 GB	No	I-frame	5.6 MB/s
ProRes 422 (LT)*	46 GB	No	I-frame	12.75 MB/s
ProRes 422*	66 GB	No	I-frame	18.1 MB/s
ProRes 422 (HQ)*	99 GB	No	I-frame	27.5 MB/s
ProRes 4444 (no alpha)*	148 GB	No	I-frame	41.25 MB/s
R3D	137 GB	No	I-frame	28 or 38 MB/s
HDCAM 720p 60 fps	396 GB	No	I-frame	110 MB/s
HDCAM 1080 60 fps	834 GB	No	I-frame	237 MB/s

Figure 8.9 Data transfer rate by video format. (Courtesy Larry Jordan, www.larryjordan.biz.)

Notes

- All AVC video formats are converted (transcoded) to ProRes 422 during ingest into Final Cut Pro. So while the AVC source video uses GOP compression, ProRes uses I-frame compression. Also, when the AVC footage is duplicated, the ProRes data rate and file size apply to the converted video.
- ProRes is a variable bit rate encoder, so file sizes will vary depending on format, image size, and frame rate. The HD specs for ProRes are based on shooting 1080i/60 and taken from Apple's ProRes white paper. File sizes decrease for 720p files or slower frame rates.
- I found that understanding the relationship between hard disk speeds and video formats greatly simplified storage budgeting and solving the dropped frame problem.
- You can just drop the R3D proxy file in the timeline to view or edit—but if you use the Log and Transfer tool to import the R3D files, they will transcode them into ProRes (HQ). The 4 K files are converted to 2 K in width, 3 K imports at 3 K, and 2 K stays at 2 K. Much like P2, it is not a fast process even with an eight-core tower.

Minimum Requirements

What about PCs? Does this process have to be done on a Mac? Final Cut Pro doesn't run on a PC. Programs that do are Sony Vegas, Avid Media Composer and Adobe Premiere.

Bob Zelin: *If you've got a PC, especially a powerful workstation like a Hewlett-Packard 8200 or 8400 workstation, yes: the same capabilities work for all of the storage. You wind up being able to pop drives into the modern computers like the Hewlett-Packard 8600s, which have plenty of slots available for eSATA drives; or, if you've got an older computer, like an 8200, you can get an eSATA card that will go into, say, slot four or five on an 8200 and then pop these external drive RAIDs on it.*

The systems are sometimes referred to as "hardware agnostic," which means you can use any disk drive you like. You can actually do multicam with just a regular 800 FireWire drive, but a couple of streams of DVCProHD are about all an FW800 can handle. You're not going to get the same performance that you would with a modern eSATA drive.

Laptop Limitations

Sometimes you just have to cut in a hotel room, on a train, or in some other exotic location, right?

You can cut multicam with a very inexpensive setup. Even a laptop will do, provided it's fast enough to handle at least one HD stream. One of the nice things about the 17″ MacBook Pros is that they have a 3–4 express card slot, which is an expansion slot, and you can buy an eSATA card that slides into that slot, so you can use an external SATA RAID at very fast speeds.

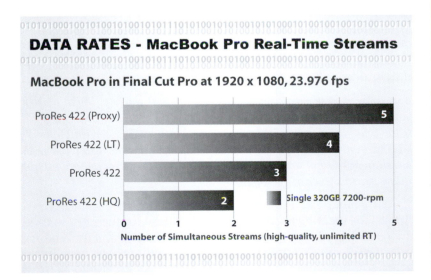

DATA RATES - MacBook Pro Real-Time Streams

MacBook Pro in Final Cut Pro at 1920 x 1080, 23.976 fps

ProRes 422 (Proxy)	5
ProRes 422 (LT)	4
ProRes 422	3
ProRes 422 (HQ)	2

Single 320GB 7200-rpm

Number of Simultaneous Streams (high-quality, unlimited RT)

Figure 8.10 MacBook Pro real-time stream comparison: Apple ProRes.

But you're definitely limited by the bandwidth of the express 3–4 bus—more than by the drives, because the express card used to connect to the external drive is limited to 120 MB/s bandwidth. You don't get full performance even if you have a drive array doing 250 MB/s. You would max out at 120 MB/s.

Full HD Playback Trick

In a minimum bandwidth situation, you can still get deliverable quality HD playback of your offline cut, provided you have enough drive space to hold the full set of HD hi-res media too. Get the bandwidth needed for editing multicam with a down-converted set, and switch to HD for high-quality playback, dailies, and sync analysis. (For a step-by-step routine for creating offline sets, see Chapter 10, Preparing the Project.)

Shared Storage

What happens if you have several editors working together in a multicam project and they need to share resources? You can use shared storage systems, of course, but they too come with bandwidth requirements. It's not just software. You have to buy a bunch of stuff to make this work, which means a server computer and disk drives and fiber channel switchers and fiber cards and cables (specialty cables). It costs a lot of money.

Bob Zelin: *Shared storage has become a major issue for many companies. Many of them have at least one or two people editing, someone else doing graphics, someone else doing audio, et cetera—and they all need to be able to access the same material, even in multicam.*

Shared storage basically means you've got a computer acting as a server and a bunch of disk drives attached to that computer. The edit suites are the clients, all of whom connect back to this central computer through either a fiber switch or an Ethernet switch to share the media. In this way, multiple people can read that multicam footage on their different systems.

Bob Zelin: *So if you're doing a multicam job and you're trying to share it, you're actually pulling the bandwidth for, let's say, 10 cameras to one edit suite, and you're pulling the same bandwidth to another computer for editing another part of the show. So where does that end? Again, you've got a certain number of streams, depending on your compression ratio, of how many streams you can pull off these systems.*

With Final Cut Pro and Premiere, it's much easier, because Apple isn't creating a special media database for the files, so there are countless shared storage solutions. Maxx Digital Final Share is one; it uses simple Apple File Sharing. And there have been lots of other solutions from companies like Pay System, Studio Network

Noteworthy

As always, the more people reading media files, the faster the drives and the more bandwidth you need. There are many options today for less-expensive shared storage solutions. Avid has three major shared storage systems working currently: Avid Unity, Terrablock by Facilis, and Edit Share.

Solutions, and Maximum Throughput. Apple itself started with a product called XSan, a powerful but expensive shared storage system.

Demystifying Multithreading

In theory, multithreading allows the application to run at a much faster throughput speed. So multithreading is a way to enable an application, or an application and a computer architecture, to run more than just one thing at a time. To understand it better, let's first consider cores.

Cores

Remember how, when each new computer came out, it was always faster than the previous one? More megahertz, more speed. Then all of sudden, and without much fanfare, the chip speeds leveled off and dual-core processing entered the picture. Intel says one problem it faced was due to leakage current. If the company kept trying to make its processors faster, the current leaked by the processor between transistors would eat up the processor's entire power budget. So Intel had to consider multiple cores instead of one very fast core.

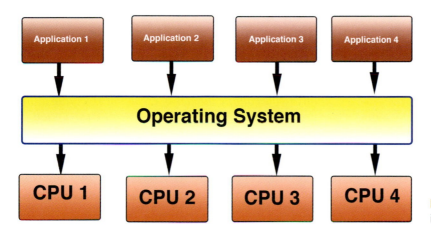

Figure 8.11 True multithreading in a four-core system.

Virtual Cores

Intel Xeon "Nehalem" processors support hyperthreading, which allows two threads to run simultaneously on each core. An 8-core MacPro presents 16 virtual cores recognized by Mac OS X. Performance is enhanced because hyperthreading enables the processor to take better advantage of the execution resources available in each core.

Threading

A thread in the operating system is a thread of execution. It's an active task.

Steve Modica: *In the old days, when you had one processor, you only ever had one thread. You didn't have to worry about things trying to use the same resource at the same time; only one thing was ever executing at the same time. Now, with threading, you have to worry about many things on the system. Three or four different threads completely independent of one another may all be trying to access the same buffer at the same time. There has to be a mechanism preventing them from stepping on each other and interrupting access.*

Definition

Multithreading computers have hardware support to execute multiple threads efficiently. These are distinguished from *multiprocessing systems* (such as multicore systems) in that the threads have to share the resources of a single core: the computing units, the CPU caches, and the translation lookaside buffer (TLB). Whereas multiprocessing systems include multiple complete processing units, multithreading aims to increase utilization of a single core by leveraging thread-level as well as instruction-level parallelism. As the two techniques are complementary, they are sometimes combined in systems with multiple multithreading CPUs and in CPUs with multiple multithreading cores.

FCP and Multithreading

Steve Modica: *So when we talk about multithreading, we're really talking about the OS's ability to have many threads of execution executing at the same time, efficiently and in a manner that doesn't cause corruption or other interference between threads.*

Bruce Nazarian: *Multithreading basically means the ability to run more than one process simultaneously—to get the most bang for your buck out of a processor or a given set of computer architecture.*

Final Cut likes to use this thing called asynchronous IO, which is a parallelized IO. It's very simple: the application gets to say, *I want to read this chunk of data off the disk, but I want to read it with six threads rather than just one.* It's not going to read it block, block, block, block. It wants to read all these blocks and it will tell the kernel, *I want you to read all these blocks and set off six threads, and just tell me when it's done,* and the OS does it.

Steve Modica: *A lot of RAIDs have a sweet spot, you know. One thread isn't enough, one core isn't enough to suck the bandwidth off the RAID.*

You need almost four to drive the RAID hard enough to max out the bandwidth.

The more cores, the more efficiently it pulls the bandwidth from the RAID.

Brian Gonosey, editor at Electric Entertainment: *RED operates very fast if you have an individual cluster on your own computer. So we created each workstation—we have pretty top-of-the line 8 cores—and we set up each workstation as its own cluster. By doing that we found maximum compression: maximum speed in terms of that transcode. You can't break apart the R3D file and then thread it across multiple computers and then put it back together the way you can so many other things using a compressor.*

References

1. Provided by Blackmagic.
2. Apple.

9

MULTICAMERA NONLINEAR EDITING SOFTWARE

As the concepts are basically the same for each of the modern-day, nonlinear edit systems, this book aims to salute their accomplishments as a whole. In this chapter, we'll consider a brief comparison of the top-selling systems' multicamera mode. It isn't a how-to. Those item-by-item menu details of the individual systems can be found in their user manuals. (There are also free tutorial links on the companion DVD). Here, we'll just look at the big picture—by comparing unique features and key differences—to help you choose the right multicam program for you.

Today's Top Systems

As this book goes to print, the top four editing systems *based on sales* are Adobe Premiere Pro, Apple Final Cut Pro (FCP), Avid Media Composer, and Sony Vegas.

Adobe sells the most systems because Premiere is bundled with the must-have Adobe Production Suite of products, including Photoshop and After Effects. Final Cut Pro sells more than Avid, whereas Sony Vegas and EDIUS are big sellers in the non-broadcast market.

All of these systems basically do the same thing with multicam. They all group clips by ins, outs, and timecode; they all allow normal clip editing, trims, and multiclip management; and they have the same audio options: audio follow video or selected track cutting. Some excel in areas where the others don't, but the primary functionality is the same, with just minor differences. And as much as these things change, they stay the same, so instead of talking about the tools themselves, we're going to discuss how best to leverage them for your maximum advantage.

Avid Media Composer

For Mac or PC

Ever since Avid multicam hit the sitcom world in 1993–1994, Avid has been the undisputed champion of multicam.

Avid has a few distinctions, including the following:

- Uses two sets of views or "banks" with 9 angles each, for a total of 18 angles; you switch between bank A and bank B to see the full group
- Switchable cadence
- Optimizes graphics card
- Media Tool has the ability to link and manage huge volumes of media
- ScriptSync with group clips

TIP

Avid started with m resolutions exclusively for multicam; Avid suggests not to use m resolutions on the software-based systems. They were designed for Meridian-based systems. There are other limitations, like the 3D tool and dissolves don't behave as you would expect. Now you can use any resolution that your system and drive speeds can support. In Multicam mode, Avid can have a groupclip that has different codecs but not different frame rates. Vegas and EDIUS can mix frame rates.

Custom Settings

A basic toolset is all you need to use multicam. The buttons in Avid can be mapped to your keyboard, and you can create custom keyboards. One improvement is that now the extended keyboards are automatically mapped for cutting angles 1 to 9 on the fly.

Tim Leavitt, an assistant editor on The Apprentice, notes: *I've got a mapped-out keyboard that's slightly evolved over the last three years. As I discover new features and realize I'm using some more than others, I rotate things in and out of my keyboard. Avid is great for having different work-spaces, where at the touch of a button you can resize all your windows a specific way, bring up a certain timecode display, change your colors, or bring up your digitized tool or your digital cut tool.*

Angle Arrangements

Avid will position its angles in the group clip by the sorted name column from the bin. So if you label your clips alphanumerically

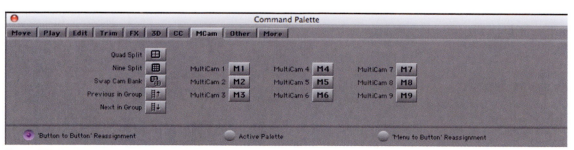

Figure 9.1 Avid's multicam button toolset.

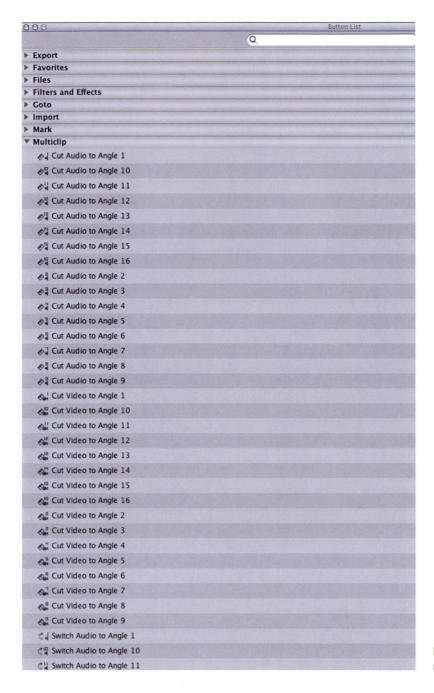

Figure 9.2 By comparison: FCP multicam (partial) button list.

and sort by name, that multiclip will have camera A in first position. The rest follow alphabetically. You can rearrange these positions directly in the source window by holding the control button down on the split screen and choosing an angle.

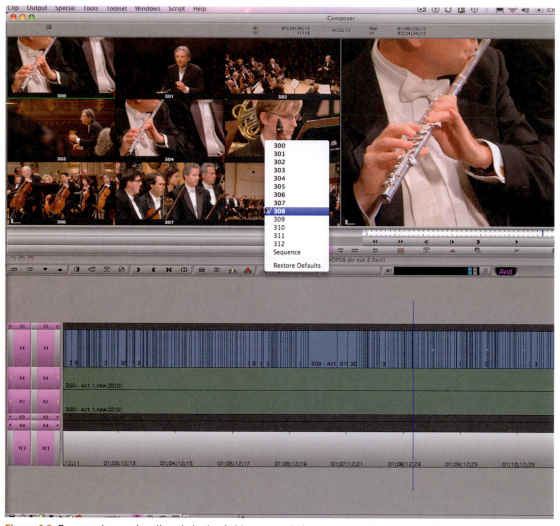

Figure 9.3 Rearranging angles directly in the Avid source window. (Courtesy San Francisco Symphony/WNET.ORG and Carnegie Hall.)

Match Frames

Here's an old friend returned. The match frame to a group clip as a source is now available as a nonsynced source clip again. It was around for a while, and then it was pulled somewhere in the transition to software-based systems. But it's back now.

Michael Krulik, Avid Technology, Inc.: *When you do a group, you'd have to be able to do a match frame back to the group and scan through the source. What usually happens when you're in multicam mode within Media Composer is it locks the timeline and the group clips so that as you scrub through the timeline, you're locked to the group, in the source. What you can do now is turn off multicam mode and still do a match frame in your timeline, and it will take you to the source.*

You still have your timeline active, and you're still at the point where you want to do a match frame, and then you turn off multicam mode, do a match frame, and it loads a match frame of the group back at the source. It match-frames from that clip from the group in the timeline, but it allows you to use standard editing tools from the group.

Graphics Card

Media Composer is using the graphics card to optimize playback. When you go into multicam, it goes into a draft resolution, to best performance. So while it still has to pull the same stream from the drives, it's not essentially displaying every field. Actually it has gone into 1/16th resolution. You're gaining speed by not taxing the system, as the graphics card is not decompressing at full quality. In the process, you're dropping the performance needed for the computer processor requirements.

Michael Krulik: *We prefer the GeForce (graphic cards) for Mac. You'll have better performance with Media Composer on Windows with the Quadro FX, the biggest and fastest card that you can get.*

Says Bob Russo, applications specialist at Avid Technology, Inc.: *Motion and Color use the graphics card. Final Cut doesn't. So there's no graphic acceleration at all in Final Cut. There's no performance improvement by having the fastest, greatest graphics card in the world with Final Cut—but with Media Composer there is, and it's a dramatic one.*

Cadence

Avid editing applications can capture footage that uses either pulldown cadence. Other editing systems might require one or the other. Media Composer can switch cadence. The project is still king in the organization, where your frame rate and video standard are set and maintained. What Media Composer allows that's far superior to all the other NLEs is that you can change the cadence of the clip that's being applied to the clip.

Bob Russo: *The perfect example would be that you're shooting P2 and you're shooting the advanced pulldown. So now you have an advanced pulldown and obviously when you remove the 3:2 it looks good, but when you leave the 3:2 in there, it looks terrible. There's no way within Final Cut to have it decide what cadence needs to be pulled out of that clip. Media Composer is going to guess, and if it's wrong you can change it. It's very simple. You can also render them. Now when you render them, of course, it's not happening on the fly and it's essentially higher quality. But you can do it on the fly in full quality.*

Noteworthy

When you launch Media Composer, you'll see along the splash screen: *Graphics card detected, Effects accelerated.* There's a line that goes on beneath it and you can tell whether your computer has a recommended graphics card. If it doesn't, it will still work, but the performance will be a notch lower.

To select the video pulldown cadence:

1. Select Output > Digital Cut.
2. Click the Video Pulldown Cadence menu, and select one of the following:
   - Standard 2:3:2:3
   - Advanced 2:3:3:2

You can also change the default pulldown phase for sequences:

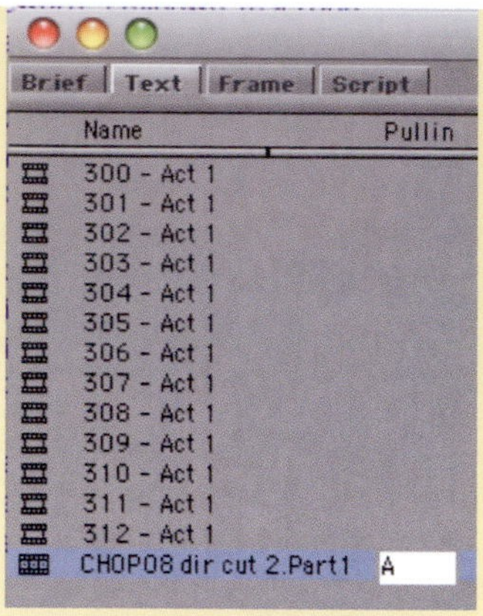

Figure 9.4 Use the pullin column to change the default pulldown phase for sequences.

ScriptSync

ScriptSync is a phenomenal feature that allows you to import your line script and link your clips or group clips to it. It's evolved over time and works very fast with voice recognition. Sitcoms or anything that shoots with multiple takes benefit from this mode without bins.

(For a full report on ScriptSync and MultiCam, see Chapter 12, Editing Techniques.)

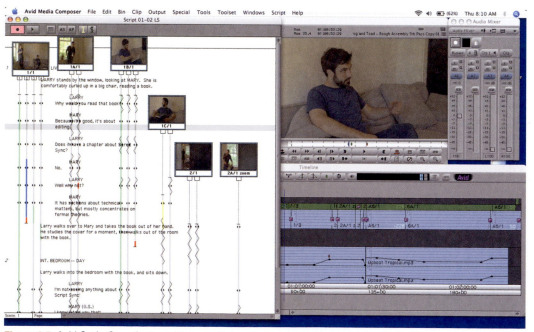

Figure 9.5 Avid ScriptSync feature. (Courtesy Robert Bramwell, A.C.E.)

Apple Final Cut Pro

For Mac Only

When FCP finally came out with multicam in version 5, it was almost limitless, allowing editors many more features than previous platforms. The workflow is also similar to that for other platforms, so it's usually adapted easily.

The multiclips have to be all the same frame rates and formats. No mixing there. So if, for instance, somebody shot P2, and one guy shot DV 25, and the other guy shot DV 50, you couldn't cut those natively as a multiclip group. You'd have to transcode one of those sets of clips to the other codec. They have to match.

Editing Multiclips with Effects

Final Cut will allow the use of effects within groups. You just throw a presaved FX right into the angle of the multiclip. You can

Noteworthy

 FCP is a smooth system that shares many of the standard features of its predecessors but also goes further, to offer many more customizable buttons and user options. You can do the following:

Resync clips

Add, overwrite, or delete clips in a multiclip

Map, switch and cut keys anywhere

Change the visible angle position after you created the multiclip

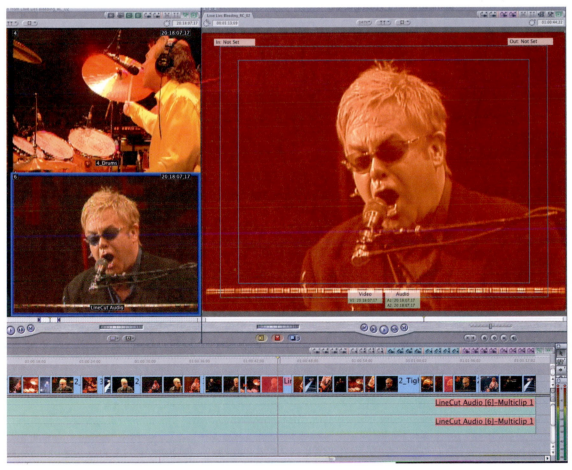

Figure 9.6 Sepia effect added to angle.

switch angles and maintain FX too. This is pretty fancy stuff, but I prefer to cut first and design FX later. So to me, the use of FX is kind of a gimmick—but a cool gimmick, nonetheless.

A better approach would be to do a rough cut, get your edit done, and then collapse all the clips and start doing your effects on a cut. As soon as you start adding processing to all those streams, you're contributing to a system bottleneck. There's really no need to worry about affecting a clip while you're making editorial decisions.

Let's say, for instance, that you have a camera with a milky black level that doesn't match the other angles. One way to add a color correction FX to only that angle throughout the sequence is to use the Find feature.

Find in Sequence

You can use the Find feature to search your timeline for clips with a similar name. For instance, if ISO 204 needs color correction, you could Find All of camera 204's shots and drop a premade three-way color effect on it. In seconds, all of camera 2's black levels will be corrected. That works with any effects. You could also use Find All to strip FX from the clip.

Figure 9.7 Find all multiclips with camera 2 as an active angle.

Resyncing

Another use of Find is to mass-slip or mass-slide shots in a sequence. I call it resyncing. If ISO 103 is off a few frames, find 103, hold Ctrl and Shift keys for a frame scrubber, and nudge the clip back into sync—or pick the slip tool and go frame by frame with the keyboard commands (, or .). This is also useful if you build sync maps and want to slip all clips in a track from a layered sequence.

Custom Settings and Keyboards

Using the keyboard shortcuts for multiclip editing saves time. Just be careful to set your keyboard up and save properly. FCP has its own default multicam keyboard, or you could either customize that or create your own. But be careful. The default keyboard is set up for switching, not cutting.

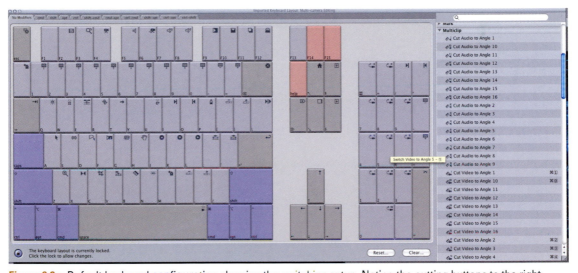

Figure 9.8a Default keyboard configuration showing the switching setup. Notice the cutting buttons to the right.

Viewing and Sorting Angles

FCP has options to view 4, 9, and 16 angles—but you can group up to 128 angles using a scrolling feature in its multicam clip to scroll up or down to see the 128 angles. You can also decide how you want your multicam angles to be positioned in the split view.

Noteworthy

In FCP, you can also preassign the angle position three different ways:
1. In the angle column of the browser, choose the pulldown menu: Edit > Item Properties > Format (or press Command 9)
2. In the browser, Angle Field
3. In the Log and Capture tool, Angle Field

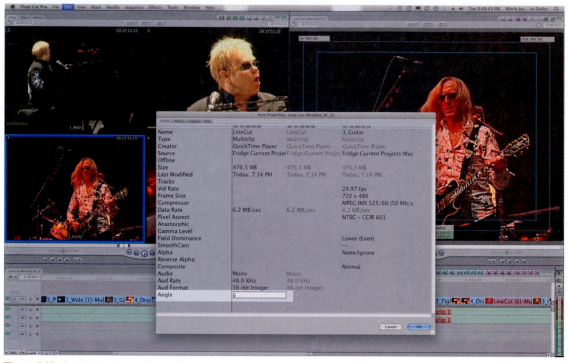

Figure 9.8b Assigning the angle position in Item Properties menu (Command-9).

Figure 9.8c Assigning the angle position in the Log and Capture window.

The three FCP options for positioning angles are browser, Capture tool, and directly in the multiclip.

You can also rearrange, add, or delete angles directly in the multiclip when it's loaded into the Viewer. Preassigned angles will automatically appear in the split where it was assigned when you made the multiclip.

Name	Media Start	Media End	Duration	Angle	Reel
Love Lies Bleeding_RC_01	01:00:00;00	01:01:13;08	00:01:13;09		
Love Lies Bleeding_RC_02	01:00:00;00	01:01:13;08	00:01:13;09		
▼ 🗀 Parts					
1_Wide [1]–Multiclip 1	20:17:20;23	20:18:38;03	00:01:17;11		101
4_Drums [4]–Multiclip 2	20:17:20;23	20:18:38;03	00:01:17;11		104
▼ 🗀 Audio					
Gain					
LineCut	20:17:20;23	20:18:38;03	00:01:17;11		100
▼ 🗀 Original Footage					
1_Wide	20:17:20;23	20:18:38;03	00:01:17;11	1	101
2_Tight	20:17:20;23	20:18:38;03	00:01:17;11	2	102
3_Guitar	20:17:20;23	20:18:38;03	00:01:17;11	3	103
4_Drums	20:17:20;23	20:18:38;03	00:01:17;11	4	104
5_Piano	20:17:20;23	20:18:38;03	00:01:17;11	5	105
LineCut	20:17:20;23	20:18:38;03	00:01:17;11	6	100
Sepia					

Figure 9.8d Assigning the angle position in the Browser.

Figure 9.9a Command click and drag to swap angles in multiclip works with non-active angles.

Notes

You can use numbers or letters, but FCP only works with the letters A through E as angle numbers 1 through 5, respectively.

Cinema Tools uses a standard clip-naming convention that contains the angle name.

For many multicam shoots, the reel name also indicates the camera angle. For example, on a four-camera shoot, reel names 1 through 4 may indicate camera angles 1 through 4. If no other angle information is found, Final Cut Pro looks at the names of the clip name, reel name, and finally the media filename to derive angle information for sorting within the multiclips. It uses the first number in the reel name or filename as an angle number. For example, you have three clips with the following names:

Camera 3_Take2

Camera 16_Take2

Camera 17_Take2

If all three clips' angle properties are empty, Final Cut Pro looks at the first number in each clip name to determine the order in which to sort the clips. In this case, FCP would sort the clips in the following way:

Camera 17_Take2: This clip is considered angle "1" because Final Cut Pro derives only angles 1–16 from a clip or reel name.

Camera 3_Take2: This clip is considered angle "3." (No Spaces.)

Camera 16_Take2: This clip is considered angle "16." (No Spaces.)

If two or more clips have the same angle number, Final Cut Pro sorts the clips in the order they appeared in your browser selection and places clips with duplicate angle numbers after the numerically sorted clips.

If Final Cut Pro cannot determine an angle number from a clip's angle property, reel name, or media filename, clips are sorted alphabetically by filename and assigned the remaining angle numbers in ascending order.

Steve Martin is the president and founder of Ripple Training. Martin has more than 18 years of experience as an editor, producer, and trainer. He is currently a lead instructor for Apple's Certified Pro training program.

Steve Martin: *The multicamera feature itself is actually pretty straightforward, and I think Apple did a tremendous job of making it very intuitive in terms of being able to take cameras and quickly sync them up for a multicam edit. They made the process the same as working with any singular clip in the viewer.*

Adobe Premiere Pro

For PC or Mac

More editors own Premiere Pro than any other NLE application, even if those editors are actually cutting on something else. As I've noted, that's because it's packaged with the Adobe Premiere

Production bundle, and almost everyone uses Photoshop and After Effects. So why isn't it used as much for cutting itself? Maybe it's because Premiere Pro only works with four angles at a time. It has a lot going for it in terms of integration and resolution independence.

Dennis Radeke, Business Development Manager, Adobe Systems Inc.: *The one thing that Adobe has is integration. Everyone knows you can do Photoshop and After Effects in Premiere and Encore and mix all this and mash it up in ways that you can't typically do with a lot of the other products.*

Integration

I think most people who use Premiere Pro use it for the Adobe-centric workflow and integration benefits. Think of Premiere Pro as a conduit that you can use to get from editing to the Adobe suite products. If you're going to cut your piece on something else, say Final Cut or Avid, and then use either the Final Cut importer or AAF to bring that into Adobe, you've got your edit for the most part. Then you can do your After Effects work or Photoshop work. Once you are in this mode, you can switch back and forth between Premiere and any of the other applications without missing a beat.

Resolution-Independent Playback Engine

One of the interesting things about Premiere is what Adobe calls a resolution-independent playback engine. In some of the other systems, you have to resolve all of those to one codec before you can actually do your edit. With Premiere Pro, it's ultimately an advantage that you don't have to lose time converting your media. You can actually just mix and match different kinds of media on the fly. The demo features 16 different types of codecs, including Red, H264, XDCAM, MXF, ProRes, and DNxHD, all mixed together with playback at the same time.

You can use different frame rates in the same group. You can use any codec, any frame rate, and any resolution that Premiere Pro 4.2 supports, including AVC-Intra native, AVC HD all flavors, DV all flavors, DVCPro 50, DVCPro HD, HDV, Red, XD Cam EX, and XDCAM HD. Long-GOP formats like AVC HD are handled natively. VOBs- also natively, right off the disk if you want. XDCAM is an MPEG-2–based codec and so is XDCAM HD, and, of course, HDV.

Dennis Radeke: *We handle everything natively. Ultimately, Premiere Pro is about never touching your pixels. That's our approach.*

Keith Anderson has been in the videography business full time since 2002. He's currently president of the Illinois Videographers Association and a five-time WEVA Creative Excellence Award winner. His weapon of choice for multicam is Premiere Pro.

Keith: *It really works well. It's pretty darn straightforward, once you understand the workflow. Basically, you take up to four different camera angles, lay them all in the timeline in one brand-new sequence, and, of course, sync those cameras up in that sequence. Now you've got one sequence created with four camera angles and four audio tracks. Essentially, what you do once you've got everything synced up is open up a new sequence and name it whatever you want.*

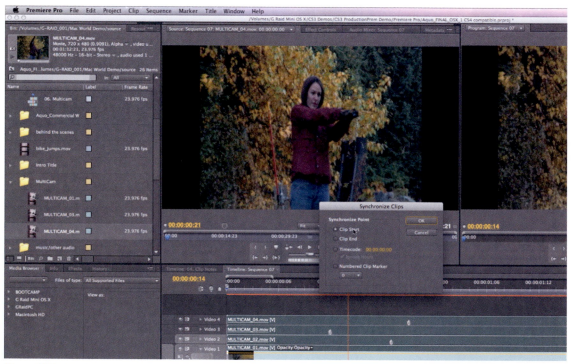

Figure 9.9b Enabling the multiclip command will enable synchronization options in Premiere Pro.

Nesting Angles and Mandatory Sync Maps

The foundation for Premiere Pro multicam is building a nested sequence via timeline sync maps. You're always going to start out syncing up your clips in a timeline by stacking them vertically. They can have matching timecode, but they don't need to.

You adjust the clips in their tracks to match a common sync point with an in, out, or audio point and then place your marks and line them up. To create the grouped clip, choose MultiCamera Enable and you'll get a nested sequence ready for editing.

Keith Anderson: *Nesting allows you to nest that sequence within the new sequence, which I call my multicam master. Then you simply right-click on that multicam master and there's a little drop-down menu that says*

"Enable MultiCam." Do that: go up to the top of your program monitor and open up a multicam monitor and then, bam! You'll see four windows open up, four camera angles within one window.

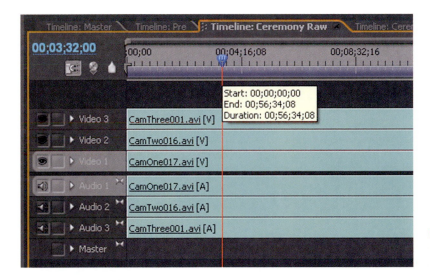

Figure 9.10 Synchronized clips stacked on video tracks 1, 2, and 3. (Courtesy of All Occasions.)

Figure 9.11 A nested multicam sequence in Premiere Pro. (Courtesy All Occasions.)

Editing

Editing is similar. Point and click or keyboard switch and edit. You can also, at any time, drag on the timeline and do an edit that way.

Keith Anderson: *It's truly as simple as playing it and choosing camera angles with either your mouse or your keyboard. It's all real time. The best part is, once you're done, it's nondestructive. Let's say you didn't like an angle that you chose; you simply right-click on the clip, and every other camera angle is hidden beneath the one that's chosen.*

Anything Can Be a MultiCam Angle

Technically, anything can be multicamera, it's just a matter of telling Premiere, "This is a multicamera clip." As that applies to multicamera—anything can be a camera. Another sequence can act as a camera angle. So I could mix a DV camera, HDV camera, an MXF P2, and another sequence that has a whole bunch of cameras I've already edited down.

In theory, you could take two nested sequences with four cameras each and turn that into one new sequence with eight cameras. But it can be a little more problematic than that. Because of the four-camera limitation, you'd have to edit in groups of four. You can view as many cameras as you want, but you really have to edit each of those four before you bring it into a master sequence.

Audio

Keith Anderson: *What I do is dump all of my audio, because it razors each cut where your keystrokes fall. It razors it all the way down through all four of your audio tracks. So typically, what you do is just delete all of the audio tracks, go back, and open up your other sequence, where all four of your audio tracks are still one long, continuous track. You simply copy and paste those over to your new multicam edited sequence. Now you've got your original four audio tracks and all of your cut-up video.*

R3D

Dennis Radeke: *We're the only major NLE supporting native R3Ds right now off a desktop. We'll use our media browser: if you're a Mac person, you call it Spotlight; if you're a PC person, it's Windows Explorer for video. So I'll go to my Red media and instead of looking at file directories and clicking on one, you see the proxies there as well as the R3D. Go up one level and it understands it.*

Premiere is actually playing the R3D, but for editing purposes you can bring down the resolution of the native file just for playback.

Dennis Radeke: *We're able to tap into the Red SDK at a deeper level than anyone else. It's a wave-based compression, so you've got fractional resolution: this is actually one-eighth of a resolution, but you can see it play.*

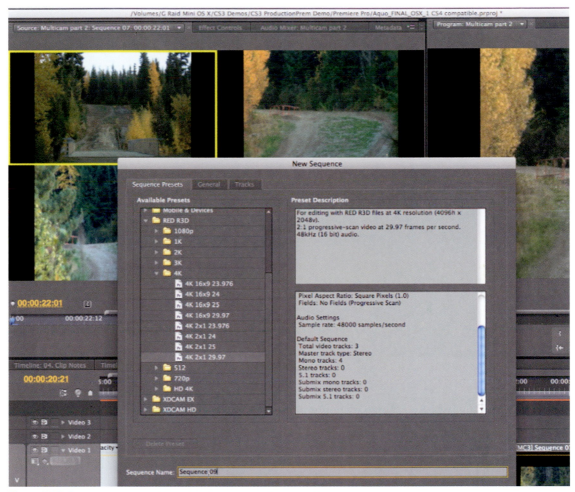

Figure 9.12 Sequence presets for Red R3D footage in Premiere Pro.

Finishing and After Effects

For finishing, there are color-correction tools within Premiere; or, if you want to export, you have an EDL export as well as AAF. Of course, you could send a finished sequence in After Effects (AE) if you want to do some color grading there. AE will divide up the nested sequence into single clips, pull them completely out of the nest, and put each clip on a separate track vertically in order.

Dennis Radeke: *That's the way you would normally do it in After Effects. Part of the idea of After Effects is that if you're finishing, you might be doing visual effects or post effects. So if you just say, okay, I want to do color grading, for example, you might go ahead and do a new adjustment layer, and we're going to call this color correction and then bring in something like color finesse.*

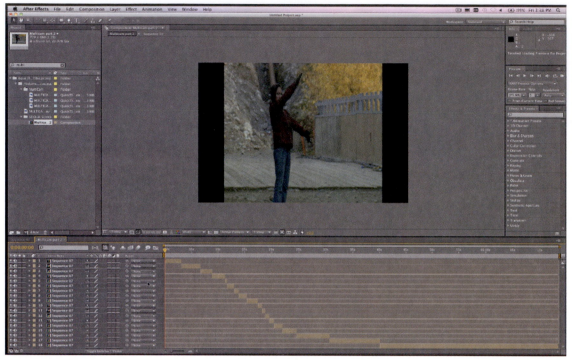

Figure 9.13 Edited multicam sequence imported from Premiere Pro into Adobe After Effects for color correction.

To conclude, Premiere Pro's main advantages are the integration of software, the flexibility of the workflows, and the deeper usage level of the metadata. With the Adobe workflow, you just bring everything in and start cutting. Adobe deals with different frame sizes by scaling to fit and automatically assigning that any image is going to scale up or scale down automatically when it's dragged to the timeline. If you're shooting 29.97 in 24, it automatically resolves that too.

Sony Vegas

For PC Only

Sony Vegas was Vegas a long time before Sony bought it. Vegas was developed by a company called Sonic Foundry, which Sony bought out sometime around 2003.

Gary Kleiner has been doing video production for more than 30 years. He has more than 530 multicam weddings to his credit. Today, he produces theatrical events, ranging from high school plays to semiprofessional ice skating shows, which he shoots with three to seven cameras. He's a Sony Vegas editor, teacher, and co-developer of a third-party plug-in called Excalibur, known for multicam editing in Vegas. He also produces a series of instructional videos on Vegas, available through his website, www.VegasTrainingAndTools.com.

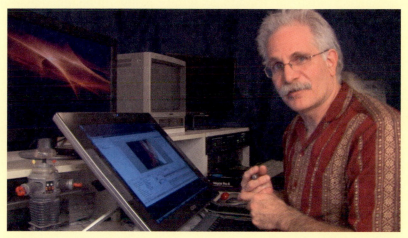

Figure 9.14 Gary Kleiner in his Vegas studio during the filming of his Vegas training series. (Courtesy www.VegasTrainingAndTools.com.)

Multicam production has always been a tradeoff between the extra gear and setup time involved to do a live switch versus the time you spend doing a postproduction switch.

I like the control of the postproduction switch, when I know I can cut exactly to the frame. For me, the pinnacle of unpredictability is shooting ice shows, because you have skaters of all different skill levels all over the place, and moving pretty fast—so you're not sure what's about to happen from moment to moment. For me, the control that the postproduction editing experience affords is really worth the effort. I'll just do them all as ISO cameras and do all my editing in post.

Gary Kleiner

Vegas's Unique Approach

Most of the editing software out there is an echo of the original Avid system, which used film production as a paradigm for the digital environment. Vegas takes a different approach. Vegas was designed from the ground up, first as an audio editor and eventually as a video editor. It offers a direct path toward getting done what you want to get done and still offers lots of features that you just won't find on the other software.

Tim Duncan is senior editor at Zoe Creative Services in Nashville, Tennessee. Zoe does it all: graphics and 3D animation, compositing short films, music and music shows, episodic reality, corporate and training productions, and everything in between. Duncan was a beta tester for Apple and a rep for the Vegas multicam plug-in Excalibur in 2004. He was also the editor for the acclaimed video publicity stunt with Sheryl Crow, in which he shot and edited a music video on a cross-country flight to Los Angeles.

Tim Duncan: *It's a very different interface. It's much easier to train somebody from scratch on Vegas than it is to bring them over from Avid or Final Cut.*

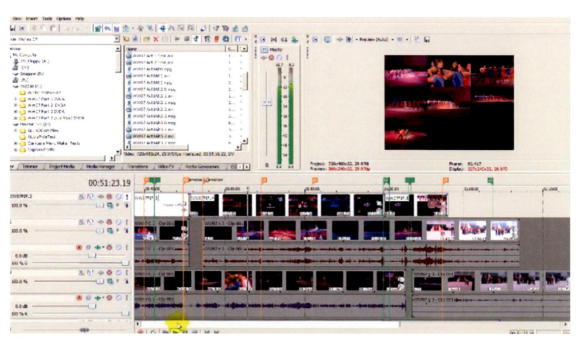

Figure 9.15 Sony Vegas interface. (Courtesy www.VegasTrainingAndTools.com.)

Gary Kleiner: *It's amusing, actually, when Avid or Final Cut or some of the other systems come out and say something like, "Look at this cool new thing we can do: we can put different file formats in the timeline without having to convert them!" That was a big thing for Avid. Well, Vegas has done that for years. Most of the new added features other programs come out with we've had for the last 10 versions.*

So why isn't Vegas as popular?

Gary Kleiner: *Why did VHS win over Beta? Who knows? Marketing? The name? Final Cut has got a really big foothold, certainly in educational circles. Final Cut is not a superior product to Vegas, though. In fact, I think Vegas runs circles around it.*

My Project's in Superfast Turnaround: As the Crow Flies

As cameras continue to get smaller, faster, and better, the footage coming into a live control room or post facility can get unwieldy, especially in tape-based workflows where you need real time to load. But with more and more productions going tapeless altogether, there are several options that allow real-time capture and turnaround and live editing, like Sony's Vegas 5.

Editor Tim Duncan used the Sony XDCAM and Vegas software to do a publicity stunt for Sony and United Airlines—to promote the launch of Sony's "Connect" online music service. The stunt? Capture and edit a Sheryl Crow performance on a flight from Chicago to Los Angeles. Talk about working "on-the-fly"!

Tim Duncan: *The original plan was to transfer the discs after the first two songs and have me working all along. But they waited until after the fourth song, which made the pressure more severe. I preset a Vegas software project to show me five angles at once. Then all I had to do was digitize the footage from each of the five cameras and sync everything. I was able to watch all five cameras, drop markers down, and tell the software how to make the cuts. I never even played it back, since I flew through the whole project.*

Only one hour passed from the time the camcorders started rolling to when Duncan presented the finished product for approval to Crow before the plane landed: a four-minute video ready for viewing by attendees of the after-party in Sony Music's Santa Monica facility.

Time Selections

Gary Kleiner: *Vegas has time selections, which is a basic but essential part of the software whereby you can instantly click and drag a selection of time and, just by hitting the space bar, it will play just that one selection in the timeline. You can delete out parts of your timeline based on that selection—unlike in the other systems, where you're hitting in- and out-points separately. Vegas has a much faster, much more intuitive workflow.*

One thing Vegas does is continue playback on the timeline even as you're making changes, trimming, adding footage, changing sync, and so on. The playback just keeps going. You can move things dynamically and hear the sync change, or make things advance or back up, all as you're playing it. While it's playing a loop, you can hear the audio get in sync or you can visually match something.

Tim Duncan: *I may drop it to 50% capacity on one track while it's playing and do that for a visual mark and play it a few times in a loop. When Vegas plays a loop, it will do a RAM previous automatically; every time it plays, it will pick up more frames until it puts everything in RAM and you're getting full-frame playback.*

Events and Takes

In Vegas, the clips on the timeline are called events. The ISO clips grouped together for multicam are called takes. Takes were originally developed for voice-over work. Grouping audio takes together for comparison editing, you set it to record mode and every time it loops back to that same point, it creates a new take over that same space across the timeline. The same is true with video. You can take video on one of your timeline tracks, drop another piece of video on top of it, and switch back and forth between those two videos— or three or four, however many you want to layer on it.

Gary Kleiner: *When you're setting up a multicam edit on Vegas, it's like a deck of cards: it's all sitting there in one space. You hit T on the keyboard, for take, and it will toggle between each of the "cards" that are layered on that one spot. You can actually play without interruption.*

In Vegas, every item on the timeline can be treated as a group clip, and you can add as many alternates as you want, even beyond the 25. You can switch between those, at will, even while playing on the timeline.

Gary Kleiner: *The beautiful thing about it is that you can cut or dissolve to each camera on the fly, so that you can see your multicamera angles, and it gives you a tally around each camera, whichever camera is the hot camera. Whether you are playing or are stopped at a particular point, you can either use the keyboard or the mouse to change camera angles during playback.*

Tim Duncan: *You can choose to go through the timeline and just do the tally system first, then hit a button and it runs the script and instantly creates the multicam cut track for you, putting it above everything else. So you still have all your other cameras vertically beneath it. You've got combinations of ways that you can use it.*

Then you can go back and fine-tune at will.

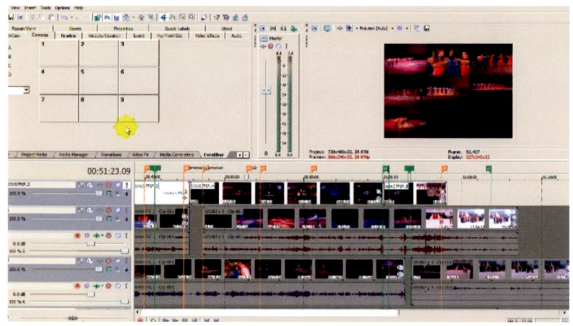

Figure 9.16 The Excalibur interface inside Vegas. (Courtesy www.VegasTrainingAndTools.com.)

Dissolves on the Fly

One of the things that you can do with Excalibur in Vegas that you can't necessarily do in Avid or Final Cut is assign four different keys for six choices: a cut, a dissolve, or one of the four transitions to set up like a switcher for live dissolves.

Tim Duncan: *You can add dissolves on the fly and then back up and watch it. While the timeline is playing back, I can jump in and out of multicam mode and see all my other camera angles and never stop playback. That is a huge advantage. Vegas does that for any clip on the timeline.*

Mixing up the Timeline

You can drop almost anything you want on a Vegas timeline and it will happily play. You can combine 24p footage with 29.97. PAL and NTSC. Mixed frame rates? No problem. Even frame rate conversions. You can mix it up however you want and tell it to display whatever timecode you want. To Vegas, these are just calculations.

Gary Kleiner: *The closer your project settings are matched to the media, the less processing has to be done to output it for preview. So the best match you have between your media and your project then you have very fluent playback, full frame playback rate. Once you start throwing things on the timeline that don't match, it's definitely going to take more CPU power and maybe make for a less enjoyable editing experience. But you can do it.*

There's a difference between simply being able to do something and *enjoying* it. Like any computer processor, the more conversion is happening on the fly, the greater the likelihood that it may drop the frame rate. So you have two options. You can drop your preview quality or you can drop the frame rate. Vegas is set up to do either, and it can do it automatically for you. It will just decide for itself what's going to be the best combination of resolution and frame rate.

Tim Duncan: *Vegas handles different aspect ratios better than any other software I've touched. I can have 4 × 3 and 16 × 9 and everything all mixed in and it handles them all beautifully. I can change my project on the fly at any point from a 720 to 480 or 486 to 720p, or to a 1080p or 1080i—Vegas doesn't care. It maintains everything's aspect perfectly. If I'm 23.98, it's going to a nondrop frame 23.98 timecode automatically. Or I can force it to show me what the 29.97 conversion would look like, what that timecode would be. And that's unique.*

Another thing Vegas can do is instantly show the original timecode of all the media and display it as a burn on all the clips, just with the click of a button: it's instantaneous.

R3D and XDCam Files

Vegas does not have the ability to render that multicam preview look, if you wanted to get full frame rate. One big advantage of using the Excalibur plug-in for multicam editing is that you can use a rendered version of your multicamera view for totally smooth playback. Vegas handles Red beautifully, but it doesn't like several Red for multicamera. It would prefer a different format.

Tim Duncan: *R3Ds will play back beautifully in Vegas, and I can even get output through my system on hardware. They added native R3D support in this last Red, and it's quite nice. But it would choke it if you try multicam with it. What Vegas is really good with is multicam XDCAM.*

Offline/Online

Tim Duncan will usually offline all of his multicam in Vegas and then do his onlines in Avid DS. That way, he can keep

Figure 9.17 A closer look at the quad-split view while trimming. (Courtesy www.VegasTrainingAndTools.com.)

everything at DV level in Vegas and ingest everything without having to keep up with it.

Tim Duncan: *Depending on the project, we choose the tool. We have Final Cut and Avid DS, Avid Media Composer, EDIUS (which has a really nice multicam), Vegas—we even have a Premiere Axio system. But of all of those, my absolute favorite tool to use—because of those takes—is Vegas. It's so quick and easy to slip and with almost anything you do you don't have to stop playback. So you're making decisions as fast as you can. I love having clients sit down with me and use it because we can make all our decisions at once, without waiting on anything.*

Scripting Engine

That scripting engine in Vegas is what sets it apart. You can do many things like automated picture slide shows and scramble all the events on the timeline and then edit all these pictures in random order—one click and you're done. Excalibur, another scripted component co-developed by Gary Kleiner and Edward Troxel, was the first option that allowed easy multicamera editing in Vegas along with a plethora of other super-handy tools.

Tim Duncan: *You take your voice-over track and cut it really tight, end to end on the timeline; you don't leave blank spaces. Then, in Excalibur, you click this button called Voice Over and it would instantly downmix the other tracks around the voice-over. You could choose and drop it down to, say, 25% volume, and then come back up at the end of the voice-over.*

Grass Valley EDIUS (and the Rest)

(Windows XP.)

A few other multicam editing systems are available, and they all have their place in the industry. One deserving of an honorable mention is Grass Valley's EDIUS. Grass Valley claims that EDIUS affords more real-time SD and HD editing performance than any other NLE.

Known for its tight code and ability to do what hardware-based systems are capable of in a software-only mode, EDIUS may very well be desktop video editing's unsung hero. Its multicam feature is known to be easy to use and offers up to eight camera angles. It's also rated as one of the most stable real-time editing platforms on the market.

Figure 9.18 The Grass Valley Edius production screen. (Courtesy Grass Valley.)

EDIUS doesn't offer the comprehensive package of its rivals, but its real-time abilities and wide format support make for a fast workflow. The chief enhancement with the Media Composer 4.0 update is the ability to mix standard and high-def footage and different frame rates all on the same timeline. This is something EDIUS (and Vegas) has been able to do for some time. It's the core real-time capabilities—and mixed-format editing of any frame rate, resolution, and aspect ratio—that make it unique.

To summarize, EDIUS allows the following:
- Tweaking for intuitive editing
- Color correction
- Mixing SD and HD on the same timeline
- Live viewing during playback, thanks to waveform and vectorscope
- 2D and 3D GPUfx
- On-the-fly conversion of frame rates, aspect ratios, and resolutions of any clip placed on the timeline (even if it differs from the current project setting)
- Seamless editing of clips in different formats without having to transcode them

EDIUS 5.1 natively supports Panasonic DVCPRO HD, Sony XDCAM and XDCAM EX, alongside Grass Valley's JPEG2000, Panasonic P2, HD, HDV 1080i, HDV 720p, AVCHD, and AVC-Intra material.

A Grass Valley EDIUS system isn't just software. EDIUS supports multithreading computer processing and a hardware-extension package. The added benefit of using EDIUS hardware is that you get full resolution and full frame rate. This is truly what-you-see-is-what-you-get editing, with everything you do on the timeline output to any connected video monitor or deck.

EDIUS 5.1 can now output the timeline to Blu-ray as well as DVD (but not with menus). In testing, it provided the smoothest playback of blended HD streams, even from disparate sources like HDV and AVCHD.[1]

So what's the best, easiest multicam system on the market? Come on! No one can say. Everyone has his or her own needs, price point, and expectations. Most of these systems have great features that make it a snap for anyone to sync up videos, switch between them, and then fine-tune edit decisions with simple, easy-to-use tools. The bottom line is this: pick a tool that works for *you*, so you can concentrate less on navigating your computer application and more on being creative.

Reference

1. *Digital Arts Magazine*. Review: EDIUS 5.1 by James Morris, Friday 06 Nov 2009; www.digitalartsonline.co.uk

10

PREPARING THE MULTICAMERA PROJECT FOR EDITING

Preparing and organizing the project for editing may be the most technical part of the whole process. As we learned from the chapters on preproduction, *organization is the key to success*. In this chapter, you will become better acquainted with the three major steps of prep: logging, loading, and grouping multicam footage for editing.

If you are fortunate enough to have an assistant, you may consider much of this chapter to break down into his or her role. In an economic downturn, however, many of us are our own assistants. Some of us have always been on our own, and others are discovering just how much they relied on assistants to do prep work in the past. Whether you or someone else does your prep, it should not be considered unimportant: prep work requires good technical specialists who can save themselves or other editors many hours of troubleshooting that can cause fatigue and slow down the creative process later on.

To keep track of the prep process, I like to keep a running text document of daily or nightly notes. A log of your progress can help you stay focused and is also good for communicating with an assistant. Another great tracking tool is a database. I use Filemaker Pro to keep a master list of all project elements. It's thoroughly searchable and allows you to export small or large clip-groups to shot logs or ALE files for batch digitizing. (We'll talk more about databases at the end of this chapter.)

Offline/Online Workflow

There are at least two forms of offline/online workflows. The standard method is to load your clips from the original tapes in lo-res, cutting and finishing with a traditional online by reloading from the sources to the deliverable format.

The alternative is to load your footage once at the highest finishing resolution and make a set of down-converted files or transcode them into a compatible format with smaller bit rates.

Doi: 10.1016/B978-0-240-81176-5.00010-1

This requires more drive space but eliminates the reloading phase. Avid has a transcode feature, and for Final Cut Pro I batch-export or media manage down-converted sets to new media with identical timecode.

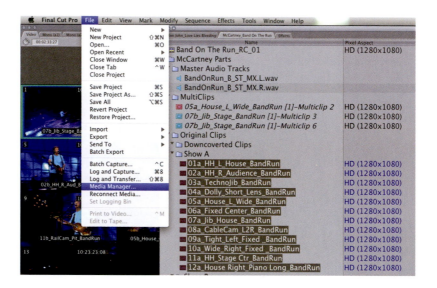

Figure 10.1 Transcoding HD master clips to a set of offline resolution clips for multicam editing via Media Manager or Batch export.

Larry Jordan of Larry Jordan & Associates: *I prefer to load your footage at the highest resolution for finishing first and then work with it from there, only because the process of doing an online from an offline can be arduous. If you're going to do smaller files, create a transcode of low-res and just cut it so you can find matching timecode and then work with small files for the purposes of creating a multiclip and then do an online shortly thereafter.*

So if you're going to do an offline/online, the instant you've completed the rough cut and before you start to add any transitions or effects, then up-rez it and do all of your effects polishing on the master. Otherwise you've got to do it twice because the settings are going to change.

Larry Jordan: *So for me, hard disks are fast enough and RAIDs are fast enough and computers are fast enough. If you can afford to shoot multicamera, you can afford to budget for a $2,000 RAID, plug it into your system, and then be done with it and not have to worry, and now you're editing at the final resolution. You and the client and everybody else can see what it looks like, and you also saved yourself a ton of money in the final conform.*

One problem with capturing everything at the highest resolution is that you're going to digitize a lot of information that'll ultimately be discarded. This takes up a lot of drive space. So you're actually better working at your offline, ProRes, DVCProHD or DNxHD 36 or 45 resolutions, so that you still have a good HD signal for the same bandwidth of SD uncompressed—good enough to finish if necessary or edited into something else. If you have the drive space and bandwidth, the obvious benefit to sticking with high-res is that you can work with effects and color from start to finish during the edit phase.

Larry Jordan: *Once the multicam edit is done and you're just into tweaking and trimming and effects and that sort of thing, I would relink back to the high-res version at that point. The farther downstream you get, then you're starting to make decisions based upon the quality of the low-res version, which may or may not be represented by the quality of the high-res version. So I would not wait until the last possible minute to relink. Also, if you relink earlier and there's a problem, then it's better to discover that when you've got plenty of time until the deadline.*

P2 and XDCAM cards have proxy files in their folder structure, which allows you to pull everything into your project as proxy files for offline. When it comes time to online, you could media manage or consolidate and then connect to the hires files off the folder. With Avid's AMA or MXF4Mac, you'll even by pass the rewrap for faster ingesting.

Michael Phillips, Avid Technology, Inc.: *It's about the continuation of file-based workflows. Our AMA structure that allows us to look at external files rather than captures, allows camera manufacturers to plug in. So we don't have to hand-tailor every codec as we go along.*

With a multicam post workflow, concentrate on maintaining consistency. It's always going to be a better post experience if everything is identical. Whether everything is P2, DVCPRO HD, or Sony HDCam—makes sure it's consistent.

In HD, you have to do this in compressed. You really can't work in a multicam environment with uncompressed content because most people just don't have that kind of throughput—they can't run two or four or six video streams at 160 megabytes a second.

In Avid, you're going to be in DNxHD; in Final Cut, you're going to be in ProRes. These are compressed, high-quality codecs that actually make editing easier. This will enable you to take your camera-native files, just the ones that are edited, and transcode those in software to something that's going to allow you to edit in multicam in real time.

Tip

The trick is making sure that you do the linking back to the online version relatively early in the effects process.

Tip

A cool trick is to FTP or use digi delivery to send low-res proxies directly from the field to the edit suite. Editing can begin immediately and later when the high-res files arrive, you can reconnect to the original media.

Using low-res offline codecs

MULTI-EXPERT APPROACH

Many codecs used as transcoded sets have sufficient quality to do finishing, editing, and compositing without much problem:

- Avid DNxHD 145
- ProRes 422
- DVCPRO HD

Popular codecs to down-convert to included the following:

- Avid 14 to 1 s
- ProRes LT
- DV50

Gary Adcock, Studio 37: *I love DVCPro HD as an offline codec. It's a very low bandwidth, very high quality; I'm still working in HD; I don't have to deal with frame rate conversions or anything else.*

Oliver Peters, Oliver Peters Productions, LLC: *So if you're shooting P2 cards at 720p or 1080i and you're wanting to cut that as multicam, even though it's a relatively light codec, by the time you slam a bunch of cameras in a clip, you need a lot of horsepower to go through that.*

If you're working with tape, you could bring it in as low-res and then go back and online it off the high-res tapes. For high-res files, make down-converted file sets.

Robbie Carman, colorist and co-owner, Amigo Media, LLC: *These files are in REDCODE codec, which is read-only. Instead, ingest the footage in Log and Transfer as Apple ProRes Proxy, which has an amazingly small data rate. Edit the show, and then use the media manager to reconnect back to the original R3D files by reingesting the Red files as Native (or even ProRes 4444) with the Log and Transfer window.*

Tip

With Red offline/ online workflow, don't edit with the proxies generated by the Red camera.

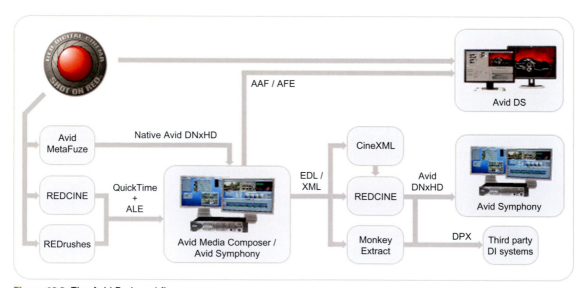

Figure 10.2 The Avid Red workflow.

The Proxy

A lot of times people use the term *proxy files* loosely when they mean transcoded or down-rezzed files to a smaller data rate codec for multicam editing.

Larry Jordan: *That would be a misuse of the term. A proxy file is simply a pointer that points back to the master file. If you're transcoding into a smaller file, then transcoding is the word to use. The reason I think it's so important is if you start to use the wrong terms to describe a technical process it is harder to diagnose the actual problem.*

So what would you call that second set of files? You just took your master and transcoded it into a different format. To transcode is simply to convert. It's not a proxy file. If you work on a Mac, then you may have made an alias of a file. An alias is a proxy; it points back to the source file. If you double-click an alias, it opens up the source file. Any changes that you make are to the source file. An alias is a proxy. If you copy that file to your desktop, and now you're making changes to the file, your source file is not affected at all; that's a transcode.

With that said, RED has proxy files that are actual pointers. But XDCAM EX, XDCAM HD, and Apple ProRes have low-resolution files called "proxys" that do not act as pointers. They work in editing environments and contain the same metadata. XDCAM and RED automatically record what they call proxies at the same time they record the high-res camera masters. But they are two different kinds of files.

Tim Duncan, senior editor, Zoe Creative: *It's a pointer file with Red, but with XDCAM it's a truly separate file, but proxy is the name that Sony gave it and it points to the full res from the proxy.*

Mixed Formats and Frame Rates

I'll say it again: *always stay in the same format.* Even software like Vegas that can mix them up will still have an easier time processing like files. Media Composer version 4.0 allows for mixed resolutions and frame rates in the same timeline but *not* mixed frame rates in grouped clips.

This rule seems made to be broken. Lots of producers and directors love to mix it up. Sometimes they have budgetary reasons and sometimes they just want a certain look—but often quite a bit of technical ignorance comes into play.

Software has caught up to handle mixed timelines, but they still vary in what they can handle. Final Cut needs all the same formats in multicam. Avid Media Composer 4.0 timelines can

Tip

If you can't avoid mixed formats, mix them as early as possible and then, on the ingest/capture, manage your project to load everything at the same format. Use standard conversions, transcode—whatever codec it takes to match everything and make it work for you.

Noteworthy

The film industry uses a convention for developing clip names that is similar to the naming convention used in Cinema Tools. "F-6-X4," for example, indicates the following:

- "F" is the scene.
- "6" is the take.
- "X4" is the camera or angle.

Tip

If you are going to be grading in Apple Color, you may want to name your angles so you can sort by Name column, because once inside Color, you can *only* sort by Name column. This will make it easier to grade like angles.

handle mixed formats and frame rates but not mixed frame rates in a grouped clip. Those need to match.

Hamish Hamilton, director, Done and Dusted: *We mix formats a great deal. Quite often we'll use little DV cameras, handheld cameras, in the crowds, because they can get to places other people can't get to. We have also mixed HD and 35 mm. But mixing formats burdens all parts of the process. There's definitely a financial burden and usually there's a practical burden as well.*

Naming Angles

When we log clips for multicam, it is a good idea to keep the angle names short so they do not take up so much space in the timeline and so you know which camera you are on with a short glance. One preferred method is to start the clip name with the camera name or abbreviation like C1 or camera 1 or Cam_1 and add a description if needed like "Cam_1_HelterSkelter" or "Cam_1_Act_1."

Scott Brock, assistant editor for Thelma Schoonmaker: *We use a special designation for A camera and B camera. We only designate the AB cameras when we are using both cameras. And, in fact, it might get a little tricky if it's designated for some reason on the set as C and D camera, because A and B were being used for some reason on second unit. This happened on* Gangs of New York *(2002). So they might have C and D camera on the main set and Thelma would designate that C and D, even though there's technically no A and B. She wants to know where all the different cameras are in case anything needs to be tracked back to an exact camera part.*

This kind of metadata is gathered meticulously on the set in case there are any shooting issues where insurance comes into play. Another important reason to know exactly which camera shot which footage involves possible registration issues with the A camera or the magazine. For example, if there were negative scratches and therefore insurance issues, you need to know not just the magazine but which camera was used. Was it the A camera?

Logging

When it comes to logging and capturing tape footage or importing tapeless footage, one thing is true in multicam: there is a *lot* more of it!

Tape-based workflows require more loading time (because of real-time digitizing), whereas tapeless is much faster, thanks to file transfers. No matter which cutting system you choose, the following workflows will apply.

Some shows just load everything (in low-res) and log/subclip from the batched clips—and it goes back to preproduction for clarification, which isn't ideal. Deliver what's needed *before* the shoot starts so everyone's on the same page. After all, everyone has to sign off on the same workflow and numbering structure. Why? For continuity. Continuity among your deliverables saves time downstream.

On logging for reality shows, Mark Raudonis of Bunim-Murray Productions says:

We don't log words like "close-up of Bill" or "Susie walks into room." We don't care about that. What we do log is "Susie and Bill kissing in the corner"; "Tom and Jill fight." In other words: we log for story content, not events out-of-context. We also log for details like trade-outs or locations. But it's basically emotional notes; we figure that that way, an editor can find the shots he or she needs.

Noteworthy

At minimum, the following items are needed to log a clip:
- Reel number
- In-point timecode
- Out-point timecode
- Name or description

Tapeless Files and Auto Naming

You may have 500 hours worth of clips that have been recorded. Every one of those clips needs to have a unique name. How are you going to guarantee that? Clips like P2 have some crazy algorithm (Universal Unique ID) that is attempting to essentially, randomly generate a unique name for every piece of media that gets recorded for however long they figure they can get away with it. But that's why the names are so crazy, because they're assuming you don't want to take the time to sit there and name every single clip before you shoot it, or after you shoot it.

Alexis Van Hurkman, author of the Final Cut Pro/Red Whitepaper (www.red.com)

The Ultimate Multicam Tape Logging Shortcuts

When prepping clips from one long, continuous performance caught on matching cameras, you could log every reel separately—or you could use this little trick for creating bins for each camera fast. For tape-based projects, each camera will require a separate log and bin. If you have a properly jam-synced production and all the timecode matches from reel to reel, the logged events for each camera will be identical (including timecode), so the only thing that changes from tape to tape is the reel name. You generally only have to log one camera's tape to get the information for all of the tapes. You'll save a huge amount of time by using the following log-duplication techniques.

FCP Shot Log Clones

In Final Cut this is easy to do. Export a shot log, and clone it for every camera. Find and replace tape names and import to new bins. Boom. Avid does it in a similar way with ALE files.

Avid ALE Header Trick

- Log the entire first-camera tape using the log mode of the capture tool.
- Highlight all the clips in the bin.
- Export an ALE file.
- Open the files in a text editor.
- In word processing, search and replace reel names with the next reel name in your production.
- Save as a new shot log or ALE file.
- Repeat for each camera log.

Now you can import the shot logs or ALE files back into the project as new ALEs/shot logs for each camera and batch-import all the tapes. Avid offers another bin-copying shortcut: unlink and relink.

The Secret Unlink Menu

This method saves you from exporting and importing logs— but it also means that you have to change the reel names by hand (i.e., without the text editor Find/Replace feature). You also need to unlink each bin and relink it after the copy process.

After the clips are unlinked, you can modify the tape names. Think about this: it may seem faster on the outset, but only if you don't have a lot of clips to work with, because you have to change every clip in the bin by hand with the modify tool. That is a lot more keystrokes than using auto Find/Replace in a text editor. A bin with 10 clips equals about 50 keystrokes to modify the tape names. Usually, ALE log sheets are the way to go.

- Unlink the clips in the first log.
- Copy and paste clip sets for each camera into new bins.
- Change all the reel names to the corresponding reels for each new bin.
- Relink.
- Batch as usual.

Tip

The Unlink command is hidden and only comes up when you hold down the Shift + Command keys on a Mac or Shift + Control on a PC. Holding these keys down will change the relink pulldown menu to the unlink pulldown menu.

Both methods will save a considerable amount of time compared to logging each camera reel separately. An added benefit is that the clips will be identical from each reel, making grouping a breeze.

Illegal and Acceptable Filename Characters

Problems with importing XML files generally arise because of illegal clip names. I tend to avoid this issue by sticking to names made up of words and underscores—that's it. (I like to use Apple Color for grading my shows, and this word + underscore habit is an old one from when the software used to be called FinalTouch HD.)

Here is a list of acceptable path and filename characters:

0-9

a-z

A-Z

Dash (—)

Underscore (_)

Space, period (.)

Open and close parentheses ()

Forward slash (/) for the separation of directories[*]

Here is a list of illegal DOS and Windows filename characters:[1]

?

[

]

/

\

=

+

<

>

:

;

"

'

The most common offender is the forward slash, which is illegal in Windows but popular with Mac users who like to include a date in the filename.

*Note that a (/) in a clip name will be considered an illegal character. Anything else is considered an illegal character and will likely botch an XML import. In Avid, you can turn on Windows' Compatible File Naming feature to help eliminate illegal characters. (In shared environments, make sure all users do this.)

Logging and Loading

Capturing

It can be a time-saver to have your assistant—or a digitizer—load everything overnight. The digitizer may even be someone you never meet but who works with the post house, where they telecine and prep and deliver your Avid drives digitized and ready to go. But a lot of editors, myself included, prefer to load their own footage. This is because it's typically your only opportunity to watch the footage from head to tail without stopping. Sure, you could screen everything later, but you might be tempted to stop for a phone call or some other distraction that gets in the way of a gut reaction. I always have an early emotional response to that footage and, just as Walter Murch recommends, I say it's a good idea to take some "gut" notes on the first screening. Fifty screenings later, we tend to get a little jaded and cynical, so it's good to have that first, truthful response.

David Helfand, editor: *In the digitizing stage, while my assistant records material into Avid, he would also be writing the timecodes on the script. He's looking at everything in real time or maybe scrolling through and logging it, putting timecodes at the top, bottom, and middle of every script page. Accordingly, I have a close reference for finding material based on the script.*

> *If I had unlimited money, unlimited bandwidth, and unlimited resources, I'd say load everything at full-res and just go to town.*
>
> **Mark Raudonis**

Says Mark: *I love to work "all in the bucket." But this isn't really an option if you don't have the drive space or time. Shows like* The Real World *generate 3,500 hours of material in one season. We simply don't have enough space, storage, or bandwidth to load it all. So in those cases, it becomes a selective digitizing process.*

Gary Bradly, Hand Made Video, Inc.: *You're paying the price to record and load all those ISOs. We load it all and never think about the tapes again. It's a huge investment. On the opera performances, like at the Metropolitan, it's 13 or 14 times three hours. That's 40 hours, times two performances. Eighty hours of load in—real time.*

Ingesting Red Files

In XDCAM, there are ways of getting around mixed formats. With P2, people are figuring out tolerable ways to work with media in its native form. But Red files live in their own world and have a unique relationship with Avid and FCP.

Robbie Carman, Amigo Media, LLC: *During ingest, you have two routes inside Final Cut Pro. In the Log and Transfer window (in the upper*

right-hand corner of the browse area) is the Action menu. Choose Preferences. From here you'll see the Red Digital Cinema category. By clicking on the Target Format column, you can choose to ingest the Red footage as Apple ProRes (either Proxy, LT, Standard, HQ, or 4444) or Native.

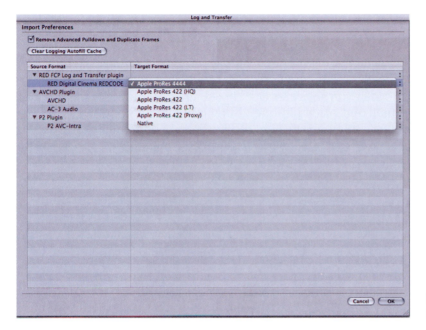

Figure 10.3 Final Cut's Red Log and Transfer mode.

If you choose any of the ProRes codecs, all of your clips will be ingested, but any 4K clips are always transcoded to 2K, as that's the maximum frame size supported by FCP's real-time effects engine. For almost any workflow, 2K files should be plenty.

Robbie Carman: *If you choose Native, the files will be ingested as Red QuickTimes that use the REDCODE codec. The advantage here is that, while they will be ingested in FCP as 2K, the 4K data is maintained. So you can send a project to color for grading and finishing and in color you'll have access to the Red tab in the Primary IN room to perform Red RAW processing. Also, because the 4K data has been maintained, you can change the project resolution to 4K and the clips "scale" to that resolution. You can then render out true 4K files and complete a roundtrip with FCP.*

Tape-and-File Hybrid Workflows

Some people are evolving hybrid workflows that make sense, but they can pose certain problems with sync and timecode. Namely, if you bring in a clip and dump it to tape, you could change the original timecode. Think of it as a digital film lab: dumping a high-end tapeless format like Red RAW to something like an HDCAM SR tape for the creation of a digital negative. Depending on your workflow, it may work—or it might create the biggest mess ever. Decide how you're going to deal with it in preproduction.

Master-Affiliate Relationships (FCP)

Angles

When you select several clips to create a multiclip, each clip is copied and placed in one of the multiclip's angles. Because each clip is copied, each is an "affiliate clip," which means the angle's clip shares most of its properties with a master clip stored in your project. If you change the name of a master clip, the names of the affiliate clips within any multiclips also change.

Multiclips

When you create a multiclip, it is called a master multiclip. When you edit, drag the master multiclip to the canvas or timeline to make a copy of the multiclip that shares properties with the master multiclip. The copied clip is the affiliate multiclip.

If you perform an operation on a multiclip that affects its angle structure—such as adding, deleting, or rearranging the order of multiclip angles—the modified multiclip loses its affiliation with the original master multiclip and a new master multiclip is created automatically.

You cannot make the multiclips in a sequence independent. Multiclips in a sequence are always affiliated with a master multiclip.

Basic Operations

Assigning the Active Tracks

When cutting in any multicam mode, you have the option to cut audio and video at the same time or audio or video only. If the audio tracks are split among different camera angles and you want to take the sound recorded with the camera, you would cut audio and video together (Audio follows video). Reality shows, interviews, and scripted pieces also benefit from this feature. When cutting music or dealing with double-system audio, it's usually best to lock your audio tracks into the timeline and switch only your video angles. Audio-only edits can also be performed as needed.

Switching and Cutting the Active Angle

The two ways of changing the active angle are switching and cutting. Switching the angle will not change any edit points; it simply changes the angle *within* the edit points. Cutting adds an edit and changes the angle to your selection. Changing the active angle in the timeline is a breeze—especially if you make keyboard shortcuts. In FCP, you can click on the angles directly in the multiclip in the Viewer. If you map the angles to your keyboard, it's even faster. Another way to do this is to use the pulldown menu in FCP's Viewer pop-up tab or in Avid by control-shift-clicking directly on the angle in the timeline (or the groupclip in the source window). Both ways will reveal a pulldown menu so you can choose which angle you want.

Locators and Markers

Locators and markers are basically notes placed directly into the timeline or on a clip at a precise timecode number with color codes. Locators and markers offer a great way to collaborate with producers and clients during various stages of production. They are also valuable tools for organizing your work.

On some shows, producers will do cut-downs and leave locators all over the timeline to, for example, *fix this shot, change that ISO,* or *redo this pull-up.* Then that cut is passed to an editor, who follows the locators' instructions. As the editor completes each fix, he or she changes the locator's color to show it's been done. For instance, an assistant or associate producer may pass to the editor a cut full of red locators. After the editor finishes making these revisions, the locators will all be, say, yellow—until an executive sees the cut and requests a new round of changes, which will be indicated by, say, blue locators. In Avid, just by clicking on a locator in the list, you can jump directly to that spot in the timeline. In FCP, you can right-click on the timeline to get your list and choose from there which note to jump to. (Another advantage to this signaling system is that you can search the timeline for words, just as you search for words in a Word document.)

When you're fixing a line cut, the locators are your notes on how to pull the show up to time. It's up to you as editor to use the ISOs to incorporate these changes in a way that makes the final result look natural, like the director shot it.

This is where your group clip comes in to save the day. Your group clip gives you all the options of the ISOs and the trim mode to make it work.

Matthew Illardo, editor: *We'll have a close-up of Rachael Ray, followed by a close-up of the guest, and then we'll have a two-shot, and then another two-shot, and then maybe two cameras on the audience (i.e., on two different audience members), and then a wide shot of the whole studio and Rachael and the guest talking.*

Get the picture? All of these need to flow seamlessly.

Match Frames

In Avid, match frames follow a logical path with reference to the hierarchy of the clip structure: master clip, subclip, or group clip. If you are working in a grouped clip in the timeline and hit Match frame, it will match to the group clip. From there you could Match frame again to the master clip. In previous versions of Media Composer, the group clip is always ganged to the master sequence, so matching back was an obstacle. Now you can remove the gang and use the full potential of a grouped clip as an independent source.

In FCP, it works like this: park on the frame in the sequence you want to match. Hit "F" to match frame to the master clip in your project or Option command-F to match to the source. For multicam clips, go to Show match frame in multiclip angle. This is in the button list under Multicam and will match frame back to the group. From there, you can match back to the source clip or stay in the group and look at alternate angles. Matching back to the group automatically turns off or closes the sync.

An Important Note Straight from the FCP Manual: If you open a source media file in the Viewer and drag it to the browser, a new master clip is created. If you drag it to the timeline or canvas, an independent clip is created in the sequence. This is true whenever you open a media file in the Viewer—either by using a match frame command or by dragging a media file from the Finder directly to the Viewer.

Reverse Match Frames

A fast way to find portions of a clip in the sequence (in Avid) is to pull a Reverse match frame. You do this by cueing up the shot in the source monitor and then hitting Reverse match frame; it'll go right into its sequence in the reverse match clip. The tricky part is that you might not be on the part of the clip where it actually appears in the sequence, in which case you might not be able to find it. Only frames in the sequence will connect to a reverse match frame.

This works with multiclips too. Click on the Reverse match frame button on the group clip and it'll find it on the timeline—whether you have the group clip or even just the ISO. From the ISO to the group clip or from group clip to group clip: it works

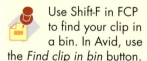

both ways. In FCP, load your clip in the Viewer and hit "F." If the frame is an affiliate clip in the sequence, it will snap to that frame.

Dupe Detection

Dupe detection is a feature whereby a colored bar appears above a clip where there are duplicated frames in the timeline. This tells you instantly whether you've already used that frame in a sequence.

Dupe detection is also a neat way to find shots or approximate times for shots nearby in the clip. (This is especially useful for finding shots fast on reality shows that shoot with multiple cameras following multiple people.) You can use it not only to find duplicated shots but also to find a section in your sequence:

Matthew Illardo: *If I need a moment that I know happened near another moment but I can't find it on my sequence because my sequence has so much stuff, I'll grab the clip I can find and lay it down … and then dupe detection will cause a red line to pop up and show me where it appears elsewhere. Then I can go right to that area and find what I'm really looking for—the other moment—in the timeline.*

Color-Coding, Labels, and Tabs

Color-coding bins, clips, sequences, and tabs makes items easy to find and allows many more options for organizing projects. One idea is to color-code cameras or performances. How about acts, rough cuts, and master sequences? Everything is better with a little color-coding. A simple glance and you're on your way to navigating the project.

While intercutting two sets of performances, I use one color for all clips grouped in one set of performance clips and a second color for a second set of performance clips. If you intercut these two sets together, then it's easy to see the difference between the two sets, right in the timeline.

Thom Zimney, editor and archivist for the Bruce Springsteen media collection: *My Assistant will set up a thing where if it's a cheat from another night, those group clips or those master clips will be color-coded a certain night so that within the timeline it will show up. I can quickly see my cheats and know that they're an issue to look at within the timeline, at these timecode numbers, so we can print out and that's ready to go.*

Gary Bradley, editor Great Performances and *The Met: Live in HD: Some shots are only available on the line cut, so we'll often give that its own color because then you'll see it immediately on the timeline.*

Mike Fay is an assistant editor for Tim Squyres, who cuts for Ang Lee and Jonathan Demme. He believes strongly in the

Noteworthy

Color codes are handy for other uses too. Some common color-coded items include these:

- B roll
- Interviews
- A-B camera
- Performance
- Scenes
- Line cuts versus ISOs

importance of color-coding in various different stages of multi-cam, in both preproduction and post.

Mike Fay: *The color-coding scheme changes based on where we are. For instance, during dailies, a circle take clip is green; a busted/no good take or a false start, red. A visual effects plate would be blue. Music and sound effect clips we generally don't color up front, but once we get into editing and working in a timeline, we designate colors for visual effects, opticals, music, sound effects, and wild tracks.*

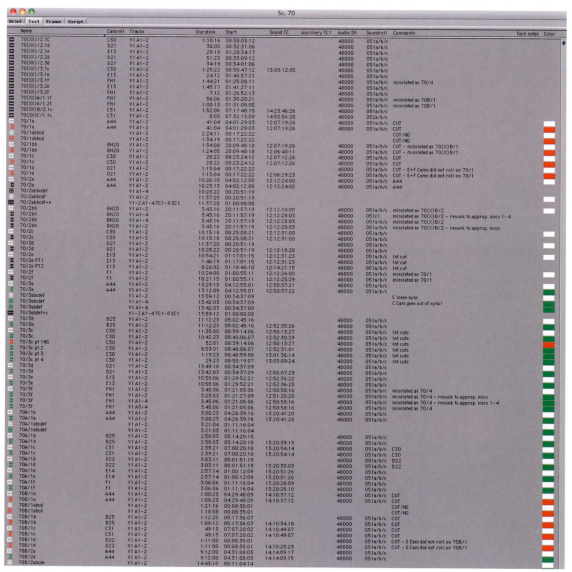

Figure 10.4 Color-coded project for *Rachel Getting Married.* (Courtesy Tim Squyres and Mike Fay.)

Tim Squyres: *I love color-coding. We usually color our interviews a certain color, our B roll a certain color, et cetera. In* Taking Woodstock, *we made visual effects cyan; opticals, yellow; music would always be cyan for audio tracks; effects based on mono or stereo would be various shades of yellow; ADR would be orange; wild track would be gray.*

Figure 10.5 Color-coded project for *Taking Woodstock.* (Courtesy Tim Squyres and Mike Fay.)

Diana Weynand is co-founder of Weynand Training International and author of the Apple Pro Training Series book *Final Cut Pro 7* (Peachpit Press). She rates color-coding tabs in FCP as the tenth best new feature of FCP 7:

Color-coding capabilities for organizing and easily identifying bins, clips, and sequences [have] been a standard feature in earlier versions of the software. However, Final Cut Pro 7 now raises the bar by implementing the color-coding of bins, clips, and sequences to their respective tabs in the Timeline, Canvas, and Browser windows.

Tip

Colored labels and tabs are just a couple of Weynand's favorite new color features. If you like these, check out her cool iPhone application, iKeysToGo, at her website, www.weynand.com.

Color Labels

You can apply a color label to any clip in the browser by right-clicking an item to get the shortcut menu then choosing Label and selecting a color. You can rename the color labels in the Labels tab of the User Preferences, although changing the name doesn't affect the color.

Figure 10.6 Labels from the Browser shortcut list. (Courtesy Weynand Training International.)

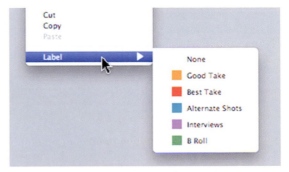

Labels from the Browser Shortcut List

Colored Tabs

When a sequence is color-coded in the Browser window, its tab in both the Timeline and Canvas windows displays in the same color.

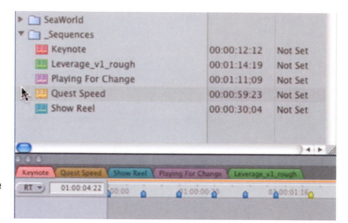

Figure 10.7 Color-coded browser sequences and timeline tabs. (Courtesy Weynand Training International.)

Figure 10.8 Viewer and Audio and Video tabs showing multiclip. (Courtesy: Weynand Training International/Electric Entertainment/Apple. (taken from the Peachpit Press book, Final Cut Pro 7, by Diana Weynand)

When you open a clip that has a color label into the Viewer, the Video and Audio tabs of the Viewer window display the same color-coding. This is particularly useful when there is a need to color-code a particular type of clip, such as multicam footage.

Although you've always been able to add a color label to a bin, now you can see that color label when you open a bin in the Browser window tab area. To review how to do that, just Option-double-click the bin in the browser and the tab appears next to the project tab. The bin will now open with the same assigned color as the bin in the browser.

You will also see something new on project tabs in FCP 7. A Final Cut Pro project file icon is now displayed on all FCP project tabs, making it easier to distinguish project tabs from bin tabs.

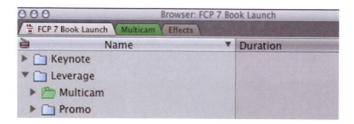

Figure 10.9 Multicam project tab icon and open bin tab. (Courtesy Weynand Training International.)

Markers

Final Cut 7 cleaned up markers to work with multicam. In earlier versions, you'd put a marker in a clip and an angle, and when you Media Managed it, the markers wouldn't be there or when you'd send it out the markers would disappear. That's all fixed now.

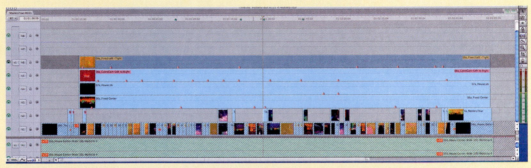

Figure 10.10 Markers in the timeline on separate angles.

Name	Label 2	Compressor	Pixel Aspect	Reel	Duration	In
▶ 📁 MultiClips						
▼ 📁 Original Footage						
▶ 📁 MHP Line Cuts						
▼ 📁 Show A						
▼ 🎞 01a_HH Stage-House Left	HH Stage-House Left	DVCPRO HD 1080i60	HD (1280x1080)	4034	00:03:10:01	Not Set
🔖 Marker 2					00:00:00:00	20:45:53:05
🔖 Marker 3					00:00:00:00	20:46:15:03
🔖 Marker 4					00:00:00:00	20:46:34:16
🔖 Marker 5					00:00:00:00	20:47:29:28
▼ 🎞 02a_HH Aud-House Right	HH Aud-House Right	DVCPRO HD 1080i60	HD (1280x1080)	4035	00:03:10:01	Not Set
🔖 Marker 1					00:00:00:00	20:45:02:12
🔖 Marker 2					00:00:00:00	20:45:08:11
🔖 Marker 3					00:00:00:00	20:45:26:28
🔖 Marker 4					00:00:00:00	20:46:00:21
🔖 Marker 5					00:00:00:00	20:46:09:29
🔖 Marker 6					00:00:00:00	20:46:35:06
▼ 🎞 03a_TechnoJib	TechnoJib	DVCPRO HD 1080i60	HD (1280x1080)	4036	00:03:10:01	Not Set
🔖 Marker 1					00:00:00:00	20:45:04:03
🔖 Marker 2					00:00:00:00	20:45:35:28
🔖 Marker 3					00:00:00:00	20:45:43:21
🔖 Marker 4					00:00:00:00	20:46:03:00
🔖 Marker 5					00:00:00:00	20:46:09:19
🔖 Marker 6					00:00:00:00	20:46:24:22
🔖 Marker 7					00:00:00:00	20:46:33:25
🔖 Marker 8					00:00:00:00	20:47:02:24
🔖 Marker 9					00:00:00:00	20:47:20:07
▼ 🎞 04a_House Dolly-Long Lens	House Dolly-Long Lens	DVCPRO HD 1080i60	HD (1280x1080)	4037	00:03:10:01	Not Set
🔖 Marker 1					00:00:00:00	20:45:04:03
🔖 Marker 2					00:00:00:00	20:45:24:15
🔖 Marker 3					00:00:00:00	20:45:30:23
🔖 Marker 4					00:00:00:00	20:45:52:17
🔖 Marker 5					00:00:00:00	20:46:20:21
🔖 Marker 6					00:00:00:00	20:47:31:03
▼ 🎞 05a_House Left-Wide	House Left-Wide	DVCPRO HD 1080i60	HD (1280x1080)	4038	00:03:10:01	Not Set
🔖 Marker 1					00:00:00:00	20:45:05:24
🔖 Marker 2					00:00:00:00	20:45:38:26
🔖 Marker 3					00:00:00:00	20:46:03:05
🔖 Marker 4					00:00:00:00	20:46:18:07
🔖 Marker 5					00:00:00:00	20:46:56:17
🔖 Marker 6					00:00:00:00	20:47:03:01
🔖 Marker 7					00:00:00:00	20:47:09:21

Figure 10.11 Markers in the browser.

Databases and Multicam Searches

Most of us will work on small programs or one-off shows like concerts that don't require extended data-management systems. But a large and growing faction of programs like reality shows or series desperately require that huge numbers of tapes and clips be managed. In cases like these, being able to share clip data is especially important. A database will allow you to search for anything not only throughout the project bins but also throughout a whole show, series, or archive. Sometimes these systems are connected to a fiber network SAN; other times they're independent systems that use internal drives or share FireWire drives. In addition to supporting custom searches, a database creates bins or shot lists that can be imported by either FCP or Avid.

Mark Raudonis has almost a hundred people working on a show at one time. All of those people need access to the media involved. Some are writing or producing, while others are editing or assisting. Bandwidth becomes an issue. Because you can read much faster than you can watch tapes, some programs use a logging method called Pilotware (www.pilotware.com). It lives on top of the File Maker Pro database software and is popular among reality show production teams.

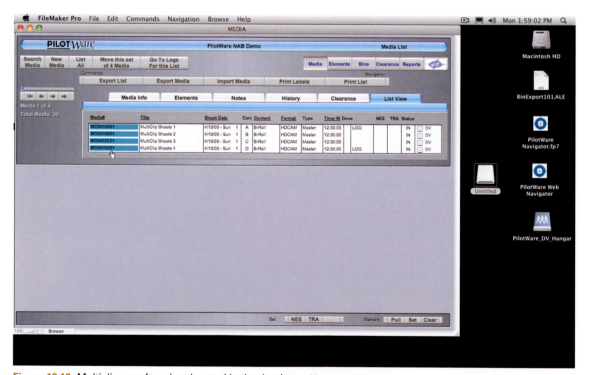

Figure 10.12 Multiclips are found and sorted in the database. (Courtesy Pilotware.)

According to Raudonis:

We have a separate server, a separate database—it's both Mac- and PC-compatible. On The Real World, *for example, we're using the XDCAM HD acquisition format and peeling off the proxies and logging to files. On* Project Runway *we're using work copies IMX 50 – based tape, and so they're logging to a tape machine. All our shows create separate searchable databases that live independently of the Final Cut system.*

Figure 10.13 Found multicam clips are grouped for screening within Pilotware. (Courtesy Pilotware.)

The information from Pilotware stays in the database and is not sent to the edit suites for capturing. And typically it's the story department guys—not the editors—who use the information. As Mark Raudonis explains, "It's like the separation of church and state. There's editorial, which is Xsan and Final Cut, and then there's story department, which is also tied into our Xsan and Final Cut but can also access this logging base."

The story department can also access multicam angles and groups. The database can create XMLs and OMFs for batch capturing or it can be imported into the bins as clips and sequences and linked back to the original footage on the server. (for more info on Filemaker Pro database usage see Chapter 20: Case Study: A Mixed-Platform Workflow)

Figure 10.14 Selected multicamera shots can be exported to FCP or Avid via XML or ALE. (Courtesy Pilotware.)

REFERENCES

1. www.macwindows.com
2. FCP manual.

11

GROUPING AND SYNCING ANGLES

Grouping angles is the key to editing in multicamera mode. Once all your footage is loaded, the next step is to group angles into multicam clips. A group clip or multiclip is a set of clips synchronized by a common sync frame and combined into one clip. Each clip within a group is known as an angle, and you can switch angles as necessary. The angle from which you can see and hear video and audio when you play your sequence is called the *active angle*.

You can also group unrelated footage together for real-time montage editing. For example, if you're editing a music video, you could group separate takes of a song as angles or add several angles of abstract visuals and cut to those clips on specific music beats.

While the active angle plays in the timeline, you can also simultaneously view all angles playing in the source window or Viewer.

A grouped clip is advantageous both to cutting and organization. Not only does a group clip allow for quick editing, it also allows for quick searches using the match frames. And you can group clips to watch more footage in less time.

David Helfand, editor, *Weeds* and *Friends: I group clips as much as possible—even when things aren't intended to be grouped or shot together. Sometimes when I'm trying to figure out the geography of a scene, having a variety of takes matched up helps me see it more clearly: maybe one camera reveals something about what's happening in the background, something I couldn't see in the background shots from the other cameras.*

Don't Stack–Group!

I see a lot of music videos that come into my suite, from editors who have only learned on Final Cut Pro. They don't know how to group and they just have these massive timelines that are stacked 50 layers deep, and I just shake my head sometimes and think, man, it could be a whole lot easier.

Scott Simmons, editor

Doi: 10.1016/B978-0-240-81176-5.00011-3

In Final Cut, a grouped clip is called simply a *multiclip*. There are additional multiclip limitations and requirements:

- Clips in a multiclip are not required to have the same duration, but they must all use the same codec, image dimensions, and frame rate.
- The same capture preset should be used for all footage you plan to make into a multiclip.
- Multiclips can be created from any clips in the browser: video and audio clips, still images and graphics, even other multiclips.
- Multiclips have a maximum of 128 angles, with 16 viewable.
- Each angle can be a clip with video and audio, video only, or audio only.
- A multiclip can have only one active video item and up to 24 active audio items at a time.
- The number of audio items in a multiclip is determined by the angle with the highest number of audio items. For example, consider a multiclip that contains three angles with the following number of items:

Angle 1: 2 audio items

Angle 2: 4 audio items

Angle 3: 8 audio items

Basic Grouping Methods

There are several ways to group angles:
- By in-point
- By source timecode
- By Aux TC
- With automation applications

If you don't have matching timecode, build a sync map and group by hand using subclip methods. (See below for SyncMap details)

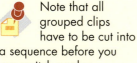

Tip

Note that all grouped clips have to be cut into a sequence before you can switch angles.

Grouping by Source Timecode

To group clips with matching timecode, choose source timecode. This is the easiest and fastest method. It works within seconds and places a new grouped clip right into your project bin. You can rename this item or presort the bin if you like; it will automatically come up with the first clip name in the group.

1. Place all the clips you want to group into a bin. If the timecode does not match, you'll need to sync by one of various other methods described in the next section.

2. Then, choose Group (Shift+Command (or Alt on PC)+G) in Avid or Make Multiclip in Final Cut Pro to create the combined clip with all the elements from the angles in one clip. Avid can use up to two banks of nine camera angles for a total of 18 angles, which can be swapped live. Final Cut can hold up to 128 angles in one clip.

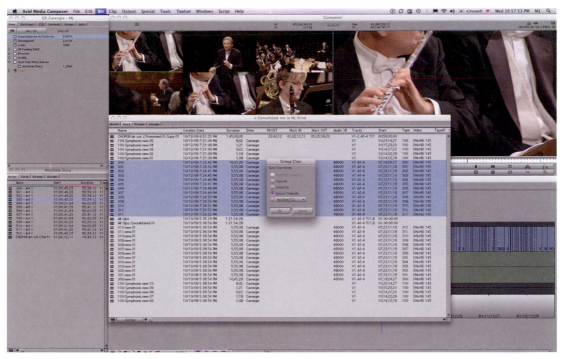

Figure 11.1 Group to source timecode. Note that the line cut is longer than the ISOs. The group will be as long as the longest clip.

3. A multiclip or group clip will appear in the bin and you can now edit that just as you would any other clip, with the benefit of optional angles at your fingertips.
4. Place the grouped clip into your sequence to activate it for editing.

If everything matched and your tapes are shot perfectly and continuously, then congratulations, you'll be home for dinner. But most likely you'll be at it all day and night, trying to sync up a big mess because production broke all the rules. Unfortunately, it's your job to fix it.

Manual In-Points

The next best thing to grouping with source timecode is grouping with manual in-points. This can be as simple as match-framing back to a particular musical beat or visual clue in the scene. The most common method is marking slates at the clap:
1. Cue up your shot.
2. Find the clap visually or match up to the audio wave and mark an in-point.
3. If you don't have slates, find a common visual or audio cue to mark.

Tip

Remember, all of these camera angles can be mapped to custom key sets for easy switching and cutting. In Avid, they are automatically mapped to the F keys, F4 through F12, and beginning in MC v.4.0 they are also mapped to the numeric keyboard, 1 through 9.

4. Repeat for every clip in the group.
5. Make a group clip using in-points.

Aux Timecode

There are a few ways to create matching aux timecode. One way is to set the auxiliary code to match LTC timecode recorded on set.

Another way to create matching aux timecode is to put the number manually into the Aux TC column before you make your groups. Setting Aux TC to the master audio timecode is a common practice; just watch out for mismatched frame rates between cameras and dual-system audio. Aux TC doesn't behave well when setting 29.97 in a 23.98 project. (See bonus chapter: How and When to use Aux Timecode)

Sync to Audio Waveforms

To manual sync to waveforms, open your clip in the Viewer, source window, or timeline and turn on the audio waveforms in the sequence settings. Find the common clapboard mark or other audio cue in the soundwave and mark an in-point. You can

Figure 11.2 Syncing by Aux TC in FCP. (Courtesy Artist's Den Entertainment and Aimee Mann.)

also pick up some speed for multiple takes by putting all takes in a sequence and ganging to the source or Viewer. This allows you to zip through the timeline without having to match frame to the original clips—just mark them and keep going until they're all marked. Then group your clips by in-points.

Omaha Wedding Video specializes in high-end weddings and events production for high school, college, and junior high dance recitals. The company typically shoots with six cameras and considers weddings to be an artistic project.

Owner Don Moran and his team sync their productions by hand using Final Cut Pro. "We line them up in the timeline, especially for the weddings," he says. "We sync to audio waveform, by having audio on all of the cameras. We're way too run and gun and we use too much multicamera to have timecode sync."

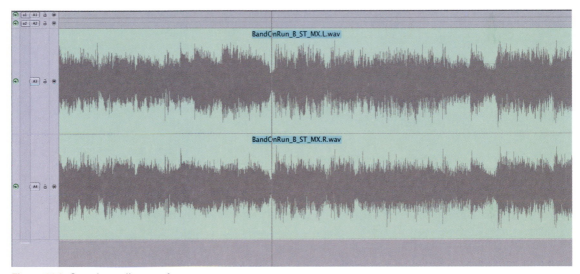

Figure 11.3 Sync by audio waveform.

Automated Applications

If you have good audio on all of your footage, you could go the quick way and use PluralEyes by Singular Systems to automatically sync your footage by the audio tracks. If not, then you are going to have to do it by hand. That's where the sync map comes in.

Sync Maps

Sync maps are sequences that consist of all of the various camera angles, multitrack audio clips, and single shots from that day stacked on top of one another, in order, over the course of the shoot day. Their function is to help editors find common sync points for footage shot without matching timecode or clips that cannot be synced easily with basic methods. Sync maps can be made for a scene or a whole day's worth of shooting. The goal is to lay out everything into the timeline so you can see the sync points and where the in-points can be. Then you can either match back to in-points or create subclips to group or multigroup later.

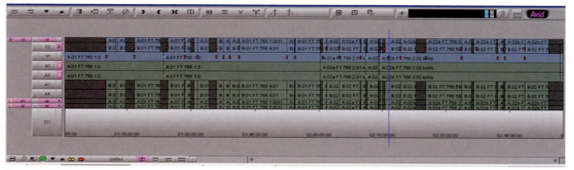

Figure 11.4 Sync map. A camera master is laid out on track 1. The B camera was turned off and on throughout the day. On Track 2, it is matched up by eye to the A camera. Track 3 shows the resulting groups at points where the cameras shot concurrently.

24-Hour Timelines

A 24-hour timeline is basically the same as a sync map except that the project media usually has matching time-of-day timecode. Under a controlled environment, your camera's starts and stops are pretty much predictable. Everyone has a collective role, and they're not too far out of bounds. When you start veering away from that production model to more of a run-and-gun reality vérité fly on the wall, your starts and stops are unpredictable, and that makes for a messy multiclipping process. The 24-hour timeline is a tool to help you address that.

You can usually see from that 24-hour timeline multiclip sequence what stuff you need to work with. You're also using the clip names, and if you've been following our organizational process with folders for A camera, B camera, C camera, the process of marking clips is pretty easy. It really becomes just kind of a very methodical mechanical detail oriented process.

Mark Raudonis , VP of Postproduction at Bunim-Murray

The A camera (i.e., the most used camera) is usually laid out first with all the clips in the order shot. If you're using double-system audio, then you could lay out all the sound first. Next, match up the B camera to the A camera on the track above it and add additional angles above that.

A basic way of grouping from a sync map is to use in-points. More advanced methods use add edits and subclips. The in-point for each camera will be different, so the first step is knowing what that point is. With Avid, I usually park my timeline marker across a common part of a set of clips with grouping potential. Next, I'll match frame back to the original clip and get a mark in-point on the source. Now I can group those clips by in-point, make a group clip, and cut that back into the sequence or continue editing with each multiclip. One drawback to this approach is that the resulting multiclips will include each camera's footage in its entirety, making the overall clip larger than it has to be. Either you have to make a subclip of the required parts or cut the grouped clip into a sequence.

Grouping from Subclips

If you are using a double-system audio workflow, chances are you have to merge clips or use Avid's auto-sync to marry the two. Sometimes you may have issues grouping merged clips. Your best bet in that situation is to make subclips from the grouped clip. This way, your in-points and out-points are equal for both the audio and video portions of the clip.

> *We subclip everything. That seems to be the magic button.*
>
> **Brian Gonosey, editor,** *Leverage*

Brian Gonosey: *We had a lot of hit and miss early on with the audio. We adopted the method of merging our clips in Final Cut with the digital audio. And so from that we would create a subclip that was one picture track and one audio track—and that's what our editors cut on. By subclipping and creating a subclip that has picture and sound the exact duration of each other, we were able to multiclip.*

Tip

FCP multiclips will work better with subclips than with merged clips. Final Cut Pro won't group merged clips without sync issues.

The ThrashGroup

Once you have a sync map in Final Cut Pro, with your clips layered vertically, you can add edits, copy and paste the clips right out of the timeline and throw them into a bin for automatic in-point grouping. I call this the ThrashGroup. Why? Uh, because I just think it sounds cool. It's really just a super fast way to make subclips.

Making a ThrashGroup:

1. Create a sequence sync map with angles stacked on tracks vertically.

Figure 11.5 Create a sync map, lining up your cameras on vertical tracks.

2. If dual-system audio, match to timecode as a base.

3. If timecode doesn't match up, sync by hand. Use markers or an audio cue.

4. In timeline, add edits cutting across all the synced tracks to mark the groups. Use arrow keys to quickly jump and add edits to the beginning and end across each clip in the sequence.

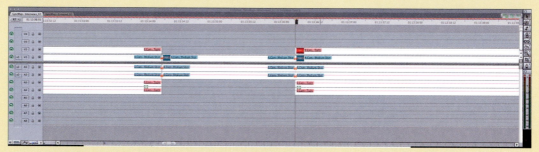

Figure 11.6 Add edits to the beginning and end across all clips.

5. Copy all clips between the add edits from sync map and paste them to the browser or a bin. This will make new master clips groupable by the first frame as in-points. No need to mark anything. I prebuild a quick folder set — one for each set of grouped clips. This is where I also save the resulting multiclip.

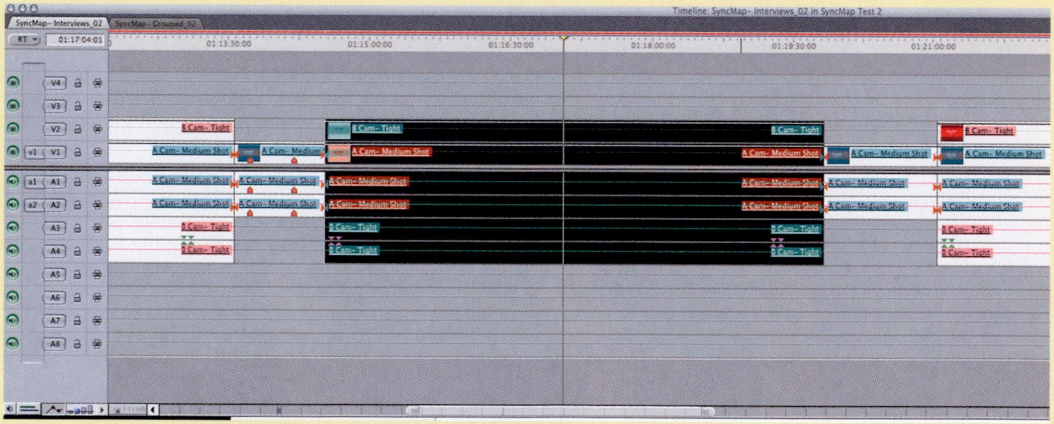

Figure 11.7 Lasso across the common parts of the layered clips and copy and paste them to the browser or into a folder.

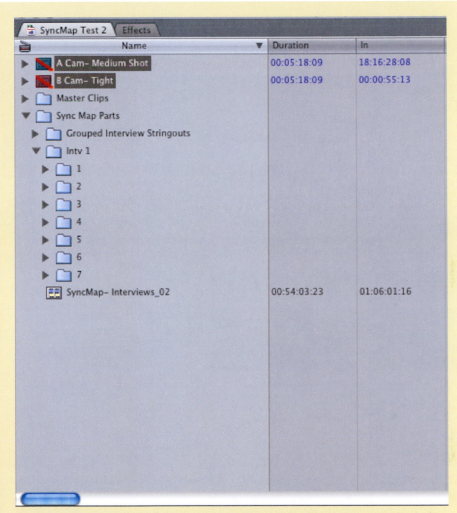

Figure 11.8 The browser now has a new master clip for each angle that was synced up in the timeline. Make a multigroup of these clips and cut it back into the sequence to test.

6. Make multiclips by in point from new clips.

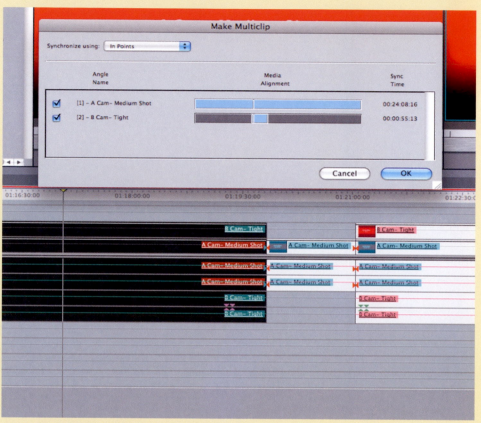

Figure 11.9 Use Make Multiclip by in-point. Notice that the timecodes do not match and no Aux TC was necessary.

7. To check, drag into track above the original stacked clips. They should be the same length and right in sync.

Figure 11.10 Optional: Add Multiclip to the sync map for double-checking sync and having a complete record of the media used.

8. Check for sync and matching timecode. Multiclips are ready to edit.

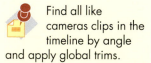

Figure 11.11 Completed sync map with multiclips on V3 over the angles that are grouped.

What's the time savings behind this? Because the new clips have automarked in-points, you wouldn't need to insert a common LTC timecode to group to, nor do you have to go through the steps of matchframing and marking ins and outs for each clip. Huge. The new in-point works perfectly.

With Avid you can get solid results using Aux TC and subclips for creating a multigroup. (See section titled "Bulletproof Multigroups in Avid," presented later in the chapter).

Tip

Find all like cameras clips in the timeline by angle and apply global trims.

Slipping Sync

Trimming has always been one of digital nonlinear video editing's greatest features. In multicam, all of your trim mode capabilities are available. You can slide your in-point, change the active angle, trim one side over another to create an L-cut, add edits, extend edits, and so on. In other words, any trimming you can do with a normal clip, you can do with a group clip.

Oliver Peters, editor and post consultant: *Let's say you're in a situation where you're syncing by hand clap and you thought you nailed it pretty closely. But you're taking your audio from one source and as you watch your sequence play out, you realize one camera looks a little rubbery in lip-sync compared to the other camera. In Final Cut, you can use the Find function in the timeline to highlight all the clips from that one angle and then use the Trim Slip and Slide function and actually slip all of those clips by however many you need to, forward or backward. Instantly all these cuts from that angle can be moved or changed in sync—and all at the same time.*

Rebuilding Nonspanned P2 Clips

Working with nonspanned P2 clips is not a common problem, but it does happen. Consider a six-camera P2 concert that was synced with a handclap. The cameras record continuously, but the P2 format creates multiple clips on the card about every 8 minutes. These clips are frame accurate and supposed to be spanned together upon log and transfer, which restores them into full continuous length clips. It's about understanding the technology and the nature of the way that P2 works.

Note that P2 cards are formatted under a Windows FAT 32 formatting system. The files break up at every 4-gig section.

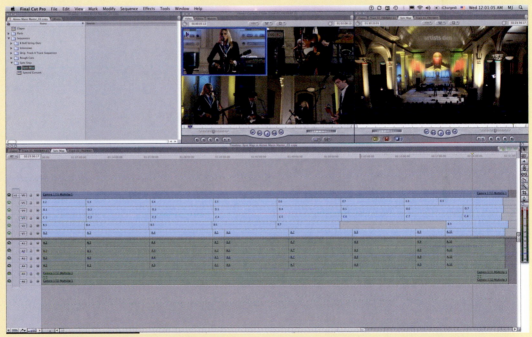

Figure 11.12 SyncMap shows nonspanned P2 clips reattached in the timeline. Each camera was resynced on vertical tracks above, and new master clips were made from each track. (Courtesy Artist's Den Entertainment and Aimee Mann.)

Because the DIT did not span the clips and the original media was not available, I was stuck with each roll broken up into 8-minute segments. These clips did not miss a frame of timecode; they laid out perfectly in a sequence.

This would be a great chance to use the ThrashGroup but, you could also export new master clips for each camera or reference movies. The sequence timecodes were identical, and each sequence zeroed out at the handclap. Each sequence was exported as a new QuickTime movie using matching timecode from the sequence. Those new clips became my master clip files. Down-converted sets, groups, subclips, and the rest all had to be made from there.

Automated MXF/P2 Sync Maps

And for when you want even more horsepower, there's metadata.

Users are getting amazing results with metadata and sequenceLiner—syncing days' worth of multicam and multitrack dual-system sound in an hour or so. But if you add an MXF4mac component to the mix, you get some real speed by avoiding log and transfer and working with the MXF natively.

The idea is to get to the creative edit as soon as possible. Most projects come with very short turnaround time—and it can take most of that time just to get organized and synced up.

Jeremy Garchow is an editor and postproduction supervisor at Maday Productions in Chicago. He's also an active leader in online forums. Once Garchow found himself syncing six hours of footage from five different cameras, plus multitrack dual-system audio—but he managed to do this in minutes rather than days, and so was able to maximize his creativity and organize and edit all elements to make a commercial for the Chicago Blackhawks in one quick week. He shares his experience using metadata for lightning-fast multicam/multitrack capture and sync and quick turnaround edits:

> We had five P2 cameras and eight channels of audio recorded to a sound device recorder 788T. We had no timecode generator and didn't jam-sync anything. We did use time-of-day free-run timecode on six different devices, but we did it on the fly: one, two, three, go—so nothing matched up exactly and one camera was actually thousands of frames out of sync!

Right off the bat, the timecode definitely needs to be offset. To prepare this project as quickly as possible, post relied on two crucial pieces of software:

- *MXF4mac.* This skips the log and transfer mode and sends P2 clips directly through to Final Cut Pro without rewrapping to QuickTime. It also allows full metadata mapping for FCP.
- *sequenceLiner.* This takes your metadata and groups everything by timecode into a target sequence, creating a sync map. (sequenceLiner is included free on the companion DVD to this book.) Garchow says:

> I had to set up all the metadata for all five cameras. I had named the clips—which meant that as soon as we were shooting, we were logging. As soon as the shoot was done, I transferred all of the P2 clips and there was no more logging to do because I had preset all that metadata. That's the power of the MXF workflow.

Truly Tapeless

Along with MXF4mac, there's a tool called and MXF Import QT for direct importing of MXF files and P2 Flow Contextual Menu, which recognizes P2 folders as P2 content for processing. Final Cut imports the metadata as an XML, marrying the video and audio and also writing XML information to all of the columns. This opens up the speed and power of tapeless.

The next application is sequenceLiner by Andreas Kiel of Spherico (www.spherico.com), a well-known developer of amazing video tools and applications. Kiel has been instrumental in the innovation of cool multicam projects like the 360° Project, which uses multiple cameras to create 360° shots, and MI8, a daily multicam soap opera in Austria that utilizes Telestream's Pipeline and LiveCut to prep more than 100 multicam setups a day—from live shoot to edit in seconds.

Sync Map on Steroids

sequenceLiner together with MXF4mac is like having a sync map on steroids. They line up multiple angles like nobody's business. Working with P2, MXF4mac, and metadata from free-run timecode, sequenceLiner is able to match up all of the cameras and dual-system audio tracks your heart desires. Even if the timecodes are off, easy fixes are done with offsets

> sequenceLiner is an application for cameras and audio HDRs running time-of-day timecode. Export your bins and one or more target sequences as XML. The application will lay down all clips into a target sequence at their TOD. Even if the TOD TC doesn't match on the cameras, the clip TOD relations within the track will match. So you can move a complete track by some frames and everything will be in sync.
>
> **Andreas Kiel**

If you have a sync point, like a clapboard, it's easy to find the offset for each clip. Next, highlight all the clips on that camera's tracks and slide them down by the number amount of frames. Once you do that for all your tracks, the entire sync map will be ready for groupings.

With luck, by the time you read this Kiel and company will have an update that automatically creates multiclip sequences from sync maps. For now, however, we have to do that by hand.

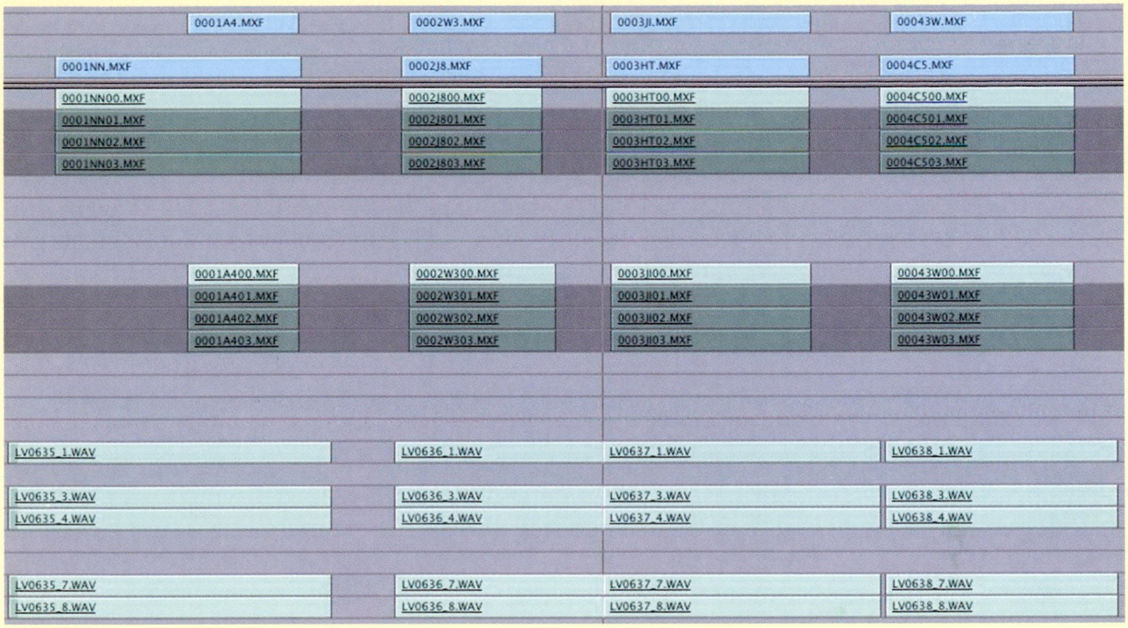

0001A4.MXF	0002W3.MXF	0003JI.MXF	00043W.MXF
0001NN.MXF	0002J8.MXF	0003HT.MXF	0004C5.MXF
0001NN00.MXF	0002J800.MXF	0003HT00.MXF	0004C500.MXF
0001NN01.MXF	0002J801.MXF	0003HT01.MXF	0004C501.MXF
0001NN02.MXF	0002J802.MXF	0003HT02.MXF	0004C502.MXF
0001NN03.MXF	0002J803.MXF	0003HT03.MXF	0004C503.MXF
0001A400.MXF	0002W300.MXF	0003JI00.MXF	00043W00.MXF
0001A401.MXF	0002W301.MXF	0003JI01.MXF	00043W01.MXF
0001A402.MXF	0002W302.MXF	0003JI02.MXF	00043W02.MXF
0001A403.MXF	0002W303.MXF	0003JI03.MXF	00043W03.MXF
LV0635_1.WAV	LV0636_1.WAV	LV0637_1.WAV	LV0638_1.WAV
LV0635_3.WAV	LV0636_3.WAV	LV0637_3.WAV	LV0638_3.WAV
LV0635_4.WAV	LV0636_4.WAV	LV0637_4.WAV	LV0638_4.WAV
LV0635_7.WAV	LV0636_7.WAV	LV0637_7.WAV	LV0638_7.WAV
LV0635_8.WAV	LV0636_8.WAV	LV0637_8.WAV	LV0638_8.WAV

Figure 11.13 P2 multicam and multitrack audio wave file clips lined up in target sequence. (Courtesy www.spherico.com/filmtools.)

So why is this workflow so cool? Why not just rent cameras and get a timecode generator? Budget restrictions are a common factor. The MXF4mac/sequenceLiner method keeps the cost down. Not having to worry about timecode is great for DPs, because it frees them up to go wherever they want and keep their mind on the shoot.

In short, using MXF4mac/sequenceLiner is very advantageous to the creative process—especially ones requiring quick turnaround.

Full coverage: MacVideo.tv: Synching the Impossible with Jeremy Garchow.

Recorded at the NAB Supermeet, by Rick Young. www.macvideo.tv/editing/features/index.cfm?articleId=3200691

Sync to What?

If there's no clapper, finding manual in-points can be the bane of existence for editors and their assistants. Rarely does everything work perfectly. This is where you really earn your money.

Many editors have a musical background, and this can come handy when trying to group clips manually. If there's music, you can find a note or beat and mark to that. If there's dialogue, you can mark to a word or line, or even use a soundwave as your in-point mark. Sometimes visuals provide good in-points—maybe even where you least expect them. You could try syncing on an actor's movement, such as when he touches his face or shakes another actor's hand. Or even something as subtle as a reflection flashing or a light turning could be a sync point.

Nick Diamano worked with Thom Zimney on the Bruce Springsteen Hammersmith Odeon concert, which was shot on film in 1975 in London. It was a four-camera shoot shot on 16 mm and recorded to a 24 multitrack machine. All of the camera reels are soundless.

Nick Diamano: *There was no LCD or timecode—those were literally all synced by eye by Matt Foglia, CAS, our ProTools editor/mixer. Springsteen songs are long, especially live, so sometimes the camera would stop and start midsong, which meant you were basically just trying to figure out what he's singing, a whole concert's worth of lyrics and angles. Everything was MOS and there were no slates, no visual references. You'd just see someone singing up there with no sound and you'd have to figure out what song it was and where that song fit into the show.*

While editing "Live and Let Die" for Paul McCartney's Backstage at the Super Bowl special, I was given a box of tapes transferred from NFL film cameras. Now, NFL camera guys are some of the best cameramen in the business. Their footage is fabulous. But they have no concern for the timecode or jam-syncing involved in a practical multicamera operation. They pretty much start and stop whenever they want and shoot whatever they see. There's no sound. So it's a syncing nightmare. The only solution is to try to sync the shots by hand.

Sometimes you can be creative. In the case of the McCartney/ Superbowl special, I synced everything from an incident of fireworks reflecting in the piano. For another show, an interview sequence, I received five cameras without matching timecode or even a single close-up—but luckily (for me anyway) one of the interviewees had a cold and kept rubbing his nose, which made a great sync point—or should I say sniff point?

The Super Groups

Multiclip Sequences (FCP) and MultiGroups (Avid) are primarily for people shooting with multiple cameras on multiple days, multiple hours, or with multiple takes in a studio-controlled environment, like a sitcom. The multigroup feature allows you to sync all the cameras into multicam groups and automatically edit them into a sequence in the same order they were shot. This is a real timesaver.

Here's the key: the cameras must have matching timecode, and it works best with time-of-day TC. If you're going to try just to sync up the clap stick or the flashlight or manually, then you're not going to want to use this feature.

Basically, a multigroup is like having a sequence of grouped clips in one clip. When you play through it, there are edit points, and if you toggle your source monitor into a timeline you can see them visually. There's a cut every time you add your edits in your sequence, because it's switching to a new group. When a new camera comes in, it's added as a new group clip within the greater multigroup. So the multigroup is like a timeline containing all the group clips in order, but the Avid treats it like it's a source clip.

Editor David Helfand: *You can have a huge group that represents the whole first act of the show. If you want to jump around and find material, you can punch in any timecode and not have to flip in or change the material you're editing with. You're editing from one massive, two- or four-hour-long stretch that had a lot of black gaps in it, where the timecode jumps happened.*

Multiclip Sequences (FCP)

In FCP, Make Multiclip Sequence will do the same thing as MultiGroup in Avid. It creates many multiclips at once and places them in a new sequence in chronological order.

The multiclip sequence command is not that intuitive and needs a little more fleshing out. To find out how to get additional help with multiclip sequences, we turned to Steve Martin, president and founder of rippletraining.com, a training company that delivers content online, via iTunes and DVDs, to help people master postproduction tools.

The company has two great video tutorials on FCP multicam: *The Essentials of Multicam,* which is also included free in the DVD companion to this book, and *Advanced Methods,* which features a great tutorial on multiclip sequences (available on iTunes or rippletraining.com). The Make Multiclip Sequence feature simplifies and streamlines the workflow.

Steve Martin: *Let's say you're shooting a sporting event over three days and you've got three or four cameras covering it. It would be a nightmare to try to sync up all those cameras using the manual method of actually finding a sync point and then creating a multiclip and editing them in your timeline or creating a sequence. What this command does is it looks at all of the timecode values of all those cameras, finds out what's common and where the overlap is, and then generates the multiclips for you—then it even places them into the sequences, saving you literally (and I am not exaggerating) thousands of mouse clicks.*

A cool feature is the timecode synchronization offset, which allows you to make a multiclip sequence with footage that overlaps or wasn't captured with exact timecode in and out. The dialog lets you adjust the overlap in terms of percentages.

Figure 11.14 Several hours of camera angles to be grouped as a multiclip sequence. (Courtesy www.rippletraining.com.)

For example, if you enter 100% in the Minimum Overlap field, multiclips are only created with clips that have the same exact starting and ending timecode numbers. Once you start the multiclip sequence process, you still have options to include or preclude individual angles in your groups. This comes in handy if the overlap forces a clip into the wrong group. You could just turn it off for that group entirely.

Steve Martin: *The multiclip sequence command isn't always going to be perfect, but it certainly gets you in the ballpark by grouping related camera takes into the same multiclip, which is a really powerful tool.*

By the way, this process of multigrouping is also great for syncing footage from cameras that are shooting different scenes at the same time of day. Once your footage is synced, into a 24-hour timeline, for instance, you could make multigroups and intercut between scenes easily, since one scene takes place at the same time as the other scene. Even if you just use this trick to find footage fast, you could always trim and assemble to tell your story later.

Tim Leavitt, assistant editor, The Apprentice: *It's perfect for reality shows where they're out shooting footage with four or five different cameras and they're all shooting basically the same stuff. You can just throw that all into one multigroup even if there's a break where there's no camera shooting.*

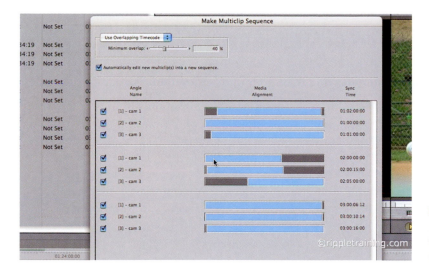

Figure 11.15 Groups of overlapping timecode adjusted for grouping camera angles. (Courtesy www.rippletraining.com.)

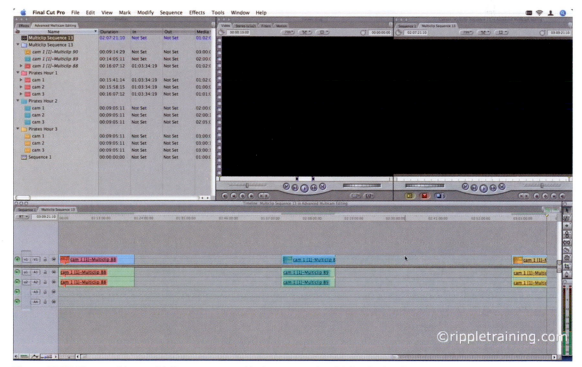

Figure 11.16 The resulting multiclip sequence with three sets of multiclips in timeline by timecode. Note the multiclip sequence folder and its parts. (Courtesy www.rippletraining.com.)

You can throw it all in one group and the multigroup can handle the jump in timecodes.

Then you have access right at your fingertips to anything, anywhere, during that day, with all the cameras right where they need to be.

Bulletproof Multigroups in Avid

(This information is reprinted with permission from the author, Tim Leavitt. It's a condensed version of the workflow. For the complete details and more cool stuff, check out Tim Leavitt's blog: http://viewfromthecuttingroomfloor .wordpress.com/2008/04/17/multigroups.)

For simple groups, like an interview filmed by two cameras, in-point grouping is the way to go. For trickier stuff, where you've got multiple cameras going in and out, stopping and starting, you really have to multigroup—and you can't get reliable multigroups except by the method I'm about to describe. (Lots of assistants seem to think there should be a "Group this sequence!" command and with just one click your sync map is grouped. Unfortunately, it's not yet quite that simple.)

Luckily, there's a way to work around all of these issues and create convenient multigroups that contain all of your footage for a given scene and are perfectly in sync. Each camera can drop in and out and the multigroup will automatically adjust and play smoothly throughout the footage's duration.

1. Make a sync map. Lay down your first and last clips of the day and add filler in between until you can match your last clip's timecode with the sequence timecode. Be sure to keep each camera on a separate video track.

Figure 11.17 Lay down clips to match timecode in sync map. (Courtesy Tim Leavitt.)

2. Decide what needs grouping. Anytime there are overlapping clips, more than one camera was shooting simultaneously. You can subclip the parts that you do want to group into their own smaller sequences (remember to reset the starting timecode to match the first frame of each).

3. Check for timecode drift. Pick a few points throughout your sequence and try playing the audio from one camera with the video from another to see if they match perfectly.

4. Sync each camera to your base camera. If there is some timecode drift, pick one camera as your "base camera." You must never move the clips of your base camera—lock its tracks for safety. Using red Segment Mode, slide each clip from your other cameras a couple frames at a time until they appear to

Figure 11.18 Timecode window showing stacked clips with V2 one frame out of sync. (Courtesy Tim Leavitt.)

be in sync. If production used a clapboard or other sync method, match the clips up using that method. Alternatively, if audio was recorded on both cameras, it is very helpful to turn on waveforms in your sequence and try to match up the clips using a sudden, loud burst of sound.

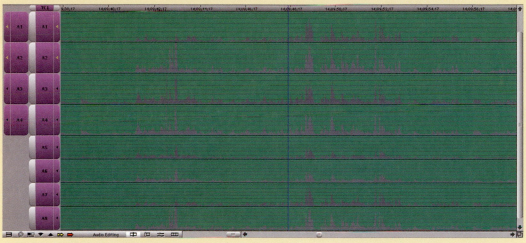

Figure 11.19 Audio waveforms matchup. (Courtesy Tim Leavitt.)

Figure 11.20 Solo tracks. (Courtesy Tim Leavitt.)

5. Set Aux TC for your base camera. Make sure your bin of master clips is set to display the field "Auxiliary TC 1." Copy the "Start" timecode from each clip into its corresponding "Auxiliary TC1_" field, but only for your base camera.

6. Adjust the Aux TC for your nonbase cameras. Make sure your bin is still sorted by timecode and then by tape name. Pick a video track (except the one your base camera is on) and solo it (Apple-click or Ctrl-click). Make sure your Composer settings are set to stop on Head frames only. Step through the edits of your sequence using the "Fast Forward" command. Enter the sequence master timecode of the first frame after each edit into the "Auxiliary TC1" field of each nonbase-camera clip.

Figure 11.21 Set custom buttons to find first frames fast. (Courtesy Tim Leavitt.)

Tip

You can copy the timecode information from the record window display and paste it into the Aux TC column in the bin.

7. Add edits at every camera start/stop point.

Figure 11.22 Add edits where clips overlap. (Courtesy Tim Leavitt.)

Make sure all of the tracks in your sequence are highlighted. Park your cursor on the first frame that any camera drops out or comes in. "Add Edit" at each of these points throughout the entire part of the sequence that you want grouped. The edit should proceed through all of the tracks.

8. Create subclips from your sequence. Now you need to turn all of these pieces into subclips, which you will use to create your multigroup. The best way to do this is to step through your timeline again track by track (using the "Fast Forward" key and "Track Solo" feature as before), and "Match Frame" back to each master clip. I recommend mapping your keyboard settings to have the following string of commands laid out in order on the number keys of your keyboard, or wherever you find most convenient.

1. Mark Clip

2. Go to In-Point

3. Match Frame

4. Go to Out-Point

5. Set Out-Point

6. Subclip

7. Fast Forward

Figure 11.23 The six buttons needed to quickly make subclips. (Courtesy Tim Leavitt.)

Turn on the "gang" button so that your master clips in the source monitor will move in tandem with your sequence. You should be able to hit buttons 1 through 6 rapidly to create your subclip. Then, simply click back in your timeline window (your bin will automatically be highlighted after creating a subclip), and hit 7 until your playhead reaches another piece of media. You cannot subclip a piece of filler, so skip over all of them.

Once you are done, you will have a bin full of hundreds (or even thousands) of subclips. The correct auxiliary timecode for each subclip should have transferred from its original master clip.

9. Multigroup by Auxiliary TC1. Sort your bin by tape name, then by Auxiliary TC1. Select all your subclips and click on "Multigroup" in the "Bin" menu. When it prompts you for a method, click "Auxiliary TC1." Media Composer will create a number of groups and one main multigroup.

Automated Macros for Multigrouping

(Reprinted with permission from Brad Cordeiro. For the full article and many other useful posts, check out his blog: http://bradcordeiro.squarespace.com.)

Here are the steps to put into your QuickKeys scripts, using your own Avid keyboard settings:

For starters, you need a certain Bin View to make these work. After the Name column, place Mark IN and then Auxiliary TC1 (or whichever Aux timecode your show is using). Any headings after that are fine, but keep them to the right of Name, Mark IN, and Aux TC.

Add your edits to the timeline you'll be grouping, make sure your sequence is at the bottom of your bin, park on the subclip you want to pull, and run the following steps (Avid commands are in italics, keyboard presses in **bold**):

1. *Mark Clip.*
2. *Go to IN.*
3. *Match Frame.*
4. *Go to OUT.*
5. *Mark OUT.*
6. *Make Subclip.*
7. **Tab** over to the Mark IN Heading.
8. **Shift + Return** to go to your sequence at the bottom of your bin.
9. Copy the Mark IN time to the clipboard.
10. **Return** to jump back to the clip you just pulled.
11. **Tab** over to the Auxiliary TC heading.
12. Paste the copied Mark IN time from the sequence to the Auxiliary TC column.
13. Send the window focus to the Timeline.
14. *Fast Forward* to the next subclip to be pulled.

And that does it. The part that usually trips people up in coming up with this on their own is applying the Aux TC to a subclip. The easiest way is to copy the sequences' Mark IN time in the bin.

Digging Deeper

Angle Placement and Strategies

You can change the visible angle position after you created the multicam group clip.

In Final Cut Pro, you can command click and move the angle physically in the Viewer until all the angles have been positioned how you want them.

There are many more tools in Final Cut Pro for arranging angles in the Viewer. The angles can be rearranged, overwritten, and inserted into a preexisting Final Cut Pro multiclip. All of them will work on any angle except the active angle:

- Overwrite.
- Swap or move positions.
- Insert new angle.
- Rearrange.
- Delete.
- Add new angles.

One of the other cool things that you can do in Final Cut Pro is resync an angle by nudging its timecode. If it's off a few frames, hold the Control and Shift keys for a frame scrubber to nudge the clip back in sync.

Figure 11.24 Resyncing an angle in the multiclip.

Recreating the Monitor Wall or Camera Map

For concerts or events, I like to arrange the Viewer window to match the director's view of the monitor wall from inside the truck. This helps me envision the director's perspective. I also take into account the camera map when creating the way angles display in the Viewer.

Sometimes angle placement is as simple as putting cameras A, B, C, and X into a quad split, with A always being in the upper left-hand corner and the rest falling in clockwise. Other times you have to take into account complicated preproduction plans intended to be carried though post.

Mini Case Study: Angle Plans

In editing *Paul McCartney: The Space Within US,* director, Mark Haefeli arranged his cameras around a circular theory. He positioned his cameras around the stage on tracks and jibs and cranes in a big circle. The direction of the show came from a deep and well-considered concept of cameras on a wheel swirling around the music.

Mark Haefeli: *We tried to establish Paul from a very circular motion. The interplanetary motion was very much part of what I was trying to establish. The way it flows felt like a big wheel constantly turning in different directions but always around Paul in the middle.*

For editing, the Viewer was set up exactly like the cameras were positioned around the stage. The 16-way split-viewer is the grid for the four inner star cameras: wide, tight, dolly with long lens, and house right. All the other cameras were positioned around that grid as if on a big wheel. I don't know if the average viewer can see or notice this; maybe they can feel it but find it hard to describe. The practical intention was to set up the workflow to match the intended plan and make the team feel comfortable about the way the show comes together.

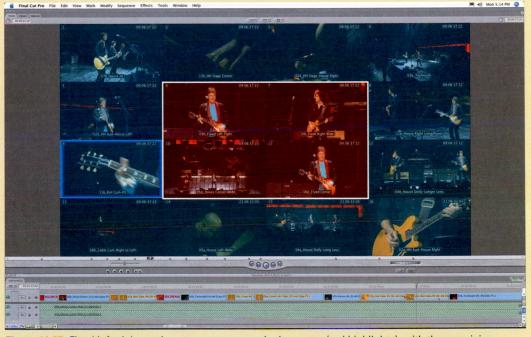

Figure 11.25 Fixed left, right, and center cameras are in the center (red highlights), with the remaining camera positions circling Paul McCartney per their original positions around the stage (blue highlights).

Editing Multiclips into a Sequence

One of the last steps in setting up a multicam project for editing is to cut the group clips into a sequence. This is where they gain their power. You can't use a group clip without cutting it into a sequence.

Once you edit a multiclip into a sequence, you can turn on the Multiclip Playback option in RT Extreme to watch all angles simultaneously in the Viewer while switching or cutting to different angles in real time in the canvas. (In Avid you need to switch into multicam mode shift: Command-shift-M.)

Real-Time Playback and Optimization

Multiclip playback will always work best when you use the fastest disks. As mentioned, the faster speed of your disk array, the better your real-time performance and the more streams you can play in a grouped clip. Avid and FCP both have additional ways of "goosing" the playback.

RT Extreme with Dynamic RT

In FCP, you can use the RT Extreme settings in the timeline to reduce real-time playback issues in the canvas. Using dynamic or low settings will help compensate for slower drive speeds. Each of the angles in the grouped clip will be affected by this setting. You could also turn off the Show Angle Effects option in the pop-up menu in the Viewer. Dynamic playback amounts to fewer missed frames, and you can switch back for hi-res playback or output at anytime.

Figure 11.26 Use RT Extreme with dynamic playback for real-time playback compensation.

Avid Full-Res Preview

If you watch your sequence with settings for less than full-resolution preview in Avid, you will reduce the amount of under-runs. Avid automatically reduces the playback quality of the sequence when multicam mode is turned on. Avid also uses the graphic card to optimize playback of all its sequences including multicam. There is code written to detect the graphics card upon launching the application. Avid then adjusts automatically to draft mode to take advantage of the graphic card for increased playback speed.

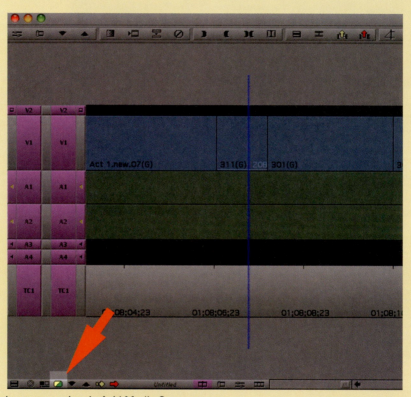

Figure 11.27 Low-res preview in Avid Media Composer.

Both systems will allow you to play back the timeline/linecut or the Viewer/source window with the angles' view to a client monitor output. Either show multiclip angles in the view menu for FCP, or adjust the settings tab in Avid for linecut or multicam output.

Organizing the Project/Browser

Whether you are preparing your own project or have an assistant to help you, getting your elements organized and ready to edit is the name of the game.

If you do have the luxury of an assistant, here are some additional ways in which he or she might be of help:

Matt Illardo, editor, The Rachael Ray Show: *We have two assistants on* The Rachael Ray Show: *one night assistant and one day assistant. They get and digitize all the ISOs and then group it at the end. Then we editors take the group clip and cut it to the sequence and go from there, cutting the show down to time and fixing all the shots.*

Peter Chakos, A.C.E. editor of The Big Bang Theory on CBS: *It's pretty cut and dry. The assistant creates bins that I like to see. He clips them and makes a multigroup bin so all of the multigroups live in there—but once they're laid in the script, I can keep that bin closed. Then I have a cuts bin and an archive where I hide things. Since we work in comedy, the most important thing my assistant does is make a laugh bin for every episode; he pulls subclips of clean laughs for me. The subclips are finite, so they can't be stretched open beyond the clean portion.*

For my part: I'm a bit of a stickler for a neat workspace. I keep two main bins: Parts and Sequences. In the Parts bin, I like bins for audio, GFX, original media, client media, and so on. I always keep separate bins for multicam parts.

And finally, after all this data and file management, it's time to edit.

EDITORIAL

12

CUTTING TECHNIQUES AND STYLES

Editors really shouldn't have a style, a style of their own. The style of the finished product should come from the footage.

Tim Squyres, feature film editor

The story is usually written three times: on the page, on the stage, and then one more time—in editing.

Cutting is a technical and personal process. No two cuts are alike. Every editor has his or her own way of tackling a job.

Thom Zimney, producer/editor, The Wire and Bruce Springsteen (various concerts and documentaries): *My interest in the cutting always comes from the storytelling. I'm not of an MTV school where I'm attached to the beat. It's much more interesting to me to try to tell a story. I want to show that dynamic Bruce Springsteen has with his audience without interrupting the flow between song to song, or between the small moments like Bruce looking over at Clarence and then Clarence breaking into the solo. It's like you give things a beat sometimes just to breathe. You just don't want to interrupt that with an edit.*

Tim Squyres is a feature film editor who has collaborated with some of the best directors in Hollywood including Ang Lee and Jonathan Demme. In 2000, he earned an Academy Award nomination for best film editing for *Crouching Tiger, Hidden Dragon*.

Tim Squyres: *I really try to let the footage inform what I'm doing. The style that's appropriate for* Rachel's Getting Married *is very different from the style that's appropriate for* Sense *and* Sensibility. *You do what's right for the footage that's in front of you, and you have to get a feel for that while you're working with it. So there might be little things that are my style in the rhythms of dialogue and where in a sentence you would cut to a reaction, but nobody would ever see that except me. You work from an emotional level when there's emotion in the footage. What audiences really appreciate in movies is emotion, excitement, things that get you involved visually, emotionally, in the story. So as an editor you have to approach it the same way.*

Daniel Cahn, A.C.E., is a third-generation film editor (his father is Dann Cahn, A.C.E.). Daniel Cahn, A.C.E. has been nominated for an Emmy Award and serves on the board of the Motion Picture Editor's Guild. He is credited with TV series such as *Saints and Sinners; Wicked, Wicked Games;* and *Fashion House*. He has also served as associate producer on a number of series including *The Secret Life of the American Teenager.* Cahn has worked on nearly every editing technology from the Moviola Monster to the Avid Media Composer.

Daniel Cahn, A.C.E.: *The material dictates the style. But you don't get in the way of the material, that's the biggest thing about style. Material drives everything. You let the actors have their moments. It's timing and rhythm. You can teach anyone to use a machine, you can teach anyone to do the mechanics, you either have timing and rhythm or you don't.*

Collaboration is another factor. Your approach to cutting may be brilliant, but if it doesn't accord with what the producer or director ultimately wants, it doesn't matter. The majority of editors are service providers who need to please their clients in combination with bringing their techniques, organizational skills, and style to the party.

Multicamera editing takes your skill set up a notch. Not everybody can look at four screens or six screens at once and know what they're looking at. It's hard to do that. It's like multitasking—with style.

Darryl Bates, A.C.E.: *Stylistically multicamera editing is a fascinating different discipline. You have to be more of a magician in terms of vision. You have to look at four screens at once and know that in a multicamera show it's entirely possible to miss a line. The guy's giving a joke and the camera guy was supposed to be there and he's not.*

Music programs, sitcoms, and talk shows all use multicam and all have distinctive styles. Cutting music may involve a live on-the-fly or purely rhythmic method; talk shows may need to be cut according to tone and pacing of dialogue; sitcoms and dramas follow scripts. Features that use A-B cameras may be cut with just camera A for story and pacing and camera B for other elements later on.

Which approach is right for you will boil down to you or your editor's preference and genre.

Oliver Peters, editor/colorist: *Usually, I'll do at least three passes on sequence just from the multicam side. The first one is cut just for feel, the second is a trim-pass, and the third one involves looking once more with a finer eye on the cameras. All remaining cuts are cutting for time.*

Noteworthy

Three basic multicam cutting styles:
1. Live on the fly
2. Start and stop
3. Add edits

Once you cut the show to time—or, for that matter, make any cuts at all—you may need to go back to make fixes to your cut. Angles may be back to back and look like jump cuts. In fact, often once you start switching angles, you subject yourself to the domino effect of having to fix many more of them than you anticipated.

Multicam Editing Styles

Cutting Live on the Fly

Coming from a live TV background, I thrive on the excitement of a live cut. (Yet even in a live cut you have a safety net: *Undo!*) Whether it's a concert, talk show, or interview, I almost always cut live on the fly for the first pass. My feeling is that the live, on-the-fly cut is the best first step, because it allows me to follow my initial instincts: to cut according to where my eye is drawn naturally when I blink, (Walter Murch's "Blink Theory").

When writers are trying to bring out the emotional quality of a story, they will often use a technique commonly called "writing from the heart." This is usually done in the first draft: the writer pours out his or her soul, as it were, plowing through the story without worrying about spelling or punctuation, so the narrative can flow freely. Then, in the second draft, the writer breaks the story down by analyzing and rewriting it. This second cut is called "writing from the head," which is a much more thoughtful, logical approach. This two-stage process benefits the story with a heartfelt tone *and* a meaningful polish.

It's okay to make mistakes in the first stage. Your first cut is not an exact science, but it should still feel "right." Try not to think too hard about it, feel it—just try to replicate your natural eye movements with the cuts, and don't stop. There'll be plenty of time to take a step back and recut based on more reflective decisions.

Tim Squyres: Rachel Getting Married *is probably the one that I came closest to what feels like switching it live. That was kind of the way I approached some of the scenes in that initially. Particularly there's a scene where a lot of musicians are performing and they shot two takes of that and each take was about 40 minutes, with five cameras, and, of course, they wanted them being film edited too. I let them play through and just switched it, put cameras in a way that felt good at the time. That kind of performance feel, a performance for them but a performance for me too. Something that Jonathan Demme one time had responded to, that the kind of spontaneity that you get that way he recognized it and liked it, that some of those things there's nothing you can really say about it except I like it. He was kind of excited, I think, by that way of editing, which I think is because he was excited by the footage.*

Tip

Get a simple USB numeric keypad that you use for accounting. They even make wireless ones with Bluetooth. Assign multicam angles to the device and cut right on the keypad.

When I'm cutting on the fly, I like to stand up and cut it as though I'm the director right in the truck: totally in the moment. *Then* I go back and clean it up. Because the first cut is in real time, the live on-the-fly method doesn't take long at all. Sometimes I can nail it in one or two takes before I do a more thoughtful trim. The second cut/cleanup can take just as long as method 2: laying bricks.

Laying Bricks: The Start-and-Stop Method

"Laying bricks" means to start and stop your cut by making careful decisions one shot at a time. I call it laying bricks because it seems to me like building a solid wall, one brick at a time. It's definitely a more logical and thoughtful approach than on the fly.

The start-and-stop approach reminds me of the days of linear editing, when every edit had to be decided right then and there, to avoid having to recut the end of the show each time a change was made. You really had to live with each decision, so more thought went into each one. Some editors prefer the start-and-stop cut to on the fly because it can feel more organic and creative. Instead of teasing out the heart and soul of the show, you *give* it its heart and soul.

Approaches to Editing

Thom Zimney: *I don't operate the multicam in the standard sort of way. I really screen the cameras like dailies. The whole thing of watching multiple cameras at once, I will do that just to get a sense of the flow of movement from what's going on stage, but I will screen cameras isolated. That comes from an approach of working in narrative film. So I treat it more like traditional dailies where I will watch camera 1 with [Bruce Springsteen's] vocal, for example, on a concert. I will spend the time just watching that through. When I get into actually cutting, I use the multicam to switch the cameras around within the timeline, but I never get into the zone of having my dailies window being multiple cameras.*

Manny Donio worked as my multicam assistant editor syncing *Aerosmith: You Gotta Move.* Now he is an editor cutting network TV shows including *Dog: The Bounty Hunter* and many others.

Manny Donio, editor: *On "Fight Quest," a multicamera vérité show I worked on for the Discovery Channel, the open demonstration and final fight were shot with four cameras and a jib. Everything I used was grouped in the edit; there was no line cut. It was start-and-stop-type editing. I prefer to "lay the bricks" and get the edits right as I go. … I'm very analytical about my editing [laughs].*

Gary Bradley, editor *The Met: Live in HD: I'm pretty careful. I look for everything to work as I go along. With this material (opera), I'm not going to step back and just roll footage and start popping cuts in. For one thing, you find that these camera operators have very specific assignments and their assignment is to give that shot and then move on to the next one, which in many cases has already been scripted, and in between they're generally finding that new subject, framing the shot up, making last-minute adjustments, et cetera. There's not all that much extra footage.*

Ray Volkema, editor, HDNet: *I start over completely. I use the line cut as a template, but in a two-hour concert there's a lot of room to fine-tune it for screen viewers. I don't often do a live punch on a timeline. I like to slow down, break it down, and take my time. The reason you're doing this is to get the best angles—and if you have nine angles, there's a lot to check.*

So "slowing it down" is a good way to work, too. But there's also a third.

Adding Edits

This method combines live on-the-fly editing with the start-and-stop method—using the Add Edit button.

With an Add Edit button mapped to your keyboard as a hot key, you can cut a multiclip on the fly and place Add edit marks without having to decide which angle to cut to right at that moment. After the live cut is done, you can go back and still lay your "bricks" (i.e., switch your angles and do your trimming). This hybrid approach allows you to get a great cut with a natural feel and rhythm while still reserving for yourself the opportunity to start and stop for more analytical decisions.

Peter Chakos, A.C.E.: *I almost never cut on the fly. I'm a bricklayer, and almost every edit is a pullup or tighten. One cut at a time. I know which camera is which, and I just start putting the show together. If I have to check coverage rapidly, I'll just arrow through it. I Add edits and use the arrow keys to switch to the next angle. Because I'm building it film style, when I stop I usually know which camera I'm going to go to because I've already seen it during the shoot.*

Dan Lebental, A.C.E., owner of Splice, Inc., cuts big studio action and comedy movies like *Iron Man* and *Couples Retreat.*

He also has an extensive history cutting rap music videos for artists like Snoop Dog, Ice Cube, and NRW. So he's an editor with a highly valuable combination of multicam skills: great comical *and* musical timing.

Dan Lebental, A.C.E.: *Before I was a feature guy, I was a music video guy and I lived in multicam. I would lay down the one cut and add my Add edits and start making cuts according to the beats, just going down my angle list until I found the best one for that moment.*

Action: Explosive Editing

If action is what you want, all you need is Robert Downey, Jr., and a couple of cameras. Bam. *Iron Man.* In this big action film that employed multiple cameras on almost every setup, the scenes are really exciting. Certainly they were exciting to shoot: often, there wasn't going to be a second chance. Chases, explosions, and fights are fun to edit and audiences love them.

Dan Lebental, A.C.E.: *Say you're going to take down a building. That's a one-er. There's no take 2. So they're going to line up as many cameras as they can and run all of them. Then multicam helps me make decisions very quickly. I can see the beginning of the explosion and, if I want to triple cut it, I can just cut one in, do Add edit, and then do roll back a few frames on the next one, and do Add edit, roll back, the next, and so on. Within a minute, I can show you a triple or quadruple cut of a huge explosion.*

The power in grouped clips is the speed at which you can find the shots you need.

Dan Lebental, A.C.E.: *Lots of times, I'm not using multicam just for sync. I'm using it as a fast way to get to footage. Now it's laid out right in front of me. Everything in that group is at my fingertips. I'm not reaching in and searching through bins for it; I've got it right there.*

Another way to use multicam (even if you don't have matching timecode) is to group the shots by a common visual—like the explosion. A case in point is a feature that David Helfand edited with huge action scenes. They were shot with eight cameras, but the cameras weren't all synced or matched.

David Helfand: *They had a few primary cameras and then they'd try and get all the different angles they could possibly grab. They'd give the producers little cameras, the director would shoot an alternate angle, they'd mix 16-millimeter Bolexes with 35 Arris, et cetera—just grabbing whatever angles they could from whoever was available. It was like, "Got a pair of hands? Here's a camera."*

But they didn't all have slates on them, the coverage didn't relate, and the project wasn't set up as a grouped, multicam project.

David Helfand: *For those kinds of scenes, I might try to find match points (like an explosion) between various takes and use some of the other options to sync all the shots together. I'd give myself the benefit of a group even though it wasn't planned that way.*

Once he'd synced everything by eye to the explosion itself, Helfand was able to use multicam to cut the scene however he liked: as a straight cut or repeating the action using triple cuts.

Quick Start to Multicam Editing

In Avid:

1. Place the clips to be grouped in a bin.
2. Sort the bin by name or tape to have the order of the angles in the group clip.
3. Select the cameras that you want to group and choose Group clips (Shift-command-G).
4. Select the grouping option by in-point, source timecode, or Aux timecode.
5. A group clip with all the elements from the cameras is created in the bin.
6. Load the group clip in the source monitor to see the split screen.
7. Edit the group clip into a sequence.
8. Turn on multicam mode (Shift-command-M).
9. Play the sequence.
10. Use mapped keyboard buttons to choose angles on the fly.

In FCP:

1. Place clips to be grouped in a folder.
2. Arrange the viewing angles in order with the angle column or sort the browser.
3. Select the cameras you want to group and choose Make multiclip (right-click on selected clip icons or use the pulldown menu: > modify > make multiclip).
4. Select the multiclip option by in-point, source timecode, or Aux timecode.
5. A multiclip with all the elements from the cameras is created in the bin.
6. Load the multiclip in the source monitor to see the split screen.
7. Edit the group clip into a sequence.
8. Open the sync between the canvas and the viewer.
9. Turn on multiclip playback from the RT Sequence pulldown menu, and adjust playback and frame rate to dynamic with unlimited real time.
10. Play the sequence and use mapped keyboard buttons or click on angles directly in the browser to choose angles on the fly.

Editing is probably the most important part of production because it's where sins are forgiven and greatness is established out of mediocrity.

Mark Haefeli, producer/director Paul McCartney: The Space Within US

Working with Line Cuts

The reason that the line cut came about, and the tradition of cutting from the line cut, was in the beginning of TV, the people who worked on sitcoms, spliced with razor blades and tape and the editors were essentially engineers who could physically splice tape but they really weren't editors, they were technicians. That's also why the tradition was established on taped shows for the associate director to sit with the editor and actually help him or her put together the show.

Darryl Bates, A.C.E.: *On* Head of the Class *I just threw away the line cut. I wasn't a technical guy. I was an editor. So I felt like that was a workflow that was part of a bygone era and said, I'm just going to throw this out and do it myself. I could do it very fast with multicam, and if I can't tell you where you should be in a show, I shouldn't be an editor.*

Fixing line cuts as opposed to recutting with ISOs is common on sports and music productions.

Some directors may allow time to load the line cut plus all the angles so the line cut is available as a guide for the recut. Yet another possibility is that the line cut is combined with one or two auxiliary angles to accomplish the necessary fixes.

Mitch Owgang, producer, *Great Performances* on PBS: *Every show is going to be different, because every line cut is different. In some cases, you could air the line cut itself. But then if you have the opportunity to make it better, shouldn't you? If you don't have to go live, you get to come back and reexamine some of those things that maybe you missed the first or second time around.*

In any case, the line cut should be treated like any other source footage: properly jam-synced and its tapes numbered, logged, and loaded.

Oliver Peters: *A trap to bear in mind when cutting or trying to patch the line cut is that you might decide that you like a certain camera angle, so you cut to that angle instead of what the director picked ... but then, lo and behold, two shots later, the director went to the same shot. So you wind up fixing not just 10% of the shots, but 30%, 40%, or even 50% of them.*

On *The Rachael Ray Show*, six ISOs and one line cut are shot and the four editors usually just fix the line cut and get it ready for output. Says editor, Matthew Illardo:

Watching the line cut, we'll just see which camera is late on a shot and sometimes the camera will move awkwardly, so we'll switch to another ISO. We also create pieces at the end of each act, as well as an open.

In remote productions, the line cut has become so common that many clients ask for one even if it isn't necessary. If the show isn't airing live or being used for any kind of quick turnaround, then the line cut may be a casual or even gratuitous experience.

Hamish Hamilton, director, 82nd Academy Awards (2010): *Sometimes clients want a line cut and I have to say, "What's the point of me giving you a line cut? I'm not going to concentrate on it because this isn't live." The vision switcher (TD) can do a line cut if he or she wants, but I don't pay any attention to it. It's a waste of time. Even without it, you can see what you've got and you can see what you're missing and I tend to make sure I've got all my angles covered.*

Thom Zimney: *I walk away from the line cut. The line cut gives me pure reality and I feel like the editor's job in these live shows is to enhance the reality and also, again, be invisible and seamless so that the music is doing the talking. After an early initial viewing of the concert. I never work off of a line cut and will not go back to the line cut.*

The Flip-Flop and Producer's ISO Tape

A line cut can also be fixed with one tape using a flip-flop ISO master. A flip-flop ISO records the preset bus of the switcher as well as the program bus. The preset bus is what camera is going to be up next.

Mark Schubin, Multiple Emmy™ award-winning SMPTE Fellow: *If you're doing a cut from, say, camera 2 to camera 5, then you'll go from camera 2 to camera 5 on your program record, and you'll go from camera 5 to camera 2 on your preset record. What that allows you to do in post is if you didn't call the cut at the right moment, or if the vision mixer didn't do the cut at the right moment, then you'll have both ends of that cut and you'll be able to move it in post.*

This enables the editor to fix the line cut with two tapes: the line cut and the flip-flop ISO.

Gary Bradley: *TV directors didn't get a lot of ISOs back in the day. They had what was called a preset ISO, which the director physically preset to the camera he wanted to go to, or he would set up a flip-flop ISO that takes the preview window—and then, when the TD hit it, it would "flop" down. You had a head and tail trim, which was very good, in a way. We would stick to the line cut, and if it were 10 frames early, we'd just go back 10 frames, add/edit, and put in the preset ISO.*

Sometimes, the producer switches his own version. The producer can select, among the cameras that aren't being recorded full time, what seems to be appropriate. Many times the editors will switch the ISO; after all, who knows best what they need to edit with?

Re-creating the Line Cut in Post

Re-creating the line cut with Add edits in order to connect to group clips and trim might seem like a slow and daunting task. But with new software options, it can be miraculously fast. One new method is to record the switcher commands from the GPI output. The metadata can be used with LiveCut to add edits to a digitized line cut in seconds. (See DVD Bonus Chapter: On-Set Editing: Live Cut.) Another way is to start with the line cut and rebuild it by hand, cut by cut.

Figure 12.1 LiveCut will record the switcher commands via a GPU interface. The resulting file can create addedits into a digitized line cut. (Courtesy Christof Halasz, Livecut.)

Gary Bradley: *I've gotten into the habit of screening the line cut and, at the same time, marking every camera cut and then going back to replace each shot from its ISO. It's a tedious process, but it does start to familiarize you with the project's problems, so it's not a total loss. It also gives you an opportunity to adjust the cuts, move them up and down, and so on.*

Many programs would never come together without a line cut serving as your basic road map—the turnaround time required would make it impossible. But there are still times you need to cut something or pull a show up to time and even the line cut forsakes you.

Laura Young, editor on *Great Performances: Carnegie Hall Opening Night*: *What I would do if I didn't like something I saw in the line cut, I would try a new shot, and then I would gang my line cut and my groups together and just look and see which one in that still frame looks better to me, and pop it in. Then see if it holds up.*

Sometimes it doesn't hold up. It's like a house of cards. You move one shot or flip a wide for a tight and the whole vibe gets out of whack. You need to go back and watch the whole song again. Sometimes you even have to throw out the line cut and start from scratch.

Laura Young: *And a lot of times, I noticed [that] by changing a few edits it would totally destroy the whole pacing of the entire song. And if I had to make that change as it was, I would have to go reedit the whole song and just adjust the pacing.*

Or you have to cheat it.

Multicam saves my ass on a daily basis.

Anonymous

Cheating a Shot

Once your show is cut to time, you can use one or more multicam "cheats" to fix the trouble spots. When you're dealing with already synced material, "slipping" a shot will cause that shot to be out of sync—but sometimes that's okay because that's how you can "cheat" it.

Figure 12.2 "Cheating" a shot by slipping.

It's called *cheating* because, in order to cover up a mistake or a cut that just doesn't feel right, you deliberately slip an angle in the group out of sync. You may be covering to pull up a moment that needs more or less time and a quick cutaway, or maybe you need to remove a distraction in the frame.

Thom Zimney: *I use markers and I really believe in the replace edits and setting up structures with add edits at times where cheats are needed—then going in and sliding things whenever necessary. So if a head turn does fall on beat, and it feels obvious, I will slide a frame just so it's a little less conscious.*

Cheating runs rampant in the edit room when you encounter continuity problems.

Matthew Illardo: *Sometimes when our host talks, her hands move around a lot—or one of the guests will be very animated and move his or her hands or head. If they get in the other person's one-shot, then we can't use it. We can't use it for pullups, because the hand will be waving, and then in the next shot you can clearly see that the hand isn't waving. So then we'll just go forward in the multicam until we find a spot where the hand isn't in the picture at all.*

Alternatively, you could try to cover it with an audience shot. Sometimes an audience shot needs to be cheated.

Matthew Illardo: *We'll scan forward to try to find a shot of someone in the audience nodding or doing something else that makes him or her look interested. Just keep slipping through the audience ISO until you get the perfect audience reaction—then make a quick tweak and on to the next edit.*

When you need to tell a story, cheating is fair game.

Thom Zimney: *I have no problem to build one cohesive version. I don't even see it as cheating, it's part of the job to tell a story and if using a shot from another night that doesn't take you out of context of the song, it's like using camera takes. "Live in New York" we covered three nights, and with the song "10th Avenue Freeze Out," I used all three nights to tell that story.*

Scott Simmons: *In music videos, in songs, it's great because you can cheat the chorus, and not necessarily the verses but just moments, you can always cheat them. So you can really get a lot of the really good stuff even if it happened all in the same chorus. So did I answer your question about splits there?*

Layering Multiclips for PiP Effects

On some shows, the directors ask for a picture-in-picture look. You know it: multiple boxes designed (or cluttered) in a frame—like the TV show *24* or the original film *Woodstock*.

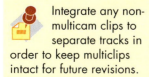

Tip

Integrate any non-multicam clips to separate tracks in order to keep multiclips intact for future revisions.

Figure 12.3 Three identical multiclips stacked for a multicamera picture-in-picture layering effect.

A really great and fast way to set this up with multicam options is to duplicate group clips and put them directly above the originals on the next track. Stack a duplicate group on each track above for every picture within the picture design. Now you have the ability to use your motion tabs to size-down individual angles within the groups to design the screen—plus you have the options to switch or decide which cameras go in there. Editing is a real breeze within the full-screen design, because you can switch any picture any time to any angle. If you save out the PiP FX parameters, then it's equally easy to resize any shot, anytime, with the same parameters of the look you design.

Ganging Pop-up Monitors

Not to be confused with those pesky pop-up windows that are always trying to sell you something online, Avid pop-up windows are just another way of looking at a clip.

If you run out of angles in Avid's two-bank/18-camera limitation or want to work with one bank and pop-up monitors, there's no limit to the number of clips you can sync up. The great

> **Tip**
>
> You can view a clip by option-clicking on the clip and up will pop what looks like a mini-source window containing all the buttons and info that you see in your regular source window.

multicam advantage to pop-up windows is that you can gang them to your sequence or group clip and keep them open during editing. But it's like a poor man's multicam: the pop-up monitors do not run continuously.

Figure 12.4 Pop-up clip of a line cut ganged to a group clip.

This way you can see the corresponding angle and cut it in if you need it. It's a perfect way to get around the Avid 18-cam limit. There are other uses too.

Michael Phillips, Avid Technology, Inc.: *Color correction has three windows, which I call previous, current, and next. And I pop up the sequence that I am actually working on as a pop-up and gang that to my existing sequence and use that to drive my whole sequence and my color corrector. I can jump anywhere I want in the timeline.*

Tim Squyres, editor, Taking Woodstock: *When I'm assembling, I use pop-up windows constantly. I don't use them much after that, but I have every tape open in a pop-up monitor. Sometimes I gang them if I'm doing something complicated. There's one sequence I was working with where I had six cameras running simultaneously and they weren't grouped, just layered in a sequence and I did a whole bunch of picture-in-pictures. The computer can't keep up and you have to knock the quality way down just so you can play through it.*

Avid ScriptSync

In my opinion, multicam is the coolest feature/mode in digital nonlinear editing. The second-coolest feature? ScriptSync.

ScriptSync is an Avid mode that allows you to automate the process of using the line script with digitized clips and group-clips. It's an editing mode that allows you to match up the script supervisor's line script with the clips, subclips, or group clips as takes and edit directly from the script.

The combination of multicam and ScriptSync is a one-two knockout punch: a deadly combination of the best in time savings and capabilities the editing world has to offer. Interestingly, it's not new; it's just not thought of very often outside sitcoms filmed in California, but a lot of drama shows and some movie editors are starting to catch on. It's a technology that Avid bought from another editing system called Ediflex, which pioneered it.

Robert Bramwell, A.C.E., has cut multicam sitcoms for years and won an Emmy for *Cheers*. He is also something of a ScriptSync guru and evangelist. Back in the day, he taught multicam on Laser Edit to fellow editors who were getting off the Moviola Monster and moving into an optical disk. Laser Edit was a big step up from film editing, but it was also a bit clunky, with timecode forcing you to enter numbers all the time. When Avid and ScriptSync came out, it was a breath of fresh air.

Robert Bramwell, A.C.E.: *I grew up in the era going from timecode-based CMX, Laser Edit, and then into the nonlinear systems. It was awesome. In addition to CMX 6000, Ediflex, Ediflex Digital, Avid, and Lite Works, I used Heavy Works on some multicam shows. The last few episodes of* Cheers, *I cut on a system called EPIX, a Canadian machine. Fred Chandler was running Paramount Post and he helped champion the use of nonlinear systems. He went around to all the shows and was looking for guys to try out Avid and ScriptSync. I couldn't wait. I embraced it. To me it's a revolution in editing. I can't go backwards and edit what we call bin-style editing. I love seeing the script right in front of me. I really don't use the bins. I'm staring at the script the entire time.*

The system allows you to import a text file and Avid will digitally "read" the script, which will then correspond to the takes that you synchronize with it. It uses phonetic voice recognition to line the script for you. It listens to the track and recognizes the script information using a phonetic engine—the same engine that the government uses to record and listen to all our telephone calls.

Nick Houy started as an intern at Post Works, worked his way up to apprentice on a film called *The Lucky Ones,* and joined the Motion Picture Editors Guild. He worked on Michel Gondry's

18   CONTINUED (2)   18

Off Stabler -- what the

19   INT. INTERROGATION ROOM #1 - NIGHT   19

Cragen, Benson with Haggerty and her attorney, Joan
Quentin, mid-30's, polished.

                    QUENTIN
          My client should be lauded for what
          she's done, not arrested.

                    BENSON
          Your client kept five 14-year-olds
          whose parents reported them kidnapped
          or as runaways.

                    HAGGERTY
          I just wanted to help them. They left
          home because their parents mistreated
          them.

                    CRAGEN
          And you know this how?

                    QUENTIN
          Mrs. Haggerty has a Masters in Child
          Psychology.

                    CRAGEN
          Then she understands that just because
          a teenager disagrees with her parents
          doesn't mean the parents did something
          wrong.

                    BENSON
          Mrs. Haggerty, who pays your salary?

                    QUENTIN
          The Foundation's board of directors.
          The funds come from charitable
          contributions.

                    BENSON
          Dr. Garrett Lang owns the building. He
          on that board too?

                    QUENTIN
          No. He started the foundation and
          provided the initial endowment. But he
          has no other dealings with the
          Foundation or any employees or clients.

                                        CONTINUED

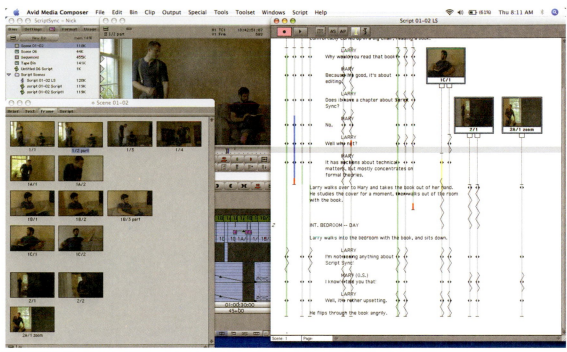

Figure 12.6 The imported line script and corresponding clips. (Courtesy Nick Houy.)

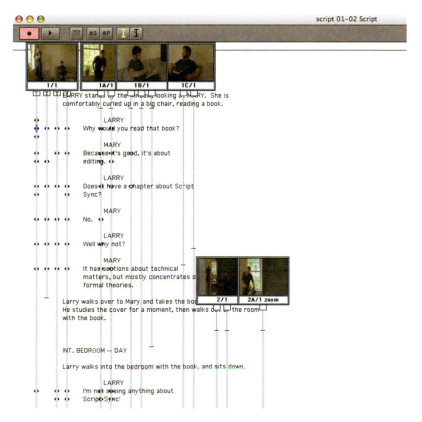

Figure 12.7 The line script imported to Avid ScriptSync. (Courtesy Nick Houy.)

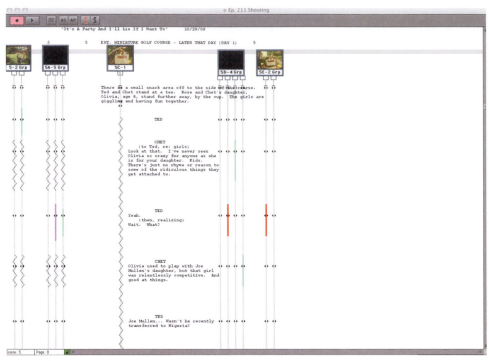

Figure 12.8 The Avid line script with group clips. (Courtesy Robert Bramwell, A.C.E.)

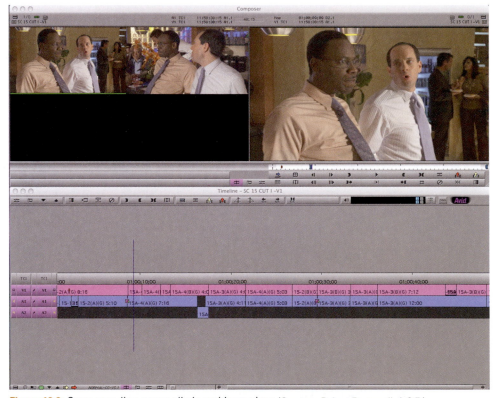

Figure 12.9 Corresponding group clip in multicam view. (Courtesy Robert Bramwell, A.C.E.)

segment of *Tokyo.* Recently he assisted on the Michael Douglas movie *Solitary Man* and is a proponent of ScriptSync.

Nick Houy: *The way to think of it is in a feature or scripted environment. You take the line script and you bring it into Avid. So it's an all-in-one sort of tool, allowing you literally to see everything that's covered visually at a glance and access the footage from that line script directly.*

Previously misconceived as a slow setup process, ScriptSync used to have to be lined manually in Avid, which was time intensive. You would follow the script somewhere near the top and bottom and add a few marks to orientate the clip with the script. Then you would add more marks throughout the script to ensure better accuracy.

Now, with the benefit of voice recognition being able to match up footage against the transcription, your nuts-and-bolts search time is reduced so much that you can't help but benefit creatively. No longer bogged down by looking for stuff, if you think of something, you find a line, and you can get to it immediately.

Says editor Scott Simmons:

This idea of script-based editing comes from feature film editing and the job of the script supervisor, who will physically line the script on set so the editor will know what the takes are, what's covered, who's on and off camera for each line, and any other information that might benefit the editor. In theory, to have an electronic lined script there in the editing application facilitates the editor's access to individual takes.

Robert Bramwell, A.C.E.: *Thank goodness it's so easy to use. You just drag the groups over into the script, run ScriptSync, and away you go—unless there are restarts, in which case you have to do the subclips. You can just click on any line of dialogue and match back from where you are to your group clips. When producers say I want to see another take on that performance—on that line of dialogue, now you just match back to the script and then you're playing the lines of the dialogue seconds later.*

Nick Houy: *I'm building a database in my script. But I would recommend breaking it up because ScriptSync can tax your system. It's just like a bin. If a bin has 60 billion items in it, it's going to start to slow down your system. That's why you sometimes put reels in separate bins: because when you open a bin and there are six reels in it and they're all full, it slows you down. It's just like that with ScriptSync. You have to think of scripts as bins, so you want to break them up into scene bins.*

It's really quite simple once you get the hang of it, and it is perfect to use with any scripted show, documentaries, and interviews with transcripts. Next time your producer says, "I need that part where the guy says [phrase]," you can search for the phrase in your script, double-click on it, and like magic it will appear in the source window, parked on the phrase requested. You can even cut directly from the script into the sequence.

David Helfand: *I've come to rely on ScriptSync and use it almost exclusively for 99% of my editing. In multicamera comedies, the way it's shot is much more structured because all your coverage is basically there together in one take—you don't have a separate line for master and a separate line for the medium shot and close-ups. It's all there in one take, which is much easier to implement.*

ScriptSync is a great feature, but a secondary notion. People don't realize until they get into it how powerful it is. For instance, try using ScriptSync for dialogue editing. It goes beyond satisfying the editor's basic need to find things fast.

David Helfand: *If I need a certain word, or even a certain consonant from a certain character. ... Let's say you can't understand a word said by a certain character—maybe I need a J or a K or something that got caught on a word, or maybe there was a big noise in the background that obscured it, and I never had it available in that particular take—if I have a whole episode, or a whole series of episodes scripting, I can just do a text search in the script looking for words from that character and immediately go to them and find them.*

The result is that you can use the Avid Scripting function to look at your scene and takes versus just typing in timecode or using multigroups.

Darryl Bates, A.C.E.: *A multicam show means we don't have to use multigroups anymore, because we don't type in timecode; we just simply click on the material in the script and that takes us to whatever take we wanted to use. So we could actually get back to using scene and take information, which is nice. In the script, you can work with anyplace in the scene that you want, without having to type in timecode info.*

Basically, with ScriptSync you don't need to do multigroups, because you can take individual group clips by take and line them to the script. If you were working with multigroups and you get a pickup shot later, you're not able to add it to a multigroup. Physically it doesn't work. Not in Avid. But with ScriptSync, you could add a pickup shot as another take to your script, any time.

Additional time-saving benefits include color-coding the scripts and the ability to do searches. You can make edits from the script, which is really great because it saves that whole step of queuing it up and cutting it in and then you can go and refine it later.

Robert Bramwell, A.C.E.: *There's nothing like ScriptSync; it's a godsend. A real revolution. And I want Avid to continue to add resources and make that product better and better. It's phenomenal what it can do. And multicam editing ... I love being able to put the multicam to your source monitor quickly and live cut. There's nothing like it.*

CUTTING MUSIC

The Symphonic Cut: Classical and Opera Television

The way we do multicam is the way television was done back in the '50s, when it was essentially invented by a few craftsmen with a score and a script.

David Horn, executive producer, *Great Performances*

One of the directors who pioneered television concert performance programs in the United States is Kirk Browning. He was the director of NBC Opera Theatre and directed many of the Toscanini broadcasts at Carnegie Hall in the late 1940s and early 1950s.

Browning was not a professional musician but, he directed from the musical score. He would decide which camera he wanted for any given measure or note and whether it should be a close-up or wide shot or two-shot, and he would write that into his score. The producers and assistants would devise their script from that.

Figure 13.1 Score from Leonard Bernstein's *West Side Story: Symphonic Dances,* featuring camera direction by Gary Halvorson. (Courtesy Leonard Bernstein Foundation/wnet.org.)

Doi: 10.1016/B978-0-240-81176-5.00013-7

Today, the Browning tradition continues, with Peabody- and Emmy Award–winning series programs like PBS's *Great Performances* and the Metropolitan Opera's *The Met: Live in HD.* They are the best in classical music and opera television in the world. They have the best crews and equipment, and every piece of the puzzle is planned well in advance. The one thing The Met *doesn't* have is a safety net. Live is live.

Pulling off a live show requires careful preparation and, most important, a script. Then it's up to the director to understand the talent and serve the performance. There are many ways to direct television, depending on whether it's a sitcom, musical performance, opera, or awards show. Gary Halvorson is one of the few directors who has mastered them all.

Gary Halvorson: *The unifying factor is that they are all driven by performance, by the artist itself. Our job is to interpret and highlight the accents or other positive contributions the performer is bringing.*

The production team has everything it needs to ensure the artistic interpretation is fully realized, thanks to what's called a no-holds-barred production.

Mark Schubin, Engineer-in-Charge (EIC), *The Met: Live in HD: The main function of the truck is for directing and engineering, plus additional functions for score reader, lighting people, graphics, and teleprompter. In the audio room, we're doing an upmix from stereo to 5.1. Just before the show, we send out multiple feeds.*

For some shows, like operas, subtitling is a big deal. Cinemas and networks all over the world expect to receive subtitles in their own language.

Gary Halvorson: *An opera script is very similar to a sitcom script. The approach is the same: you script the shots according to the action in the story. You start with the story and you work your compositions and your shot movement and everything else to tell that story the best way you can, pictorially.*

For symphonies and other musical performances, in lieu of a worded script, you would use a score and score reader.

Interpreting the Score as a Script

Many seasoned directors methodically plan every shot, every move, every cut. Being familiar with the score, a director doesn't have to keep a camera on the percussionist for 40 minutes if the percussionist is going to hit the cymbal or triangle only once. The director knows exactly when that hit is going to be—and when a camera operator needs to be ready to shoot it. The "score as a script" technique takes us back to the beginning of television production.

Figure 13.2 Shot 104, camera 9, on snare drum and shot 105, camera 12, on trumpets. Score from Leonard Bernstein's *West Side Story: Symphonic Dances,* featuring camera direction by Gary Halvorson. (Courtesy Leonard Bernstein Foundation/wnet.org.)

John Walker, producer, *Great Performances* on PBS: *In the '50s and '60s, networks worked in a set methodology. Whether it was a studio shoot or a remote shoot with a multicamera truck, all three networks generated the same type of ethic for shoots. And that included whether it was an arts program, sports program, or a live event. It was all done in the same way.*

When PBS was started, many of the people who came to PBS originally came from the networks and brought with them the method that they knew worked. The difference was the content. WNET, producers of *Great Performances*, pledged to the artists to make the programming on par with or better than anything a viewer would see on the networks.

David Horn is executive producer of *Great Performances* and a director of many of its classical TV programs.

David Horn: *Pioneering multicamera directors had to do live television and storytelling. You could not just wing it.*

Director Gary Halvorson and coordinating producer Cara Constentino (who acts as a liaison between Halvorson and the crew, including editors) work from an amazingly detailed shot-by-shot script based on the actual symphonic score.

Figure 13.3 Shot 106, camera 3, on conductor with a dolly move and pedestal up. Score from Leonard Bernstein's *West Side Story: Symphonic Dances,* featuring camera direction by Gary Halvorson. (Courtesy Leonard Bernstein Foundation/wnet.org.)

In other words, Halvorson decides what shots he wants based on the music and produces his shot script by writing those shots right into the score.

Gary Halvorson: *Most directors of televised symphonic music are trying to interpret a score. What's important is to build the overall arc of the piece. You may want to hear the countermelody; that might be more important to you. I read music, and without seeing it I'm lost. I work on a piano vocal if it's an opera, or on a full conductor's score if it's a piece of orchestral music.*

David Horn: *I direct primarily with a score because, particularly if you have a limited amount of rehearsal, the score is always right. You have to be respectful of the music and its dramatic moments and at the same time help to tell its story. You need to think about when you need to be wide, when you need a two-shot, when you need to be focused on a person performing an important moment, rather than looking at background. Foreshadowing plays into it. It's a process. A craft.*

The Score Reader

A score reader prepares the score for scripting and, during production, sits in the TV truck and tracks where the performance is in the score, so the director—even one who does not read music fluently—can glance down at any time and see where he or she is. Obviously, a score reader must be proficient in reading music.

The score reader starts by typing up a shooting script—which in the case of an opera, which has a libretto, involves identifying word cues. In any case, score readers must ensure that every line ends on a musical note so that directors know whether or not they are ordering a musically appropriate cut.

Figure 13.4 Technical director Emmett Loughran reviews his shooting script.

Mark Schubin: *She'll provide lots of extra space in there for times when there might be a musical interlude and the director might want to have several shots. Then that's distributed to the director and assistant director, and they enter their notes on that.*

Figure 13.5 Adding notes to shooting script.

When the script is ready, the AD interprets the score into a shooting script for all crewmembers who don't read music. This is done by highlighting lyrics or counts or beats of a specific instrument—or points in the score when a new instrument is about to solo.

John Walker, producer, *Great Performances: The AD is always considering the shot coming up, always one step ahead. Then the director sees the shot and calls it to the technical director. Ideally, all three people—the director, AD, and TD, who's pushing the buttons—are musicians who can read music comfortably. (The TD has the score in front of him, too.)*

Figure 13.6 Score for opera at the subtitle station.

In opera, there is a passive score reader, one who just keeps a finger on the score so the director can note where he or she is. On symphony shows, there's a more active score reader. That reader is counting down the tempo of the score for each shot. So if it's shot 256, the reader will say, in tempo, *256 in 3, 2, 1*—and everyone knows that on *zero* it's time for the appropriate cut. Everyone gets a feel for it.

Mark Schubin: *The camera guys like to listen to the score reader, whose cues come along a program feed into their headsets. Usually they have two different controls: one tuned to the program and one to the intercom, so they can hear as much of the score reader as they want.*

The shooting scripts are also divided into a shot list for each camera operator. The AD can produce a timeline of shots and then, with this rudimentary shot-sheet program, separate out each camera's shots and print individual scrolls called camera rolls.

Camera Rolls

Great Performances is never shot with zone coverage. It's scripted with numbered shot sheets. Each cameraman is on all the time. You can never make a move that isn't airable.

Gary Bradley, editor

Camera rolls are used more often in classical productions precisely because they scroll. However, this method of tracking shots is unique to New York and even more specific to classical music concerts. On the West Coast, camera operators tend to use shot cards instead. They write out their shots on long, thin pieces of cardboard, punch a ring through the stack, and keep the cards near the camera controls.

The camera operator puts the camera roll into a small box equipped with rollers. Designed by Jake Ostroff, these rollers are basically MacGyvered from an electrical outlet box (available in any hardware store) fastened with rubber bands and toilet paper rollers. They are mounted just above their cameras' viewfinders with a jerry-rigged reading nightlight clamped to the side so you have a little bit of light.

Figure 13.7 Camera with shot roll in makeshift scroller box. (Courtesy Mark Schubin)

The wait between focusing on the cellos and the violins can be 40 minutes in a musical piece, and the camera operator can't spend this entire time flipping cards. During the shoot, camera operators use one hand to scroll through the shots and the other to manipulate the camera. Once a shot is done, a camera operator scrolls to the next one and sees, *my next shot is a three shot of the hero.* Or of the soprano. Or, *my next shot is a full figure; two dancers, they break; carry the left dancer as they break.* Then the camera operator scrolls again, and the next shot might be a close-up of this dancer or that singer. The camera operator is always prepared.

This method isn't easy, but Great Performances' producer, Mitch Owgang says it works. It's an old design that we all kind of laugh at, but if it works, don't change it. If it isn't broken, don't fix it.

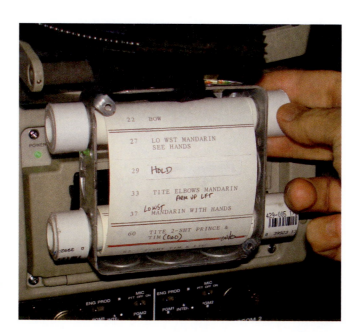

Figure 13.8 Close-up of scroller and shot sheet roll. (Courtesy Mark Schubin)

Mark Schubin: *I think they're the best. No one has come up with anything better. There was a German machinist who saw the shot sheet rollers and said, "Oh, this is a wonderful idea but it could be so much better." So he machined up this absolutely magnificent beautiful thing and they made multiple ones for the camera guys to use on their show, and then they got a ways into the show and every single camera guy couldn't get to the next shot. They tried and tried, but the inventor hadn't realized that the paper was going to build up more on one roll than the other. The rubber bands were fine with that because they were a perfect clutch, but the gearing couldn't deal with it, so now we're back to the rubber bands and it works fine.*

Meticulous Preparation

After the concert is shot, the footage is prepped by the production team at WNET headed by Sean Riordan and production coordinator Jermaine Pinnock. They organize the elements and digitize the clips at 4 to 1s for the editors. The tapes are given unique IDs, and the clips are meticulously labeled. It's all loaded at low-res and then the online is done in HD using DNX 145— spitting out to HD Cam 1080i tape.

Laura Young co-edits the Met and Carnegie Hall shows with Gary Bradley.

Laura Young: *It's a really big deal when you're working on a series like* Great Performances at the Met. *You can't just call things "Act 1," because every opera has an Act 1. So we have to say "Aida 1." You'll see what we call our bins and clips: at Carnegie Hall it's the handmade version of multicam identification. I don't think everybody uses our kind of labeling.*

ISOs are called CH (Carnegie Hall) OP (opening performance) 10 (the line cut) 11, 12, 13, 14, and so on, in ascending order of the ISOs.

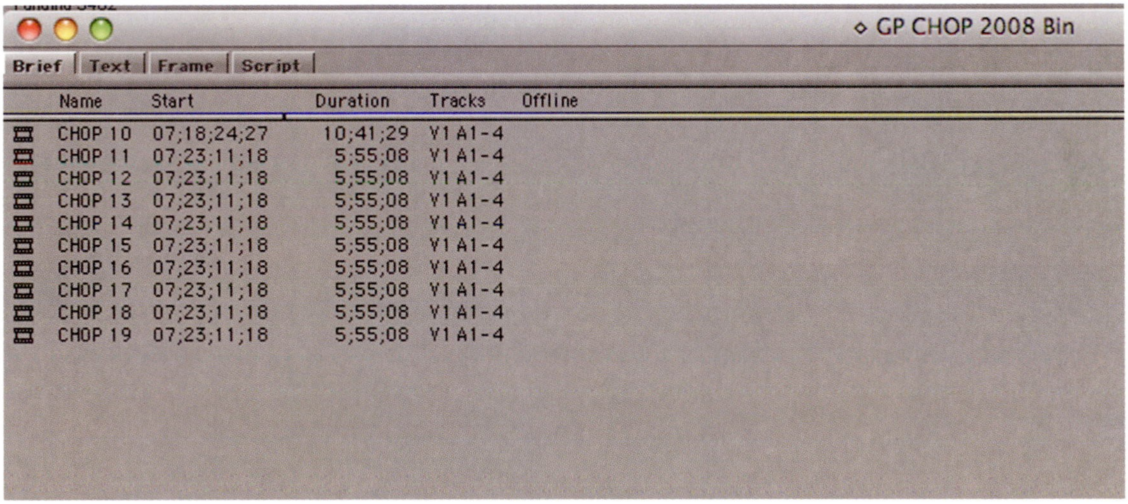

Figure 13.9 Avid bin with clips from line cut and each ISO.

Laura Young: *A lot of people will use the ABCD identification for cameras, but we've just gotten into this numbering system because it falls in line nicely in the bins and is easy to see in the quad split. When you hit the Alt key (Control on Mac), you get that drop-down menu and you can see what your ISOs are called. It's a really short, quickly identifiable version.*

In four letters or less I know exactly what camera and show I'm on. From AI13, I know I'm on Aida camera 3. Tosca TO14? Tosca camera 4.

Cutting from "The Book"

For the Carnegie and Met shows, Gary Bradley begins working with director Gary Halvorson to cut the concert while Young begins the interview sessions. They recreate the line cut basically by adding edits at every cut and then grouping them to the camera ISOs so they can switch and trim. It all starts with the director's original score notes—or "The Book," as they call it in post.

Gary Bradley: *That's the director's starting point. He'll mark the score up bar by bar with places where he thinks he's cutting to a new camera—or a place where he thinks he's starting a camera movement. You'll see these vertical markings dividing the score into visual after visual.*

Figure 13.10 Line cut recreated and grouped to ISOs with Add edits.

Laura Young: *We adjust everything either to make it match the director's script or to make it a little more musical, because they're late in the truck, or whatever else has happened.*

The 20-minute opening piece, the *West Side Story Symphonic Dances*, had 400 to 500 scripted live cuts. And then, in post, the editors added even more cuts for things that couldn't be done live.

Gary Bradley: *Let's say there's a 20-frame insert from a snare drum or pizzicato string instrument. How are you going to get it right on the beat in the line cut?*

Figure 13.11 Score notes from "The Book" for quick cuts (each circled numeral is a camera cut).

They get as much as they can in the line cut, but you really do need the opportunity to get that kind of precision right in post.

Gary Bradley: *When I'm working and I don't have Gary Halvorson (or whoever the director is) with me, I'll sometimes refer to the (score) book, because otherwise what you see in the line cut doesn't make any sense.*

Maybe the live cut has fallen behind the music. Or communication in the truck—among the score reader, the assistant director, the director, and the technical director (who's actually taking the shots on the video switcher)—has broken down. Often the problem is just that every cut is late by a second, in which case, referring to the book can sometimes help everyone reconstruct things more quickly to match the music.

Laura Young: *Mostly what I'm doing is just trimming the cut. I know that for the next five minutes I'm just trimming 10 to 15 frames and each cut is a little bit late, a little bit late, pulling things back just a little bit. I know that most of my camera angles are correct, so I'm just going to edit and trim until I get to an area that's no good—and then I'm going to have my ISOs available if I need them.*

Young likes to view full-frame shots in trim mode and switch to multicam as needed. She just watches until she finds the next edit and steps forward to the next edit, to the next edit, and so on.

Laura Young: *I'm in trim mode, but I'm not actually trimming. I want to watch in full screen, so I work with this trim on the 30-minute postroll and I can just keep playing as long as I want to. I'm trying to see what the director had in mind, because I don't have him sitting in the room with me. I want to see what he had in mind and then see what doesn't work and then what I have to edit to fix that.*

Slave to the Performance

No matter how hard we try to stay on the script, somehow we are slaves to the performance.

Gary Bradley: *Sometimes it's a script and sometimes it's not. You might have a script that's not working. In an opera, if the lead singer forgets a scripted moment and goes left when she's supposed to come right, to camera 1, you're sunk. You have to improvise. Your cuts have to follow the performance, which means you have to anticipate the unexpected.*

Laura Young: *We can have whatever we want in the script, but if the actors cross at the wrong time in a lyric, that angle is not going to work. It won't work even if it's in the script—because now, say, the singer's back is to us now when she's singing that lyric, so I can't use that shot anymore. We have to do something different.*

And then there are language barriers.

Laura Young: *You have to become very familiar with being able to hear certain words, or when a lyric begins, but it took a long time for me to get to that point, because I don't speak French, Italian, or German.*

In opera multicam, because the performance is so carefully mapped out in advance, when it *does* go as expected, the editors can tweak decisions or enhance them wherever possible.

Laura Young: *If you can find a better angle, try to use it. Sometimes, on a live event, the director in the truck didn't see that better angle and you want to give him that opportunity. You want to present him with something he couldn't see in the heat of the moment. Often we'll give him those little cutaways that he didn't get.*

Gary Halvorson: *I show the countermelody. Nobody ever sees the countermelody. And guess what? When you see the countermelody on television, you hear the countermelody. You always hear the melody; you may not see it, but you hear it. But rarely do you hear the basses, for example. Countermelodies are the driving soul of what makes a melody what it is. They enhance the violence, or anger, or love, or sweetness—whatever the emotions in a piece, the countermelodies and the accompaniment are behind them. They're what's making that flood of emotion come up through that single note.*

Sometimes, because an auditorium is so huge, you can't see certain things in the house. The editor and director are there to help you find a moment you may have missed live because there were too many cameras.

Gary Halvorson: *I don't show the obvious; I show the not-so-obvious, which in turn shows the genius of the composer. When you see all the inner workings of the orchestra, like the timpani player ready to go—and he's looking, and then he hits it—it builds a more emotional response to that moment in the music. Suddenly it's even more interesting.*

Syncing up the Theaters

Mark Schubin: *We're transmitting over satellite, which introduces a delay. We're going into a digital encoder, which introduces a delay. We're doing frame rate conversion, which introduces a delay. So we need to make sure that the audio is in sync and we're doing audio encoding of AC3, which introduces altogether, encode and decode, about seven frames of delay. We've calculated what the delay should be and we're subtracting that on our encoder, because it does more of a video delay. So we make sure the audio and video arriving at the receivers are in sync, but then those go into the theatrical systems that might have their own delay systems.*

Figure 13.12 A slate and a hand mic are used to generate sync tests to theaters over a satellite.

Cameras aren't the only things that need to be in sync for worldwide live opera transmissions. There's also the lip sync! After trying a number of lip-sync mechanisms, production teams all over the world agree that the basic clapboard works best. Back to basics.

Mark Schubin: *We do five minutes of opera and then five minutes of clapboard. Acoustically, depending on temperature and humidity, 37 feet is approximately the same as one frame of lip-sync error in the United States. It's a slightly different number outside North America. We don't have any body mics, so there will be some acoustic delays involved. Also, someone on a camera in the back of the cinema might be 150 feet back, which amounts to several frames of acoustic lip-sync delay, so that has to be adjusted for as well.*

The Lucy Leader

One of the many great things about *The Lucille Ball Show* was that Lucille Ball always made such exaggerated facial expressions. Now, more than 50 years later, those expressions are coming in handy again—in opera! The footage of *The Lucille Ball Show* was played at the top of the test tapes that were transmitted to the theaters. The exercise was to see if the lip sync was off between the picture and the sound and how much it varied from the first and last rows of the theater.

Mark Schubin: *The way she talked was a perfect lip-sync device. You can't do it with anybody else. We used to have this thing we called the Lucy Leader, and we'd just put it on the front of the tapes and from that we could tell whether lip sync for transmission was going well.*

Music-Cutting Techniques

Here are some common ways of cutting musical performances:
1. Cutting on the beat
2. Cutting before the downbeat
3. Cutting on the action

Cutting on the Beat

Sometimes the artists have a preference. I've had band members tell me they like cutting on the "2 and the 4." This means, for example, that in a 4/4 music time, the cuts are made on the second and fourth beats, as opposed to on the first and third. A common pattern is to hear a snare drum on 2 and 4 and a bass drum on 1 and 3. But if you do cut every single thing exactly on the beat, what you can end up with is mechanical and predictable.

Martin Baker started his career with the BBC in London fresh out of college. His background spans 14 years as a broadcast offline/online editor. He went on to become a director and editor at the ITV Network. Baker started on the Avid in 1995, and in 1999 he began his own company, Digital Heaven, which among other things developed the software package called Multicam Lite, a predecessor to the multicam feature in Final Cut.

Martin Baker: *One of my pet peeves in editing multicam music is that it's not editing law that you have to cut exactly on the beat, [although] a lot of beginners always assume you have to cut everything on the beat. It's more about the feel, which is actually what I prefer, to cut as I watch. I would just play the sequence and I would just cut on the keyboard where I felt I wanted to get this shot, where I wanted to go with that shot. And basically I'd do multiple passes. I'd go through it again, over and over again, and just basically refine it each time.*

Cutting Before the Downbeat

This technique is used a lot in symphonic music, but it can be applied to any genre. If there are four beats in a measure, then counting by sixteenth notes would sound like this: *one-ee-and-a-two-ee-and-a-three-ee-and-a-four-ee-and-a.* Instead of cutting on the 2 and the 4, you cut on the "a" just before it. This "softens" the cut.

David Horn: *So the picture arrives before the music happens, before the frame starts. And often during live rock and roll, they'll have to ride on the beat, and that's kind of the essence of how that music is done. Then, cutting before the downbeat isn't jarring. If the cut's late and it's jarring, that's usually because it's not properly positioned in the rhythm.*

Cutting on the Action

Sometimes it works better to avoid the beat altogether and cut on the action or vibe of the performance. When Steven Tyler does his world-famous stage spins and dance moves, he *is* the music. So I just follow his moves and cut on the action to enhance the natural excitement that he provides.

Thom Zimney, editor, *Springsteen's Wings for Wheels: The Making of Born to Run:* *With multicam, it's great to work with the movement of the performers, the way people cross the stage or move with the music. That's when I feel like the magic happens, because you really tap into what's going on onstage at that moment. You're not working with just the beat of the song or the drive of the song; you're working with the energy of the performers.*

Tip

Avoid Nesting

If you try to cut one sequence into another sequence in Final Cut, it will automatically become a nested sequence in the new sequence. You can assemble sequences without nesting by Command + dragging and dropping sequences from Viewer into the canvas to retain edits. You can also Command drag and drop into the insert or overwrite buttons to achieve the same effect.

Cutting Concerts: Track by Track

For concert productions, I like to cut each music track as a separate sequence for assembly into a show master later. This technique also works for separate sequences of scenes, acts, or segments of any kind. When assembling a show in Final Cut, I'll take those song sequences and cut them directly into the time-line (without nesting) by Command dragging and dropping into an insert or overwrite mode. This cuts the entire segments into the assembled master, leaving all edits intact. Otherwise, these segments would be cut in as a nested segment, hiding the edits. *Avoid nesting*. Nesting can be a considerable disadvantage in the conforming stage of the project because of the media management issues it enjoins.

Multicam tracks are logged and loaded onto the hard drive one angle at a time. My logging preference is to log one tape (angle) first, track by track, with handles for spoken banter between songs. This creates a "road map" for the entire show; the first tape log will be the same as each corresponding angle's tape log in the group. This same principle applies even if you've had to change tape reels midshow. Just remember that you must always log the first tape in a reel group. Now you can export your first log and duplicate it for each additional angle's tape. This technique only works if the timecodes match. Simply changing reel names creates new shot logs. Everything else stays the same. (See Chapter 10: Preparing the Multicamera Project for Editing.)

I call this method the track-by-track method. It helps to have camera reports to find the tracks in the show. The main reason for doing this with a concert program is that it mirrors the way artists are accustomed to working: song by song, or track by track. That's how they record, and that's how they break down and arrange their performances and CDs. Using this method also creates smaller files on the drive, which helps with media management. It can also alleviate the headache of losing a file; you have less material to load or move around. I also make a set of low-resolution proxy files for editing on my laptop or off slower drives. You can cut with either set of files and match back to high- or low-res anytime.

Ray Volkema, HDNet: *Everything is one song at a time. I'll go through a song the first time very slowly and try to see all the angles until I feel I've got something correct, then come back, play it again in multiclip mode, and continue to watch what I have, fine-tuning it the second time to make sure I didn't miss anything. Third time, I'll come back and turn off multiclip so I can see it in the high-res format and watch my cut without looking at all the other angles—and at this point I'll just watch it without stopping. Then I'll feel where, okay, that felt uncomfortable, and I'll go back again, make those fixes, watch it one more time, and if I'm happy at*

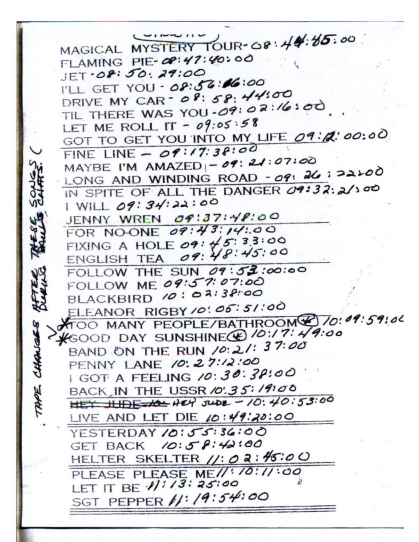

Figure 13.13 Set list is track by track with time-of-day timecode corresponding to videotapes. (Courtesy Mark Haefeli Productions/mhp3.com)

that point I'll move on to the next song. And obviously, when I'm finally done with the concert, I'll watch it altogether and try to get an idea of whether something still isn't right.

After all the tracks are cut, you can start to assemble the show. Take all of those separate track-by-track sequences and copy and paste them into the first full rough-cut version of the concert. (Don't forget to use the Command + drop method to avoid nesting.) You aren't really worried about cutting to time yet; your focus is to get everything on the same timeline. From there, you can start to pull up the time between songs.

Name	Duration	In	Out	Media Start
Final Sequences				
Amazed RC 016	00:05:25;11	Not Set	Not Set	01:00:00;00
Blackbird RC 008	00:03:49;06	01:00:00;00	01:03:49;05	01:00:00;00
DriveMyCar.RC11	00:03:11;22	01:00:00;00	Not Set	01:00:00;00
FlamingPie.RC18	00:03:18;26	Not Set	Not Set	01:00:00;00
FollowMe.RC07	00:03:10;06	01:00:04;29	Not Set	01:00:00;00
FollowTheSun.RC08	00:04:22;12	Not Set	Not Set	01:00:00;00
GetYou.RC15	00:02:53;07	01:00:00;00	01:02:53;06	01:00:00;00
GoodDaySunshine.RC10	00:02:55;09	01:00:00;00	01:02:55;08	01:00:00;00
Hey Jude RC 012	00:02:14;09	Not Set	Not Set	01:00:00;00
IntoMyLife.RC09	00:03:25;28	Not Set	Not Set	01:00:00;00
JennyWren.Master.08	00:03:58;02	Not Set	Not Set	01:00:00;00
PennyLane.RC06 AUD v2 Becky	00:03:35;08	01:00:00;00	01:03:35;07	01:00:00;00
People/Bathroom.RC21 BG	00:05:39;19	01:00:00;00	01:05:39;18	01:00:00;00
Roll It.RC09	00:05:56;01	01:00:00;00	01:05:56;00	01:00:00;00
ThereWasYou.RC14	00:02:43;06	01:00:00;00	01:02:43;05	01:00:00;00
Will.RC10	00:02:16;00	01:00:00;00	01:02:15;29	01:00:00;00
OMF Output 1	01:10:27;14	Not Set	Not Set	01:00:00;00

Figure 13.14 Final sequences track by track.

Project Status-Paul McCartney US Tour 05

5/30/06

#	Element Name	Capture Scratch Show A	Capture Scratch Show w	Proxy File	Sync Audience Cine Alt	Sync Audience Vari ca	Sync nce HD's	Misc Audi enc	Other B-Roll	Syn Mas te	Alt Camera Loca tor	Audience Maste	Audio Mixes	Marker Note	Macca Notes	Notes	Cutting Priority Rating	File Location	RoughCut Modified	Final Approval	ROUGH QT OUTPUT	MixDown Clip Version	New OMF AUDIO Output	OMF AUDIO Output	Conformed
1	Mystery Tour	x	x	x	x	x	x		x	x		Audience v.2	ReMix v2		Screened by PM 3/10 Screened by PM 6/1	wide shots of crowd 6/3 Girl Sync "Waiting to..." fusilly solo, wicks at 2:20, cheat wide- reverse menu reorg	****	on Firewire	8-Jun	screen	15-Jun	NuMystery Tour.28	15-Jun	30-May	
2	FlamingPie	x	x	x	x				x	x		Audience v.2	ReMix v2	sync issues, spot rework shots see-markers	Screened by PM 4/18 Screened by PM 5/9	audience/reverse		on Firewire	5-Jun	6/6 MH	6-Jun	FlamingPie.RC18		30-May	x
3	Maybe I'm Amazed	x	x							x		Audience v.2	ReMix v2	spot rework shots see-markers	Screened by PM 4/18 iScreened by PM 5/9	issues; bald spots rework shots see-markers, change out audience-		on Firewire	7-Jun	6/8 MH	6-Jun	Amazed RC 010.mj	30-May + 4-Jun		x
4	Eleanor Rigby	x	x							x		Audience v.1	ReMix v2	Added BG BETTER AUDIENCE	Screened by PM 4/18 Screened by PM 5/9	Better audience- "Haunting Eyes"	****	on Firewire	15-Jun	screen	15-Jun	Eleanor Rigby RC 013	15-Jun	4-Jun	
5	Let Me Roll It	x	x							x		Audience v.2	ReMix v2	replaced Done JP Need- Check Sync of	Screened by PM 4/18 Screened by PM 5/9	at Sync, More Paul Solo on Jim H guitar, Hold on		on Firewire	5-Jun	6/6 MH	8-Jun	Roll It.RC07 AUD v3 JP		30-May	x
6	Drive My Car	x	x							x		Audience v.2	ReMix v2	and choices...good Fixed Dancing	Screened by PM 4/18 Screened by PM 5/9	Hold shot at 01:00:39;10 longer		on Firewire	1-Jun	6/5 MH	6-Jun	DriveMyCar.RC9 JP		30-May	x
7	Got To Get You Into My Life	x	x							x		Audience v.2	ReMix v2	intro banter- countdown @ top is off	Screened by PM 4/18 Screened by PM 5/9	cut to banter		on Firewire	1-Jun	6/5 MH	8-Jun	IntoMyLife.RC07		30-May	x
8	I'll Get You	x	x							x		Audience v.1	ReMix v2	added audience BG	Screened by PM 4/18 Screened by PM 5/9 Screened by	Band Curls bo Plodding, more life-pull ups 6/1- Check for Intro Banter- 6/3 Abe Younger Faces-see markers		on Firewire	7-Jun	6/8 MH	8-Jun	GetYou.RC11.mj		30-May	x
9	Till There Was You	x	x							x		Audience v.3	ReMix v2	added audience BG	Screened by PM 4/18 Screened by PM 5/9 Screened by PM 6/1	Change out audience, some larger groups-check sync Abe 01:01:30;17, 6/3 Check open-Vocal 6/3 Check Sync		on Firewire	7-Jun	6/8 MH	8-Jun	ThereWasYou.RC11.mj		30-May	

Figure 13.15 A song status checklist keeps track of digitizing, syncing, versions for audience pass, screening notes, priorities, approvals, and outputs.

For *Paul McCartney: The Space Within US*, we loaded all the tapes through the AJA Kona 3 board set to capture our original 1080psf/23.98 footage, adding a 3:2 pulldown to DVCProHD 29.97. This decision was made long in advance, when we proposed the post workflow. That's when we decided that since the deliverable masters were eventually going to HD 29.97, all the sources would have to match to that frame rate. So we pulled it down on the original capture, which made it easy to mix formats—everything had the same frame rate. Some shows, a lot of shows actually, use DVCProHD as actual master codecs, but later we reloaded everything at 10-bit uncompressed for color correction and final conforming. (See Chapter 20: Case Study: A Mixed-Platform Workflow—Paul McCartney: The Space Within Us).

Editing with Multiple Performances

Many producers make a habit of shooting the same show twice over two nights. This is a great option if you've got the budget. Not only can you drop a bad performance by shooting a second show, you can also double your angle choices by moving some or all of the cameras the second time around. Sometimes you can substitute a dress rehearsal as a "second performance." It's like having a safety net.

"You always want to shoot more than one performance," Mitch Owgang says. "Always, always, always. Otherwise: if a singer just sang the wrong note or the lead trumpet solo wasn't there ... where you going to go? We always strive to shoot at least two, if not more."

Editor Craig McKay consulted Jonathan Demme and editor Lisa Day with production for *The Talking Heads: Stop Making Sense.*

Craig: *We shot over three nights at Pantages Theater in Los Angeles and each night they had six camera setups, but Jonathan wanted to do every performance live. So the question then is, how do you cut all that stuff together? I gave him the idea to feed the drummer a click track. Create a click track for every song and then every night use that click track as a guide for the multiple cameras.*

The click track kept all three performances within a frame or two most of the time. If you look at the film, you'll see the drummer keeping the beat in sync. Sometimes rehearsals will suffice as a "second performance." It may be your only saving grace in the edit room.

Cara Constentino is even more of a proponent of rehearsals. "We usually try to have at least two rehearsals," says Constentino:

One is a rehearsal where they're not really dressed, it's sort of a look-see, and no stock is burned; it's just a DVD. That's the first time we sit around and talk about the shots. Then there's the dress rehearsal, where tape is burned, and by that point we'll be on plan.

Some producers prefer to tape a show over several nights of performances and then combine them into one show. Each show has a multicam setup of its own, complete with jam-synced timecode. But each night's timecode is different from that of the others (see Figure 13.20). There are a few ways to handle this. You could sync a scripted show or musical performance by using in-points. If the shows fall out of sync, then they need to be resynced each time. Another way is to pick one show as your master and only cut in moments from the alternate shows if they work better at telling the story. These moments could also be multiclip groups or single-camera angle fixes.

Lighting director Jeff Ravitz worked as a consultant with director Jonathan Demme and cinematographer Ellen Kuras on Neil Young's *Heart of Gold*. He helped with a lot of angle choices at Grand Ole Opry Ryman Auditorium in Nashville, where the team built a nine-camera show and shot it twice, changing up angles the second night.

Jeff Ravitz: *We were very, very careful not to impose any of those camera angles that would be totally contrary to the mood and look we were trying to create with Neil and the background performers. It was cued out very precisely—moment to moment. There was absolutely nothing left to chance.*

By switching up the angles the second night, the team could effectively achieve 18 camera angles in all. There were a few that were virtually consistent from night to night, but a good number of them were moved around.

Combining Performances

All of this said: if you do find yourself shooting over two or more nights, bear in mind that it entails additional timecode considerations. The two nights will have different timecodes and there's no way to sync precisely two live shows shot over two nights. One method is to mark in-points and keep your shows in sync as long as the performances allow (see Figures 13.16 and 13.17). But then some pullup editing will still be necessary, simply because it's live and no one's perfect—even in the tightest bands. These pullups determine new sync points for manual in-point matching between the two shows.

We did the same thing on *The Space Within US*. Each night the positions or lenses of the 13 cameras were changed out, for a set of 26 unique camera angles. We were asked to group all the cameras as one show. We used several methods to do this, depending on the need for the song and the band's ability to stay in sync with itself over two nights. Amazingly, the band performed the same tracks nearly identically on both nights. Occasionally the band would drift out of sync and we would find sync points to match them back up, but most of the time, they were right on the money!

After all the clips were loaded from both performances, they were grouped together as one multiclip. Grouping one set of cameras with matching timecode to themselves is easy. But to group two sets of nights together, you need to find sync points to the music manually and mark in-points to match them up.

DVD Exercise

Group two performances as one. Timecode matches for show A independently from matching timecode from show B. Can you sync them? Use the clips provided on the companion DVD to create one multiclip out of show A and show B combined.

The Preferred Performance

Another method for cutting two shows together is what I call the "preferred performance" or "selective viewing" technique. For this approach, you use one performance for a base cut. Then you manually cut in selected shots from the alternate performance vertically on tracks above. Each alternate angle is screened separately and marked for the best part of the track. I call this mark "the sweet spot." Then you whittle away the unused parts of the clip and eventually collapse them into a second track (see Figures 13.18 and 13.19).

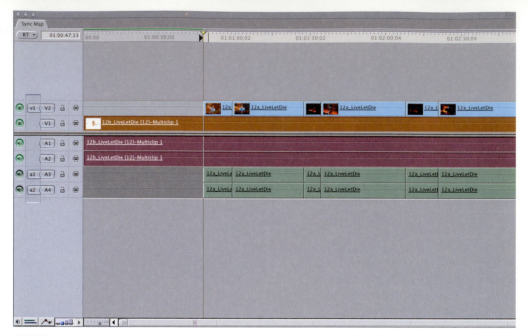

Figure 13.16 To find matching sync points, cut the second show on top of the first show where they match to the music. This will allow you to determine where the in-point for each set of cameras will match.

Name	Duration	In	Out	Media Start	Media End	Tracks	Good
▼ 🗀 Original Footage							
▼ 🗀 Show A							
🎞 01a_LiveLetDie	00:05:01:19	22:48:58:12	Not Set	22:48:10:00	22:54:00:00	1V, 2A	
🎞 02a_LiveLetDie	00:05:01:19	22:48:58:12	Not Set	22:48:10:00	22:54:00:00	1V, 2A	
🎞 03a_LiveLetDie	00:05:01:19	22:48:58:12	Not Set	22:48:10:00	22:54:00:00	1V, 2A	
🎞 04a_LiveLetDie	00:05:01:19	22:48:58:12	Not Set	22:48:10:00	22:54:00:00	1V, 2A	
🎞 05a_LiveLetDie	00:05:01:19	22:48:58:12	Not Set	22:48:10:00	22:54:00:00	1V, 2A	
🎞 06a_LiveLetDie	00:05:01:19	22:48:58:12	Not Set	22:48:10:00	22:54:00:00	1V, 2A	
🎞 07a_LiveLetDie	00:05:01:19	22:48:58:12	Not Set	22:48:10:00	22:54:00:00	1V, 2A	
🎞 08a_LiveLetDie	00:05:01:19	22:48:58:12	Not Set	22:48:10:00	22:54:00:00	1V, 2A	
🎞 09a_LiveLetDie	00:05:01:19	22:48:58:12	Not Set	22:48:10:00	22:54:00:00	1V, 2A	
🎞 10a_LiveLetDie	00:05:01:19	22:48:58:12	Not Set	22:48:10:00	22:54:00:00	1V, 2A	
🎞 11a_LiveLetDie	00:05:01:19	22:48:58:12	Not Set	22:48:10:00	22:54:00:00	1V, 2A	
🎞 12a_LiveLetDie	00:00:11:17	22:48:58:12	22:49:09:28	22:48:10:00	22:54:00:00	1V, 2A	
🎞 13a_LiveLetDie	00:05:01:19	22:48:58:12	Not Set	22:48:10:00	22:54:00:00	1V, 2A	
▼ 🗀 Show B							
🎞 01b_LiveLetDie	00:06:20:01	10:49:00:00	Not Set	10:49:00:00	10:55:20:00	1V, 2A	
🎞 02b_LiveLetDie	00:05:32:18	10:49:47:13	Not Set	10:49:00:00	10:55:20:00	1V, 2A	
🎞 03b_LiveLetDie	00:05:32:18	10:49:47:13	Not Set	10:49:00:00	10:55:20:00	1V, 2A	
🎞 04b_LiveLetDie	00:05:32:18	10:49:47:13	Not Set	10:49:00:00	10:55:20:00	1V, 2A	
🎞 05b_LiveLetDie	00:05:32:18	10:49:47:13	Not Set	10:49:00:00	10:55:20:00	1V, 2A	
🎞 06b_LiveLetDie	00:05:32:18	10:49:47:13	Not Set	10:49:00:00	10:55:20:00	1V, 2A	
🎞 07b_LiveLetDie	00:05:32:18	10:49:47:13	Not Set	10:49:00:00	10:55:20:00	1V, 2A	
🎞 08b_LiveLetDie	00:05:32:18	10:49:47:13	Not Set	10:49:00:00	10:55:20:00	1V, 2A	
🎞 09b_LiveLetDie	00:05:32:18	10:49:47:13	Not Set	10:49:00:00	10:55:20:00	1V, 2A	
🎞 10b_LiveLetDie	00:05:32:18	10:49:47:13	Not Set	10:49:00:00	10:55:20:00	1V, 2A	
🎞 11b_LiveLetDie	00:05:32:18	10:49:47:13	Not Set	10:49:00:00	10:55:20:00	1V, 2A	
🎞 12b_LiveLetDie	00:05:32:18	10:49:47:13	10:55:20:00	10:49:00:00	10:55:20:00	1V, 2A	
🎞 13b_LiveLetDie	00:05:32:18	10:49:47:13	Not Set	10:49:00:00	10:55:20:00	1V, 2A	
▶ 🗀 Parts							

Figure 13.17 Show A timecode is matched up to show B by manually changing the mark in-points as determined by the sync map (notice show A is on military 24 hour clock and show B is on a 12 hour clock).

Usually, preferred performance is chosen by the artists, based on the show with the best sound, not the show with the best look or the best camera moves. (That would be too easy!)

Zoran Jevremov, editor: *You're always cutting from your good night, when the performance was spot on and the band sounded at its best. Then you use that as your main cut and trust that when you use the shots from the other night, you may have to slip and slide shots visually to get them to work.*

Another way would be to cut the two performances as individual shows and layer them vertically to compare and contrast. Making multiclips is easy, because clips are grouped only with like timecode. The downside is having to cut the show twice.

Oliver Peters: *When doing multiple performances, rather than integrate all the cameras, I tend to cut the two performances as their own cut and stick one on top of the other and then combine the two and see what I want and don't want to keep. In a concert, you tend, obviously, to keep one audio performance and use the best camera angles and use ones from the other show. In something like a sitcom, people will go back and forth between the best delivery of a line.*

Noteworthy

An additional way to make groups with a sync map is to stack all the camera angles in sync on the timeline and use the ThrashGroup method as described in Chapter 11, Grouping Clips.

Figure 13.18 The excess parts of each additional clip are whittled away, leaving just the sweet spot.

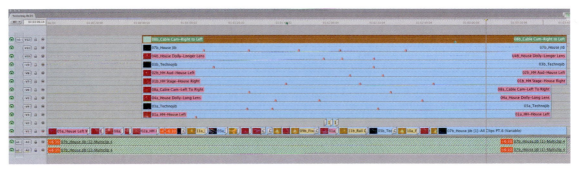

Figure 13.19 Show A on track 1 is a multiclip of the preferred performance. Tracks above are from show B for selective viewing. Notice the markers are located inside each alternate clip as a chosen sweet spot.

Figure 13.20 Different timecode between two shows.

Ganging the Group

Looking at more than a quad split can be hard for some people to process. Watching huge multicam shows on monitors is tough; being able to keep track of everything and call these shows in real time is an amazing skill. Sometimes it's easier to break it down and analyze smaller parts, shying away from splits. Using group clips as sources ganged to the record monitor is a good way to accomplish this goal.

Scott Simmons, Avid/FCP editor at the Filmworkers Club in Nashville (www.scottsimmons.tv): *I use the ganging more than splits. When I find something good, I throw it in the timeline. Since the source monitor's ganged with the record monitor, right when I find a good moment I can mark my in and my out and just drop it in the timeline. Since I'm ganged with the group clip, I'm dropping the group back into the timeline. I just may have three or four different layers of all these little moments that I really like.*

The process is tedious but necessary if you care about performance. By watching the individual takes (in groups) one at a time, you can see more obviously where the magic moments are.

Scott Simmons: *Whether it's a music video or a multicam concert, I feel the duty to the job and the artist and the performance to watch everything. On a music video, when artists are lip-syncing, there are certain moments when the artist really connects and you can see it clicking in his eyes and face. I try to watch all that at least once from beginning to end, to find those moments.*

What you end up with is a sequence of your selected takes in their group on multiple tracks. If there are several selects for a particular line of a song, you can decide which one will live and kill the others—then start collapsing. The result is an edited track with the groups intact for further refinement.

Music Videos

Using Takes as Angles

A really cool way to use multicam is to cut single-camera music videos by grouping takes as angles. If the production shoots with a smart slate and timecode that matches the playback source, all of the takes will have common-source timecode and each take will group easily in multicam.

> *It's not uncommon in a music video edit to have 58-plus angles to sync.*
>
> **Scott Simmons**

A major difference in this mode is that music videos can shoot many more takes than a typical live show would have angles. So you could end up with more than 50 angles to sync up or cut individually by finding the sweet spots.

Scott Simmons: *A video is a different type of sync beast from a multicam concert. Instead of 2, 4, 6, 8, 22, 24, 26, or 28 different cameras to sync, you often have 52, 54, 56, 58-plus angles to sync. I say* plus *because that number can move to the triple digits. A beast indeed.*

Figure 13.21 Assistant camera operator Roger S. Jacobson readies the smart slate to sync film cameras for a Billy Idol music video (1990).

Figure 13.22a Billy Idol in signature poses for music video cameras (1990).

Figure 13.22b The camera is set in the middle of the arena (1990).

The more angles or takes in the project, the more tracks in your timeline and the more choices for selected shots to be whittled down.

Playback

A music video production has a soundtrack at its core. The soundtrack is striped with timecode, starting the track at 01:00:00:00 and dubbing for playback on location during the shoot. The artist hears the music and lip-syncs the track to stay in time.

Playback comes from the sound team. Traditionally it's been done on open-reel tape, then 3/4, Beta, HDCAM cassettes, DATs, and now digitally from Pro devices and iPods or even iPhones. The timecode is fed to a smart slate. Another method is to feed the playback timecode

Figure 13.23 Smart slate for Billy Idol music video.

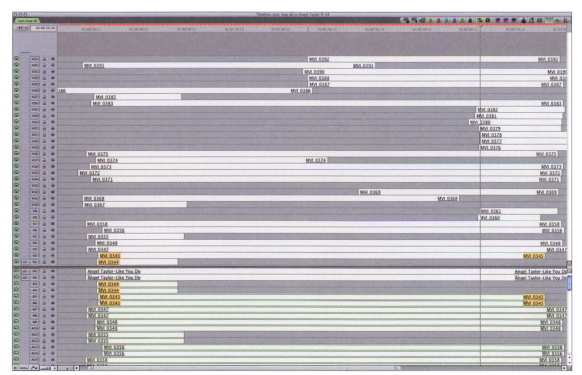

Figure 13.24 Sync map for a music video with 33 takes matched up to master audio tracks. (Courtesy Scott Simmons.)

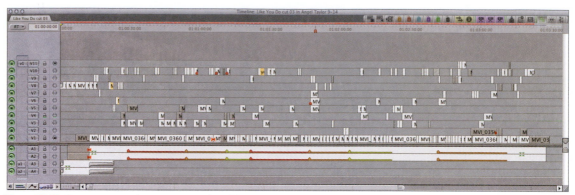

Figure 13.25 Sync map cut down to 11 tracks with select shots. (Courtesy Scott Simmons.)

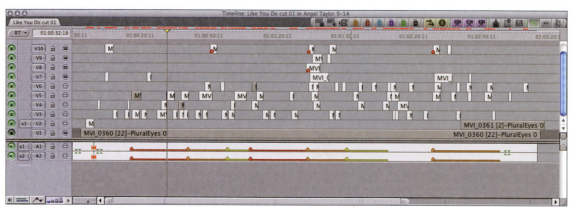

Figure 13.26 Sync map cut down to 10 tracks. (Courtesy Scott Simmons.)

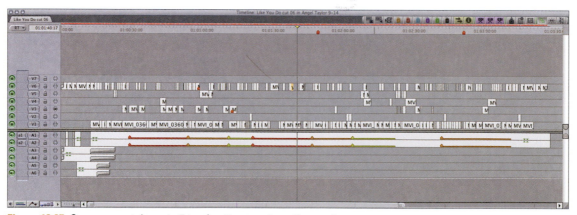

Figure 13.27 Sync map cut down to 7 tracks. (Courtesy Scott Simmons.)

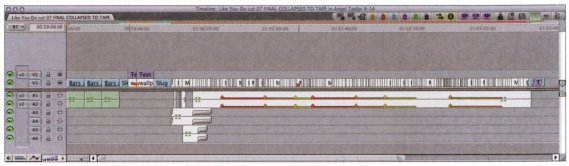

Figure 13.28 Sync map cut down to 1 track with only select shots. (Courtesy Scott Simmons.)

via LTC to an alternate track on the camera. During post, the LTC is converted to Aux TC to match playback TC while still retaining continuous record-run TC on the camera master. During the shoot, the slate will show visible TC at the top of the take.

Directors who want to do a take with only the chorus or a verse or solo can play back from the middle of the song—but any time you see that slate, you have that piece of master audio in your timeline, basically digitized from that master audio pack tape.

The theory is that the timecode on that audio master in your timeline matches exactly the timecode on that slate.

Using Subclips and Aux TC

In Avid, try using auxiliary code in grouping to do a music video; doing it one time will convince you of its value. Music video production is shot single-camera film style with individual takes; it's a good plan to pull subclips of the selected takes, assign an Aux TC to match the sequence, and group the subclips.

Scott Simmons: *You can still use an auxiliary timecode, even if you don't have a smart slate. If you have no slate whatsoever, you rip audio right off a CD, drop it in a timeline, stack out 10 individual takes; you can still use auxiliary timecode; it's just that the timecode itself comes from the timeline.*

Drop the CD audio in a timeline, and the song starts at one hour; you can still use that as the auxiliary timecode to assign to your other takes that you shot, even without a smart slate. The smart slate just makes it easy, but the numbers themselves can come from anywhere.

Scott Simmons: *I always choose the last readable frame of that slate before it was pulled out and make that the frame that I put the timecode on. Once you have all of these takes with your auxiliary timecode, which came from that timecode on the slate, you group your clips together by auxiliary timecode and it pretty much just drops the clips into your timeline. It slips them around by that auxiliary timecode, which matches that slate. So in theory, everything you have there is in sync.*

The method used for Avid differs from that for Final Cut. On Avid, if you're doing film transfer, you have maybe a two-hour reel of takes and you digitize it in one two-hour chunk. Then you can just subclip out every take of the song. The subclip will be from the slate to when the subclips stop to the beginning of the next slate. So you would have all these subclips.

Scott Simmons: *If the first frame of that subclip is, say, the last readable frame of that slate, then when you put the auxiliary timecode in, the first frame of that auxiliary timecode is going to match up to that slate. In Avid, that first frame of the subclip is going to be the first frame of that Aux TC. You just type it into the auxiliary timecode and there you have it in that Avid subclip.*

Unfortunately, Final Cut doesn't quite work the same way. As this book goes to press, there have been issues with the Aux TC resetting, making this process ripe for a workaround.

FCP and AuxTC: NOT

In Final Cut, if you have a two-hour piece of tape and you pull subclips from that tape, every time you assign a new Aux TC it's going to ripple the auxiliary code through all the subclips pulled out of that master clip. You can see that, at that point, it becomes useless for editing music videos with subclips.

Scott Simmons: *In Final Cut, I would pull my first subclip, make my Aux TC, move to the next one, and then when I type in a different code it would change the auxiliary code of that first clip. If you're 20 clips in and you change it, it's going to change the auxiliary code on all those 20 clips.*

The workaround comes into play during the prep phase. If you're coming from tape, it's going to be a more logging-intensive process—you log the tape from the slate to the end of the take and then have Final Cut digitize master clips for every take. No subclips, no problem.

PluralEyes

Another way to group these takes is with PluralEyes. PluralEyes analyzes the audio tracks and makes a sync map and group clips. One thing to look out for here is that natural-sound audio tracks

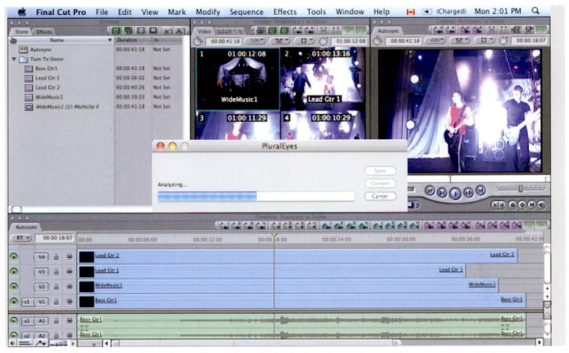

Figure 13.29 PluralEyes analyzes the audio tracks on individual angles and syncs them up automatically.

vary with delays, as the source sound may be recorded at various distances to the microphones on the cameras.

Scott Simmons: *The audio on a music video shoot can be quite a cacophony of sound. There's the official playback of the band's track being lip-synced to by the band, and then there are the sounds that the band makes while going through the motions: singing, guitars, drums, et cetera. Add to that commands shouted by the director and the volume fluctuations as a handheld or camera dolly moves closer to or farther away from the band. You can see how it might confuse PluralEyes.*

If you don't have common sync and you send a mix track to each camera, the groups will be more accurate when grouped by sound waves. It may be a little tricky at first, but once you get the hang of it, PluralEyes works fast and well. How accurate is it?

Scott Simmons: *On another recent video, the production had used a proper smart slate for syncing—but I was curious to know how close PluralEyes would get the sync to the smart slate. I ran the clips through PluralEyes and it placed all of the clips within nearly a single frame of the smart slate, if not right on. Considering how it works, I thought that was pretty damn good. Automagic indeed.*

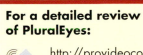

For a detailed review of PluralEyes:

 http://provideoco-alition.com/index.php/ssimmons/story/automagic_part_i_pluraleyes/P0/

14

SITCOMS AND COMEDY

The Reinvention of Sitcoms

James Burrows is considered by most people to be the master of multicamera American comedies. "I think Jimmy Burrows is the king," his original mentor, Jay Sandrich, said of his former protégé. "He's gotten so many shows on the air."

Burrows comes from a theater background, growing up under the wing of his father, renowned Broadway impresario Abe Burrows. When James Burrows finally got into TV in 1974, he began reinventing the sitcom almost immediately.

Burrows is a 10-time Emmy™ Award–winning television director and is widely recognized as one of the best sitcom directors in the business. His career includes great shows as *The Mary Tyler Moore Show, The Bob Newhart Show, Rhoda, Friends, Taxi,* and *Cheers.*

Figure 14.1 Panavision Cameras X and A shoot the chipchart and grab a slate on set of Cheers (1993).

James Burrows: *What I do [on TV] is theater. I do a play every week, and the cameras are just recording the play. So all of my theatrical knowledge is in my work every day, combined with the technical side of cameras and editing, which you can learn. It's not the technical side that makes the show a success; what makes the show a success is the story and how funny it is.*

His directorial style is to work with the sounds of the actors' voices as if he were working on a radio play. He concentrates on the jokes, not the cameras. He doesn't even watch the monitors during the taping.

James Burrows: *It's about listening. Timing. If somebody screws up on the way to a joke, you try to stop them before they get to the punch line, so the audience only hears the punch line when the joke is delivered correctly. Surprise is 90% of humor.*

Daniel Cahn, A.C.E.: *If I look at anything that Burrows has done, it's pretty much the same style of editing. I think it's just because Jim directs like he's a stage director. The show has dictated its own style. You're not cutting* Cheers *differently every week. That's the style that's been bred editorially.*

Burrows's training ground was MTM, Mary Tyler Moore's company, where he learned the business from Jay Sandrich—who started as an AD on *I Love Lucy*. Burrows worked his way up the ranks to the Danny Thomas Company, where he became one of the industry's top directors, responsible for *The Golden Girls, The Cosby Show*, and *Two and a Half Men*.

James Burrows: *At MTM, you had to play by their rules. I was doing shows that I didn't create. The first job of a director coming into a show that's already up and running is that you play by the rules. Only once you do that can you can slip in what you want to do.*

It was different when Burrows did *Cheers*, because he was one of the co-creators. He could do a lot more, because now *he* was setting the rules.

James Burrows: *I shortened the rehearsal process, for one. The actors were so good, you didn't want to bore them. So you just made sure you weren't rearranging deck chairs on the* Titanic. *You didn't do scenes you knew would be changed. I also broke down walls by encouraging collaboration between the writers and actors, which for years hadn't been done. For years the writer was the boss, the tyrant. On my shows, everybody talks about what might make the show better. It's not about who's the boss. A lot has changed, now that everything is done twice. Every show, you do every scene twice. In between, after the first take, you rewrite if necessary, or you just do it again and change it a little, tweak the performance. Writers like to have two options in the editing room, two different performances.*

Many sitcoms are a producer's medium. But then many producers are writers too, and Burrows likes to allow for the actors to collaborate as well.

James Burrows: *When the producers are also the writers, they work really hard on the script. But the actors, most actors, would like to contribute, rather than feel like parrots saying the writer's words. So you have to find a happy medium wherein everybody tries to do what's best for the show, and without slapping someone else in the face.*

Blocking

There is an audible rhythm to comedy. You're not required to watch. You can feel it and hear it, and when it's really cooking, it's undeniable—sweet as music. To me, comedy and music are the same.

Gary Halvorson, director

Burrows is really good with cameras and physical blocking.

James Burrows: *I look at the actors and the cameras a little bit and make sure they're pointing at the right person—and I can tell by how the camera is pointing whether it's a master or a close-up. I have a memory for every shot I need; it's a curse and a blessing. If you have a quad split, the producers tend to watch that and come over and say, "These shots don't match" or "I saw a boom in the shot," rather than worrying about whether we're telling the right story.*

Peter Chakos, A.C.E.: *James would block the show out and never look at the video feeds again while we were filming it. So I would have to be his eyes, to make sure that cameras were where they were supposed to be and that we had everything we needed. He shoots blind, for the most part. He just watches the stage and listens to the actors. That's a unique way of working. Now everybody sits around the monitors.*

Gary Halvorson is just as at home with comedy as with music. In addition to directing some of the finest music programs, he has an uncanny feel for comedy and has directed many sitcom productions, including 75 episodes of *Friends*. The jokes are his priority too. Neither Burrows nor Halvorson does a real line cut. But while Burrows never watches the split-screen monitor, Halvorson finds that both approaches work for him.

Gary Halvorson: *I watch everything. I watch the cameras and tell the cameras exactly what I want. Because I do live TV, I'm a little more versed at watching splits. But sometimes I'll catch myself in run-throughs, walking behind all the executives as they're laughing, and I'm just looking at the ground, not even watching the actors. But I'm scoring on these jokes, so I know I'm okay. I can relate to it in musical terms.*

They say that you cannot learn or teach comedic instincts; they have to be there naturally. I find that its visual styles are simple. Just make sure the audience sees the jokes. I know exactly where the shots are in comedy, and so does Jimmy. It's formulaic. What's not formulaic about it is the directing. Making a joke work. There's no formula for that. You cannot teach an actor to be funny, but you can help an actor.

I can help a dramatic actor be funnier, but I can't make somebody funny, period. Helping someone become funnier [is something] you accomplish with blocking. You can make the joke work if it sounds funny by moving that actor around and picking up the phone and going blah blah blah blah and there's your joke. When a joke is good, that joke has been studied. When art is true, understanding it is easy, simple. But it's also the hardest thing to hit.

Daniel Cahn, A.C.E.: *You can't do anything with it. It plays. You know with the read-throughs when it's working. I've heard of episodes that were disasters in blocking, but [by] the time that the night shooting before the audience came along, they had worked it. That's what Jim does. But it's certainly up to the cast too. It's a real team effort.*

Burrows says, "Know your technical aspects with cameras."

James Burrows: *The worst possible thing that can happen to a show on camera days is that you take forever blocking. Your cast gets bored and the crew gets bored and there's no spontaneity. In the old days, I used to take a lunch hour. I'd start at nine and finish at three, with a break in the middle. Now we go from ten to one. It takes me three hours to block the cameras. That's on camera day and I know I have the next day (Tuesday, say), which is shoot day, when we come in at noon and I know I can run each scene twice again, so if I screwed up the cameras I can fix them then.*

It's as Easy as A, B, C, and Sometimes X

On *I Love Lucy,* there was the occasional fourth camera. They called it the "D" camera, as it was traditionally referred to on film sets. It was used for big scenes with a lot of actors.

Ted Rich, A.C.E., original assistant editor on *Lucy: Then sometimes there was a fourth camera and we could attach an additional head (on the Moviola Monster) to handle it. The cameras were lined up across the stage, left to right: A, B, C, D. "B" was always the master camera. "A" was one close-up and "C" was the other. "D" would be just a fourth camera. Only the center camera had a zoom lens. The two on the side were 100 mm.*

Camera D was treated like a single camera and not synced up for the Monster. It was only cut into the multicam cut as needed. As the show progressed, D was used less and less. Eventually it was packed up and put away for many decades—until James Burrows came along and added it back in again. Except this time, the name and placement changed.

Figure 14.2 Cameras X, A,B and C on the Cheers set with full cast (1990).

James Burrows: *I added it back in on* Taxi. *I had done a couple of four-camera shows before that, pilots. But the set for* Taxi *was so huge and there were so many people in the cast that I thought there'd be no way I could cover it, get all the jokes the first time through, with only three cameras.*

He called it the X cam. But no, that doesn't stand for "extra" camera, as most people guessed.

James Burrows: *We already had A, B, and C, and you don't want the fourth to be called D because D sounds like B. So we called it X. Shooting the first scene of* Taxi, *I had the extra camera on the left, so for me, for years it was XABC. Now it's just ABC and X.*

Typically, X had been used to pick up extra actor shots, but Burrows discovered a more cinematic use almost by accident.

James Burrows: *I wasn't sophisticated enough at first, and I tried to get my masters in the center, but eventually I found that the masters from the sides, from the X and A cameras, looked really, really good. So I started to use those a lot.*

Quad Splits and the Editor Behind the Curtain

James Burrows: *In the old days, I used to mark my scripts so that every line had a camera on it. I don't do that now. I haven't done that in 30 years. You just go in and you know what you have to do. On Cheers, we never did everything twice. On Cheers, we went through the scene and I only reshot jokes that didn't work or I went back and picked up shots I missed. In those days, there was no video monitor, so the cameramen had to tell me when they missed a shot.*

The video monitor is also known as the quad split because it is a single monitor that has four equal size pictures visible, one for each of four cameras. The feed comes from video taps that are attached to film cameras or split feeds from ISO tapes combined into a single screen. Burrows had a policy: because of his success, he could prevent studio or network people who might be at the taping from looking at the quad split. He didn't want anyone looking over his shoulder and second-guessing what he was doing.

Daniel Cahn, A.C.E.: *I think all editors should cut the film and not cut for anyone's ego or politics. Unfortunately, nowadays there's 12 producers on the show and you have heavy network influence; everyone's got their hand it and everyone uses the editing room as the hub to act and control. And everyone thinks that they're an editor. And really until you get in there and you have to do the tricks and the magic and everything, that comes from experience.*

James Burrows: *My editor has a quad split under the stands, and he'll come to me if something is really wrong, but usually I already know. I can tell from rehearsal whether the cameras are doing the right things. I've had the same crew for about 10 years now and it's all shorthand. They could block it themselves.*

David Helfand: *He created this little room under the bleachers with the four cameras on a quad split and with a big curtain behind me so that no one could see behind my back or know where I was. Basically, I had to watch all four cameras in a little cave. He really restricted anyone from seeing anything but the audience's line cut. During a taping like that, there will be somebody in the back doing a very rough, live cut of the cameras, and that's all he'd let people see. And if I had a note, I would have to emerge and talk to him about it and we would discuss it. That was just part of his method, to maintain control and eliminate interference during the shoot.*

Cutting Comedy

If it doesn't work in front of the audience, it's not going to work in the editing department.

James Burrows

The Moviola Monster was the first multicam editing machine, and although it gave filmed television nearly 30 years of loyal service, newer forms of technology inevitably began to replace it. First there was tape, then digital laserdisc, then the real game changer, Avid multicam (see Chapter 22, A Thumbnail History of Multicamera Production and Editing). Regardless of the technology involved, however, well-edited comedy has a global resonance that moves us at a higher level: laughter.

Figure 14.3 The Moviola Monster with three picture heads and one head for sync sound. (Courtesy Dann Cahn, A.C.E.)

Figure 14.4 Producer and editor Ted Rich, A.C.E. with his lifetime achievement award from the American Cinema Editors (A.C.E.). Rich, A.C.E. was one of the first assistants to work with the Moviola Monster on *I Love Lucy,* and he went on to run all of postproduction for MTM.

Daniel Cahn, A.C.E.: *I can guarantee you that if you were doing film today, on the Monster, it would be the exact same process; the shows would be just as funny.*

James Burrows: *If it doesn't work in front of the audience, it's not going to work in the editing department. So the most important thing is to make it really funny in front of the audience. If the story works and the audience laughs, the actors' eyes light up and you can't duplicate that.*

Ted Rich, A.C.E.: *You have to know comedy. You have to know how much of a laugh to leave and when to make a reaction cut. And the editing is different from single-cam to multicam. Interestingly, I could put a comedy editor on a drama, but I could not put a drama editor on a comedy. Very few people have a good sense of humor. And comedic editors know timing better than drama editors.*

Daniel Cahn, A.C.E.: *A comedy has certain basic rules. You don't cut away from the joke. Things that you would do in dramatic dialogue or in action, you would not do in comedy. And the thing is, you can pretty much take any comedy show and put it together and there's certain things that you see happen. The reaction is king.*

James Burrows's teachers include Doug Hines, who edited *The Mary Tyler Moore Show;* Pam Blumenthal, who edited *Newhart;* and Michael

Zinberg, associate producer of *Newhart* and a cutting legend. Then Burrows teamed up with Andy Chulack, the first editor of *Cheers* and now the editor of *Gary Unmarried.*

> *The editor then has to cut the show, and it's pretty apparent which way to cut it. Then the producers come in and the hardest thing is to take time out of the show. Sometimes we come in six minutes long and that's a quarter of a show overtime. So you've got to cut out some jokes and do some edits.*

James Burrows

Cutting Comedy

MULTI-EXPERT APPROACH

Daniel Cahn, A.C.E.: *Half-hour live comedy or audience-oriented shows are very difficult because they have the timing inherently built into them. What I call the set timing, the director's set timing. So whereas timing and rhythm in single camera is very much editorially manufactured, when you have a live audience show, you can't go through and take a frame off of everything; you'd throw the laugh track off and everything that goes with it. Even taking two minutes out of a half-hour comedy is very difficult. It's a real skill.*

James Burrows: *I end the shots, so I have to know where you can cut and where you can't cut and where I have to back a line up if somebody screws up. The editors are creative people too. I'll go with their comedic instincts in editing, and I'll look at the cut after that. Usually, they pretty much nail it.*

Peter Chakos, A.C.E.: *I go through the whole show by myself, do a first cut. Then I give it to the director and he has a handful of angle changes or something for me. Then it goes to the exec producers. They run through it once with me and we figure out what other changes we're going to make, and then, once I've made them, we're pretty much done. It goes to the studio network for approval, but typically by then the show is so tight that there are virtually no notes.*

Darryl Bates, A.C.E.: *You're trying to patch together the best performances. Sometimes you pull a reaction shot you don't want to pull, but you have to because you have to patch together where the actor comes in and forgot a line. The editing style is a little more patchwork than in a single-camera show.*

David Helfand: *You're trying to blend the best performances from different takes and also trying to build the pace. There's a big conflict in multicam comedy editing, and comedy editing in general: weighing the audience laugh versus pacing, preserving the best pace for the show. The audience is like an additional character in the stories you edit. You have to account for their laughter; their participation is part of the comedic rhythm. My challenge was exactly the opposite on* Friends *and* That '70s Show, *which were both very popular and funny and had strong audiences. They involved sort of fighting with the audience, trying to pull things up and not let the televised laugh last as long as it actually did, because if it did it would really slow down the show and you wouldn't be able to tell as much of the story or as many of the jokes within the given time period.*

For years, multicam editing had a reputation for being a much easier medium for assembling a coherent scene or effecting a cut in a shorter period of time. But that's not exactly the case.

David Helfand: *Certainly I believed it was easier before I got into multicam on* Friends. *You think that, basically, a couple of takes are shot and people randomly selected from among the various camera angles. It was only after I got into it that I realized it was more complicated than that. Except on the most simplistic shows, there's a lot of additional coverage, including single-camera footage, that goes into multicam.*

It all goes back to the original notion that multicam is just a way to collect a lot of coverage at once, as opposed to doing one setup at a time, in a sequence—but you're still approaching each angle as its own shot.

David Helfand: *As sitcom cutting became a little more refined—like in* Seinfeld, *for example—you could see that there was active editing, choices being made, because you could see slight mismatches. You could see slight changes that made it obvious that not just one take was being used.*

Those are the tough decisions, but in editing you have a safety net.

Daniel Cahn, A.C.E.: *It's all about storytelling because that's really what editing is, storytelling. Our job is not to get in the way; it's to accentuate everything that goes on there. But the whole nature of the job has changed. The half-hour multicamera, film-based shows are edited in what I would call traditional Hollywood style. But when you're shooting a* Cosby Show, *live, someone's calling the cuts from the technical booth. Then an editor comes in and sweetens that show, makes a pass at the first pass. When you're doing a film-based show, no one is really calling the show at that time. So I think you see a very big difference between that and the live shows or assistant director–edited versions of the shows.*

Improvisation

Improvising. ... It's an editing nightmare so, I always ask the sound people to record the offstage dialogue, especially when they're overlapping. It saves me.

Maysie Hoy, A.C.E.

In features, comedy filmmakers consider multicam production necessary to help them protect themselves from overlapping lines in post. Any time actors improvise or talk out of turn (e.g., step on someone else's lines), a second or third camera can be a lifesaver.

Judd Apatow, the writer, director, and producer *of The 40-Year-Old Virgin, Knocked Up,* and *Funny People,* among many other credits, says:

I'm a fan of shooting multicam. It helps to make our scenes funnier. We roll two cameras for a little bit of improv. We look to do it especially at the end of scenes, where we can drift off into the actors' crazy worlds, and a lot of times great things happen. It definitely helps to use more than one camera. I endorse it.

Says Dan Lebental, A.C.E. editor of *Iron Man*:

Robert Downey, Jr., does some amazing improv … and I can very quickly cut between the two cameras, so I'm not caught. I don't hit a blind alley that I can't use. Without having organized in multicam, it would be incredibly time consuming to go to the matching camera and find a way to cut back without sound pops and things like that. But with multicam, I can instantly go between actors while they're improvising and talking over each other and use the same piece of sound underneath to cut very quickly.

Maysie Hoy, A.C.E. worked her way up through the edit suite as an assistant for Robert Altman. Soon she was cutting his best movies. She also cut *The Joy Luck Club* and many other big studio pictures including *Madea Goes to Jail* and *Bad As I Wanna Be* for producer/director Tyler Perry.

Maysie Hoy, A.C.E.: *It's a big advantage to have more than one camera. Because actors improvise, they don't do the same thing take after take. And so if they do something really great and you only have one camera, you're committed. If the one camera is on a close-up of the actor and he's improvising and doing something great, you might have to cut away, because the actor you weren't covering has to have some kind of reaction to what the first actor did.*

The annual A.C.E. EditFest in New York and Los Angeles is an action-packed weekend with the world's top editors discussing their craft in roundtable forums. Here is what a couple of them said about multicam editing and improvisation:

Stephen Rotter, editor of *What Women Want and Enchanted*: *With improv, using multiple cameras is really the best, because I can't tell you how many times an actor has done an improv and there was no camera coming from the other side, which means you either have to group something or create something. It's hated, but it's an advantage.*

Michael Berenbaum, A.C.E., *Sex and the City*: *I would start out with a grouped clip, but sometimes you find that, for some reason, you've made a cut that's a continuous frame from another angle and it doesn't match as well as if you cut it in a different frame. So it's a good starting place, but you don't always end up with cuts from a multiple clip.*

15

THE MAIN EVENT

Multicam editing is not just for broadcast TV. Technology is constantly getting smaller, faster, and cheaper. Increasingly, complex multicamera production systems that were once the exclusive domain of major recording acts, broadcast networks, and film studios are now available to just about anyone with a message and a live show. Meanwhile, more and more venues are calling for multicam production, which means one thing for everyone reading this book: more jobs.

When arena rock ruled the country, the "big screens" started appearing in stadiums. Giant towers with screens positioned about halfway back in the crowd gave last-row fans the same views the high rollers enjoyed up front. If you were in the back of Trump Plaza in Atlantic City in 1989—when the Rolling Stones closed out their Steel Wheels Tour—you didn't have to squint to see the special guests brought onstage by Keith and Mick for "Salt of the Earth": the monitors clearly showed Axl and Izzy from Guns 'N' Roses.[1]

Figure 15.1 Paul McCartney, IMAG at Citi Field in New York City. (Courtesy Paul Becher and Nocturne Productions, Inc.)

Doi: 10.1016/B978-0-240-81176-5.00015-0

Figure 15.2 Elton John. (Courtesy Elton John and HST Management, Ltd.)

To survey the potential of live event multicam, we'll start with a look at image magnification (IMAG) and how U2 uses it on its state-of-the art 360-degree screen to connect with fans throughout a stadium. We'll also look at the other end of the spectrum: corporate events, weddings, worship TV, electronic press kits (EPK), satellite media tours (SMT), and daily multicam shows in the school system.

Figure 15.3 IMAG screens featuring the Dalai Lama. (Courtesy Todd Gillespie.)

Image Magnification (IMAG)

Image magnification or IMAG for concerts began in the late 1970's when Nocturne, a live-event production company (co-founded by Journey manager Herbie Herbert and guitarist Neil Schon), started adding cameras and big-screen projection to concerts for the band Journey.

Paul Becher has been directing live events for Nocturne since the 1970s. These days, he usually only tours with artists that have the "Sir" prefix i.e.: Elton and Paul McCartney. There's a simple distinction between shooting IMAG for the audience in a venue and shooting for broadcast or home video/DVD. Although these formats might use the same or similar gear for each situation, the shot choices set them apart.

"When you're shooting IMAG," says Paul Becher, "you're basically shooting for the person sitting in the last row of the venue. So you're concentrating on close-ups: facial expressions, fingers plucking the guitar, hands on the neck of the guitar, drum hits, and other tight shots."

Figure 15.4 Director Paul Becher. (Courtesy Nocturne Productions, Inc.)

Figure 15.5 Sir Paul McCartney, IMAG system inside Dallas Stadium. (Courtesy Paul Becher and Nocturne Productions, Inc.)

Figure 15.6 Director Paul Becher and Sir Paul McCartney during an equipment setup. (Courtesy Paul Becher and Nocturne Productions, Inc.)

Figure 15.7 Elton John in concert with hanging image magnification (IMAG) screens. (Courtesy Elton John and HST Management, Ltd.)

There are no wide shots in IMAG, because that viewer in the back row is already living the wide shot. Showing a wide shot to these viewers would defeat the purpose.

"It's all about close-ups," says Peter Moll, a video director who's toured with the likes of Elton John, Velvet Revolver, and Guns 'N' Roses. "Close tight face, tight hands on the guitars, tight hands on the keyboards, that kind of stuff." Moll likes to think of what the show looks like from specific seat locations at certain times in the show, so the fan can see what he can't see from his seat. Even with the huge screens, a wide shot would look like a postage stamp.

Figure 15.8 Director Peter Moll of Gray Matter Entertainment, www.Gmatter.tv.

Peter Moll: *I'm going to show you what's going on at any given moment onstage. There's one instrument that's the highlight for that moment, for those four bars, or the guitar solo. I'm going give you that—up close and personal.*

By contrast, when you're recording for broadcast, you're recording to the person who's at home—whose living room is the "front row." According to Paul Becher, you still want to give the viewer the intimate feeling of a live show. So you want to capture the ambiance and flavor of the entire event, including the audience, wide shots, little things happening onstage, and relationships between different people.

The idea of IMAG hasn't changed since the late 1970s, but the technology of the screens has come a long way, baby.

U2 360° Tour: Not Your Average Big Screen*

I drew it first, the concept of trying to play in 360 degrees, and then I built a model with forks at a dinner table.

Bono

Figure 15.9 U2 360° screen with color bars during ESU. (Courtesy Live Nation/MHP3/www.U2.com.)

In these live applications, IMAG helps to drive the sense of connection and intimacy between a band and its audience. From the Zoo TV Tour to the 360° Tour, nobody does it more creatively than U2.

Video is integral to the U2 360° Tour, both as a design aspect and a technical element. Central to the experience of seeing this show is an elliptically shaped video screen that, through clever engineering and construction, can stretch and open up to offer a 360-degree view of the band to everyone in the audience.

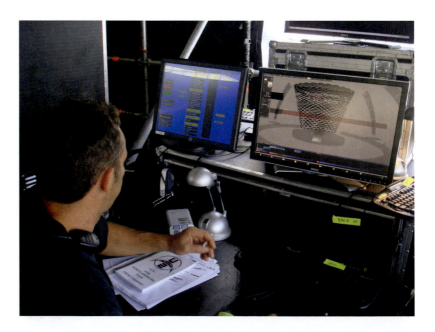

Figure 15.10 The video screen computer controller. (Courtesy Live Nation/MHP3/www.U2.com.)

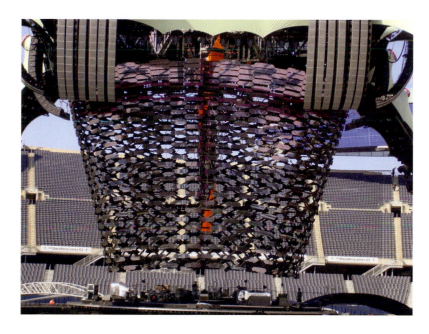

Figure 15.11 Expanded video screen test. (Courtesy Live Nation/MHP3/www.U2.com.)

With this screen, U2 envelops its fans and brings them right into the middle of the band's experience. There really is no bad seat in the house.

Willie Williams, show designer/director, U2 360° Tour: *Instead of making it smaller, we made it so big it actually becomes part of the stadium.*

This screen is a far cry from the gigantic screens that hovered over London's Wembley Stadium in the Live Aid era. It's made of a million different pieces: 500,000 RGB pixels, 320,000 fasteners, 30,000 connecting cables, 60,000 off-the-shelf items (connectors, bearings etc.), 90,000 custom-fabricated components, 25 kilometers of cable, and 3 kilometers of aluminum profiles. Altogether, the screens, trusses, and winches weigh more than 74 tons.

Mark Fisher, architect/designer, U2 360º Tour: *We have here probably the largest rock and roll touring stage production that's ever been put together.*

All this adds up to a flexible LED screen that's about the size of a tennis court and can morph into a seven-story-high, cone-shaped structure that encircles the band even as it extends. (Owing to its shape, it has been nicknamed "The Frietzak," after the cone of paper Belgian *frites* are served in.) The scale is amazing and blurs the line between video screens and scenery, band, and fans.

Setting aside for now the years of development and engineering that went into creating a modern marvel like this, how do you use it? That task fell to video technical director Stefaan "Smasher" Desmedt, who has elevated U2 video since he started with the Zoo TV tour.

Desmedt has at his control 12 manned cameras that shoot live feeds for the screen: two at the front of the house, on the follow spot towers; one on each leg of the "claw"; one at the rear, facing the front of the house; three rail cameras on the outside ring; two rail cameras on the main stage; and one up at the drums.

Figure 15.12 Desmedt's switcher and monitor wall. (Courtesy Live Nation/MHP3/www.U2.com.)

Since the band likes to play "in the round," the end result of all of this coverage is that there is no "back" to the stage—no one is left sitting in some high, left-side, partially obstructed-view seat where the sound is muddy and the only intimate glimpse possible is of the drummer's back.

In its fully extended state, the screen provides a place for some carefully chosen art that augments the performance. But 90% of the time, Desmedt uses it for IMAG.

When the band plays "No Line on the Horizon," the screen displays content created by the Japanese artist Hiroshi Sugimoto. Sugimoto designed the album cover for *No Line on the Horizon*, using photographs of the sea, sky, and horizon. Combining his art with the live shots is an art in itself—like, for example, in a preset segue from "I'll Go Crazy" into "Sunday, Bloody Sunday."

Figure 15.13 The view from vide village. (Courtesy Live Nation/ MHP3/www.U2.com.)

Figure 15.14 Video engineer Jeroen "Myway" Marain shades the cameras. (Courtesy Live Nation/MHP3/www.U2.com.)

Stefaan "Smasher" Desmedt: *There's a design with an eye of a girl and the middle of her eye is IMAG. When we zoom out, it reveals the whole face of the girl. It's quite amazing.*

This IMAG screen is truly the one to beat.

Figure 15.15 The U2 360° "Claw" Opening Night of the 2009 North American Tour in Chicago, Illinois. (Courtesy Live Nation/MHP3/www.U2.com.)

Additional U2 360° Tour video credits:
Show designer/director: Willie Williams
Video screen kinetic design: Chuck Hoberman
Production architect/designer: Mark Fisher
Video director: Tom Krueger
Video technical director: Stefaan "Smasher" Desmedt
Video screen LED system: Frederic Opsomer, Barco
Video screen technical management: Richard Hartman
Production director: Jake Berry

*Special thanks to Live Nation (U2.com) & Mark Haefeli productions (mhp3.com) for EPK material and Michael S. Eddy (eddymarketing.com) for excerpts from his article in LiveDesignOnLine.com

The Electronic Press Kit (EPK)

When it comes time to delivering an integrated video package of the 360° Tour to the worldwide media, U2 and other top touring artists turn to director Mark Haefeli of Mark Haefeli Productions (www.MHP3.com). Haefeli helped to pioneer the simultaneous integration of touring IMAG systems adding multicamera packages to tour productions to make compelling electronic press kits (EPKs) and satellite media tours (SMT) for major artists like Paul McCartney, the Rolling Stones, The Police, and many others.

Figure 15.16 Director Mark Haefeli (right) backstage at the U2 concert with camera crew during a preproduction meeting.

A number of years ago, Mark Haefeli and his team were asked to shoot performance footage for the Rolling Stones, capturing the band's stadium concert experience for news organizations and promotional purposes: everything from selling tickets to creating commercials. Although Haefeli knew there were already cameras in place at these shows, he realized there were a few missing ingredients.

Figure 15.17 The stage set with the IMAG screen for the Rolling Stones' *A Bigger Bang Tour,* opening night at Fenway Park in Boston.

Mark Haefeli: *Back then, it was just cameras out there shooting the action as it happened and going directly to the big screens. There weren't even any recording devices to record the feed. They recorded the audio, but they never recorded the mixed master of all the cameras mixed together, which we now know as the line cut.*

Haefeli and his team found a way to piggyback the EPK production with the IMAG setup to turn around video packages quickly and cost effectively. Haefeli figured that if he could simply record the mix of the line cut going to the big screens and add a couple of cameras for wide shots and cutaways, he'd be able to capture the bands show without spending the kind of money they'd have to spend starting from scratch.

Mark Haefeli: *They've got all of these cameras, a switcher, and all the equipment you need—except a record deck. We can just place three or four cameras strategically around the venue to capture the scale of the production and shoot various wide shots and then integrate what we shoot into the IMAG line cuts with the close-ups. This has become standard operating procedure for recording concert EPKs. It's a great way to save a tremendous amount of money.*

Figure 15.18 EPK crew readies gear and prelabels tapes.

The U2 360° Tour is all about the grandeur of the spectacle. The band likes its public imagery to look cutting edge and wanted Haefeli to find a way to bring that experience to the masses.

Mark Haefeli: *We had eight cameras switched already for us on a hard drive and eight additional supplemental cameras, unmixed, of wide shots. Essentially, we walked out of there with a complete show under our belts. With remixed audio tracks, as well; half an hour after the show was over we were able to go right into post and edit what ultimately looked and felt like a multimillion-dollar concert production of tremendous size.*

Figure 15.19 U2 camera operator controls a robotic camera during the show.

Figure 15.20 EPK camera operator shoots reverse angle shots of crowd to complement the tour camera angles.

Adding cameras to an IMAG setup is a very efficient example of how modern technological advancements bring down the costs of producing, replicating, and distributing quality programming. This is appealing to potential clients; it's also appealing to rock 'n' roll fans.

As the concert was shot and afterward into the night, Mark Haefeli and I edited the U2 EPK backstage, combining the show cameras with our multicamera footage and adding graphics and mixed audio.

Mark Haefeli: *Everyone's objective is for the fans to benefit. As the agents say, the fans put their bums in the seats and pay for the tickets; the fans buy the music and the fans spread the word by mouth. It's all for the fans.*

Figure 15.21 Director Mark Haefeli and Mitch Jacobson edit the EPK for the U2 360° Tour backstage at Soldier Field in Chicago.

Figure 15.22 The on-set editing system for U2 EPK.

Figure 15.23 Helicopter shot over Soldier Field, opening night of U2's 360° Tour, Chicago, Illinois. (Courtesy Live Nation/MHP3/www.U2.com.)

Going Corporate: From the Boardroom to the Ballroom

While rock bands and other entertainers are applying multi-cam stage and video craft to their product launches, the corporate world's been gearing up too. Les Goldberg of LMG Show Technology, who's been producing events for 25 years, says that there's a lot of crossover among TV, touring events, corporate meetings, and sports production, so people who know the basic fundamentals of multicam can work in any genre. He says that 90% to 95% of the events he produces with video have at least two cameras and everything they do is at broadcast quality.

Figure 15.24 A multicamera concert for a corporate presentation. (Courtesy LMG.)

Les Goldberg: *About 15 years ago, the most tech involved in a corporate presentation was usually a PowerPoint deck on a big screen and maybe a video playback on the same screen. But now, people are used to seeing high levels of production and the technology that runs arenas and concert halls has been adapted to the boardroom and ballroom.*

Figure 15.25 Behind the scenes at a ballroom presentation. (Courtesy LMG and Rob Lee.)

Today, the expectations for live, staged corporate events are similar to those for broadcast TV. Many of the components cross over. Many multicam practitioners could do broadcast television any day of the week. We have the same talent and equipment and we leverage it with HD because that's what people want—on TV and at live events.

Figure 15.26 Video village. (Courtesy LMG.)

Figure 15.27 Technical director switches a multicam shoot with graphics roll-ins. (Courtesy LMG.)

A corporate event, just like a concert or any other event, is about communicating a message to an audience: conveying an experience or understanding of the meeting's goals. IMAG and multicam switching allow you to do exactly that.

Figure 15.28 A corporate presentation video setup with camera shading. (Courtesy LMG.)

Many corporate presentations rely heavily on creativity. For instance, at a recent event for Animal Planet network, the producers brought in a special weapon: the HamCam (a pig with a wireless camera on his back).

Figure 15.29 The HamCam for Animal Planet. (Courtesy LMG & Animal Planet.)

Figure 15.30 HamCam testing the live wireless video feed to IMAG screens. (Courtesy LMG & Animal Planet.)

Les Goldberg: *The more you can make the show dynamic or interesting, the more differing perspectives you can present from different angles—the presenters', the participants', the audience's—that's when the tool really works.*

Multicam works well for corporate communications, but it also has taken its place from an inspirational level: Worship TV.

Worship TV: Enrapturing the Audience

As we've seen, multicam and IMAG techniques connect music with the fans in a way that inspires devotion and action.

So does Worship TV. The churches, big and small, have made that connection too, putting on weekly shows that are as technically advanced as any network TV show.

Figure 15.31 In-the-round service and production at The Second Baptist Church, Houston, Texas. (Courtesy The Second Baptist Church, Houston, Texas.)

The Second Baptist Church in Houston, Texas, counts more than 50,000 members spread over five locations in and around the city.[2] In 1979, the church launched a weekly broadcast of edited worship services on local television, with the mission of growing membership and spreading the gospel beyond the church's walls.

That show begat a weekly, national radio show, which begat books, and today, Senior Pastor Dr. Ed Young's "Winning Walk" has become an international television, radio, and Internet outreach effort.

Figure 15.32 Master control for the Second Baptist Church, Houston, Texas. (Courtesy The Second Baptist Church, Houston, Texas.)

To distribute its heavenly message, the church relies on the terrestrial talents of director Keith Brown, a former promo producer at a local TV station. He's responsible for preproduction, live direction, postproduction, distribution, and promotion, as well as coordinating production simultaneously across the church's multiple locations in a global video initiative.

The effort is the result of a multiyear plan and investment to embrace video as a tool to communicate the church's message. Brown designs and specifies all of the church's acquisitions, from cameras to distribution, edit systems, and data transport and standardization across locations.

Keith Brown: *We're set up a lot like a postproduction facility or like an independent production company. We have a 30-minute broadcast that we produce each week. We do 52 shows a year.*

Worship TV is not necessarily just a couple of guys shooting camcorders and editing with iMovie. Brown's system would rival any network news facility or monster truck. He captures each weekly sermon with 10 cameras in the round, recording in HD 1080 60i with matching Ikegami cameras, recording ISOs and a line cut. As more campuses are connected, more cameras will be added. Brown hopes ultimately to have a system of 18 cameras capturing direct to disc.

Figure 15.33 Audio Suite, The Second Baptist Church, Houston, Texas. (Courtesy The Second Baptist Church, Houston, Texas.)

The production design derives from that of major broadcast events like awards shows and concerts. The latest set design was done by the same production designer who redid *The Tonight Show* set for Conan O'Brien. Lighting and staging were inspired by a source that might sound at odds with a worship service: Las Vegas.

Keith Brown: *Our pastor and technical director took a trip out to Vegas, so there's a lot of influence from touring acts, especially in the lighting and video projection.*

Figure 15.34 Special lighting design inside church. (Courtesy Jeff Ravitz/www.visualterrain.net.)

With all this technology at his fingertips, Brown has a major hand in helping the pastor and the church spread their message. And there are plans to grow the digital ministry. Brown's facility also produces Vacation Bible School DVDs, original theatrical productions by the children of the church, and is planning a full digital curriculum that could be franchised to other churches around the world, proving that the greatest story ever told will continue to be told for generations to come.

Weddings: Everyone's a Star

As the public has become more accustomed to what a major event looks and feels like, it's no surprise that regular people want to bring these production values to one of the most important events in their lives. Just as worship TV is no longer the exclusive province of interns and camcorders, wedding video is no longer

Figure 15.35 Wedding video demo at WEVA Expo. (Courtesy John Zale/WEVA.)

exclusive to moonlighting ENG guys trying to earn an extra buck with their beta rigs.

According to John Zale, director of education development for the Wedding and Event Videographers Association (WEVA.com), there were approximately 3 million weddings in America last year, and some 30% of those were professionally videotaped. Zale also believes that between 80% and 90% of those shoots involved more than one camera on location.

John Zale: *It's very difficult for one camera to cover all the angles, so the more, the merrier. You always want to have backup. The people I know, even the one-man shops, usually shoot with a second camera in the back of the room or up in a balcony so they have cutaway shots to go to.*

There is definitely a market here for talented people to get noticed and land regular work. Zale observes that there is a wide range of people working, from 20-year broadcast veterans to new people getting into the business every day, as the cost of professional-quality equipment goes down.

Don Moran runs Omaha Wedding Video, a high-end company in Omaha, Nebraska. His multi-cam packages start at $4,000, and shooting runs from 8 a.m. to midnight with three Sony Z1 cameras. "The Omaha Wedding Video is a big grand cinematic fairy princess wedding," Moran says. He likes to be flexible with gear to meet the client's demands and can shrink to single-cam or expand up to a six-camera production.

While Moran live-switches two-camera shoots like events and ceremonies, for larger weddings he prefers to go more run-and-gun and sync up in post. It takes more time to produce, but it gets that vérité feel that a lot of folks like, making their wedding video look more like a reality show.

John Zale agrees with this approach and thinks most of his members do all of their syncing in post. In a wedding context, he notices that producers place more value on capturing audio, because you don't want to miss the vows—and at a Jewish wedding you really want to capture the sound of the glass breaking.

Don Moran: *Most people in our industry will mic the officiate, whether it be a minister or priest or rabbi or justice of the peace, and also mic the groom with wireless, just in case the officiate doesn't happen to be close enough. So it's not uncommon to have two or three audio sources at a wedding. Sometimes more.*

"I'm definitely a postproduction editor," says Gary Kleiner, a producer of more than 530 wedding productions in a 30-year career.

Gary Kleiner: *In the event videography world, things are happening in a spontaneous way, especially weddings; they're totally unscripted, and you don't know what's going to happen. I think it's always been a tradeoff between the extra gear and setup time involved to do a live switch versus the time you spend on a postproduction switch. I like the control of the postproduction switch, when I know I can cut exactly to the frame.*

Gone are the days when it took 6 months to get your wedding video. Increasingly, wedding videographers are cutting and turning around video on the same day or the next day, just like traditional broadcasters.

Figure 15.36 A wedding video edited in Premiere Pro by Illinois Videographers Association president and five-time WEVA Creative Excellence Award winner Keith Anderson. (Courtesy Keith Anderson.)

The future in wedding video may be even more in line with TV and webcasting. The pace of change has accelerated from yearly to monthly. The next frontier is livestreaming. John Zale says that's probably going to be the next big thing in weddings.

John Zale: *I was testing out a system for a friend of mine who had a wedding in Chicago. The groom's father became ill at the last minute and couldn't come from Boston. So they took one of the cameras and did a live stream so he could watch it from the hospital back in Boston. He watched the ceremony and the first couple of hours of the reception.*

Who needs a monster truck when you can shoot and switch a wedding live online, with a couple of cameras, a MacBook, and WiFi?

In-School TV: The Kids Are All Right (Maybe Even Better Than You)

Most of us have seen the commercial where the 3-year-old girl takes a picture with a digital camera, crops it on a computer, and makes a high-quality color print. There are millions of people 20 times her age who wouldn't be able to do that without calling for help.

It's just a commercial, but it makes a valid point. Younger generations are growing up with technology that as recently as the early 1990s was available only to multimillion-dollar broadcast productions. It's as natural today for a high school kid to submit an assignment on video as on loose-leaf paper.

With media literacy and production classes increasing at high schools and colleges across the country, the children and grandchildren of the Baby Boomers will be entering the workforce.

Figure 15.37 An ENG crew conducts an interview for a high school news program. (Courtesy Debbie Rein/Osceola Fundamental High School.)

They will be unburdened by such concepts as rendering time, down-converting for SD, real-time tape transfer—even tapes, for that matter.

In New York City, schools chancellor Joel I. Klein has started a program called the Blueprint for Teaching and Learning in the Arts: The Moving Image, a guide that outlines clear expectations for the study of film, television, and animation from early elementary school through high school graduation.

It can't be a bad idea to encourage ongoing partnerships between schools and cultural organizations that will allow students access to studios, museums, and film and broadcast venues across the city.

In a press release, Chancellor Klein said:

The media arts profoundly shape our culture and our daily lives, and we look forward to seeing New York City public school graduates lead the next generation of filmmakers, screenwriters, producers, editors, grips, broadcasters, and animators.[3]

While the Big Apple school system is looking forward, some other schools are already there—like Debbie Rein's TV and Video class at Osceola Fundamental High School in Seminole, Florida.

Figure 15.38 The studio set at Osceola Fundamental High School. (Courtesy Debbie Rein/ Osceola Fundamental High School.)

Rein oversees a not-so-mini broadcast center with 40 Avid Media Composer stations, Final Cut Pro stations, and a studio in which the students produce a live morning show every day and record a live-to-tape multicam show called *Teen Talk* for a local broadcast channel. Rein teaches them the basics, then they're on their own, rolling four cameras live with locking timecode, switching live, and posting packages.

Figure 15.39 Students edit multicam videos using Avid and Final Cut Pro. (Courtesy Debbie Rein/Osceola Fundamental High School.)

The kids write, produce, direct—they do it all, says Rein. Audio, video, hookup computers, direct, run cameras—they run everything.

Figure 15.40 Audio mixing and computer graphics workstation. (Courtesy Debbie Rein/Osceola Fundamental High School.)

Many of the students who find their way into her class get there with little or no interest in TV production and leave with keen interest and a set of real career skills. In the 1970s they would have been in auto shop, but now they're making television. Says one 18-year-old student named Jacob:

I had no interest in TV before this. It actually ended up on my schedule as an accident. I got stuck in this class, and I've been in it for four years now.

Figure 15.41 Student directors call the shots to the TD using NewTek TriCaster. (Courtesy Debbie Rein/Osceola Fundamental High School.)

And now Jacob and another student, Kyle, have taken the skills they learned in Rein's class and landed professional work. They just shot a three-camera wedding and are looking to pursue careers in broadcasting. Look out world!

Satellite Media Tours (SMT): Guitar Hero: Aerosmith's Sweet Promotion

Concerts are no longer the only place for bands to reach out to their fans. New gaming systems like Rockband and Guitar Hero allow every air-guitar virtuoso to jam along with his or her favorite artists. Such totally immersive experiences demand a concert-like immersive kick-off event. In June 2008, Aerosmith escalated the music-gaming arms race when, toting road-honed multicam and IMAG techniques, the band took over Times Square to promote the debut of Activision's Guitar Hero: Aerosmith.

Figure 15.42 Aerosmith at Guitar Hero launch party/press conference. (Courtesy Kevin Mazur. www .kevinmazurphotography.com)

The launch was a big deal: it was broadcast live to the building-size screens at the crossroads of America and sent via satellite to the world.

Figure 15.43 Video presentation on Nasdaq monitor in Times Square.

Whether shooting a concert, a car race, or a press conference, Keith Garde is guided by the same principles: be true to the artist you're covering and let the action lead your shot choices. Keith Garde is president of the celebrity services group for Paid, Inc. Garde has been in artist management and entertainment production for more than 25 years, is an early Internet pioneer of digital distribution of entertainment, and serves as special projects manager for Aerosmith. It was natural for the band to hand him the task of turning a video game release into a major event.

"It's not so much following the action as knowing where the action really is and letting it lead you," says Garde, who takes issue with the fast-cutting style that has taken over much of music video production:

Figure 15.44 The author with Keith Garde and Andy Martel inside a TV truck.

If Joe Perry is moving across the stage playing a lead, a director guided by the music alone will cut to what he thinks is a fast pace. Mine is a style that conforms to the performance. If somebody's doing something compelling, you want to stay with them and not worry whether you're making a cut on the downbeat.

Why apply so much style to an event as banal as a press conference? The answer should be clear: press conferences can be dull.

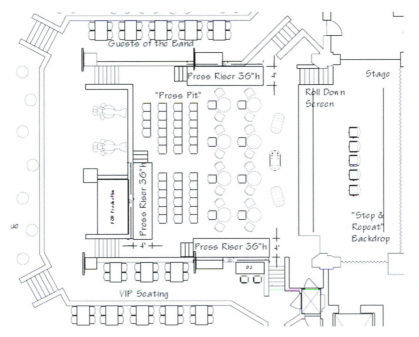

Figure 15.45 Camera map for the Guitar Hero Aerosmith press conference. (Courtesy Jack Morton Productions.)

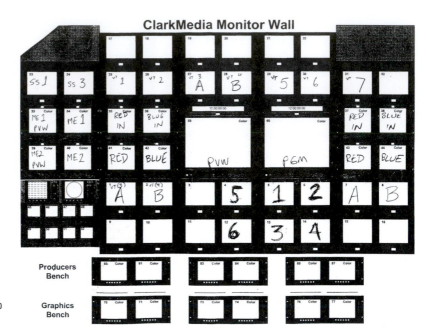

Figure 15.46a Monitor wall map for Guitar Hero Aerosmith.

Figure 15.46b Mitch Jacobson directs the press conference with cameras direct to the Telestream Pipeline system. (Courtesy Kevin Louden/Telestream.)

A multicam production, broadcast live and large to the world's most famous intersection, automatically generates excitement. When you're doing a live show, you can't stop and start and do overdubs. When you have multiple cameras, you're catching everything. It's live; it's exciting.

Keith Garde: *It's great to watch that live energy of what's happening when human beings infused with creative spirit are expressing something altogether. It's a coordinated display of how beautiful and harmonious collaboration can be—but it's also filled with tension. It's live and at any moment anything can happen.*

Of course, the marketing effort recorded and touched up the event for distribution to international media outlets, but capturing the live event with multicam was essential.

Figure 15.47 Camera prep with chip chart.

The main problem was how to capture, digitize, and edit the six-camera, 90-minute performance for a super quick turnaround package for a satellite feed within an hour after directing the press conference. It was important to management to review and have access to all the ISOs. If I had to wait to capture all those angles to tape, it would have taken all day and into the night. Maybe we could have cut tape, but that was only our backup. Fortunately, we didn't need backup.

To have a fully digitized set of ISO and a line cut, I brought in the Telestream Pipeline system and specialist Kevin Louden of Telestream.

Figure 15.48 Kevin Louden of Telestream sets up the Pipeline system on-set for Guitar Hero Aerosmith.

Figure 15.49 Engineer Gary Templeton plugging SDI feeds into two pipelines ganged together.

Figure 15.50 Pipeline and AJA iO employed to record ISO feeds.

Pipeline encodes multiple camera streams onto a single MacPro tower and allows editing to take place concurrently with the capture process. No waiting. The system pulls SDI feeds from each camera. It reads house timecode through the SDI cable. HD units can record two feeds and SD units can record four per unit and units can be ganged to accommodate as many cameras as necessary.

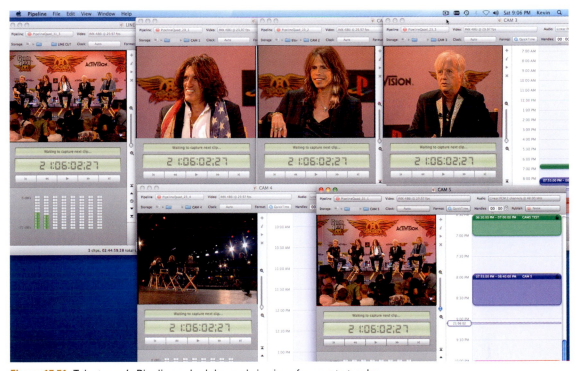

Figure 15.51 Telestream's Pipeline schedules and viewing of separate tracks.

The individual feeds can be pregrouped into a multiclip sequence for cutting live directly in Final Cut Pro. Then, as the show starts, the QuickTime files grow as frames are captured. The advantage is that all the ISOs get loaded directly and in real time to the editing codec of choice. This allows for superfast turnaround for editing live shows, publicity, or webcasts.

As I directed the show live to a line cut, the Pipeline was recording five cameras, and the line cut directly into a multiclip sequence into a timeline in Final Cut Pro on a MacBook Pro with a portable eSata Raid.

Andy Martel, director of artist relations/client manager at PAID, Inc., marked the FCP timeline in real time for approved sound bites. When the show wrapped, I took the markers and made them into subclips and started cutting. All the ISO reels were grouped and synced into the sequence, so if I needed an alternate angle, it was right there. Even loading four angles of selects would have taken an hour or more.

By cutting immediately after the show, we were able to get on an earlier satellite feed. Without a direct-to-disk multicam ingest while editing on a system like Pipeline, I would not have had the time to make our quick-turnaround deadlines. Pipeline allowed me to get the job done by providing a cost-effective way to encode and edit simultaneously with very little setup time using off-the-shelf equipment. That was a huge benefit to making the package available to the widest audience in the quickest amount of time. Multicamera madness!

References

1. www.youtube.com/watch?v=zzZXXCDakjY.
2. www.second.org/VisitorInformation.aspx.
3. "New York City Announces Publication for Blueprint for Teaching and Learning in the Arts: The Moving Image," Press Release, October 15, 2009, www.nyc.gov/html/film/html/news/100109_blueprint_moving_image.shtml.

DELIVERABLES

16

CONFORMING THE MASTER

Conforming a multicamera show involves only a few extra steps not needed in typical single-camera productions. Otherwise, the procedures are virtually the same.

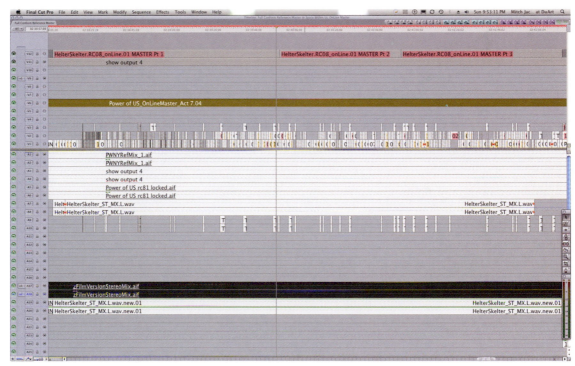

Figure 16.1 *Helter Skelter* timeline with all post elements prior to conformed output master. Sequence includes all multiclips, B roll with original natural sound, layered effects, reference mixdowns from offline, production mix, music master, and alt mixes plus original live board mix.

The main difference would be collapsing and removing .xml info from the multiclips (FCP) or using Enable Commit Multicam for grouped clips (Avid) to send out projects for color and sound. Once the master sequence is collapsed, the standard techniques are employed to deliver the masters.

Leverage is a TNT show produced by Electric Entertainment, Dean Devlin's production company. Devlin is a director and a Hollywood special effects wizard and *Leverage* is an action show shot with a minimum of three RED cameras. Brian Gonosey is the show's editor.

Brian Gonosey, editor: *What we did with our two-episode finale was to go back in and redigitized using the 2K native res—log and transfer—and bring that in native. We decomposed the sequence in Media Manager, then relinked to the native and sent it to color. We had about 5% of the total edits that we had to go back in and work over by hand.*

20-Minute Reel Sizes

Many editors choose to work in sequences smaller than 20 minutes. One reason for this has to do with workflow. Because film editors have generally worked in terms of 20-minute act reels in film, this has become a common sequence length.

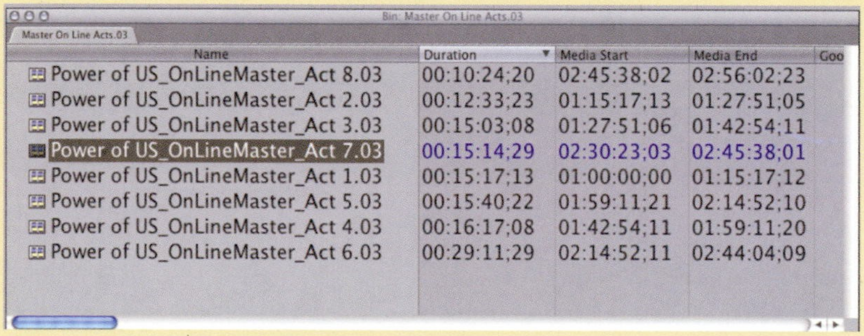

Name	Duration	Media Start	Media End	Goo
Power of US_OnLineMaster_Act 8.03	00:10:24;20	02:45:38;02	02:56:02;23	
Power of US_OnLineMaster_Act 2.03	00:12:33;23	01:15:17;13	01:27:51;05	
Power of US_OnLineMaster_Act 3.03	00:15:03;08	01:27:51;06	01:42:54;11	
Power of US_OnLineMaster_Act 7.03	00:15:14;29	02:30:23;03	02:45:38;01	
Power of US_OnLineMaster_Act 1.03	00:15:17;13	01:00:00;00	01:15:17;12	
Power of US_OnLineMaster_Act 5.03	00:15:40;22	01:59:11;21	02:14:52;10	
Power of US_OnLineMaster_Act 4.03	00:16:17;08	01:42:54;11	01:59:11;20	
Power of US_OnLineMaster_Act 6.03	00:29:11;29	02:14:52;11	02:44:04;09	

Figure 16.2 Feature is divided into act sequences of 10 to 30 minutes in duration.

Ray Volkema, HDNet: *I like to break it down to 20-to-30-minute segments for drive reasons—so that if you get one bad clip you're not toasted for an hour and a half of reloading. I think the computer runs better with 20-to-30-minute clips, max, so I just group all of those that way. Maybe you're doing a 20-to-30-minute sequence in multiclip, when you've got 10 cameras; it's a lot for the computer to keep up with. So I try to keep my sequences short, too.*

Usually, when you get a locked picture, after finishing the edit you can manage the media. Start with collapsing the sequence. You want to lose any references to multicam for EDLs, XML, OMF, and AMA.

Collapsing Your Edit

Before using the Media Manager in FCP, you want to collapse all of your multiclips. This will alert Media Manager of the angle that you want to use in the final show, so you can recapture only the one angle that you need, not all of the angles that make up the multiclips. When you collapse a multiclip, it's replaced by the

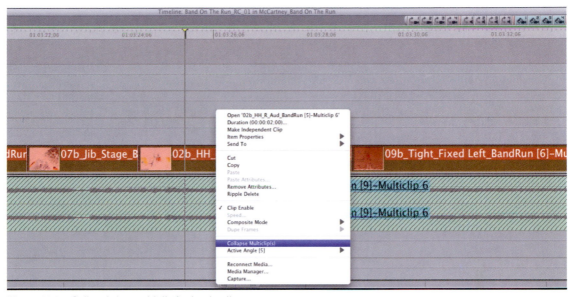

Figure 16.3a Collapsing a multiclip in the timeline.

active angle of the multiclip. This is useful when you want to send a sequence to a color correctionist or effects artist and you want him or her to focus only on the angles you chose during editing.

Collapsing a multiclip is not permanent, which means you can expand the active angle at any time to return to the full multiclip, even after you close and reopen a project. You could use it as a temporary lock to prevent switching of angles during a screening or between rough cuts by collapsing a multiclip down to its active angle. Collapsing multiclips also improves performance, because less video is streaming from disk.

Scott Simmons, editor: *These days, the offline/online world is very blurred, as opposed to what it used to be. I'm cutting the show at full ProRes resolution, so there's no "online"—but say you're cutting at ProRes Proxy or working on a RED job and you transcode it to low-res files to edit, then conform with the R3D files?*

You need to collapse that sequence down to as little media as possible in the timeline, as you go to a conform in online. One reason is that you don't want to digitize or capture or transcode media that you don't need. It takes time, disk space, and money.

Another reason is that, if you're going to do a color correction or a color grade in Color or DaVinci, it will save you time and money if you pull an EDL of that edit and load the EDL into the DaVinci, which gives the edit points. Otherwise, it has to go through and play back in real time and autodetect the edits.

Figure 16.3b Pulling an EDL.

Scott Simmons: *Say you have a 90-minute show that you want to color correct. That's an extra hour and a half that you have spent playing that thing back to autodetect those edits. If they're similar camera angles and lighting, sometimes they can't be autodetected. So by pulling that EDL, you've saved yourself a lot of time shuttling around and in DaVinci. Just collapsing the thing down as low as you can will really save a lot of effort down the line.*

By collapsing the multiclips, you can still uncollapse them and go back and change an angle if you need to; it just gets rid of all that stuff and improves the performance of your machine, the video goes back to full quality, and so on. But a multiclip is still a multiclip. It's different from an individual master clip from a single media file. So that does seem to affect how the code is going.

On the Avid side, you're not really sending out to another application except for Pro Tools. But you'll still need to Enable Commit Multicam to consolidate the grouped clip audio before sending it to Pro Tools.

Enable Commit Multicam

You can remove the grouped clips in a sequence and replace each of them with its selected original clip by committing

Collapsing Multiclips

To collapse one or more multiclips in the timeline, select the multiclips you want to collapse in the timeline and choose Modify > Collapse Multiclip(s) or Ctrl-click one of the selected multiclips in the timeline. Then choose Collapse Multiclip(s) from the shortcut menu. The selected multiclips are collapsed to the clips of their active angles.

To expand one or more multiclips in the timeline, select the multiclips you want to expand in the timeline and choose Modify > Uncollapse Multiclip(s) or Ctrl-click one of the selected multiclips in the timeline. Then choose Uncollapse Multiclip(s) from the shortcut menu. The selected multiclips are expanded to the clips of their active angles.

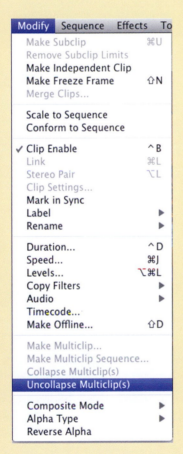

Figure 16.4 Uncollapse Multiclip.

multicamera edits. This might be useful if you experience poor performance with a complex multicamera sequence on a slower system, for example, a sequence that uses many multicamera clips and many effects or color corrections.[1]

It also allows matchback directly to a clip and not a group. This is necessary when color-correcting multicam shots or sending OMFs to an audio session. Don't use it if you still want to edit with groups, because it will break links to the groups in that sequence.

To commit multicamera edits:

1. Select the sequence you want to affect.
2. Right-click the sequence and select Commit Multicam Edits.

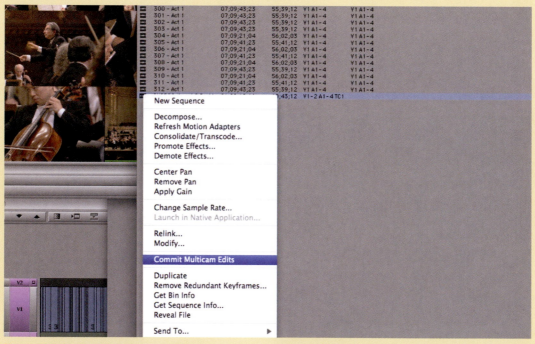

Figure 16.5 Commit Multicam Edits flattens out your sequence and links back to the original clips for sending out to audio or color grading in Symphony.

Your Avid editing application duplicates the sequence and then replaces each grouped clip in the duplicate sequence with its selected clip. The original sequence is unaffected and still contains the grouped clips. A message will appear: Enable Commit Multicam is on.

Using the Console Command

Enable Commit Multicam is an Avid command that previously needed to be entered into the console that would make a duplicate of your sequence without groups in it, essentially flattening the sequence for finishing and collaboration.

You should know that if you are working in MC 3.5 or above, the Enable Commit Multicam function is always enabled. Earlier versions contain a workaround, so for those of you doing multicam on previous versions of MC, you will still need to make the command manually.

Before exporting a multicam edited project, open the console and type: enablecommitmulticam. (No spaces.)

Reconforming

Everyone has his or her own media management horror stories. No NLE is perfect. The idea is to consolidate your sequence so that you're dealing only with the clips that appear in the cut—no ties to multicam and no shots that don't appear in the final master. First delete all of the disabled clips and merge all of your clips into one track, if possible. Then take your final collapsed sequence and media-manage it.

Mark Raudonis, VP postproduction, Bunim-Murray Productions: *There are three shows currently going around, so we have to work offline. It's an unfortunate byproduct of the volume that we have to deal with.* Project Runway *is digitizing about a hundred hours of media a night. (Multiply that by the number of production days.) A hundred hours, that's a lot of drops. And* Real World *is bringing in an equal amount.*

Consolidating and Decomposing

In Avid, that's consolidating or decomposing, depending on how you go. Consolidating will break your show down with or without handles and relink to a new set of media to match a new sequence. Decomposing is the same thing, but your new sequence doesn't create or relink to any new media. All the media would be offline. It's like a skeleton of your project, requiring you to reconform all the media from scratch.

Avid's been doing it a lot longer and seems to be robust, with its mega database. Occasionally, however, you have problems.

Mark Raudonis: *We media-manage a sequence (in FCP), basically creating independent new clips that shed the excess amount of media, i.e., anything that's not in the cut. And then we basically redigitize that sequence. That's if everything goes well. We have a lot of checks and balances. Once the up-res process is done, we do a picture-in-picture split-screen and compare the low-res to the offline. Low-res to the full-res. Frame by frame, cut by cut. In general, there'll be 75% of the shots that will need an adjustment.*

Media Manager

In Final Cut, it's using Media Manager. Final Cut tends to be a little more fussy, particularly in multicam and when relinking media.

In FCP7, many issues have been resolved. But Final Cut tends to be more sensitive to the path of where you stored the media and what the computer wants to see as the path to its own media management. Don't try to outsmart it with your organization of the media folders. Sometimes it's very happy and allows you to be as free form as you want and you don't get into trouble. Other times, you get burned, and there doesn't seem to be any rhyme or reason as to why.

If you're using Media Manager, in the offline/online workflow, you can manage to an off-line sequence where you're creating new master clips. Then either recapture or, in a file-based workflow, reconnect or relink.

Oliver Peters, editor/colorist: *As much as everybody's trying to get away from the time-honored edit decision list of the last 30-odd years, in many cases that still seems to be the most rock-solid, straightforward way of doing this, particularly in a multicam show where you don't have a lot of effects. It's more about the cutting and less about the filters you throw on, and with that EDL works very well. So if you named your reels and clips properly, if you're organized, EDL should be fine, even making the transition between versions of Final Cut.*

If you're using Final Cut's Media Manager to throw everything away except what you want to use in the cut, you have the choice of doing that with or without other angles in the multiclip angle. If you deselect this option, only the media files from the active angle will be processed, saving you a ton of time and hard-drive space on a multicam show. But know when to do that. Is the picture really locked? If you think at some point down the road the

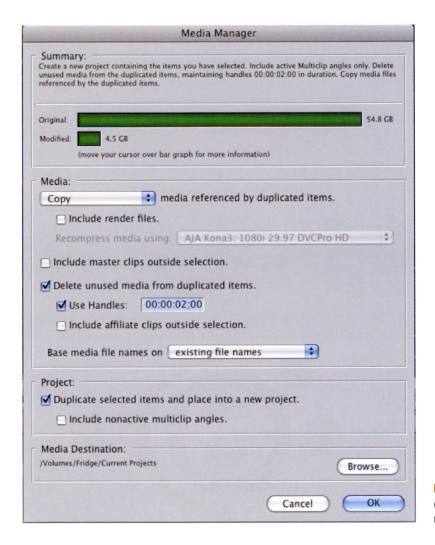

Figure 16.6a Media Manager option to include nonactive multicam angles (not selected).

director is still going to want to change his or her mind at the last minute and go to a different camera angle, you need to preserve that possibility during your media management: by keeping the other angles.

Log and Capture or Transfer

After collapsing, use Media Manager to create an offline version of the project to redigitize your high-res footage. In FCP, use either Log and Capture or Log and Transfer, depending on whether you use tape or files. In Avid, use AMA to relink/transcode file-based media or the Capture tool to reload off tape.

AMA stands for Avid Media Access, which does the following:
1. Extends Avid's support of media formats
2. Accelerates Avid's adoption of new formats
3. Streamlines file-based ingest
4. Allows for plug-in architecture for camera manufacturers
5. Currently supports Sony XDCAM and Panasonic P2
6. Offers direct access to recording formats (SxS and P2 cards)
7. Allows for virtual volumes
8. Archives in an Avid bin view on the volume

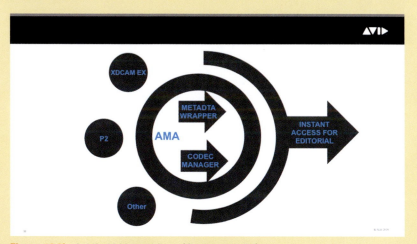

Figure 16.6b Avid's AMA workflow. (Courtesy Avid.)

Tip

For file-based offline/online workflows, use the Log and Transfer tool's cog icon on the upper-right-hand corner to reveal options for any given formats' codec and ingest resolutions.

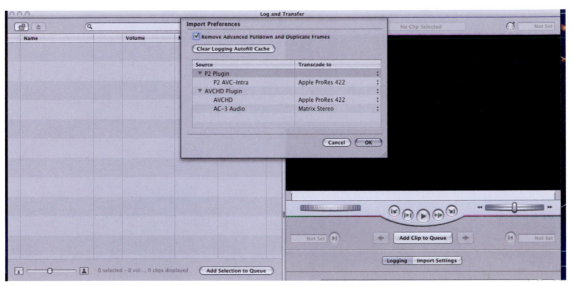

Figure 16.7 Log and Transfer settings in FCP.

Reload from Original Media

Because storage is so cheap these days, many people are bypassing the offline/online process and opting to digitize or ingest everything at an online codec with a low bit rate suitable for broadcast-quality mastering—and they are skipping the conforming stage altogether. However, in multicam, you may still need to drop the multicam clips to a lower bit rate codec to play simultaneously. In this case, simply use the transcode method and only reconform the multiclips.

If you've done a fly-pack shoot or the cameras weren't jam-synced and the timecode is all over the place, doing an online conversion—going back and redigitizing the master tapes—would be a nightmare. You or your assistant editor is going to have to go through and find every bit of tape from every camera and make sure it's correct. It probably won't be. And that may add as much as a week or two to the online process.

Gary Adcock, Studio 37: *The highest quality, however, is always going to come from going back and capturing via HD SDI from the original masters. That's a simple process, if all the timecodes are synced.*

RED Post Workflows

What is R3D? The file format created by the RED ONE Camera. It records in 2K, 3K, and 4K (and larger frame sizes in the future).

1. RGB 4:4:4 at 12 bits.
2. It's a compressed format (JPEG 2000) recorded as RAW.
3. It uses a Bayer-type encoding to recreate an RGB image.

Tip

Go to red.com/ support for product manuals, plug-ins, firmware, and other solutions for Avid, Adobe, and FCP.

Read the RED Final Cut white paper that comes with the Final Cut Studio RED installer. (It's also available separately.) Written by colorist/author Alexis Van Hurkman, this is a must-read.

4. Color is applied as metadata to the RAW image.
5. The R3D file itself is encrypted and needs components available from RED or licensed tools to decode the image.

FCP and RED

Download the Final Cut Studio plug-in for RED (red.com). That will allow you, in Final Cut Pro, to ingest your RED footage when you're in the Log and Transfer window.

There are two main RED/FCP ingesting workflows worth noting:
1. Many people shoot in RED 4K but do not need to finish in 4K.
2. You can plan to work in proxy files and still finish in 4K if necessary.

Shooting in 4K looks gorgeous, but for broadcast jobs, it's overkill. Networks don't broadcast in 4K. Most projectors don't show 4K either. So you could down-convert the 4K into 2K proxies right off the bat and have master clips for finishing.

When you do that, something interesting happens. Any time you ingest RED footage to a ProRes codec, because Final Cut Pro only supports a maximum resolution of 2K, anything shot in 4K is down-sampled to 2K on ingest. So what you end up with is 2K Apple ProRes Proxy files. Now, those are still bigger than high-def files, so they're going to take up a little bit more room, a little bit more bandwidth.

Robbie Carman, colorist: *When you're in the Log and Transfer window ingesting your RED footage, you can choose to ingest that footage to any of the Apple ProRes codecs, so when you do you can just follow along on that sort of offline/online workflow and ingest all of your RED footage as Apple ProRes Proxy.*

If the project is going theatrical, then perhaps finishing in 4K native would be a good solution.

Robbie Carman: *The one difference I would suggest is that when you go back to do that, create those offline files and then reingest the high-res RED footage. Or, if time allows, you could ingest RED footage as native. You would edit it offline using Apple ProRes Proxy, create an offline project, go back and reingest your original RED footage, and you can choose RED native. Now, the problem with that is that it takes a while, because you have to do it for every card. This assumes that you've backed up every card.*

On *Leverage*, Mark Franco is the "anything that has to do with technology" guy and has been going through all the permutations, gestures, and gyrations as the technologies develop. He is constantly walking on that razor's edge to incorporate the best workflows for the show.

Figure 16.8 Mark Franco of Electric Entertainment. (Courtesy Electric Entertainment.)

Mark Franco: *The pilot for the series was shot on the Genesis. We can't buy a Genesis, but we can buy a RED, so we immediately purchased two RED cameras. We also incorporated additional cameras—Dean [Devlin] likes to shoot with a lot of cameras. We get a big feature-quality look from our work, and one of the ways we achieve that in the time constraints is to have three or as many as five cameras running at the same time on a given day. We want the results to look like a big movie, but we don't have time to take one camera and shoot six or eight setups. That's why we use so many cameras when we shoot.*

Electric Entertainment has been a pioneer of tapeless workflows and has helped to push the industry into new territory.

Figure 16.9

Figure 16.9 and 16.10 In-house post facilities at Electric Entertainment. (Courtesy Electric Entertainment.)

Mark Franco: *We shoot 24p, unless we're doing some sort of stunt or something that requires slow motion. The 24P RED RAW files are captured to ProRes as an intermediate codec.*

Brian Gonosey: *We were feeding the QuickTime proxies pointing back to the R3Ds into a compressor. We set up a script in Compressor to take it from the 16 × 9, 4K dimension to a 1920 × 1080 ProRes HD. We got around the render times on transcoding from RED into ProRes by processing our dailies at night, when the editors were down. So we had a swing shift come in at night and essentially set up camera rolls on maybe 12 different workstations.*

As for color on the edit proxies, it's baked in with the DP's look from the set. It's not RAW; it's the look that was dialed into the camera with the metadata. From there, it's just a standard Apple ProRes HD offline/online workflow.

Brian Gonosey: *These are basic workflows. A couple of years ago, when we started working with multiclips, we'd just take those ProRes dailies as offline clips and make our multiclips and cut the show. Not only can you switch it live, on the fly, but you can make your edits live, on the fly. The show gets a lot of accolades for its multicam style.*

Cinema Tools and R3D

A new process in Final Cut Pro 7 and Color 1.5 allows you to use Cinema Tools as a match-back vehicle.

Matching back to R3D Files with Cinema Tools is amazing. The only problem is that it's limited by what EDL supports. Basically, here's how it works. Instead of having to do that offline/online version of a project and go back and find every card and reingest it at high-res, what you can do (if you've ingested all of your footage into Apple ProRes Proxy or some other compressed Apple

ProRes codec) is export an EDL of your final sequence from Final Cut Pro and then take all of your original RED footage and drag it to Cinema Tools to create a new Cinema Tools database. Then, in Color, instead of pointing back to the original media, point it back to the Cinema Tools database and, in one click, all of your offline files, your ProRes Proxy files, now become the native RED RAW files.

Robbie Carman: *Essentially, you create an offline edit export and EDL from FCP. Then take all of your RED sources and create a Cinema Tools database. In Color, you then open the EDL and point Color to the Cinema Tools database and ... voilà! All of your clips reconnect to the original R3D files. This is much quicker than using Media Manager, but really limited, because EDLs only support a few different types of transitions and one video track and no audio.*

So now you can grade all of your RED files in true native fashion using the RED tab in Color. It's really quick, but there's one danger, in that it's really just cut to cut. Don't use more than one video track. It's best suited to concerts.

Avid and RED

Avid has always been a leading choice when it comes to media management. Working with RED and other file-based systems in Avid proves no exception. There are many variations on the theme, but one thing is always true: Avid has a solution for you and your RED workflow. You can offline in SD or HD and online in HD or 2K/4K or native R3D with Mac and Windows. Avid has an easy import solution that allows the ingest of picture, sound, and metadata from the RED ONE camera. It works in the native file format, which will eliminate QuickTime file wrapping from the process, making the imports faster.

There is native R3D support in Avid DS and with MetaFuze. You can use Avid MetaFuze to transcode R3D files to Avid DNxHD and customize your workflow. And when it comes time to conform, finish with Avid DS, which also has native file capabilities, including the ability to keep original color parameters created by REDrushes passed through to the conform stage.

For a complete, step-by-step guide, go to the Avid download page at www.avid.com/red. Workflow tools are also available.

Here are a few workflow advantages in Avid:

- Metadata tracking
- Native MXF wrapped DNxHD from R3D transcodes
- Both ToD and edgecode (REDrushes)
- Short, medium, and long filenames in separate columns
- Ability to change clip name once imported

- Color parameters
- AutoSync for double-system workflows
- Cross-platform support for Mac and Windows
- R3D and DPX conform via AFE in Avid DS

One cool thing about clip naming in Avid is that you can edit with your customized descriptions for clip names, scenes, and takes, without restrictions. It also uses XML representation of the sequence metadata for use with third-party programs.

MetaCheater

MetaCheater, created by Jabez Olssen, lets you extract time-code and reel ID metadata from QuickTime movies and save it out as an Avid Log Exchange file (.ALE).

MetaCheater supports both SD and HD workflows and lets you select one or more QuickTime movies. Through a variety of settings, you can work with any number of workflows, depending on the metadata extracted. It's a great way, for example, to work with QuickTime files associated with a RED camera workflow.

Michael Phillips, Avid Technology, Inc.: *ALE, as many of you know, is an Avid log file format that has become a de facto standard in the post industry. It's a text-based metadata exchange format used in telecine to standalone logging applications and is supported by many NLEs on the market today. The Avid Log Exchange format is based on a TAB delimited file format and is therefore easily extendable.*

It runs on both OS X and Windows XP and is offered as a shareware application at www.staticpictures.com/metacheater.

MetaFuze

MetaFuze is a free automation application that transcodes many files types to native Avid DNxHD, including R3D. It can scale via scripts and XML to be used on render farms. Although it is optimized for the PC, it can run on a Mac via Bootcamp or Vmware, but the performance is not great.

ROCKETCINE-X will most likely be the application of choice for R3D, but MetaFuze has its advantages:

- Frame rate change (frame for frame) 24 as 23.976, 25, 24, and so on
- Lower cost to scale to faster than real-time encode than REDROCKET
- Supports taking advantage of existing hardware in render farms

RED Cine-X

RED Cine-X is a free application from RED that will open REDCODE RAW (.R3D) video files so you can do initial light color corrections and export to any number of output options. Specs include the following:

- Works on both Mac and Windows
- Supports trimming of R3D files via subclips
- Supports scale and X/Y offset
- Renders with color correction
- Creates Avid DHxHD 175x and 180x only
- Can create a DVCPRO HD workflow (via MetaCheater)
- Uses Avid's REDCINE_ALE.xsl file to create ALE

Another feature, Hybrid Workflows, allows the use of a combination of tools for additional functionality. For example, on a Mac you can use QT ref + REDCINE metadata and create QT wrapped DNxHD files in REDrushes. On Mac *and* PC, use a DVCPRO HD workflow and transcode with REDrushes or REDCINE directly to DVCPRO with burn-in. You could also use MetaCheater to create an ALE file with proper timecode conversion.

Color Correcting

These days, editors are more involved in color correction than they were in the past. After all, color correction is more than just matching camera angles; it's establishing control over the stylistic look and treatment. The integration of editing with products like Apple Color makes the process even more feasible for nonspecialists.

Color-correction methods vary from show to show and budget to budget. Most broadcast shows have traditionally gone to tape-to-tape color with DaVinci or digital systems like Clipster. Many inexpensive products have come along with powerful features, changing the game. Between Apple Color and Scratch, everyone should have the power to create a pretty picture.

The process for color-correcting a multicamera show is the same as coloring any show. By now, the angles have been collapsed and the clips up-rezzed, and the sequence information has been prepped to move on to the color phase. One thing apparent now is that there are several broken shots from each master camera. If they have been named strategically for editing, those names carry through into color and this makes it easier for the colorist to apply grades to each angle. Other than that, it's as traditional as it gets.

If you work on a studio production with engineered shading cameras, most of the angles are going to match. On the lower-budget productions, however, you may have cameras that aren't dead-on, or different types of cameras, which are never going to match perfectly.

Tip

Color-correct the angles before grouping. As you play it, you see your cut with the color correction applied, which is nice, especially when you're working with a client in the room. It's a little bit of a trick:

1. Straighten together a couple of shots on a timeline.
2. Match them first.
3. Take the filter you've applied to each one and copy and paste it to the browser.
4. Paste it to the source clip.
5. Group it.

Of course, there may be many elements to conform in a program other than multiclips, so the first step is to send your project off to the color phase.

XML Round-Tripping with Color

a

b

Figure 16.11a and 16.11b Color-correcting in Apple Color.

Until the most recent release of Color and FCP, dealing with multicam XML round-tripping was a very sketchy move. You had to kill all references to the multiclip. It used to be a hugely painful process. If you had multiclips on a sequence, you had to match-frame back to the original angle and then recut that back into the sequence, so it was no longer a multiclip. You have to prep the project for any finishing. Now, in Final Cut Pro 7 and Color 1.5, multiclips are supported for doing the color correction and that part of the finishing process.

Figure 16.12 Author's cut and color workstation.

Alexis Van Hurkman: *So multicam now round trips just fine. So hurrah for us, we don't have to deal with prebaking everything just because it's multicam. This is predictable because of the way Color works, but you send your multiclip-constructed sequence to Color, Color sees all the proper clips, you do your grade, and as always Color renders a new set of media, which is then the master media for your project. So when you go back to Final Cut Pro you don't have multiclips anymore, you just have QuickTime Clips.*

Robbie Carman: *If you have multiclips in your sequence, whether they're collapsed or uncollapsed, and you send that to Color, the active angle shows up in Color and you can grade it just like you would any other clip. Then, when it comes back to Final Cut Pro, obviously the clip is no longer a mult-clip; it's just that one angle that you graded.*

If you are working on a previous system, you can still do multicam with Color; you just need to prep the sequence to break any links to multicam in XML. For instance, if you're sending Final Cut sequences to Color and multiclips are a problem, you could go through and manually match-frame every camera angle and replace the multiclip version of that camera with the original media file.

Figure 16.13 Controlling Apple Color with J.L. Cooper "Joy Balls". (Courtesy Mark Foreman www.screeningroom.com)

Or you could use this method of removing multicam from the .xml:

Workaround for Multicam Before the Release of Color 1.4

Apple has fixed most multicam bugs when round-tripping to Color with FCP 7; however, there can still be issues. Managing multiclip sequences in FCP 6.04 and prior versions for use in Apple Color requires a workaround. All of the multiclip information needs to be removed from the .xml file before it is sent to Color or the round-trip process will not work. Here is an example workaround to remove the .xml info from the sequence:

1. Lock the picture.
2. Make all of the clips independent clips.
3. Collapse multicam clips in sequence.
4. Apply other prep as needed: bake-in timewarp shots and stills as necessary.
5. Media Manage sequence to a new project and create offline. Do not select multicam angles and do not delete clips.
6. In the new project, reconnect clips to original media. This will break all ties to multiclip sequences.
7. Media Manage to a new project, but this time copy clips and delete with handles.
8. Send final sequence to Color and grade shots. Render and send back to FCP.
9. Open sequence (sent from Color) and finish conforming your master.

TNT's Leverage and Color

Brian Gonosey: *We're bringing clips in with the ability to strip off the DP look, but when you bring it in, you're looking at the metadata from the DPs on top of the RAW file. It's essentially a check box in Color that they've added. It just applies that look to the RAW footage. So when you see it in Color, you're seeing exactly what we created and baked in the ProRes, only now we have the ability to work, to massage it there, after the fact.*

Everything is zeroed out except for the red tab. By adding the red tab, they've enabled these fields that let the metadata that was in that R3D file come in. It's got saturation, Kelvin, tint, exposure.

It's essentially giving you what you get when you open something as a RAW file in RED alert: I get gamma color space and the ISOs. So I can manipulate that here. We just had a screening on our 2K projector last night, and what we saw is that we're increasingly able to apply that grade to a RAW file—and this gives us more latitude. A lot of latitude, a lot more pop.

When we render out, we're rendering out 2K ProRes HQ. So when we go back into Final Cut, that's where we apply our titles and essentially still use Final Cut for speed changes and any complex effects. I just generated the files I needed in Color, then went back into Final Cut and rebuilt some complex moves. Reconformed it with the audio master and then output from Final Cut to tape.

Avid Color Correction

One big advantage to Avid's method of color correction is that it's all done inside the application. You don't have to send it anywhere—and, as an added bonus, you can start coloring before you lock picture and come back to shots during and after the editing cycle.

DaVinci and Clipster

Traditionally, sitcoms and many other shows have gone the tape-to-tape color-correction route. Multicam shows have changed very little since the late 1980s. With the advent of DaVinci Color Correction, in the early 1990s, everyone jumped on the digital component bandwagon. Dailies were transferred for multicam shows, mainly sitcoms, to digital beta cam, and then the show was onlined in a linear online bay. They put all the shots together and then, before air, they brought the finished tape, without titles, to a DaVinci color-timing bay to color-correct from digital video. Then the colorist would just go through, shot by shot, with an editor providing EDL, and make corrections.

Marc Wielage of Cinesound/LA has been color-correcting sitcoms this way for *Will & Grace, Caroline in the City, Dave's World, Two and a Half Men,* and *3rd Rock from the Sun.* All of those shows were shot on film, edited on tape, and color-corrected digitally through DaVinci.

Marc Wielage: *It's actually quite a challenge to color-time sitcoms. We typically have about four hours for the color-correction session per episode, for about 20 to 23 minutes of footage. Which means about three hours for doing the actual color-correction work and then another hour or so going over the footage and laying it down to video tape for the producer to approve. We're also hampered by the number of cuts in the show. I'd say that typically a 22-minute sitcom has 250 to 300 edits.*

It's funny how cinematographers don't want modern multicamera shows to look like an old-fashioned sitcom. They still want to introduce drama, contrast, and deviations from the soft lighting that makes everything look even and flat. People have been trying to get away from that look for years. Don Morgan, a fine cinematographer, figured out precisely how the backlight for one character from the angle to the left would become the key light for the other character, when shooting from the right—a more natural look.

Another issue colorists must contend with on multicam shows is the differences in lenses.

Figure 16.14 Assistant colorist Maizie Mac guards a DaVinci color room at DuArt Film and Video in New York City.

Marc Wielage: Lenses themselves each have their own color. Even the same lens can change color. For example, if you have a zoom lens, a typical 10-to-1 lens from 25 to 250 mm, you'll park on a wide shot and the shot is reasonably exposed and, let's say, looks fairly well-balanced; then you'll zoom all the way in to the end of the zoom at 250 mm on a close-up and the picture will be maybe 15% darker and slightly yellow. The lenses tend to go either a little yellow or a little blue at the extreme ends of the focal length. This is something that we have to correct in the final color-correction process.

Usually, it ends up in a digital NLE system no matter what format it was shot in, and at that point you're dealing with footage that is file based. Everything in our business is going completely file based, although some network series still wind up on some form of tape, usually HD Cam SR. (That's also what's used for the final output format.) But this is rare. The trend is moving toward 100% file-based footage. One of the most popular systems to use nowadays is probably DVS Clipster, a fine hard drive–based playback system that mimics a tape machine.

Marc Wielage: A hard-drive source like that acts just like a tape machine, but it's digital files on the server. It's wonderful to be able to back-and-forth quickly through the entire show, even if it's a one-hour show. You get 40 minutes into the episode and the director says, you know, our opening shot looks kind of like this, could we go back and take a look at that? Rather than grab a digital still of that image, we'll say, sure—and hit one button and there we are, sitting immediately on the frame he wanted to see. Then we can compare those shots and say, Oh yeah, they look close enough, that's fine, let's keep going. Or no, let's add a little bit more green and make it a little darker.

Once the file is loaded and checked, the color correctionist ensures it's the right version and the right cut for loading the EDL into the DaVinci.

Marc Wielage: *We like the DaVinci 2K for television, because it requires no rendering, so anything we do on it is absolutely instantaneous. We can have up to six power windows; we can do large groups of dissolves; we can make instantaneous changes to the entire show at one time with a global edit; or we can make just small, incremental changes to each shot, as required.*

Post Processes: Film to 24p with Double Sound

Until recently, film has been used extensively in TV sitcom production. *Cheers* was shot on film with four cameras. Sitcoms go through the same processing, printing, and telecine transference as any feature—and wind up cutting on an NLE and finishing to tape masters or matching back to film.

David Helfand, editor: *These were all 35, 3-perf or 4-perf film shows, and each camera had a video tape that would be fed throughout the studio, but it would be pretty poor quality. Most of the time, the footage is sent to the lab, then sent to the post house, where it's telecined. If there are four cameras, they transfer the soundtrack with the timecode onto the tapes first. Then, when the film is ready, it's developed and they sort of look at the clappers and check out the timecode on the clapper and sync that up visually to the preexisting timecode of the videotape.*

If you have a four-camera shoot, you'll have an A, B, C, and X camera. You'll also have an A, B, C, and X tape. Each tape is identical; it has the same sort of sound bed and timecode bed on it, and in telecine they will just insert the picture from the various cameras related to the various tapes: A, B, C, or X.

With the advent of digital technology, the post workflow has become a lot more complicated. There are more formats, codecs, and workflows than ever before. The idea of having fantastic quality without the added expense of film processing, transfers, and matchbacks has been a great leap forward.

Every show has its own workflow. Here is one for *Rules of Engagement*, courtesy of co-producer Cheri Tanimura:

We shoot on HD cam, 24p. I will send those tapes out to be down converted to a DV cam with 30 frame, nondrop timecode. We digitize the 30 frame DV cams at 4 to 1 m into the Avid. Our editor will work with that footage and then once the show is locked, I will get an EDL. We do an assembly at our post facility with my Master HD cams.

For audio, we use a double system and record to a DVD RAM and to a DA88. Once we get our DVcams, we use our DA88 for our audio and bring that in simultaneously with video from the DVcams as we digitize into the Avid. So the audio in our Avid is our final audio.

Some shows will bring in audio from their low-res DVcams, but we'll actually use our DA88s so that we have the access to all eight tracks. If we go on location and our mixer has the RF ISOed on the tracks, we will import all of that into the Avid so it's available at the mix and they don't need to go back to our dailies to try to find the RFs. We'll digitize everything.

After we lock picture, our online facility will convert the EDL and assemble the show using our 24p masters. As a temporary audio track, we will take the audio from the DVcam Avid check cassette and lay that onto the high-def master to double-check against it. The audio that's now on that master is not used. It's just a temp track because the audio straight out of our Avid in the OMF will go to the mix. That's the audio that we will use in the mix and that will eventually be laid back on to the final master.

Cheri Tanimura, co-producer, *Rules of Engagement*

REFERENCE

1. Avid.

17

AUDIO IN POSTPRODUCTION*

Sound professionals are often unsung heroes who work their magic in isolation. They make the production sound great but are often undervalued. Many times, the sound mix is the last part of the production process, and the mixers are the last people to andle the finished product. Additionally, sound editing has morphed into becoming more a part of the picture edit session.

Matt Foglia is the former chief audio engineer of Post Works New York, and for 14 years, he worked on award-winning live musical performances, documentary programming, reality programming, independent films, and tons of other productions. He was involved in combining a workflow between Pro Tools and the Avid. He has won two Cinema Audio Society awards (he was nominated for two others) and has two Emmy nominations. He is a voting member of ATAS (Emmys), CAS, and the Recording Academy (Grammys). Foglia is currently an associate professor at Middle Tennessee State University just outside of Nashville, Tennessee.

Matt: *I might talk with the editor at the very end of the cutting, when they say, "Hey, how am I going to get you the media for this? What format would you like this in? What format do you need your picture in?" things of that nature. Additionally, the producer/director will give me a deliverables list indicating what they need from me when I'm done. That's very important information as far as how I lay out my mix.*

The Re-Recording Mixer

A credit usually given on larger film and network TV programs for the person who actually blends all of the sound together in postproduction is "re-recording mixer."

Matt Foglia, CAS: *It's a funny name because it's like you're mixing a mix again. But what you're doing is mixing all the final sound elements associated with the project together, including those of the production*

> **Noteworthy**
>
> The re-recording mixer can also be called the dubbing mixer (Europe), postaudio mixer, or any variation of that term.

* Co-edited by Matt Foglia, CAS.

© 2010 Mitch Jacobson. Published by Elsevier Inc. All rights reserved.
Doi: 10.1016/B978-0-240-81176-5.00017-4

Tip

Work with 48-kHz Audio

For the most part, your audio sampling rate (also known as sampling frequency) should be set to 48,000 Hertz (48 kHz) since it is the standard sampling rate for sound for picture; 44,100 Hertz is the standard for audio CDs. For video, any video or film applications, we're always doing things at 48,000 Hertz.

mixer. So it's as if you're recording what was recorded initially (by the production mixer) back onto tape. In Europe that person is called a dubbing mixer because they mix on what is called a dub stage. That is a term that we use here in the States, but it usually refers to the very large rooms where films are mixed.

It's great to send volume and fade information, but don't render effects or EQ into the mixes because it limits the re-recording mixer's ability to work with the best quality.

Matt Foglia, CAS: *If I receive a file that has a rendered EQ, it's like receiving a file that's been messed with. It's like trying to color-correct a file that's already been color-corrected. So that can become a little difficult.*

Double System Audio

Double system audio (sometimes called dual system audio) refers to needing a second recording device in order to capture both picture and sound. Often a second system is utilized even if a video camera has audio inputs. The recorders usually have multitrack audio capabilities and superior specifications to the onboard camera audio inputs. Feature films were the earliest double system users. A double system allows you to have more channels and more flexibility.

Double system audio started when sound was added to film productions.

Matt Foglia, CAS: *If you're thinking of film, you can't record audio anywhere on the film; it just holds the visual. So you need something to record the audio. That means that you need two systems, or a "double" system: one for sound and one for picture.*

With the advent of video cameras, we now have audio tracks available onboard the video camera. A lot of budget productions will use the built-in audio channels and record the picture and sound in one place, on one piece of tape or in one file. However, it's not the best (or safest) way to go. So productions will often use a separate (known as "double") system where a production mixer can be in charge of recording and monitoring levels. The production mixer's mix will often be sent back to the video camera (often via wireless transmitter) so that the editor can load the picture into the editing system and have a reference mix to cut against. Some location recording systems have up to 16 audio tracks, but a double system could be as simplistic as a stereo flash recorder.

TAI Audio in Orlando, Florida, sells, rents and services audio systems for the film and TV industry. Joe Guzzi, the company's president, says:

It's about ISO track recording. For instance, in a reality show they'll take two audio bags with four wireless mics in each and then they would have a bank of receivers only so that they can get ISO tracks, rather than going right into the camera where they're only going to be able to get two to four tracks. They'll isolate the tracks so that the editors are going to be able to pick apart whatever they need, track by track. We've done shows as big as 64 independent tracks.

One of the major benefits of a double system is that you know there's a person paying attention to the sound and making sure that the audio is getting to where it's supposed to go.

Carmen Borgia is vice president of audio production at DuArt Film and Video in New York City. DuArt has a rich history in filmmaking as the first motion picture lab in the United States; 80 years later, the company is keeping up with the digital age. This sound team does it all: sound design, Dolby surround-sound mixing, sound editing, audio restoration, and layback of final master audio.

Figure 17.1 Carmen Borgia, vice president of Audio Production at DuArt Film and Video, NYC. (Courtesy Carmen Borgia.)

Carmen Borgia: *Multicam is interesting because there's this kind of notion that you're going to have all these cameras and sound and something's probably going to be good, and that might be true. My experience is that if you're going to go to that much trouble to record it with cameras that way, then you should also be using a separate system for sound, which is going to have its own multitrack elements. The place where things get ugly is when people make errors and they have mismatches between the cameras and audio, say one recording at 24 fps, one recording at 23.98 fps, one recording at 29.97 fps.*

With most location audio recordings, you're going to have media delivered, usually on a compact flash drive, SD media, or things of that nature, or maybe even a DVD-R. Controlled environments, such as for your standard multicam comedy, often have tape-based machines like the Tascam DA88. This eight-channel, digital audio machine was developed for postproduction in particular.

Manufacturers may sell a camera for $50,000 but only allocate a couple of thousand dollars to the audio processing. This is why it is important to have the audio pros handle the sound. Even if you are on a limited budget, you can still set up an inexpensive mini double system using something like the Zoom H4n Handy Recorder.

Figure 17.2 Deva 5.8 on location.

Matt Foglia, CAS: *Zaxcom is a company that makes one of the more common location recording systems, called the Deva. Other big companies are Sound Devices, Fostex, Tascam, and, on the inexpensive end, there are the zoom recorders. The H4 can record four tracks at once using a built-in stereo microphone and two XLR inputs. High fidelity for a very cheap price (around $300).*

The Zoom H4n Handy Recorder

Whereas professional productions usually utilize double system audio, pro-sumer projects employing additional tracks will benefit from double system use too. For example, DSLR multicam almost always needs something like this. Additionally, multicamera weddings typically record with four mics or more. Wire up the priest or rabbi, bride, groom, and audience; add more for music.

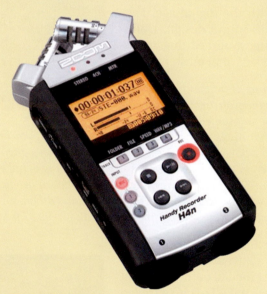

Figure 17.3 Zoom H4n Handy Multitrack Recorder.

Some shows still use the camera's internal audio tracks. If a taping needs multiple tracks to accommodate the mix, dialogue, effects, music, and audience left and right mics, they would be patched to multiple groups of four channels on the camera ISO tapes. For instance, cameras A and B will each have four channels with some combination of mix, dialogue, effects, and music. The X camera may have an audience laugh track and audience ISOs. Problems can arise when those tapes are down-converted to DVCam tapes with limited audio tracks because there is a high potential of the tracks getting mixed up in duplication.

A better way is to use a separate sound team to record everything with a dedicated audio recording system.

Cheri Tanimura, producer: *We record to a DVD RAM and to a DA88 because I want all eight tracks. Once we get our cameras and digitize them into the Avid, we use our DA88 for our audio and bring that in simultaneously (since it has the same timecode as the video ISOs) so that we have access to all original eight tracks. If we go on location and our mixer has the RF ISOed on the tracks, we will import all of that into the Avid so it's available at the mix. That way, they don't need to go back to our dailies to try to find the RFs. We'll digitize everything.*

At this point, the editors are now working with down-converted low-res footage that's married to the original digital audio tracks. It will be these actual tracks that eventually make it to the audio post session for mastering (mixing). Once the picture is locked, OMF files are sent out to the audio mix while an online session creates a 24p master from an EDL.

Cheri Tanimura: *First we record the temporary audio track from the DVCam Avid Check Tape onto the high-def master so that we can double-check it against picture. Then we lay in the final mixed soundtracks back to the master as a deliverable show.*

Keeping Track of Tracks

Keep Track of Tracks

Timecode usually works out, but it will kill you.

Carmen Borgia

Peter Chakos, A.C.E.: *I have four channels. The dialogue comes to me mixed on channel 1. Channel 2 is usually any playback effects, and [channels] 3 and 4 are stereo laughs, although you get a lot of bleed of the audience laughter in the dialogue mics. What I generally do, if I find something where the picture has been a little slow or missed a cue so something's slightly off mic, I can always go back to the DA88s and get back the single, individual mic tracks. We'll have two or three booms working at a time and they'll be ISOed somewhere, so I can get the ISOs and lay them in if I need to.*

Eli Tishberg, director: *When I edit, I'll cut my show with the stereo line mix of the show and I'll make lists for the audio; then someone else will remix it to picture in another audio room. I will sit in on the mix to picture—if I took things out between songs, if I cut to night two or a second version of the song, we'll do all that, and we'll also do audience sweetening for transitions between songs.*

Mark Raudonis, VP postproduction, Bunim-Murray Productions: *You have an offline cut that's locked and it has only the four channels of audio, which is basically whatever you digitized. We will then sync up the dual-system ISO tracks to whatever the final offline cut is. So you'll now have four channels of audio and then typically eight to ten additional channels that are available for the re-recording mixers to pull out the ISO mics. We've found that there is a significant enough difference between the ISO tracks and the line mix that it's worth doing.*

Fishing for ISOs

Mark Raudonis, VP Postproduction: *We digitize four channels of audio and picture for each angle. We multiclip everything together. You can have 10 camera angles and 40 audio channels. We'll go with the production mix for most of the offline ... then go fishing if we need something.*

Track layouts usually come from production. The production mixer will assign talent on tracks 1234, other talent on 5678. The biggest help in offline editing is to have what we call a "flying mix" or a production mix (line mix) on all cameras all of the time. So at least one channel is a live mix. That means that you can now go to town editing without having to find ISO tracks.

Matthew Illardo, editor: *Yeah, we have the studio audio tracks. Each ISO has its own tracks of audio that are different and that's all matched in the group clip. I usually keep the line cut audio and once I realize what I need to do, if I'm looking for a certain audio thing and I don't know where it is or I don't know how it sounds best, and I'm trying to isolate it, that's when I'll switch to the audio follows video. I'll go back to the group clips just because it's easier to find.*

0.1% The Magic Number

When film is put through the telecine process, the film is slowed down so that the 24 frames per second plays at 23.976 (often referred to as 23.98) frames per second. This translates to 29.97 frames per second in standard-definition video. Like the picture, the audio is slowed down 0.1% so that it stays in sync and can be viewed on a video monitor.

Speed is a major factor in frame counting because there's speed and then there's counting, which are two different things. We're counting this at 23.976 frames a second or we're counting it at 29.97 frames a second, and they're running at the same speed.

Matt Foglia, CAS: *Everything is based off of the American power line frequency of 60 Hertz (Hertz=cycles per second). Here in the States, black-and-white TV ran at 30 frames a second (half of the 60 Hz line frequency). This was great until color TV was introduced, because manufacturers needed to make sure that those folks with the black-and-white TVs didn't have to go out and buy new TVs. To allow color programming to be broadcast and viewed on black-and-white TVs and color TVs, a subcarrier was introduced into the broadcast signal. The subcarrier contained the color info. Color TVs could "decode" the color info, and black-and-white TVs just ignored it—not having the "decoder" built-in. However, in order to include that color subcarrier into the signal, the speed, or frequency, of the broadcast signal needed to be slowed down ever so slightly because at 30 fps, there were modulation issues with the audio. The speed variation is 0.1%.*

Carmen Borgia: *There's a difference between frame rate and speed. The whole reason 23.98 was invented was to match the speed of 29.97. So I think of 29.97 and 23.98 as generic video speed. I think of 24 and 30 as film speed. This is from the Way-Back Machine, because in the old days when you shot film, all the cameras ran at 24, and when you transferred it to video, to make a clean 3:2 pulldown transfer, you'd end up at 29.97.*

Production sound mixers will sometimes record in the field 0.1% faster (48,048 Hz) so that the final sampling rate of the sound in postproduction will be 48 kHz. They're speeding it up on location because they know it's going to be slowed down in post.

Project Interchange

Definitions

AAF metadata interchange will be based on Avid's Open Media Framework Interchange (OMFI). OMFI is widely used in the audio industry for exchange of audio files that must synchronize with edited video and film productions.

OMF is an edit data interchange format introduced by Avid Technology in 1990. OMF is a binary file format using object-oriented technology.

OMF and AAF are file transfer methods that transpose data from one system to another. They contain all of your raw file information plus the metadata associated with your sequence.

Matt Foglia, CAS: *One of the large benefits of OMF and AAF is the ability to share metadata. Metadata basically means "data about data." It is an aspect of the file protocol that allows me to see, for example, timecode information, how you laid out your tracks, volume information associated with your sequence, what your clips are named, et cetera, so that we can have further conversations about the sequence. If there's an issue with a particular track, I can indicate to you what track or clip it is and you will know what I'm talking about, as opposed to a clip getting a generic name like "clip 1" or "clip 2," that doesn't necessarily mean anything.*

OMF and AAF allow the mixers or editors to view the original source timecode of the file in case they ever need to reconform or fish for more info, like tracking down a corrupt or poor-sounding file. Maybe something was loaded into the system improperly and there is phasing or imbalanced levels; I can let the editor know which files are problematic and the files can be redigitized.

On the post side, with your standard, nonmajor network or film project, we get an OMF or an AAF that contains all, or nearly all, of the audio elements for the show. We will split things into at least three categories: dialogue, music, and effects. If there are additional deliverable requirements, like the voiceover (narration) as a separate track, then we can do that at the start. It's good to know beforehand what we have to separate our tracks out into.

Sending out Audio

Not every facility has the infrastructure with offline and online under one roof and a centralized machine room for five online and three mix rooms to all share, so most of us are sending the audio out-of-house. When that time comes, you'll have to clean up your tracks and send your soundtrack to an audio post facility for mixing and final laybacks. Your audio team will provide exact delivery specs that will make their job easier, such as having you embed the audio into the OMF format using 300 frame handles and providing a QuickTime reference movie. Or the team could request an EDL and DigiBeta tape. It makes sense to ask.

a

b

Figure 17.4a and b Audio mix room theater at Electric Entertainment. (Courtesy Electric Entertainment.)

Featured Applications

Automatic Duck

Automatic Duck, founded in 2001 by Harry Plate and Wes Plate, is a software developer based near Seattle known for its plug-ins that translate edited sequences between Final Cut Pro, Avid, After Effects, Quantel, Pro Tools, and other professional digital video editing tools.

Automatic Duck's first product, an After Effects import plug-in that could read Avid OMF exports, was called Automatic Composition Import and shipped in April 2001. Since then, many new products have come to the market to support interchange between many different applications including Final Cut and After Effects. The plug-ins have improved over the years with the amount of information translated as well as adding support for newer file formats such as AAF, MXF, and XML.

Here is a look at the current lineup:

- Pro Import AE 4.0. Import your Avid or Final Cut Pro timeline into Adobe After Effects.
- Pro Export FCP 4.0. Export AAF files for export to Avid or Quantel editing systems as well as the Pro Tools digital audio workstation.
- Pro Import FCP 2.0. Import OMF or AAF compositions from Avid editing systems, Toon Boom's StoryBoard Pro, or Pro Tools into Final Cut Pro.
- Pro Import Cmb 1.0. Import your FCP, Avid, or Premiere Pro timeline into Autodesk Combustion.
- ProDate DV. This FxPlug plug-in for Final Cut Pro and Final Cut Express displays the DV datecode recorded onto your DV tape during shooting.

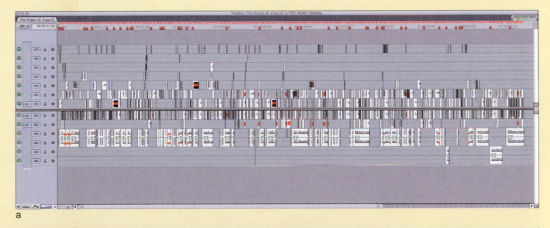

a

b

Figure 17.5a and b Using Automatic Duck's powerful timeline translation plug-ins, it is possible to move an edited sequence between Avid, Final Cut Pro, and other applications.

Wes Plate: *Our plug-ins do not create a multiclip/group clip representation in the destination system. Instead, the currently selected/enabled angle is translated. So if you're importing an Avid AAF into After Effects or Final Cut Pro, the active angle from the group clip will appear in the timeline. Similarly, if you're exporting a sequence from Final Cut Pro, the current selection from the multiclip is exported.*

digiGO! Boris XML

Boris FX has released Boris XML Transfer, a new Adobe After Effects plug-in designed for the seamless transfer of Apple Final Cut Pro program sequences to Adobe After Effects. Boris XML Transfer preserves all aspects of a Final Cut Pro project, including effects, audio, media clips, transitions, and geometric transformations, and it takes special care to preserve multiclip edits.

Matt Foglia, CAS: *Sometimes editors will ask, "If our sequence has audio laid out with on-camera sound clips and interviews on channels 1-4, sound effects builds on 5-10, and music tracks on 11-16, does that work for you?" I appreciate that kind of stuff because if I know where things are going to be whenever I get an OMF or an AAF, it saves me time separating the files and, in turn, saves the client money.*

There are several ways to share projects between systems and applications. Here is a quick look at a few.

OMFI

Open Media Framework (OMF) or Open Media Framework Interchange (OMFI) is a platform-independent file format intended for the transfer of digital media between different software applications. It may be exported from digital video editing or audio workstation (DAW) software. Because OMF files use a standardized format to store audio and video data, they are commonly used to share projects between multiple applications.

An audio project saved in the OMF format can store multiple audio tracks, volume and pan information, and references to audio files; however, not all settings, such as insertion effects and channel routing options, can be saved in an OMF file.

Carmen Borgia: *At the end of the edit process, we are given an OMF; 100% of the audio that's going to be used, that was acquired on the shoot, is in the OMF. That's the simplest workflow.*

The following applications are known to support OMF importing or exporting:
• Adobe Premiere CS4
• Avid Media Composer

- Avid Pro Tools
- SONAR
- Cubase
- Final Cut Pro
- Logic Pro
- Nuendo
- Pro Tools
- Digital Performer
- SADiE
- Automatic Duck

AAF

Advanced Authoring Format (AAF) is a cross-platform, multimedia file format that allows the interchange of media and composition information between AAF-compliant applications. These applications are primarily content-creation tools such as Avid editing applications, Avid DS, and Sonic Foundry's Sound Forge, to name a few.

There are two general types of data in an AAF file:
- Media such as audio and video
- Composition information (metadata)

Exporting Methods

OMF and AAF provide two basic methods for exporting files.

Method 1: Compositions with Linked Media

Matt Foglia: *With this method, there is a folder that houses all of the associated media (audio and/or video) and an .omf/.aaf document that contains the metadata information (timecode information, telling the media where to go in the sequence, et cetera). For delivery, you provide the two parts, the file and the media files folder.*

Method 2: Compositions with Embedded Media

Matt Foglia: *With this method, the associated media and the metadata are wrapped into one file. This is the easiest method from a management standpoint, but the files cannot exceed two gigabytes, so be careful when trying to export a 14-track, hour-long audio sequence using this method. Be sure to break the sequence into two (or more) parts.*

XML

XML (Extensible Markup Language) is a set of rules for encoding documents electronically. For Final Cut Pro, it's an open, standards-based XML Interchange Format—a feature that allows developers to create and interface new products to improve the editing process. The XML protocol is designed from the ground up as a way of describing every aspect of a Final Cut Pro project—from clips, bins, and sequences, to edits and transitions, effects, color correction settings, and keyframes. Whereas XML provides an open, transparent, plain-text format, other systems often generate black or opaque binary metadata.

This means that Final Cut Pro users can share comprehensive information about a Final Cut Pro project with an other nonlinear editing system. In fact, they can share that information with any application or system that supports XML, including database systems, broadcast servers, outlining software, HTML and web authoring tools, and graphics applications.

Important: Final Cut Studio includes the Final Cut Pro application and companion applications such as Cinema Tools, Compressor, Color, DVD Studio Pro, Motion, and Soundtrack. Color, Cinema Tools, and Final Cut Pro itself make use of the Final Cut Pro XML Interchange Format.

EDLs

David Helfand, editor: *On* Friends *we would just give the sound department an audio EDL and they would recut all of the audio tracks from the original. Certainly, in those times, things were recorded to DA88 (an eight-track digital audiotape machine). They would recreate and reedit all the tracks, making sure everything was clean. The laughs, for example, were recorded live, so those would be on separate channels. They would come across and be assembled and, then in the sound mix, the mixers would determine what laughs needed to be smoothed out.*

By having all the tracks in the NLE, picture editors are the first audio editors as well. They set up the tracks, sync them, and sort them out for the mixers.

Zoran Jevremov: *Because the mixer is not familiar with what the audio tracks are until you give them the cut, you have to actually place them in the timeline for him or her. And even the songs or the soundtracks that I use under a documentary, bits are often all cut up. The audio mixer can move them around a little bit to make the beats work better or whatever, but basically has all the audio there for them.*

Peter Chakos, A.C.E.: *When it's done, I would have locked picture. My picture-cutting job is done. My tracks and all my sound effects go as they are to an OMF, and then they're tightened up and cleaned-up by the sound department using all their EQs, filters, compressors, and such. I don't do much EQing in the edit unless it's for a particular effect or a joke.*

18

DELIVERABLES

When you finish your final mix, and you've got your final picture and there are no more tweaks to do, you're halfway done—because now you have to QC it. You have to provide deliverables masters.

Carmen Borgia, VP, DuArt Film and Video, NYC

Deliverables are what the networks or client needs when a project is finished and ready for presentation. In the simplest terms, they are the master tapes or files.

In addition to a master mix, there's a whole other suite of deliverables that you may need to do:

1. Split tracks for dialogue, music, and effects.
2. Full mix back for making trailers and cutdown versions of the film and promotional material.
3. If you have a 5.1 mix, you will always include a stereo mix with it.
4. Foreign language M & E (also called a DM & E), short for dialogue, music, and effects. The original language is completely stripped out of the film.
5. You might have different lengths of the film. There might be a 30-minute version and a 60-minute version. There might be a theatrical release.
6. You might have a modified mix for the Web. Obviously, levels are going to sound different on the Web than they do if you're in a theater.

Once everyone has signed off and the mixes are approved, then it is re-laid (or "laid back") to tape or recorded as a master file.

Laura Young, editor: *We have to format it for PBS. We have to format it for DVD. We have international. We have multiple versions. We have subtitles. They subtitle it in the truck when they shoot it and feed it out high def on satellite, live in at least eight languages. Then we get a file from them, a changed file, because once it's reedited, we adjust the subtitles to match our cuts, because we're perfectionists and we don't want it to cross over cuts. We might change words here and there to better suit our needs. We'll put the subtitles in at the very, very end. It's one of the last things we do.*

> **Noteworthy**
>
> Avid now has the SubCap Generator for Subtitles. As your deliverables are concerned, audio needs to have every mix separate so they can be isolated for outputs. Says Matt Foglia, CAS: "Because we're not dealing with the video, we assign the mix, or other required variations, to the videotape's audio inputs and insert the audio mixes onto the videotape. Depending on what the deliverables list specifies, we watch the show down that many times, keeping our ears open for technical anomalies as well aesthetic preferences."

Doi: 10.1016/B978-0-240-81176-5.00018-6

To keep your tracks from being laid out all over the place, try arranging them under the three main categories of audio postproduction split mixes: dialogue, music, and effects—or DME, which is often one of your deliverable requirements:

1. Dialogue
2. Music
3. Sound effects

Various versions of the soundtrack are made in addition to the regular full mix. Split mixes have dialogue and music and effects on separate tracks. Sometimes it's a full mix on channels 1 and 2 with audience reactions on 3 and 4. Other times, it's a mix without the dialogue. Each show will have its own requirements.

Matt Foglia, CAS: *We often have to marry some form of split out audio to the textless master with maybe mono dialogue on channel 1, mono effects on channel 2, and stereo music on channels 3 and 4, or some variation of that.*

Brian Gonosey, editor, Leverage: *We have our own mixing stage in-house and they give us the 12 tracks that we need, and all that gets married to the picture and we produce a 12-track ProRes QuickTime. It's six tracks of surround, then the (stereo mixdown of the 5.1) Lt/Rt mix and the mix minus.*

The very last stage, after the final mix has been inserted on the color-corrected master tape with all the titles and information the network needs, is to take the tape and create an actual air master for delivery. Deliverables are the output masters that the clients give to the distribution partners. Deliverables these days could mean anything from a podcast to a broadcast.

There are separate versions for domestic and international audiences, where certain things, like dialogue, are stripped out. Currently for network television, the final air master is going to be HDCAM or HDCAM SR videotape.

Some shows deliver file-based masters.

Ray Volkema, editor: *At HDNet, we have everything as files now. Once my show is finished with 5.1 and the stereo audio files and all of the color correction and everybody's happy, I export that file as a DVC Pro HD QuickTime file that we can air directly out of master control.*

Brian Gonosey: *Our network deliverables so far have been to an HDCAM SR 60i tape. We produce our 24p QuickTime, and we take that to another facility, and have that inserted on to a 60i tape. And that's the only piece of the entire puzzle that happens outside of our roof. And I think one big reason we didn't go and adopt the strategy to bring in that hardware is, our feeling is that those tape delivery days are numbered as well.*

File-based delivery is also happening to the theatrical releases as well.

Laybacks

Traditionally, laybacks, where the audio is inserted back onto the master videotape, was done by the audio team. However, many soundtracks are being relayed in the edit suite as well. It is coming down to "Who has the video deck?" Are you going to buy or rent a machine worth $100,000+ or go to a facility that has one all set up?

Carmen Borgia: *At DuArt we have HD decks: D5, HDCAM, and HDCAM SR. If you have to put the audio directly back onto one of those, we do that here. If it's going back to a more down-home or digital only output, often we'll just hand it back to the editor and they'll output from their edit bay.*

It's a good job for the audio engineer to be the last person who hears the audio go down. Because the audio engineers have been living with the show and they're used to looking at the sync, it gives them one last chance to catch goofs, errors, or omissions.

Carmen Borgia: *Keeping track of the picture is its own challenge. Do you have any dropped frames? Is the color-correct approved? Did all of your real-time effects or wipes or dissolves that you put in, work correctly? Did everything get remembered? Did the system cough on you when it played back?*

Tip

Watch your final DVDs on many different players to check compatibility.

Laying Back Concert Mixes

For concerts, people who work with the artists usually do the music mixes. Not all the time, but usually. Those mixes are combined with various other show audio elements to create the tracks that become the full program mix. In my experience, band music mixes are constantly being updated and must be replaced several times.

Ray Volkema: *The audio is just a part of the concert, really. It is recorded in the field by each artist on hard drives and sent to our truck as a house mix. This gets recorded on the tapes, and that's what I edit to. Sometimes we get a decent front-of-house mix, but basically you're always editing to a very rough mix, which is kind of unfortunate, but at least you know that there's something there if you can tell quickly. But the audio is basic. I usually just grab it off the line cut, and then the physical edit on the timeline is just the line cut audio along with all of the multiclip video.*

A house mix is sent to all the ISO tapes. Sometimes, individual audio tracks or different mixes are also recorded on the ISO tapes. So keeping the house mix in sync is easy because it's already part of the video clip. But this rough mix does not sound ideal because it was mixed for a live venue. However, it's good enough to cut a rough cut with. Most of the time you will just use the soundtrack from one of the angles and switch just the video with the intent of replacing the soundtrack later when you get the final music mix.

Sometimes mixes are going on simultaneously to the edit. You may receive various mixes along the way. I like to refer to these mixes chronologically as the "house mix," followed by the "rough mix," followed by the "final mix," followed by the "real final mix," followed by the "final final mix, etc."

Each time these tracks are replaced, they have to be hand-synced unless they have matching TC. It's not hard to match it up with a 2-pop (see below). But it is a consideration for losing sync each time a track is replaced.

Ray Volkema: *Those WAV files actually do not have the same timecode as my show ... but there's a sync at the top where they give me the code of that file that matches to the start of my show or the start of that countdown or the start of bars or whatever we work out. And so there have been times where I've had to do estimates where they've had some issues in the syncing where I could still, in Final Cut, try to fix certain songs that may be slightly out. I drop it in the final sequence and life is good and we've got a match.*

If you're given files, Broadcast Wave Format files (BWF) are what you'd really like to get. With BWF, the file contains metadata embedded into it. The most important piece of metadata is the timecode information. If the mixer uses the timecode that was initially recorded to the files, then you should be able to spot or relink the BWF files containing the newer mixes with ease. You don't get the metadata with WAV or AIFF files.

Matt Foglia , CAS

Outputs from the Edit Suite

The magic happens in the mix room, the effects are done, the sound design is done, everything is enhanced, and then there's the mix. Then what? Delivering back to the editor for layback?

There are some extremely creative and awesome picture editors who are so talented cutting dialogue, FX, and music.

On certain budget productions, I found myself doing the layback and outputs at the edit suite. In these cases, I am delivered stems or audio files provided by the re-recording mixer to sync up with the show.

Matt Foglia, CAS: *We will deliver the stereo file of the mix, maybe a stereo file of music and effects, stereo music tracks, stereo effects tracks, mono dialogue, mono voice-over, deliver all those files.*

So how do you sync these new files to your master? The time-code doesn't usually match the original sequence.

Matt Foglia, CAS: *Having all of the files actually start at the same time is the key. Maybe the narrator doesn't come in for three minutes, but we're going to make sure that the narration file starts at the exact same time as the other files, either the first frame of the show—FFOA, first frame of action—or two seconds prior to the FFOA. In that case, we would put a 2-pop in, just like you would in film.*

Carmen Borgia: *If we're going back to the picture editor and they're out-putting from their system, say they're going to make a DVD for a screener or they're going to output to their own DVCam deck or they're going to out-put some high-def file or something, we will make either stereo or 5.1 files that we return back to them. We want to make sure that there's a reference, a dumb reference, that's on every file, which is a 2-beep at the head and a 2-beep at the tail. The 2-beep is a 2-pop that's on the timeline.*

The 2-Pop

The 2-pop, or 2-beep, is a one-frame tone that is used to sync picture and sound. As those of you doing countdowns will know, that's whenever the three turns into the two and the frame disappears. The 2-pop is the audio equivalent of the two on your countdown. It is placed 2 seconds before the first frame of action (FFOA), the show start, and that's why you hear the pop; it is the audio syncing with the visual reference.

Used in television and film postproduction, a 2-pop is a 1-kHz tone that is one frame long and placed 2 seconds before the start of program. For example, in a video program, the FFOA starts at 1 hour (typically 01:00:00:00 in the United States and 10:00:00:00 in the United Kingdom). Preceding that, one frame (or the 2-pop) of tone would be placed at timecode 00:59:58:00 or exactly 2 seconds before first frame of video.

Whereas laying down bars and tone before the start of the program establishes video and audio calibration levels on the tape, the 2-pop is primarily used for picture and sound synchronization. Therefore, while the loudness of the 2-pop may be the same as the bars and tone, this is not a requirement. The loudness level should be sufficient to be heard clearly.

Associated at the same point in the timeline with the audible 2-pop is a visual flash frame. Together, the 2-pop and the flash frame are used to synchronize the audio and video tracks when more convenient methods are not available.

Matt Foglia, CAS: *In film, when synchronizing reels, we also include a "tail pop." This is, essentially, a 2-pop that is placed two seconds after the last frame of action (LFOA). This is used to ensure that no audio/visual drift occurred during the playback. It is also used as a synchronization tool when combining multiple film reels into a composite master.*

Make a 2-Pop

- Render out a big number 2 and just stick it in your timeline for one frame, 2 seconds before your first frame of action.
- Add an audio beep that goes with that the number 2 and is one frame long.
- Copy and add the frame at 2 seconds after the last frame of action to create a tail pop.

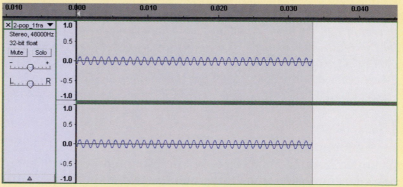

Figure 18.1 This is a sample waveform of a 1-kHz sine wave lasting for one NTSC television frame (1/30th of a second). (Courtesy David Sutherland/Wikimedia.)

Archiving and Backups

As we mentioned in our discussion of preproduction, it is not only important to back up everything but it may even be a legal deal breaker requirement for insurance. Many people use LTO drives, but everyone has a system of hard drives that suits backup and budget needs. Back up on anything. Just back up.

Michael Philips of Avid describes the current truth about backup solutions:

1. Only near- to medium-term solutions exist.
2. The long-term solution is still 35-mm film.
3. FireWire drives have high failure rates after a year or so.
4. Other drive formats need to be exercised on a regular basis.

5. Optical is still too small and slow for most high-value productions.

Tape (LTO):
6. The tape format is not guaranteed past 15 years.
7. Newer-generation readers do not support tape beyond two generations.
8. For example, LTO1 will not read in an LTO4 device, LTO2 will not read in an LTO5 when released.
9. Assume new device every 3 years – 9-year life on being able to read.
10. As with drives, one must keep a system that can mount drives, drivers, and so on to be able to pull off a file.
11. Backing up is costly.

For archival, HDNet uses HDCAM SR tape, record the stereo mix on channels 1 and 2 and encode Dolby 5.1 on channels 3 through 8.

Leverage runs an LTO tape that is archived on an almost daily basis. It has a 28-terabyte X-SAN in-house that runs a backup every night.

There's a differential backup of the entire SAN. So we always have that for the archival medium, and we have a 24p master that we strike as our master-master.

Additionally, they back up each show and its elements. With RED footage, they maintain a series of portable FireWire RAIDS on set. Each week, they have a redundant copy hard drive that has all of the master 4k files from the RED.

Matt Foglia, CAS: *We back up at the end of the show, with another series of 2-terabyte drives. For the ProRes files that we use to actually edit with and deliver with, as well as all the project settings and all the business that goes along with the sound, the music, and FX, this gets backed up to yet another hard drive. So you end up with a 2- or 3-terabyte drive with your master source files; you end up with a 2- or 3-terabyte drive with your project files; and then, as an overall backup, we have the LTOs that work on a constant basis.*

MULTICAMERA MADNESS® CASE STUDIES*

*The following case studies have been condensed to fit into the printed version of
this book. For the full in-depth case studies, bonus chapters, multiclip videos and and
free applications see the companion DVD included with this book or download from
www.MasteringMulticam.com

19

CASE STUDY: A HYBRID 10-CAMERA RED 4K AND EFP HD PRODUCTION—*JOURNEY: LIVE FROM MANILA**

Advice: Think outside the (matte) box!

Steve Gibby, director of photography

Figure 19.1a Journey live from Manila. (Courtesy Pam Gibby/www.cut4.tv.)

I was jazzed to learn about this production because of the show's hybrid nature: 10 Red cameras on the rock band Journey in Manila in the Philippines. It may be the most exciting case study of this book, because it exemplifies great craftsmanship executed with passion and a bit of risk-taking in order to ratchet the entire industry up a notch.

A great big mash-up, the Journey/Manila show combined Red 4k with 720p HD-SDI video, traditional video lenses with cine

*Portions of this chapter have been reprinted from Red's "Journey" to Manila. Used with permission by Steve Gibby. The following case study has been condensed to fit into the printed version of this book. For the full in-depth case study, see the companion DVD included with this book or download from www.MasteringMulticam.com.

Doi: 10.1016/B978-0-240-81176-5.00019-8

and SLR lenses, was directed for live IMAG and a feature-length edited concert, and employed crew members from around the world. And now, thanks to the team's generous communication with me, this study can help to clear the way for future Red 4K-EFP hybrid productions to evolve.

Steve Gibby: *For the challenge-driven, this was Nirvana—because we were on the leading edge of changes in a converging industry between the EFP world, the former film world, and the still photography world. We had to use technology from all three in order to pull off what we were trying to do.*

Figure 19.1b Executive producer Dan Barnett making a crew announcement from the stage. (Courtesy Pam Gibby/ www.cut4.tv.)

Dan Barnett, executive producer of Wizard Entertainment and producer of the Journey/Manila concert and film, has decades of experience working as a concert promoter with the biggest names in show business. He has a passion for video and a keen eye for creativity and integrating talent and technology for a seamless production. After analyzing Red 4K camera technology with DP and Red owner Champe Barton, Barnett determined that he could get the best quality resolution and logistical flexibility by going with a hybrid EFP-Red 4K multicam production.

Champe Barton, owner HD Suite, Inc.: *Shooting Red gave us not only the opportunity to capture in 4k RAW, it also gave us the ability to ISO ten cameras. We shifted the critical decision making for edits, color, and overall look to the post process, where we have the luxury of more time.*

Dan Barnett: *Basically, with Red you get a higher-quality production at a more affordable price and you're delivering 4k resolution. The final edit of this show would be able to go theatrical or to IMAX, based on the resolution.*

When the basic equipment decisions had been made, Barnett set out to assemble an amazing crew, starting with veteran director/editor Eli Tishberg. Tishberg comes from the editing world and directs for the edit (when there is one) but also does a live cut.

Eli Tishberg: *I firmly believe that a multicam show should be directed with a live line cut and not just 10 cameras being watched on 10 monitors. I find that the camera operators are reacting both to the music and to me talking in their ear, and they can hear where I'm going, what I'm doing, my pace—and they match their moves to that.*

Figure 19.2 Eli Tishberg, Dan Barnett, Oli Laperal, Jr. and Steve Gibby in an impromptu preproduction meeting. (Courtesy Pam Gibby/www.cut4.tv.)

The show also had not one but two directors of photography: Steve Gibby and Champe Barton.

Steve Gibby: *There were two DPs because there was such a massive amount of coordination and tech to wade through in order to integrate what is essentially a digital cinema camera system with modified equipment into a traditional, EFP-style production. We had to balance out which lenses to use, which techniques, which shoulder rigs, what frame rates, everything down the line—it was just a lot of work. So we double-teamed it. It was great to work with another DP; two really good and experienced minds are better than one when you have a lot of problems to solve.*

Figure 19.3a Shooting Journey from both sides of the pit. (Courtesy Pam Gibby/www.cut4.tv.)

The rest of the crew was brought in from all over the United States and merged with the local Manila crew, which was overseen by Oli Laperal, Jr., of RSVP Films.

4K Capture Plus IMAG

Event programs like this one have traditionally been shot using 2/3-inch HD camera systems. Though the end product would be HDTV, Blu-ray, and DVD, Journey's band members and the production team wanted to future-proof the acquisition format by taking it up to the next resolution level: 4k RAW, or what's known as format 4k HD. When processed correctly, 4k down-samples beautifully to color-saturated 1080p. With its high quality and low cost, Red One was the logical camera to use. Red shoots in 4k, 3k, and 2k, and can be used with cine lenses, 35-mm still lenses, or B4 2/3-inch lenses (2k only).

The production featured a fusion of cine-style techniques executed with the Red cameras, along with multicamera television-style production techniques.

The Red drive will hold 3 hours of 4k HD footage, so the team could get it all on a drive, no problem. To simplify production further, they kept two backup drives while recording in the camera, as opposed to external decks. But the cameras still had to be wired for audio, video, communications, timecode, and so on, and these signals were all on different connectors. There was still all the same signal distribution to the router, switchers, and monitors. Red batteries last about an hour and a half. However, there is a drawback:

Figure 19.3b The Red One camera. (Courtesy www.red.com.)

Steve Gibby: *We'd send a PA around to each camera when they were getting a little low on battery and we'd plug in with a battery belt and hot-swap it real quick.*

All cameras were set to shoot 4k HD. Because the band members were going to move around a lot, they used a frame rate of 29.97 fps and a shutter speed of 1/100th second. Timecode was jam-synced to all cameras. Each camera was hard-lined to the control room via HD-SDI, which was live-switched throughout the concert for audience viewing on the huge IMAG screen above the stage.

Director Eli Tishberg was calling the live show for the line cut, as well as calling the cameras' coverage for the edit and the IMAG to ensure there were no conflicts or interference.

Eli: *It's interesting that it ended up with three handhelds on stage, a small jib on stage over the keyboard player, a 40-foot-long jib arm in the audience, a dolly camera, two wide cameras, and a camera up in a one of the lighting towers. The tenth was a lock-off camera behind the drummer. The dolly rode on 60 feet of track in front of the mix position—in the back, behind the crowd. Not in the pit. I generally don't like dollies in the pit.*

The camera operators used the handheld cameras EFP-style with Nikon lenses and Mantis shoulder mounts and viewfinders. The external zoom motors they had for the Nikon lenses didn't work quite right on the shoulder-held rig cameras, so the camera operators performed all lens functions manually—definitely a challenge, but the Red image is RAW and has a lot of latitude in post, and no camera shaders were necessary.

Figure 19.4 Dolly setup from house right. (Courtesy Pam Gibby/www.cut4.tv.)

Figure 19.5 Wide shot from crane. (Courtesy Wizard Entertainment/Dan Barnett.)

Ground Control: Fly Packs and Trucks Versus Red

Going with Red instead of rolling a truck or a full fly pack actually saved money. It's considerably less expensive to shoot in Red than to shoot in HD cam. Observes Dan Barnett:

If you rent 10 Red cameras, which means you have drives on the cameras, you've just saved $3,000 in tape stock.

With Red cameras, the control room can focus more on quality control. You still hard-line back to the control room and set up a large monitor with your 8 or 10 cameras on it, so you can see the imagery of each and ensure the settings are accurate, but you're not doing any recording in there; the footage is actually being recorded right on the camera.

And there are even more savings—in post:

In post, you take your drive and download directly onto another large drive, and when you're done with this digital transfer, which is bit-for-bit perfect, you have all your media on this second drive and you're ready to edit. You don't have to pay anyone to roll tape and digitize and it looks so much better.

Switching and Monitoring

Each Red camera acquired footage to its own drive in isolation from all the other cameras. But the team members also had the 720p outputs from their cameras going into a switcher, and a monitor wall, so the director could call a "traditional" live show. Everyone involved could see immediately from the line cut how the show looked.

Mike Knowles, from Orlando, Florida, engineered the fly-pack portion of the show.

Mike: *I had all 10 cameras hard-lined via HD-SDI 720p back to the to the control room through reclocking DAs to two switchers: the line cut and the IMAG.*

The eight input Panasonic HS400 switchers have a built-in multiviewer.

Mike Knowles: *There's an output that gives you a preview program and then the multiviewer eight inputs all in one; you can either route it out to a VJ output or an HD-SDI output or the DVI output. I had a 32-inch plasma in front of each switcher, and I gave them their preview program and the eight inputs.*

Figure 19.6 Multiviewer output from Panasonic HS400 switcher. (Courtesy Oli Laperal, Jr.)

Sync

An hour before the show started, the techs locked a Lockit box and took it around from camera to camera to jam-sync free-run time-of-day timecode. They toyed with the idea of hardwiring TC and genlock, but they decided against it.

Steve Gibby: *This was like a non-hard-line EFP shoot, except we were hard-line for intercom and HD-SDI out to the IMAG big screen.*

Mike Knowles: *The idea was that we'd hardwire the cameras that we could, but obviously the handhelds would be tough to hardwire. Next time, I'll definitely hardwire everything.*

The Jib Shot

One more big standout on this show was Dave Hilmer, a Los Angeles–based 43-year veteran crane operator with nine Emmys to his name. Hilmer shoots most of the big awards shows, from the Grammys to the Academy Awards; he also does jibs and cranes for music, big-duty shots with the 40-foot crane.

Figure 19.7 Reverse angle from stage showing the crane in the background. (Courtesy Pam Gibby/www.cut4.tv.)

Dave Hilmer: *I was called to do a jib, and as it turned out they were able to supply us with a crane with a Toma head on it. Basically, the camera mounts out on the end of a 40-foot arm, and the cameraman operates from a tripod with a monitor and a zoom and focus. So I'm back on the ground, looking in a monitor and panning and tilting and zooming and focusing, and it's all done remotely and transmitted up to the camera.*

Recording on Red

With direct-to-disk recording and no tape backup, producers are sometimes apprehensive about losing valuable footage. In this show, there were many angles as backup but no drives went down, so the team had no problems whatsoever. The Red cameras performed flawlessly.

Figure 19.8 Recording 4K directly to hard drives onboard the Red camera. (Courtesy Pam Gibby/www.cut4.tv.)

Even with tape-based shows, the reality is that you're going to have a tape change at some point anyway. By contrast, tape changes weren't necessary in this case. Each camera had two extra backup drives.

Dan Barnett: *We made sure that we had new drives. We tested them the night before and verified they were recording properly. The unique thing about these drives is they go two and a half hours at 4k—so the entire show lives on one drive. Plus, we have production insurance.*

On some TV shows, insurance bonds require backing everything up to LTO drives or special setups to guarantee that the footage is archivable. After the concert, a designated team spends the next 18 hours recording drives to backups and prepping for edit.

Working in Manila

A key element to any production is capable, on-location support and dependable equipment rentals. The Manila support was top-drawer.

Mike Knowles: *One of the big concerns for this particular show was that overnight freight to the Philippines isn't cheap, so we had to try to keep things as light as possible. I took only exactly what I needed plus a couple of spares.*

Figure 19.9 The Manila crew with Oli Laperal, Jr. (Courtesy Pam Gibby/ www.cut4.tv .)

Oli Laperal, Jr: *I proposed a redundant system, so that it would be fail-safe. In other words: if we're in the middle of a concert and we have a BNC HD-SDI fail, or somebody trips over the cable and it fails, provided there's a double redundant system, then it's just a matter of unplugging a BNC and plugging it in and with luck we're on in about a few seconds, rather than running around among 50 people to try to find out where the cables are.*

Shooting for the Edit

It's really important for camera operators to shoot for the edit in a situation like this, where everything is being recorded and it's all going to editing. They need to have in mind what they're going to need in post. So they have to listen to the director and also hear the AD telling them what's coming up, like the end of songs.

Dave Hilmer: *At the beginning of a number, I would always be wide and push in to at least a waist-shot of the performer; then I would come back and refocus to wait for a chorus, let's say. Then I'd start on the chorus so that in editing there would be a move there for them.*

This is the mindset of great camera operators: they are always considerate of where the other cameras are and how the footage might fit together in post.

Lighting

Figure 19.10 Jeff Ravitz gets a light meter reading on stage. (Courtesy Pam Gibby.)

If you're using Red cameras and the type of lensing the Journey/Manila team used, you need a very hot light on stage throughout the show. Two LDs were responsible for this: Jeff Ravitz, from Visual Terrain, who oversaw TV and audience lighting, and Kevin Christopher, Journey's LD, who adapted the live show.

Jeff Ravitz may be one of the best TV LDs in the world. The last project he did prior to Journey in the Philippines was Bruce Springsteen's halftime show for the Super Bowl.

Jeff Ravitz: *As planned and practiced on rehearsal night [for Journey/Manila], we were able to light the stage area to an average off 5.6, thus providing plenty of light for Red One to get very good images.*

Moreover, TV lighting is different from theatrical stage lighting. Sometimes the two schools clash, but when they're tweaked to work together, the results make the difference between a good show and a great show. In Manila, for instance, there was a tour lighting designer whom Journey had hired and who travels with the band. Journey's LD designs the band's own lighting systems and personally operates the console to create that special live vibe every band needs.

Jeff Ravitz: *I come in more or less as a consultant. Somebody who then has to say, "Well, your show is great but it needs this, this, and this to be viable for television." And I make some of those decisions based on my own set of aesthetics and I make some of them in conjunction with the producer and director, who tell me what they want to see, and that's ultimately what drives the project.*

The camera team was using some fairly long lenses in order to get front-of-house portrait-type close-ups, and those lenses are considerably slower than the sports lenses you can put on broadcast cameras. Accordingly, they need approximately *six times* the amount of light that a show like this typically requires.

Jeff Ravitz: *We were told that we needed 130 foot-candles for this show and the weak link was our key light: our main front key light, which came from follow spots on towers 140 feet away from the stage. They were just way underpowered for what we needed, which required us to double and triple up to get a number of lights. So we did find ourselves running into some very, very serious issues with Red, and that was probably the main*

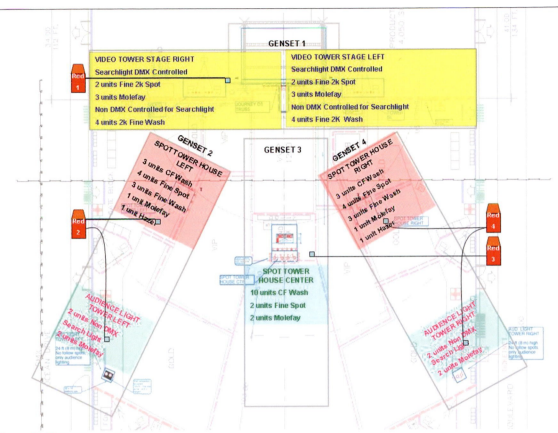

Figure 19.11 Diagram of lighting tower locations, camera positions, and instruments used. (Courtesy Jeff Ravitz/ www.visualterrain.net.)

thing. Red had no problem with any of the color—the rock 'n' roll color you ordinarily see—and it had no trouble with any other issue, except sheer intensity.

Working along a steep learning curve, the crew gradually improved the output of the follow spots and used the lens extenders less and less.

Editing

After the show, two backup drives were made and sent back to the United States with separate people to ensure delivery.

Eli Tishberg switched from director to editor and Champe switched roles from DP to post supervisor. He had all of the native R3D files transcoded to ProRez 422 and had all the ISOs loaded into Final Cut Pro and synced up. Multiclips were made, and the whole project was sent to New York for editing by Eli Tishberg.

Eli Tishberg: *The footage looked great. I directed the show live, which enabled me to get the pacing down. I get a better show that way because the cameras are reacting to me and know there's a drum solo coming up or whatever.*

For Tishberg's first pass, he cut in real time using the start-stop method for picking shots from the 10 cameras. Then he would ride that camera until he felt motivated to switch.

Eli Tishberg: *I basically would do it in four or five song segments. So I'd do the songs and then I'd start a new sequence about every 15 to 20 minutes of program time. As I would do each chunk, I would put it aside for a day or two and I would make a Blu-ray disk to watch on my regular TV.*

The cutting proved to be straight ahead, allowing the true spirit of the band to shine through. No tricky cuts but some digital camera moves were added.

With a locked picture, the project was sent back to Champe Barton and Dan Barnett where they onlined and color-corrected from the 4K native files.

The Wrap

In short, integrating a digital cinema camera like Red One into what has traditionally been an EFP camera production posed a lot of technical and operational challenges—but the Journey/ Manila crew accepted those challenges with excellent and encouraging results. Red can and will continue to be used widely in hybrid productions, in the name of better-quality footage and final cuts. The Journey/Manila team put many of the techniques particular to hybrid productions to the test, helping to enhance Red's potential benefits to the world of multicam.

Figure 19.13 The crew wraps one of the most uniquely designed 10-camera Red shows. (Courtesy Pam Gibby/www .cut4.tv.)

20

CASE STUDY: A MIXED-PLATFORM WORKFLOW—*PAUL McCARTNEY: THE SPACE WITHIN US**

Multicam editing is great for concerts. I have the most fun when I'm cutting to music. In this special chapter, we'll look at the mixed-platform techniques my team used to create the television program and multi-platinum DVD *Paul McCartney: The Space Within US*. It was extremely rare and successful to mix platforms the way we did in this case, so it's an ideal case study. Not to mention that it's not every day your executive producer is a knight.

Sir Paul McCartney is a living legend, of course. Moreover, he's no stranger to filmmaking, especially of the musical variety. He's been part of the movie business since 1964 when he starred in *A Hard Day's Night*, directed by the legendary Richard Lester—a pioneer in both cutting film to music and multicamera production. Just watch the train scene in that movie, when the Beatles are playing cards. The music for "Love Me Do" sneaks

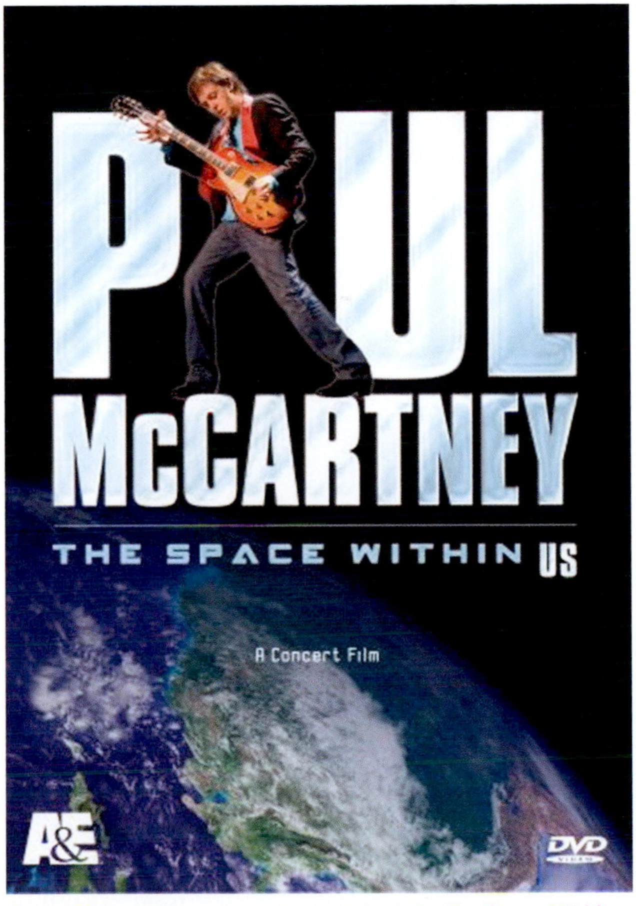

Figure 20.1a DVD cover for *Paul McCartney: The Space Within US*. (Courtesy A&E Home Video.)

*The following case study has been condensed to fit into the printed version of this book. For the full in-depth case study, see the companion DVD included with this book or download from www.MasteringMulticam.com

Doi: 10.1016/B978-0-240-81176-5.00020-4

Paul McCartney: The Space Within US

Broadcast special and DVD distributed by A&E Television Networks.

Copyright: MPL Publishing, Ltd.

Executive producer: Sir Paul McCartney

Producer/director: Mark Haefeli

Edited by: Zoran Jevremov and Mitch Jacobson

Studio: A&E Home Video

DVD Release Date: November 14, 2006

Run Time: 115 minutes

Figure 20.1b Sixteen camera split from *The Space Within US*. (Courtesy MPL Tours Inc.)

up as a score, and then, thanks to an L-cut, the band members suddenly have their instruments in hand and are performing the song MTV-style, nearly 20 years before MTV was even born.

Consequently, Lester has been called the father of MTV, although he never seemed too thrilled with this title. "If I'm the father of MTV," he said, "then I want a paternity test."

McCartney went on to star in several other movies with the Beatles and even took a turn behind the camera to direct *Magical Mystery Tour*. Within hours of his first visit to our studio, I could tell he's a seasoned filmmaker with a sharp eye for everything from sync issues to art and color palettes to software and, of course, music. He even sketched out our first mockup of the DVD box art.

Figure 20.2 Director Mark Haefeli discusses camera angles with Sir Paul McCartney inside the production truck. (Courtesy Mark Haefeli Productions)

Similarly impressive was our producer Mark Haefeli, a maverick producer and director who specializes in high-end legacy-type music TV and DVD projects. I had worked for him on other music projects, including collaborations with Aerosmith and Keith Urban, and work on the Newport Jazz Festival. *The Space Within US* would be my third project with Sir Paul McCartney and the fourth in a series, including *Back in the US, Paul McCartney in Red Square,* and a special Emmy-nominated concert that appears on the *Red Square* DVD, titled *Paul McCartney in St. Petersburg.* But *Space* would prove our biggest and most complex job so far. It would last almost a year and would eventually generate hundreds of hours of tour documentary footage plus a 26-camera multicam performance. All hands on deck!

Now just as a plumber brings a full box of tools to a job—sometimes a wrench, sometimes a plunger, sometimes a hammer, or all three—sometimes combining two or more systems is the only way to achieve the desired product. In the case of *The Space Within US,* one system wasn't enough.

We used Avid *and* Final Cut. Why? Unfortunately, in 2005, Avid couldn't yet handle HDTV, which the major networks were only just starting to require as part of deliverables, but our concert offline and dailies were in HD. Because Apple had just released multicam in Final Cut Pro and it did HD, it seemed like a good time to upgrade. But our trusty Avid Symphony was not ready to retire. So my team was caught in the transition: we had to figure out how to put not one but two platforms to the test, which also meant working with a special new technology designed to bridge the software gap.

Previously, we had always cut on Avid Symphony. But because this year HD was coming on strong, we got the green light to produce in the new format. This meant making some post-workflow

Figure 20.3 Chart showing the postproduction workflow used to share media between Avid and Final Cut Pro.

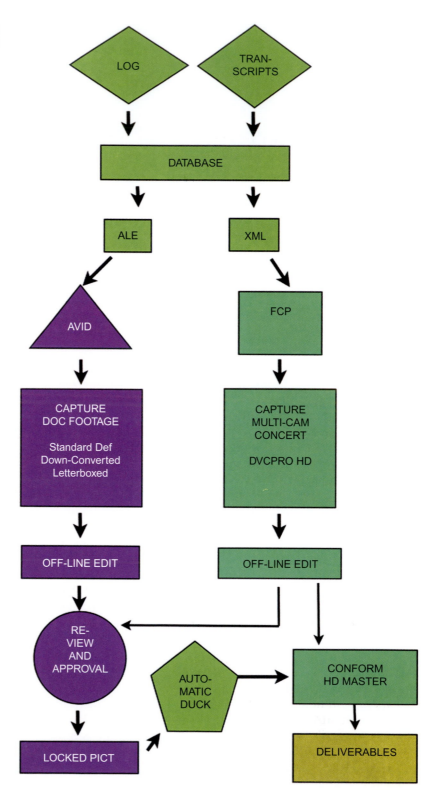

decisions, namely, whether to upgrade our Avid or employ Final Cut HD. Unsurprisingly, it came down to cost. We certainly had our work cut out for us, because the concert was set to be recorded in San Jose with 26 camera positions over two nights, and the documentary tour would be covered over 3 months with the Sony HVR-Z1U.

My editing partner was Zoran Jevremov, who won the Emmy™ Award for best multicamera editing on *Paul McCartney in Red Square*. On *Space*, it was his job to cut on Avid, focusing mainly on the documentary segments and master assemblies, while I cut 30 of Sir Paul McCartney's legendary songs offline in HD in Final Cut. Then we swapped songs and segments between the two systems, using Wes Plate's Automatic Duck software, which converts Avid OMF timelines to FCP .xml timelines and vice versa. We also used Automatic Duck for audio exports to Matt Foglia, CAS, and his Pro Tools system at Post Works/NYC.

Preproduction

The whole process started with a preproduction meeting to talk about the technical issues of concern. Including various HD and SD formats and frame rates, we discussed live performance format and compatibility with the other formats and frame rates being shot for the documentary.

The director's treatment required the use of audience members in the music segments. We called this part of the job "casting." Haefeli wanted to see a diverse mix of people—folks from every walk of life—singing and swaying along to the music. Of course, they all had to be singing in sync, even though they were filmed from over 90 different shows over the course of 3 months.

I developed a "post proposal" and presented it to the director and engineers for approval well in advance of the shoot. Typically, a post proposal has all production elements organized in a way that proves the workflow will be technically sound.

Additionally, our post proposal addressed format conversions and ultimately the postproduction workflows across multiple platforms, dailies delivery, conforming, color correction, final mastering, and deliverable formats.

When the proposal had been approved, we established our timeline.

We didn't use anything fancy or customized. We just tried to get the fastest, most current model we could find of each kind of software. The RAID for the FCP system *had* to be fast in order to run 26 streams in HD. Fortunately, DVCProHD has a very low bit rate and worked like a charm. Granted, FCP can run 128 streams, but it can only show 16 at a time.

Noteworthy

Deliverables

The deliverables included mastered elements in this order:

1. Network trailer promo in standard definition (SD)
2. Set of broadcast TV promos (also SD)
3. Set of Web clip teasers, one 2-hour DVD feature (HD and SD)
4. Set of five DVD bonus features (HD and SD) and one 43-minute A&E Broadcast Special (HD and SD)

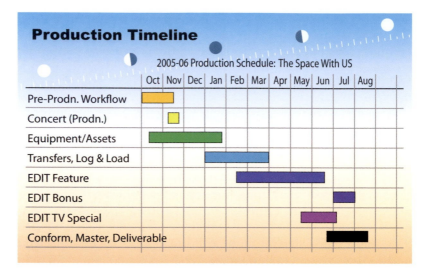

Figure 20.4 Project timeline.

Figure 20.5a Sir Paul McCartney with the postproduction team. From left: Joe DeAngelus, line producer; Zoran Jevremov, editor; Sir Paul McCartney; Claudia DeAngelus, coordinator; Matt Giffen, graphic artist; Mark Haefeli, producer/director; and Mitch Jacobson, editor. (Photo Courtesy: Mark Haefeli Productions.)

This was our hardware breakdown (2006):
- FCP on Apple G5 Dual 2.6 gigahertz computer
- Avid on Compact PC
- Dual 4 gigabit FIBER Channel Card
- Roark 8TB RAID (300 MB per second)
- J.L. Cooper Spectrum/MCS-3000 Color Controller
- Dell 19-inch monitors

A basic breakdown of how we handled the systems, followed by a complete breakdown of the post workflow:

Edit 1

Avid Symphony (v.4.x) (SD)

Zoran Jevremov, editor, with Evan Langston, assistant

1. Manage and cut documentary packages.
2. Assemble screeners and dailies.
3. Assemble final master for approval.
4. Load footage via HD decks with down-convert mode to SD.
5. Convert letterbox sequences from OMF to .xml with Automatic Duck for conforming in Final Cut Pro.

Edit 2

Final Cut Pro HD (v5.01) (HD)

Mitch Jacobson, editor, with Rich Kaplinski, assistant

1. Offline-edit 26-camera concert.
2. "Casting" audience members.
3. Conform final master.
4. Correct color.
5. Lay back audio.
6. Create deliverable masters/outputs.

Figure 20.5b Final Cut Pro edit suite with 21 TB of hard drive space.

Assets

The Space Within US ultimately involved more than 200 hours of mixed-format documentary video. You name it, we had it: Beta SP, PAL VariCam, HDCam, DigiBeta Anamorphic, and HDV. In addition to the doc footage, we had two beautifully shot and perfectly synced 13-camera concert performances, which gave us 26 unique camera angles recorded to HDCam1080psf/23.98 from two different nights.

In *Space*, over two nights, we shot 26 different camera lenses/positions, as follows:

Show A: 13 cameras (right heavy, short lens)
Show B: 13 cameras (wide heavy, long lens)

If you have a show longer than 90 minutes, you will need part A and part B and sometimes part C show reels, thus doubling and tripling your concert assets. Now, double that for a *second* performance and combine that with hundreds of hours

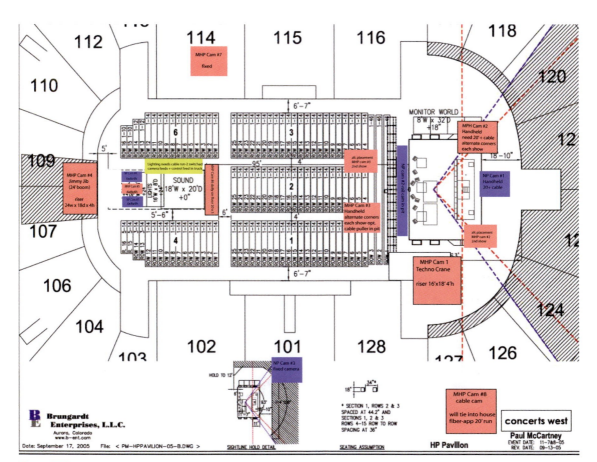

Figure 20.6 Camera map. (Courtesy Mark Haefeli Productions/MPL Tours Inc.)

of documentary and you have the perfect job for a database in postproduction. For the concert performance, we used one switched cut, one line cut, and 13 camera ISOs with two loads each per night, which actually meant about *60* HDCam tapes.

Database

We used FileMaker Pro to catalog all of our shots and tapes from the logging process through to the tape library. The database can also print labels for everything, making everything organized and legible. The logs were pulled and formatted for .xml for the FCP and OMF for Avid. Then we imported the shot logs and batched media into both systems.

Audio Assets

For the concert audio, Sir Paul McCartney recorded every show with a remote 72-channel Pro Tools Rig. The music was produced by Grammy Award–winning producer David Kahne, with re-recording/post audio mix by Matt Foglia, CAS at PostWorks. The Cinema Audio Society awarded the production sound team as winner of Outstanding Achievement in Sound Mixing for Television – Non-Fiction, Variety or Music – Series or Specials (2007).

1	2	3	4	5	6
Bill Mahr bobs head to "Band on the Run"	00:40:58:00	00:41:23:00	1093	Celebrity	Band On The Run
Mom and daughter dancing together	00:41:24:00	00:41:51:00	1093	Audience	Band On The Run
Mom and daughter dancing together	00:41:24:00	00:41:51:00	1093	Audience	Band On The Run
Mahr clapping, singing "Band on the Run"	00:41:52:00	00:42:20:00	1093	Celebrity	Band On The Run
Ladies dancing	00:42:21:00	00:42:56:00	1093	Audience	Band On The Run
Little kid clapping, smiling	00:42:59:00	00:43:17:00	1093	Audience	Band On The Run
Older woman clapping looking up	00:43:18:00	00:43:36:00	1093	Audience	Band On The Run
Woman dancing 60s moves	00:43:37:00	00:43:45:00	1093	Audience	Band On The Run
Chubby girl hollering	00:43:45:00	00:43:57:00	1093	Audience	Band On The Run
Blonde girls, guy air guitaring	00:44:05:01	00:44:34:00	1093	Audience	Band On The Run
Very bright great smile	00:44:36:00	00:44:44:00	1093	Audience	Band On The Run
"Band" - Little girl held by parents, yawns*	01:07:32:00	01:07:50:00	1088	Audience	Band On The Run
audience/ couple dancing/ group clapping Band On The Run	01:07:41:00	01:08:20:00	1036	Audience	Band on the Run
"Band" - family nods, cheers and dances	01:07:50:00	01:08:18:00	1088	Audience	Band On The Run
sign: hand raises LP 'Band on the Run'	01:08:09:20	01:08:23:23	1037	Sign	Band on the Run
"Band"-fans clap, Brian on stage, CU of hands clap	01:08:18:00	01:08:46:00	1088	Audience	Band On The Run
little girls dancing	01:08:25:00	01:09:10:00	1036	Audience	Band on the Run
mom and daughter, smiling jumping, pan across to an asian	01:08:38:19	01:09:20:22	1037	Audience	Band on the Run
"Band" – woman dances to music	01:08:45:00	01:09:03:00	1088	Audience	Band On The Run
"Band" – 2 women dancing, singing, 1 holds up cell	01:09:01:00	01:09:43:00	1088	Audience	Band On The Run
MCU lady / man w/ glasses singing	01:09:12:00	01:09:46:00	1036	Audience	Band on the Run
"Band" Mom, teenage daughter sing along	01:09:45:00	01:10:13:00	1088	Audience	Band On The Run
woman clappling/ guylong hair singing/ couple singing/	01:09:58:00	01:10:32:00	1036	Audience	Band on the Run
"Band" –CU, women singing, cheer at end*	01:10:12:00	01:10:26:00	1088	Audience	Band On The Run
men dancing/ audience / end of song	01:10:37:00	01:11:09:00	1036	Audience	Band on the Run
"Band"- Boy w/ PM T-shirt makes a sign, couple*	01:11:22:00	01:11:49:00	1024	Sign	Band On The Run
"Band"- 2 singing girls sway, wave arms	01:11:52:00	01:12:14:00	1024	Audience	Band On The Run
"Band"- woman nods, woman sings: We Paul sign	01:12:12:00	01:12:31:00	1024	Sign	Band On The Run
"Band"- couple clapping	01:12:30:00	01:12:38:00	1024	Audience	Band On The Run
"Band"- Mother, son nodding	01:12:41:0	01:12:52:00	1024	Audience	Band On The Run
"Band"- women dancing, couple dances, sings*	01:13:02:00	01:13:25:00	1024	Audience	Band On The Run
"Band"-people dance, mother, daughter dance*	01:13:23:00	01:13:41:00	1024	Audience	Band On The Run
shot of crowd lots of people clapping, very nice light band on	01:13:32:05	01:14:05:17	1005	Audience	Band on the Run
"Band"- Girl w/ b'day sign, boy w/ Beatle T sings*	01:13:40:00	01:14:12:00	1024	Audience	Band On The Run
fans on the run sign	01:14:05:18	01:14:07:17	1005	Sign	Band on the Run

Figure 20.7 Raw data from the Filemaker Pro database sorted by audience shots and song title.

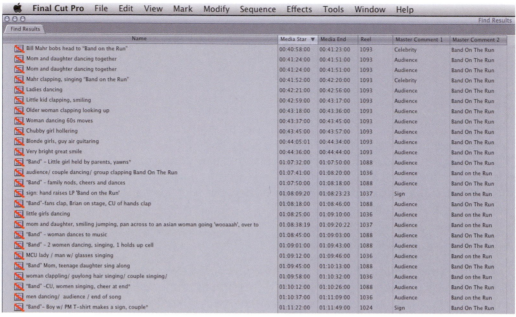

Figure 20.8 Same data as figure 20.7 imported into FCP as a shot log ready to batch-capture.

Additional Assets

- Live show graphics (onstage screens): Beta SP
- IMAG nightly recordings (60+ shows): DigiBeta Anamorphic
- Switched masters: BetaSP Anamorphic
- ISO Originals: BetaSP Anamorphic
- Miscellaneous additional material (i.e., photos, audio mixes, and a graphics package)

Noteworthy

Concert Performance Assets

- 13 Sony HDCAM F900 cameras 1080psf/23.98 per night/26 total angles (captured via Kona 3 to DVCPro HD 29.97 with 3:2 pulldown added)
- 15 Sony HDW-500 tape decks for 13 cameras and one line cut and one protection master

Paul McCartney The Space Within US
Tape and Camera Configuration
15 VTR's: Sony HDCAM HDW-F500

First Half of San Jose Show Chart

	Show A			Show B	
Tape#	Camera #	Position	Tape #	Camera #	Position
4034	1	HH-House Left	4065	1	HH Stage-House Right
4035	2	HH Aud-House Right	4066	2	HH Aud-House Left
4036	3	TechnoJib	4067	3	Techno Jib
4037	4	House Dolly-Long Lens	4068	4	House Dolly-Longer Lens
4038	5	House Left-Wide	4069	5	House Center-Wide
4039	6	Fixed Center	4092	6	Fixed Center
4040	7	House Jib	4093	7	House Jib
4041	8	Cable Cam-Left to Right	4094	8	Cable Cam-Right to Left
4042	9	Fixed Left-Tight	4095	9	Fixed Left-Tight
4043	10	Fixed Right-Wide	4096	10	Fixed Right-Wide
4045	11	Rail Cam-Pit	4075	11	Rail Cam-Pit
4046	12	House Right Long (Piano)	4076	12	House Right Long (Piano)
4047	13	HH Stage Center	4077	13	HH Stage Center
4048	14	**Line Cut MHP**	4078	14	**Line Cut MHP**
4049	15	**Line Cut MHP**	4079	15	**Line Cut MHP**

Figure 20.9 Tape assets recording plan (note that the show exceeded a 90-minute tape and doubled the amount of assets needed.)

Needles in the Haystack

Many additional assets were provided to us for use in post. The tour video crew, headed by director Paul Becher of Nocturne Productions, Inc., recorded the show with a multicamera fly-pack system every night—and we had access to these tapes. Most were on hand for the library and catalog and weren't intended for use in the DVD, but sometimes reviewing additional assets like these is nevertheless valuable.

During a concert in Tampa, Sir Paul McCartney fell into a hole in the stage just before performing "Fine Line." He was unhurt—and even told the story to the camera for one of our concert dailies. It was hilarious, especially because McCartney didn't try to hide it.

Then I had a eureka moment. I went to the database to find the Tampa show, and there it was: a wonderfully directed scene with Sir Paul tumbling backward into the piano hole, still clutching his Hoffner Beatle Bass. Of course, I *had* to cut it in. First it was just for fun, to see how it might come together: McCartney tells the story and then, in a surprise moment, we see it for ourselves. It came out pretty well, and I showed it around the studio where it got some great reactions, so we sent it to McCartney for approval. He liked it. He wanted it in the show. Not too many superstars would want to be seen in a blooper like that, but Sir Paul was cool with it.

Mixing with the Doc Segments via the Script

The Space Within US is fundamentally about the emotional power of music—and, of course, a man who has successfully shared his musical gifts with countless other people.

Mark Haefeli: *Music is what moves the story along. So this isn't just strict concert production, but pure documentary concert production. We try to appropriate the right song and the right place with the right dialogue, so that it all makes sense and ties in—so that the songs become part of the story.*

We had two big boards in the editing room. One board showed the tour schedule, the cities, and the songs (basically, all of the songs) in the order that they were done in the concert. The second big board basically showed the script, and that's constantly changing, so we were always blocking out—like, intro documentary segment, first song, second segment, second song—and then we were constantly erasing sections and moving them to another place.

Zoran Jevremov: *So we'll have a little documentary segment, and then try to find a song that naturally leads off with what that subject was. Then when that song ends, it's another documentary segment, which leads to another*

Figure 20.10 Production storyline and music chart. (Courtesy Mark Haefeli Productions. www.mhp3.com)

song. Then you start playing with exchanging songs and exchanging segments to get the best kind of impact.

Casting

Another emotional element of music documentaries can be found in fans' reactions to the show itself. McCartney loves his fans and likes to show them in his films. This project is called *The Space Within US*, and the fans put the "us" in US. Accordingly, we logged through 3 months' worth of shows to find the best faces, expressions, and bursts of energy from fans all over America. It was completely databased and pretty much treated as a separate workflow that we called casting.

We had to choose from among thousands of people, categorized by four main criteria.

Singers

These are fans actually singing along with the concert. This is the hardest category to work with because the fans have to be synced to the music. Watching one televised song, you might see footage of fans singing in 10 different states—although it looks as though they're all at the same show.

Clappers

These are fans applauding, usually before and after a song. This category isn't dealt with until you are polishing work, when you need to smooth out song transitions.

Swingers and Swayers

These are fans moving around or dancing, but typically not singing—perfect for anywhere that needs a fan or to cover a cut that doesn't need to be in perfect sync. Tempo is the main thing to match here.

Age

We also subgrouped people by age, to emphasize the music's multigenerational fan base.

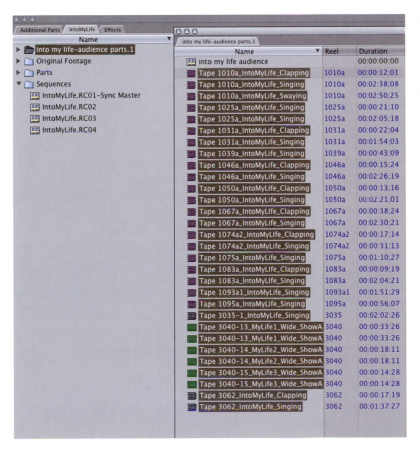

Figure 20.11 Audience members that made the grade were logged and categorized by song so they could be manually synced to the music they were singing. (Courtesy Mark Haefeli Productions.)

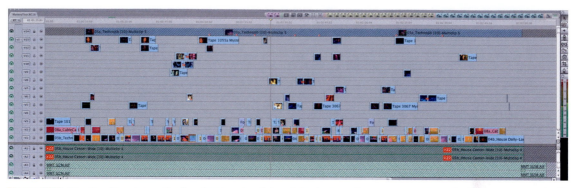

Figure 20.12 The timeline shows the band cut on track 1 and the best audience moments stacked in sync on vertical tracks above. (Courtesy Mark Haefeli Productions.)

Figure 20.13 Set list with the timecode log from show night. (Courtesy Mark Haefeli Productions.)

MAGICAL MYSTERY TOUR - 08:44:45:00
FLAMING PIE - 08:47:40:00
JET - 08:50:29:00
I'LL GET YOU - 08:56:06:00
DRIVE MY CAR - 08:58:44:00
TIL THERE WAS YOU - 09:02:16:00
LET ME ROLL IT - 09:05:58
GOT TO GET YOU INTO MY LIFE 09:12:00:00
FINE LINE - 09:17:38:00
MAYBE I'M AMAZED - 09:21:07:00
LONG AND WINDING ROAD - 09:26:22:00
IN SPITE OF ALL THE DANGER 09:32:21:00
I WILL 09:34:22:00
JENNY WREN 09:37:48:00
FOR NO-ONE 09:43:14:00
FIXING A HOLE 09:45:33:00
ENGLISH TEA 09:48:45:00
FOLLOW THE SUN 09:53:00:00
FOLLOW ME 09:57:07:00
BLACKBIRD 10:02:38:00
ELEANOR RIGBY 10:05:51:00
TOO MANY PEOPLE/BATHROOM ✒ 10:09:59:0(
GOOD DAY SUNSHINE ✒ 10:17:49:00
BAND ON THE RUN 10:21:37:00
PENNY LANE 10:27:12:00
I GOT A FEELING 10:30:38:00
BACK IN THE USSR 10:35:19:00
HEY JUDE 10: HEY JUDE - 10:40:53:00
LIVE AND LET DIE 10:49:20:00
YESTERDAY 10:55:36:00
GET BACK 10:58:42:00
HELTER SKELTER 11:02:45:00
PLEASE PLEASE ME 11:10:11:00
LET IT BE 11:13:25:00
SGT PEPPER 11:19:54:00

TAPE CHANGES AFTER THESE SONGS DURING BALLS CHARTS (

Audio

All of the audio recording was handled by the show team who records everything, every night. We took a feed to the truck and sent that in sync to all of the tape decks, loading it in with all the angles for a scratch track. This is the track on which I then did all of the rough cut editing. I would work with the show mixes until Sir Paul's music producer David Kahn was able to get me his first set of rough mixes. These new mixes are cut into the timeline under the show mixes so I can compare sonic quality and watch for sync issues. Concurrent mixes are also layered into new tracks. Eventually, I would get the final approved mix and cut that in. All of the new mixes are matched in by hand unless their timecode matches that of the show, but this is unusual. Most mixes are exported without regard to original timecode and need to be matched up manually.

Syncing to Different Shows

The real trick to matching two shows to one track is sync. In this case, the band is so tight it's fairly easy to stay on time. If sync slips from moment to moment, I'll usually stick with the already synced show and pull up the others by resetting in-points, making a new multiclip, and cutting it back in sync.

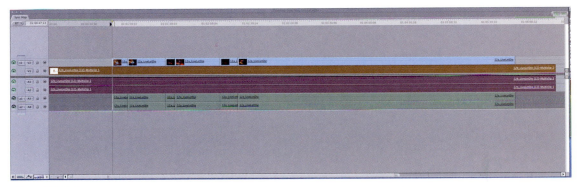

Figure 20.14 Sync map with show B matched up to show A. (Courtesy Mark Haefeli Productions.)

Re-Recording, Mixing, and Laybacks

After the show was locked, I took my timeline with final master soundtracks—complete with final music mixes, natural sound from documentary clips, interview and dialog audio, and sound effects—and exported an OMF file along with embedded audio and a QuickTime reference master in 20-minute reels. Then Matt Foglia and his team at PostWorks in New York City took it from there, for the mix and laybacks.

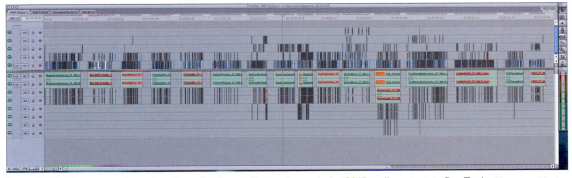

Figure 20.15 Master timeline with all production audio tracks ready for OMF audio output to Pro Tools. (Courtesy Mark Haefeli Productions.)

Conforming the Master

Concurrent with the mix, I continued to conform the final video master. First we took an OMF from the Avid and pulled in the master assembly to Final Cut Pro, reel by reel in seven parts. A reference master of the low-res Avid sequences was also exported for me to lay over the final master and check shot by shot. We used the Automatic Duck software to convert the Avid OMF to the FCP .xml.

The final sequence was a 10-b it uncompressed HD 1080i/29.97 master. The 23.98 concert footage took a 3:2 pull-down right out of the deck and was recaptured at full res for bump outs to commercial breaks.

The color needed only a few minor primary corrections. The documentary footage, however, was in rough shape. But, it was nothing that expert colorist Bob Sliga couldn't handle. Shot in several formats and under varying lighting conditions run-and-gun style, it required lots of prep—including changing out illegal character names, deleting all indications of multicam in the master clips, stripping out picture-in-picture effects, slow motion, and time warps. We needed more than double our drive space because the new graded-color media would render out new QuickTime files and more than double the amount of media.

At last, the final master was finished and laid off in-house. Then the tapes went back to PostWorks for final audio layback to the master and then off to the network and DVD compressionist for delivery to the world.

I collapsed for 2 weeks. Then I was back to work on the next big adventure. And I confess: even after all that time spent listening to Sir Paul and the Beatles, over and over and over and over again, I *still* love them. Now *that's* the power of great music.

21

THE FILMED CONCERT WORKFLOW: THE ROLLING STONES' *SHINE A LIGHT**

Oliver Peters

It's fun to look at the challenges working editors face every day on real projects. Multicamera films are an especially good study, because they often take the form of large events, spectacles, and concerts. There's no better example than *Shine a Light*, Martin Scorsese's concert film featuring the Rolling Stones, which was released in both standard 35 mm and IMAX. Scorsese was instrumental in inventing the rock 'n' roll concert film genre as an editor on *Woodstock* and the director of *The Last Waltz*. Here he continued his passion for the art form by teaming up with none other than Mick and Keith to bring you up close and personal with the world's greatest rock 'n' roll band.

Figure 21.1 The Rolling Stones perform at the Beacon Theater in New York City for the filming of *Shine a Light*. (Courtesy the Rolling Stones, Shangri-La Entertainment, and 20th Century Fox.)

*The following case study has been condensed to fit into the printed version of this book. For the full in-depth case study, see the companion DVD included with this book or download from www.MasteringMulticam.com.

Doi: 10.1016/B978-0-240-81176-5.00021-6

This wasn't your average production. Scorsese pulled together an Oscar-winning crew, headed up by cinematographer Robert Richardson (*The Aviator, JFK*). Live recording was handled by Grammy-nominated recording engineer Bob Clearmountain. Rounding out this ensemble was editor David Tedeschi, who had also worked with Scorsese on the acclaimed Bob Dylan documentary, *No Direction Home: Bob Dylan*.

David Tedeschi is a New York–based editor who mainly works on feature films, documentaries, and music projects. He first hooked up with Scorsese on *The Blues*, which was being posted while Scorsese was working on *The Aviator*. Something must have clicked, because Tedeschi was tapped to cut *No Direction Home: Bob Dylan* and then *Shine a Light*. Tedeschi was happy to discuss Scorsese's approach to this production:

Marty didn't want to film a Rolling Stones concert in a huge arena. He wanted a smaller, more intimate. It's really a very positive and exciting film about how these four guys go out and make music. They are the real deal, with Mick singing and moving around on the stage like a 20-year-old and Keith, Ronnie, and Charlie going out there every night with great passion. That really comes across in Shine a Light.

18 Cameras: No Waiting

Shine a Light was filmed in a smaller theater over two performance nights. Given the resolution of modern HD cameras, you would have thought that this would have been a natural application for the Sony CineAlta models, as Robert Altman had done on *A Prairie Home Companion*. Instead, Scorsese and Richardson opted to stick with film. In fact, 17 35-mm cameras rolled along with one Panavision Genesis during both nights. More than 100,000 feet of film ran through the gates—as much for as a typical dramatic production—shot over several weeks and months. *Shine a Light* did that in just two nights.

David Tedeschi: *For the key cameras, they needed backup cameras, because they're going to be changing rolls of film during songs. There's no way around that. It's a live concert, so you can't say, "Okay, cut! Everybody change your film!".*

The general editorial workflow Tedeschi followed was to first review dailies with Scorsese in much the same manner as a scripted film. Next,

Figure 21.2 Director Martin Scorsese and cinematographer Robert Richardson talk with Mick Jagger during rehearsals. (Courtesy the Rolling Stones, Shangri-La Entertainment, and 20th Century Fox.)

clips were synced and grouped within Avid's multicamera routine into sets of nine camera angles within each group. Tedeschi then reviewed each camera angle and added locators (markers) at points in each angle with particular interest to be used in the cut. Once this was done, he was able to start cutting the performances by editing between the various options. Tedeschi was aided in his task of keeping the footage organized by Nick Damiano, the first assistant editor. Damiano, a graduate of the Berklee College of Music, was chosen for his experience with various music productions, including Bruce Springsteen and Dave Matthews Band concert programs. He was also in charge of loading and grouping clips on the U2 3D film.

Organizing the MultiCamera Beast

Nick Damiano described some of his organizational steps on *Shine a Light*:

In the beginning it was a real nightmare to catch up and to get it all organized. The workflow was to shoot on film and then transfer to an HDCAM-SR tape in 4:4:4 logarithmic color space. That HDCAM-SR tape was color-corrected and laid back to a regular HDCAM tape. There were hundreds of hours of film dropped off to a lab, literally within a couple of days, and they had to develop it and transfer it. Unfortunately, this came back to us out of shooting order. Marty wanted to start screening at the beginning, meaning that he wanted to start looking at dailies from "Jumpin' Jack Flash." We'd have half the song, and the assistant director didn't want to watch until Marty could see everything.

In the end this was straightened out and post continued on a more even keel. Standard definition DVCAM tapes were also created to load into the Avid system for cutting.

Damiano explained how he prepared the content for editing:

We received Flex files [film transfer logs] from Technicolor and would load everything. I'd then build a sequence that had every camera angle, all 18 cameras in a row and in a specific order. Anything Marty was going to screen, would always be batch digitized at high resolution from the color-corrected HDCAM tapes. He screened it in a screening room using a high-end Digital Imagery projector and literally would watch the 18 angles in a row, one after another. David was at the screenings and he would have lyric sheets that I prepared for him, 18 of them numbered according to the camera. As Marty was watching, he'd make notes. If he said, "Oh that's great. Look at the way that's shot," David would add a little note for that camera angle. Then after they screened, David had that sequence in his Avid and he could go back there and add Marty's notes via locators to the sequence.

Damiano discussed his strategy for grouping multicamera clips in Media Composer:

Once I had all the 18 camera angles I needed for a single song I would drag them into a new bin for that song. Then I'd build a timeline with a different video layer for each camera. Next, I'd literally sync each camera by eye, using the number from the LED timecode displays shot by the camera operator as my starting reference point.

I would nudge shots until I felt it was the best possible sync. Sometimes it would be a guitar, sometimes it would be Charlie Watts in the back where he hits a cymbal.

Once that was done I'd make a subclip of that group clip from just the start to the end, because you don't need all that extra stuff. Finally I put that into another bin labeled "group masters." If camera rolls stopped and started, at that point I had to make a second group clip. The most was four group clips for one song.

Making a Movie

The edited film is about 2 hours long, based largely on the running length of the songs in the concert. Tedeschi explained:

Getting to the two-hour length was an intuitive process. The second night was a much better performance, so 98% of the cut came from that second night. The set list was not exactly the same between the two nights. The first night started with "Start Me Up." So that alone changes everything, including the continuity of clothing. You can't cut "Start Me Up" between the two nights, and you can't cut "Jumpin' Jack Flash" between the two nights.

I know from experience that no matter how many cameras you have, you still run into situations where you want another angle. David Tedeschi laughed:

Yes, I ran into that too, they did have a modified zone coverage plan for the cameras, and Marty was in radio contact with them, of course. But he had such faith in them that he was able to trust their instincts and let them explore as well. As a result, the performances and the shots they were able to get were more spontaneous than just a series of planned camera moves.

It's about the spontaneity that they do onstage to reach that audience. You can say 18 cameras seems like a lot, but the truth is, as crazy as it sounds, there were times where you had one camera capture it right. It would be a different camera each time. So say, when Keith and Mick share a microphone—that was really captured by one guy who was smart enough, because he saw it out of the corner of his eye and he got it when he needed to get it. And Keith coming out in "Jumpin' Jack Flash," Keith spitting out his cigarette, all that crazy Buddy Guy stuff. More often than not you had one camera guy able to get it and it was usually a different guy for the things that I think of as the great moments of the film.

Sync

Shooting both 35-mm film and 24p HD video introduced a number of sync issues. They debated between recording at 24 fps and 23.98 fps, but in the end they decided to operate the Genesis camera and the film cameras at a true 24 fps. During post, the recorded audio track and the Genesis video was "pulled down" to synchronize at the video-friendly rate of 23.98 fps. All of the film negative, which was shot as 3-perf 35 mm, was transferred to videotape. As is standard for telecine operations, the 24-fps film runs through the scanner at a slightly slower 23.98 fps. This means that in the end, all sources would run at the proper speed and be in sync with each other.

The master clock with time-of-day timecode was being generated from Dave Hewitt's mobile recording truck. Timecode slates were mounted on the walls, in the audience, and backstage. Whenever a camera operator started a new roll, the operator would shoot the slate. The editorial team had scratch mixes from the live recordings of each night complete with timecode, so that visuals were synced against this. This included the Albert Maysles behind-the-scenes coverage, which also matched the same timecode.

Nick Damiano: *The master timecode generator that was feeding Bob Clearmountain's Pro Tools rig also fed four to six LED screens in several different positions throughout the stage. The idea was that while the film was being shot at the very beginning or at the very end of the reel, that was going to be how we would sync the audio to the film, because obviously there were no slates. We discussed if the project was going to be a true 24 or 23.98 fps. The mixer recorded at 96 kHz, 24 bit. When he actually mixed, he just set his Pro Tools to pull down—a process where it's slowed down by .01%. Then when he remixed, he gave us stereo mixes and surround mixes that had already been matched by speed to the HDCAM tapes.*

The Basement

Postproduction followed a rather unique path thanks to Scorsese's frequent visual effects collaborator Rob Legato (*The Aviator, The Departed*). Legato is a proponent of many desktop tools and operates a small visual effects facility out of his house, known as the Basement. Legato explained their approach:

Sparkle, Bob Richardson's preferred colorist at Complete Post, transferred all the film dailies to HDCAM-SR tape in the 10-bit RGB 4:4:4 mode, which becomes the equivalent of a digital negative. He also provided SD dailies for David to capture into the Avid. During the course of the editing, we would take David's Avid sequence and boil down the nearly 300 source tapes into only two main source tapes. These were basically clones of the originals, so there was no quality loss in this step.

The Basement's editor, Adam Gertel, used an Apple Final Cut Pro workstation and a Sony HDCAM-SR deck to do this. Their MacPro was configured with a high-speed Ciprico MediaVault RAID and a Blackmagic Design Multibridge Extreme capture/output unit, ideal for handling the data throughput and preserve the color integrity of the 10-bit 4:4:4 media. The key to this method was to create new Avid-compatible logs so that it was easy to locate any shot on the new tapes, as well as find additional shots on the original transfer masters, if needed.

Rob Legato: *Our final color correction was done on a daVinci. Since the source was tape and not media files from a hard drive, any last-minute updates could be made in Final Cut, output to HDCAM-SR, and then color-corrected on the daVinci in real time. Although the HDCAM-SR format is only high definition (1920 × 1080) and not a true 2K film file, it's still more than acceptable for a film-out.*

Completing the Cut

David Tedeschi did all his cutting on an Avid Media Composer Adrenaline HD system connected to Avid Lanshare shared storage. Tedeschi explained the rationale to cut in standard definition:

I had to use the multicam feature all along the way, and that simply works best on Adrenaline when you stay in standard definition. For one song, I could go through and we could view it with nine cameras playing at the same time. I needed the responsiveness for Marty and by staying in standard def we were able to see nine camera angles at any given time playing back in real-time.

Nick Damiano: *David Tedeschi would get a first rough cut, and Marty wanted to screen it. At that point the media was already loaded, including the HDCAM footage. I only had to decompose, switch my project settings over to HD, and relink the media from the SD to the HD files. I would add a 1.85:1 mask, render the one song, and output it for the screening. We did that literally for the whole concert, which was about 20 songs. Each song was a separate sequence, and generally he would average two songs in a week. When we got through the halfway point, we actually assembled them all together and Marty screened the first half of the concert. When David had a rough cut of every song, we put the whole thing together and Marty screened that. Once David had his first pass on all the songs, that's when they started playing with archival footage and the intro.*

David Tedeschi: *The concert was completely cut from beginning to end by the time anyone saw anything. We did our screenings in high definition, though, using Avid's DNxHD 220 resolution. We would do these screenings at least once a month—and sometimes once a week. The image looked wonderful. The edit lasted 10 to 12 months, but in spite of the time, David tells me there were no surprises.*

In closing, Tedeschi offered:

The thing that took the longest, interestingly enough, was to make Shine a Light *feel like a movie. In other words, I felt going into this that the biggest challenge was going to be using 18 cameras and cutting music. I love music, and I've been cutting a lot of music. So I felt the challenge would be the music, but Richardson and Marty captured the concert so well that the challenge became something else too. This was much more time consuming, which is to shape it in such a way to give it elements that weren't just about the live performance—even though the movie is about the live performance. The first 10 minutes and the archival element was much harder. It took a long, long time, but to be honest with you, that was all fun.*

Shine a Light was being released by Paramount Classics as well as by IMAX and is available on DVD.

Figure 21.3 The Rolling Stones' core members: Mick Jagger, Ronnie Wood, Keith Richards and Charlie Watts sign off to the crowd after filming. (Courtesy the Rolling Stones, Shangri-La Entertainment, and 20th Century Fox.)

22

A THUMBNAIL HISTORY OF MULTICAMERA PRODUCTION AND EDITING*

There has been multicamera madness since the first-documented multicamera shoot in 1898, followed by the first multicamera live broadcast in 1928. Inventors, craftsmen, and film-makers have been experimenting and perfecting multicam techniques. Multicam film editing started in 1951 and electronic editing grew between the early '70s and 1999. In 1992, when Avid introduced multicam editing for nonlinear digital edit suites. In 1998, Patrick O'Connor, Tom Ohanian and their team won the Emmy™ Award for multicamera editing software on the Avid and paved the way for a new chapter in postproduction—and this book.

Origins of Multiple-Camera Production

Cinéorama (1898)

Multiple cameras in production can be traced back to the Cinéorama, in 1900 at the Exposition Universelle Internationale in Paris. Its inspiration came from the cyclorama.

In 1898, French inventor Raoul Grimoin-Sanson filmed Paris from a balloon with 10 cameras and presented the results on a circular screen.

> A cyclorama was a 360-degree painting inside a building that depicted a landscape or a battle, and visitors would stand in the middle and feel as if they were inside the event. (Any Trekkies reading this might think of it as the first hold deck.)

*The following case study has been condensed to fit into the printed version of this book. For the full in-depth case study, see the companion DVD included with this book or download from www.MasteringMulticam.com.

Doi: 10.1016/B978-0-240-81176-5.00022-8

He called it Cinéorama, which was somewhere between a film and a ride, perhaps most similar to an IMAX experience. Actually, it was a flight simulator that gave grounded viewers the sensation of taking a ride in a hot-air balloon over Paris. It created a sensation at the 1900 Paris Exposition.

Grimoin-Sanson locked 10 cameras together with a single central drive. He put them in a hot-air balloon and filmed as the balloon rose over the Tuileries.

Playback for the expo-goers was provided by 10 synchronized 70-mm movie projectors, projecting onto 10 9-by-9-meter screens arranged in a full 360-degree circle around the viewing platform, which was a large balloon basket capable of holding 200 viewers.

Since then, many film directors have used more than one camera to cover a scene. *Howard Hawks: Angels with Wings* (1939, Columbia) used many cameras to capture the action.

TV was soon to follow with multicamera live telecasts and kinescopes.

Figure 22.1 The Cinéorama camera configuration.

The Queen's Messenger (1928 (TV))

The use of multiple video cameras to cover a scene goes back to the earliest days of television. Three cameras were used to broadcast *The Queen's Messenger*, in 1928.[1] The BBC and NBC routinely used multiple cameras for their live television shows from 1936 onward.[2]

W.G.Y. 467

Figure 22.2a *The Queen's Messenger* (1928) was the first broadcast live TV show and the first to use multiple cameras. Here, director Mortimer Stewart is shown blocking the actors with the cameras. (Courtesy Chris Hunter/Schenectady Museum & Suits-Bueche Planetarium, www.schenectadymuseum.org.)

I Love Lucy Sets the Stage (Desilu, 1951)

The term *multicam* is often used synonymously with *sitcom*, but in fact the former term is frequently misunderstood. Multicamera situation comedy is the correct full term for what we're talking about here. Multicam can mean shooting with two or more cameras in any genre. It also refers to our favorite editing mode.

Shooting three or four cameras at a time was pioneered in the earliest of television production for live shows even before videotape and timecode. It boils down to the same notion as capturing a live event and maintaining an engaged audience while getting all the coverage you need at the same time, instead of shooting multiple takes over and over again.

Although it's often claimed that Desi Arnaz and cinematographer Karl Freund pioneered the multiple-cam setup for television on *I Love Lucy* in 1951, it had in fact been used by other

Figure 22.2b Desi Arnaz at the apartment set of the *I Love Lucy Show* with three cameras and a boom mic. He is also holding a handheld microphone (1951). (Courtesy CBS/Getty Images.)

live (filmed, but not edited) television shows, including another CBS comedy, *The Amos 'n' Andy Show,* filmed at the Hal Roach Studios and on the air 4 months earlier. The technique was developed for television by Hollywood short-subject veteran Jerry Fairbanks, assisted by producer-director Frank Telford, and it was first seen on the anthology series *The Silver Theater,* another CBS program, in February 1950.[3] Desilu's more high-profile innovation was to film multicam in front of a live studio audience.

The First MultiCam Team: A New Hybrid

The team that formed *I Love Lucy* developed the multicamera TV system that we continue to use today. The *I Love Lucy* team consisted mainly of a new hybrid, perfectly suited to the emerging television business. The performers, including Desi Arnaz and Lucille Ball, were from the stage; the writers and producers came from radio; and the director, Mark Daniels, came from live TV. From the feature films she had done, Lucille Ball brought in the remarkable DP Karl Freund and editor Dann Cahn, A.C.E. Later, Bill Asher would take over from Mark Daniels and apply more of a movie technique. But when the show was first formed, the provenance of its actors, writers, and producers contributed greatly to its unique style and success.

Dann Cahn, A.C.E. was the first editor to cut with synchronized multiple cameras on film and is considered to be the grandfather of multicamera editing. He got his first lucky break the day he was born. He grew up, literally, under the *Hollywoodland* sign and came from a long familial line of filmmaking experts—so you could say that editing was his destiny. It would be his son's, too. In fact, Dann Cahn, A.C.E. is in the middle of the only three-generation family in A.C.E history. His father, Phillip Cahn, had a long career at Universal, mainly cutting Abbott and Costello comedies.

His son, Daniel Cahn, A.C.E., is a picture editor for TV and film productions, including *The Novice* (2004) and *Tremors* (2003).[4]

Daniel Cahn, A.C.E.: *I literally believe that I have a family comedy gene. The fact is that I come from a generation [of] skilled film assistants that were trained by master editors. It is still the thing that I like doing the best.*

Dann Sr. paid his dues early, persevering through an 8-year-long apprenticeship. When he finally got his International Alliance of Theatrical Stage Employees (IATSE) card from the Motion Picture Editing Guild, he was cutting features. His second big break was landing his job on *I Love Lucy*, where he would help invent the way multicam sitcoms are still shot and edited today.

It was Karl Freund and Desi Arnaz who set the studio for staging, camera blocking, and the live audience. The lights were hung instead of stationed on the floor, film style, and a new feature was added to the dollies: crabbing. This allowed the cameras to move from side to side on the sets quickly and easily.

Under Dann Cahn, A.C.E. in the editorial department were his assistants Bud Molin and Ted Rich, A.C.E. Ted Rich, A.C.E. also went on to do great things in TV, including becoming head of production for MTM.

Ted Rich, A.C.E.: *Desi was the one that came up with the idea to use multicam, so they could shoot in front of an audience and get actual reactions. Actors react better when they hear the audience reacting and laughing, like in a theater.*

They were also the first to edit multicam style.

Ted Rich, A.C.E.: *Desi would say, let's play it that way, it'll play better. Or, I like that angle better. Lucy never got involved. Not in the production, not in the end product. She never sat in on editing; she was the actress; that was it.*

Sync 'Em Up

Dann Cahn, A.C.E.: *We had ABC cameras and they had this bloop-flashing system, instead of a clapper.*

George Fox came up with a bloop-light sync, which would flash a sprocket on a frame and simultaneously flash the sound-track. The soundtrack was on regular motion 35-mm stock film. The light would flash and a series of linear marks would occur on the soundtrack frame. You could read the soundtrack to see where the mark was and sync it up to the light flash on the cameras for editing. The problem was that it wasn't accurate and the sound pop was always out of sync plus or minus two frames with the flash.

Dann Cahn, A.C.E.: *So we dispensed with the camera system and I went down to the Mill (workshop) to build an old-fashioned clapper, like you see on a movie set, only it was big enough that three cameras could see it. We had the assistant cameraman clap that big thing for three cameras and we had perfect sync; no problems.*

Back to basics.

We laid down the Bible for multiple-camera sitcoms.

Dann Cahn, A.C.E

a

Figure 22.3a Dann Cahn, A.C.E. at the Moviola Monster in 1951. (Courtesy: Dann Cahn, A.C.E.)

The Evolution of Multicamera Editing Technology

Enter the Moviola Monster

When I had signed up for the I Love Lucy *job and arrived in my cutting room, two guys came in wheeling this new edit thing and I said to my assistant, "What are we going to do with this monster? It won't even fit in the cutting room." So we put it in the prop room and used it there. It was a Moviola with four heads—three for picture and one for sound. Its new name—the Monster—stuck.*

Dann Cahn, A.C.E.

Syncronized multicamera editing started in the film world with the advent of the Moviola Monster, a custom four-headed machine used for three picture reels and one audio reel. Dann Cahn, A.C.E. used this machine on the *I Love Lucy Show* (1951). It was retired on *Designing Women* in the late 1980s.

Eventually, the Monster would be retrofitted for five heads, to include a soundtrack and a fourth camera called the "D" camera (later renamed the "X" camera by James Burrows; discussed later).

The Monster technology may seem more like a horse-and-buggy than a Model T, but it was used for about 30 years before being replaced by computers and CMX editing (and eventually Avid and FCP). That was long enough for Dann Cahn's son Daniel to work his way up in the business and use it to cut hugely popular sitcoms.

Daniel Cahn, A.C.E.: *I used both the three-headed and the four-headed, and most had been upgraded to the four-headed version. You could very easily cut three cameras on the Monster; you can look at the center picture head and peripherally see left and right, to the first and third camera, so to speak. Once you start integrating the fourth camera, you're really jogging between watching two at any one given time, so there's a lot more forward and back in editing for comedy.*

b

Figure 22.3b Dann Cahn, A.C.E with the Moviola Monster 2009. (Courtesy: Dan Cahn, Photo by: **Carrie Puchkoff**).

CMX Linear Editing

Beginning with CMX linear editing, which appeared in the early 1970s, you could easily do multi-cam, provided you had enough tape decks. It involved a two-inch machine, a one-inch machine, a 3/4-edit worktape, and a lot of knowledge about the analog video signal. Next up were systems like the EditDroid, Montage, and Ediflex, which actually used multiple tape decks or laserdiscs to mimic random-access editing. They had the same material on each deck, so they could get to shots much faster. Another system that came into play around this time was Spectra System from Laser Edit, a multi-cam pioneer. LaserEdit used laserdiscs.

Laura Young finished her music and arts education at NYU. She has used every type of major nonlinear multicamera system from CMX to Avid. Today, she is a renowned broadcast editor and part of the world-class team that brings us *The Met: Live in HD* and PBS's *Great Performances*.

Laura Young: *In the old days, I would sit in a room with four one-inch tape decks stacked up together with timecode and roll those together, then cut*

The EditDroid

The EditDroid was a computerized analog NLE developed by Lucasfilm in the early 1980s and together with the SoundDroid, spun off in 1985 into The Droid Works - an independent joint venture between Lucasfilm and, and, the Convergence Corporation. The venture was the first to introduce Hollywood to nonlinear editing. The EditDroid software was eventually sold to Avid in 1993—but primarily as a marketing deal, not a technological development. The controller, called the TouchPad, featured a KEM-style shuttle knob and a trackball. The EditDroid pioneered the use of the graphical display for editing—introducing the timeline as well as digital picture icons to identify raw source clips.

References: droidMAKER: George Lucas and the Digital Revolution and Nonlinear, written by Michael Rubin. (droidmaker .blogspot.com)

and make a list in EDL. Then we would take that EDL—which would be on eight-inch floppy disks—and go into an online room, plug that into a CMX 3600, and, one at a time, put up those one-inch tapes, then auto-conform from one inch and make our master.

Random Access

Although it used the same data-storing method as the 3600, the LaserEdit controlled dual-headed laserdisc players stacked together instead of doing tape dubs. For multicam editing, you could sync-roll the decks with multiple ISOs and actually make cuts or dissolves through a switcher to a record deck—and the computer could remember and recreate those edits.

Digital Nonlinear Editing

Once things became computer-based and digital, nonlinear editors gained many advantages—but in a sense we also took a step backward because tape systems were full resolution and played back simultaneously. The early computer-based systems didn't have the ability to play streams fast enough to obtain multicam capability.

HeavyWorks

In 1994, Lightworks came out with a well-received system called Heavyworks, which offered digital nonlinear-based multicam.

Scott Brock assistang editor: *It's actually pretty similar to Final Cut multi-cam setup. You have a gallery, which is the equivalent of an Avid bin or a Final Cut bin, and you would drag [the clips]into a special gallery that was known as a sync gallery. You could select which of the ways you wanted to sync them up by. And then they would all play.*

Avid

Then along came Avid multicam (code-named Mustang) in 1995–1996—taking on the market with a tiny team of five and some serious competitive disadvantages, like not being able to play more than four cameras in real time. Still, it went on to crack Hollywood's multicam comedy-editing market and gave Heavyworks a run for its money.

Jeff Bass: *We were editing using the Avid on a show called* Dinosaurs *in 1992–93 and seeing that it had some grouping capabilities. We started thinking that it could be useful on some of the multicamera shows that we were doing at the time, and contacted Avid, got in touch with Tom Mohaney, and asked him about some abilities for the product to do a multicamera-type process.*

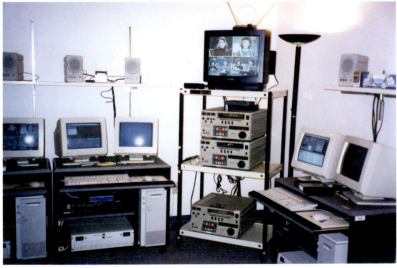

c

Figure 22.3c The first Avid ingest station (1993). (Courtesy Jeff Bass.)

Tom Ohanian came up with the nomenclature. The star Avid concept was presented as the group clip.

Tom Ohanian: *What we had in the first version was the ability to take multiple angles from multiple clips from multiple cameras—and with this we created the group clip. And from there, of course, we were able to create a multigroup clip.*

Avid went on to win an Emmy Award for its multicam system. It also won an Oscar in 1998

Final Cut

Final Cut Pro has offered multicam editing only since version 5. Before that, there was a application called Multicam Lite from Digital Heaven that provided multicam functionality.

Figure 22.4 The timeline used to simulate multicamera editing in Final Cut Pro before version 5.1. All video tracks are laid out in sync map. The layers are mixed down with PIP FX to get a single clip with all angles. The chosen shots are placed above to build a sequence. (Courtesy Donald Kilgore/www.image202.com.)

Chronological History of MultiCam Editing Systems

Film

- Moviola Monster (1951; used on *I Love Lucy*)

Tape and Disk

- CMX 600 - (1971) Non-linear with a stack of disk platters that held 5 minutes each. The platters looked like a horizontal bread slicer. Cost: $30,000.
- Ediflex (1983) 1/2" VHS sources. The Ediflex system earned Cinedco, its manufacturer, an Emmy Award for best design of electronic editing systems in 1986. It uses an array of 10 domestic VCR players, all cued up to different camera angles or takes of a shot. Editor, Herb Dow was the guy behind Ediflex.

The Montage and EditDroid debut at NAB in 1984.

- EditDroid (Laserdisc, 1984) (See the sidebar.)
- Montage (17 1/2" Betamax Sources. and lasardisc-1984) In 1989, Zoetrope defined industry standards by editing *The Godfather*, Part III using Montage Picture Processor.
- Laser Edit' Spectra-Ace (Laserdisc, 1984) A proprietary linear system that used two-sided laser disks. Directly marketed to multicamera shows.
- CMX 6000 (Laserdisc, 1986) The 6000 could roll a simulated master in all directions and all speeds without going to videotape.
- BHP's TouchVision (9-12 VHS Decks, 1986) Had a unique touch screen controller.
- E-PIX (Laserdisc and Tape, 1988) Officially called E-PIX Hybrid Editing System because it had a hybrid mode where you could edit both tape and disc, the theory being that you' use disc when the cuts got too fast on tape.

Digital Nonlinear

- Avid/1 with multicam software (1991)
- Premiere Pro (1992) This is United Media's plug-in for Premiere Pro 1.5.
- Lightworks' Heavyworks (1994) First viable digital non-linear editing system for traditional multicamera television programs. This system was predominantly designed by engineers and computer guys, not editors.
- Final Cut Pro (1999) Final Cut Pro was sold to Apple in 1997 and the software received an technology and engineering Emmy Award in 2002.
- Vegas (2000)
- Discrete Edit (2001)
- Liquid (2004)
- Velocity HD (2004)
- Grass Valley EDIUS (2007)
- Media 100 (2009)

References: *droidMAKER: George Lucas and the Digital Revolution* and *Nonlinear*, written by Michael Rubin. (droidmaker.blogspot.com)

References

1. "The Queen's Messenger," at Early Television Foundation and Museum.
2. "The Alexandra Palace TV Station," at Early Television Foundation and Museum. "The Birth of Live Entertainment and Music on Television, November 6, 1936," at History TV.net. "Telecasting a Play," *The New York Times*, March 10, 1940, p. 163.
3. "Flight to the West?" *Time*, March 6, 1950.
4. From Editors Guild Magazine, story by *Michael Kunkes*.
5. www.editorsguild.com/V2/magazine/archives/0705/news_article03.htm.

INTERVIEWEE LIST AND BIO INFO

First	Last	Title	Credits/Bio Info
Gary	Adcock	President, Studio 37	Gary Adcock, President Studio 37 in Chicago, which offers Consultation Service for Film and HD Production and Post Production needs
Jim	Alfonse	Owner, Tri-Sys Designs	Jim Alfonse is owner of Tri-Sys Designs, is a Systems Integrator with twenty-five years experience in the Broadcast Industry
Keith	Anderson	President, All Occasions Video	Keith Anderson has been full-time in the videography business since 2002. He's currently President of the Illinois Videographers Association and a five-time WEVA Creative Excellence Award winner.
Jon	Aroesty	President, Playback Innovations	Jonathan has over 25 years experience in television production and is the President and Founder of Playback Innovations in Los Angeles.
Martin	Baker	Managing Director, Digital Heaven	Martin Baker is the Founder and Managing Director of Digital Heaven and has 13 years of experience as a broadcast editor. His extensive work with Final Cut Pro includes post production for the BBC and Channel 4. Martin has been an Apple Certified Trainer since 2006.
Randy	Baker	Producer, Director, and Cameraman	Randy Baker is Founder and Owner of Randy Baker Productions, a full service digital production company located in Central Florida specializing in directing and shooting high-end film style video production for both broadcast and corporate clients.
Dan	Barnett	Executive Producer & President, Wizard Entertainment	Wizard Entertainment's President, Dan Barnett has been booking and producing entertainment events for over 25 years. Wizard clients include: Journey, Southeast Toyota, Seminole Hard Rock Hotel & Casino, Gulfstream Park, City of Hallandale, Absolute, LXR Luxury Resorts, City of Fort Lauderdale, Image Entertainment and Kid Rock.
Champe	Barton	Owner, HD Suite, Inc.	Champe is a top, High Definition cameraman in Florida area and Owner of HD Suite, Inc.
Jeff	Bass	Editor	Veteran Multi-cam Editor and Owner, J/KAM Digital in Hollywood

(Continued)

First	Last	Title	Credits/Bio Info
Darryl	Bates, A.C.E.	Editor & Director	Emmy nominated editor whose work includes series such as "90210" and "Gilmore Girls"
Paul	Becher	Paul Becher is co-CEO of Nocturne Productions, Inc in Illinois.	Paul Becher is co-CEO of Nocturne Productions, Inc in Illinois. Nocturne provides expert live entertainment and corporate production services at the arena and stadium level. Paul has overseen live visuals for Paul McCartney for some 200 performances.
Glenn	Bekovitz, CAS	Mixer	Glenn Berkovitz is a Freelance audio mixer at Spinning Reel Sound in Los Angeles. He has over 20 years of experience as a sound mixer.
Kyle	Bell	Student, Osceola Fundamental High School	Student, Osceola Fundamental High School in Florida
Carmen	Borgia	VP of Audio Production, DuArt Sound Design & Mixing	Carmen Borgia is VP of Audio Production, DuArt Sound Design & Mixing. He currently supervises audio production for the North American English Language dubbing of Pokémon. Carmen is also a singer, songwriter, as well as a sound mixer and film sound designer.
Gary	Bradley	Editor	Editor and Owner, Hand Made Video, Inc.
Robert	Bramwell, A.C.E.	Editor	Editor, Robert Bramwell, A.C.E. has worked for 20th Century Fox, NBC Universal and Sony Pictures Entertainment Television. He is currently editor for Barking Dogs Productions. Robert is a huge proponent of Avid ScriptSync.
Scott	Brock	Assistant Editor	Scott Brock is currently Assistant Editor for Martin Scorsece's Sikelia Productions in NYC.
Keith	Brown	Director	Second Baptist Church, Houston, TX
Daniel	Cahn, A.C.E.	Editor	Film Editor/ Post-Producer/ MPEG Board Member/Editing Instructor at Inner City Filmmakers in the Greater Los Angeles Area. Father is editor Dann Cahn, A.C.E.
Dann	Cahn, A.C.E.	Editor	Dann Cahn is an American film editor who has received the Career Achievement Award from the American Cinema Editors (ACE). Cahn is best known as the head editor of the TV series, I Love Lucy and for his work as the head of post-production of comediene Lucille Ball and Desi Arnaz's Desilu Playhouse. Cahn is known as the father of multicamera editing for his innovation with the Moviola Monster.
Robbie	Carman	Colorist, online editor, author and Apple Certified Trainer	Robbie Carman is a Colorist and co-owner of Amigo Media LLC a small finishing boutique located in Washington, DC with a focus on broadcast television and independent film finishing. Robbie has 12 years of experience in SD and HD projects including dozens of programs for Discovery Networks, National Geographic, PBS, MSNBC and others.

First	Last	Title	Credits/Bio Info
Otto	Cedeno	Livestream, Producer	Otto Cedeno is a Producer at livestream.com and a freelance photographer.
Peter	Chakos, A.C.E.	Editor	Emmy Award nominee, Peter Chakos has produced, directed and edited TV shows such as Will & Grace and The Big Bang Theory and the movie Breakfast of Aliens.
Lew	Comenetz	Engineer, Digital Imaging Technician	Broadcast/HDTV Engineer & Digital Imaging Technician
Jacob	Coonfare	Student, Osceola Fundamental High School	Student, Osceola Fundamental High School in Florida.
Cara	Cosentino	Coordinating Producer, Great Performances, WNET.ORG	Coordinating Producer, Great Performances, WNET.ORG
Sam	Crawford	Director of Engineering, Henninger Media Services	Director of Engineering at Henninger Media Services, Washington, D.C.'s premier production and post-production media company.
Nick	Daimano	Editor	Nick Diamano worked on the Bruce Springsteen Hammersmith Odeon Concert, which was shot on film in 1975 in London.
Mark	Doering-Powell	Director of Photography	Mark Doering-Powell is an Emmy-nominated Director of Photography, a member of the International Cinematographers Guild, Television Academy and Visual Effects Society.
Emannuel "Manny"	Donio	Editor	Freelance editor whose carrer includes working for History Channel, A&E, and WE
Eric	Duke	Owner, All Mobile Video	Eric Duke is Owner and President of All Mobile Video, the country's premier provider of end-to-end video and audio solutions for entertainment, sports, and news programming and events
Tim	Duncan	Editor	Nashville based editor whose experience covers a broad range of linear/nonlinear editing, engineering, systems design, color correction as well as multi-camera video and film production.
Alan	Falkner	Tape Op	Freelance Tape Operator
Mike	Fay	Assistant Editor	Mike Fay is an assistant editor who has worked with directors Ang Lee and Jonathan Demme
Jim	Feeley	Documentary Producer	Jim Feeley is a producer, journalist, and occasional audio mixer at POV Media, a northern California production company.
Matt	Foglia, C.A.S.	Re-Recording Mixer	Matt Foglia's 15 year experience includes being a sound engineer for Sony Music Studios and Chief Audio Engineer for PostWorks New York. Matt has mixed hundreds of hours of television programming for networks such as Bravo, Comedy Central, Discovery, ESPN, HBO, MTV, PBS, the Sundance Channel, truTV and VH1. Matt is currently Associate Professor, Middle Tennessee State University, Sound For Picture Digital Audio Technology Recording Studio Techniques.

(*Continued*)

First	Last	Title	Credits/Bio Info
Jerry	Foley	Director, The Late Show with David Letterman	Jerry Foley has been directing the Late Show with David Letterman since 1995. He has received five Emmy nominations and six Directors Guild Award nominations. In May of 2003 he became a Producer of Late Show while continuing as Director.
Mark	Franco	Head of Electric FX, Electric Entertainment in Los Angeles	Mark Franco's career in visual and special effects spans almost thirty years. He has worked on some of the most epic films of all time including global blockbusters "Titanic" and "Independence Day." Franco's additional credits include special-effects driven films like "Armageddon," "How the Grinch Stole Christmas," "The Patriot," "Batman Forever," "Batman & Robin," and many more.
Ron	Friedman	Associate General Counsel at Adobe Systems Incorporated	Associate General Counsel at Adobe Systems Incorporated
Jeremy	Garchow	Editor & Post Production Supervisor, Maday Productions	Jeremy Garchow is an Editor & Post Production Supervisor at Maday Productions. Jeremy has been working on high end corporate communication pieces, commercials and promotional material for clients like Harley - Davidson and also local spots for Chicago based businesses. Jeremy also completed a documentary headed up by a budding Chicago producer for PBS in late 2006.
Keith	Garde	Founder of PKA Management	Keith Garde, founder of PKA Management, brings over 25 years of experience in recording/touring artist management, serving as co-manager from the late 80's through to 1995 for the internationally renowned rock group Aerosmith and continues to consult for the group today. His experience includes: business development; organizational systems, structure and processes; strategic alliance management; branding and imaging as well as having architected fan club management subscriptions and fan experience programs.
Steve	Gibby	Multiple Emmy Award winning television producer/director.	Multiple Emmy-winning television producer/director. Over forty national television awards. Contributor as a producer, director, editor, scriptwriter, and cameraman to over 700 national television programs that aired on ESPN, Fox Sports Net, OLN, NBC, UPN, TLC, A&E, Speed Channel, and Comcast.
Les	Goldberg	Owner, LMG Inc.	Les Goldberg, Owner LMG Inc. in Orlando, FL, nationwide supplier of video, audio, and lighting support services for Fortune 500 companies across the nation.
Brian	Gonosey	Editor, Electric Entertainment	Brian Gonosey is editor at Electric Entertainment, a full-service film, television and new media production company and studio in Los Angeles.

First	Last	Title	Credits/Bio Info
Peter	Gray	Director of Photography and Digital Image Technician	Veteran Director of Photography, Writer, Producer, and Director whose experience in the Film and Television inductry spans over 30 years
Barry	Green	Producer	Emmy®-winning producer and resident tech guru at DVXUser.com
Joe	Guzzi	President, TAI Audio	Joe Guzzi is President at TAI Audio, which provides audio and communications solutions for the broadcast film and video industries. Their clients include network television producers, production companies, special event and convention groups, sporting event companies, churches and law enforcement.
Mark	Haefeli	Director & Producer. President & Founder of Mark Haefeli Productions.	Mark Haefeli is President of Mark Haefeli Productions in NYC, an electronic marketing firm specializing in video and film production for corporate and entertainment communication platforms.
Evan	Haiman	Executive Producer, Music & Entertainment at HDNet	Evan Haiman, Executive Producer, Music & Entertainment at HDNet, leads development and production of concerts, music shows, and entertainment specials, and will review pitches and develops new entertainment programming for the network. Haiman oversees productions of HDNet's current original entertainment series, including "Hollywood HD," "Higher Definition," and "Get Out!"
Christof	Halasz	Multicamera Workflow Supervisor	Workflow Supervisor at www.Livecut.at in Vienna
Gary	Halvorson	Director	Gary Halvorson is a world renowned director that has excelled in three of the top multi-cam categories, music, sit-coms, and live events. Credits include: The Met: Live in HD, Great Performances, Friends, The Macy's Thanksgiving Day Parade
Hamish	Hamilton	Director	Hamish Hamilton has directed several concert DVDs for U2, Britney Spears as well as the MTV Video Music Awards, MTV Europe Music Awards and Victoria's Secret Fashion Show in 2008. He was also the director of the 82nd Annual Academy Awards.
Richard	Harrington	Founder of Rhed Pixel in Virgina	Richard Harrington is an author and certified instructor for Adobe, Apple, and Avid, Rich is a practiced expert in motion graphic design and digital video. His producing skills were also recognized by AV Video Multimedia Producer Magazine who named him as one of the Top Producers of 2004. He is the founder of Rhed Pixel in Virginia

(*Continued*)

First	Last	Title	Credits/Bio Info
Alan	Heim, A.C.E.,	VP of American Cinema Editors and VP of Motion Pictures Editor's Guild	With a career spanning over 30 years, Alan Heim, A.C.E. is one of Hollywood's most distinguished editors. Alan won an Oscar, BAFTA and Eddie award for All That Jazz. He was also nominated for an Oscar for Network. Alan began his editing career on Sidney Lumet's The Seagull, and went on to cut Lenny, Hair, American History X, The Notebook and many more. He has worked with Mel Brooks, Milos Forman, George Roy Hill, Nick Cassavetes, Martha Coolidge, John Hughes and Stephen Frears. He is currently President of American Cinema Editors (A.C.E) and the producer of The Cutting Edge: The Magic of Movie Editing.
David	Helfand	Emmy-nominated Editor	Emmy-nominated Editor who worked on Friends, Weeds and That 70's Show.
Dave	Hilmer	Emmy Award Winning Camera Operator	Emmy Award Winning Camera Operator
Philip	Hodgets	President, Intelligent Assistance	Philip Hodgets is President of Intelligent Assistance. He is a technologist, editor, industry pundit, podcasting veteran and specialist in new distribution systems, Philip Hodgetts has 25 years experience in production and post, more than 10 of them in the digital realm.
David	Horn	Executive Producer of Great Performances PBS series	Executive Producer of Great Performances PBS series
Nick	Houy	Assistant Editor and Sound Recordist	Assistant Editor and Sound Recordist
Maysie	Hoy, A.C.E.	Editor	Maysie Hoy, A.C.E. editor at Tyler Perry Studios
Matthew	Ilardo	Editor	Editor at the Rachel Ray Show
Zoran	Jevremov	Editor	Zoran Jevremov is a Primetime Emmy Award Winner for Outstanding Multi-Camera Picture Editing for a Miniseries, Movie or a Special for "Paul McCartney in Red Square"
Larry	Jordan	President, Larry Jordan & Associates	Larry Jordan & Associates, Inc. provides high-quality, engaging training and information through a variety of media worldwide. They cover video production and post-production for practicing professionals and students, with an emphasis on Apple's Final Cut Studio.
Andreas	Kiel	Software Developer	Andreas Kiel is a software developer at Spherico.com which specializes in consulting, sales and postproduction for digital video
Donald	Kilgore	Cinematographer, Editor, and Visual Effects Artist	Donald Kilgore is an experienced Cinematographer, Editor, and Visual Effects Artist with over 10 years of industry experience.

First	Last	Title	Credits/Bio Info
Gary	Kleiner	Editor	Gary Kleiner is producer of training videos for Sony Vegas® and Sony DVD Architect®, and original co-author of one of the most popular plugins for Sony Vegas, Excalibur which can be accessed at vegastrainingtools.com
Michael	Krulik	Principal Applications Specialist - Avid Technology	Michael Krulik is Principal Applications Editor, Avid Technology Inc.
Oli	Laperal Jr	President RSVP Film Studios	Oli Laperal Jr. is President of RSVP Film Studios in the Philippines which is responsible for the production of hundreds of local film spots for all the major advertising agencies, foreign feature films, documentaries, MTV's and news strings. Laperal operates the largest, most complete and most comprehensive film production facility and rental house in the Philippines.
Tim	Leavitt	Freelance Assistant Editor	Assistant Editor at Brad Lachman Productions and Khartoum Films. Credits include The Apprentice.
Dan	Lebental, A.C.E.	Editor, Owner, Splice, Inc.	Dan Lebental, A.C.E. is an editor and Owner of Splice-inc.com based in Hollywood. Credits include Iron Man 1 & 2
Meredith	Lerner	Producer	Meredith Lerner is a field producer for broadcast television programs.
Roger	Macie	Owner, Macie Video Service	Roger Macie is Owner of Macie Video Service, which has been serving the Broadcast and Professional Video Industry in Massachusetts since 1990.
Steve	Martin	President and Founder of Ripple Training.	Steve is the president and founder of Ripple Training. Steve has over 18 years of experience as an editor, producer and trainer. He has taught workshops at NAB, Macworld, DV Expo, QuickTime Live and the American Film Institute. He is currently a lead instructor for Apple's Certified Pro training program
Craig	McKay	Editor	Craig McKay is a renowned film editor who was nominated for an Oscar for "Silence of the Lambs"
Karen	McLaughlin	AD, Met Cinemacasts, The Metropolitan Opera	Intermissions Associate Director of the Met cinemacasts, The Metropolitan Opera, New York
Steve	Modica	CTO - Small Tree Communications	Steve Modica is the Chief Technical Officer of Small Tree Communications. Mr. Modica brings over 15 years of experience in the field of high performance operating systems to the company.
Peter	Moll	Director	Peter Moll is a veteran rock-and-roll video director who's toured with Van Halen, Guns 'n' Roses, and Elton John
Don	Moran	Owner, Omaha Wedding Video	As the owners of Omaha Wedding Video, Don Moran and his wife Miriam are committed to producing the highest quality wedding and event video productions for their clients.

(*Continued*)

First	Last	Title	Credits/Bio Info
Nelson	Navarro	Editor and EVS Operator	Nelson Navarro is an editor and EVS operartor with more than 10 years of experience.
Bruce	Nazarian	The Digital Guy	MPSE, award-winning DVD producer, DVD consultant and author and President of the DVD Association.
Mike	Noles	Video Engineer	
Chuck	O'Neil	Director, The Daily Show with Jon Stewart	Emmy nominated Director of The Daily Show with Jon Stewart
Tom	Ohanion	Editor and inventor	Thomas A. Ohanian is an accomplished strategist, designer, and inventor of digital media products and workflow solutions with over 23 years in the digital media industries. He is an Academy Award® and a two-time Emmy® recipient. An founding employee of Avid Technology and designer of Avid Media Composer's multicam mode.
Mitch	Owgang	Producer, Great Performances Series, PBS	Producer, Great Performances Series, PBS
Pilot	Peppler	Founder of Los Angeles based PilotWare	Founder of Los Angeles based PilotWare, database system for film and TV.
Oliver	Peters	Owner, Oliver Peters Post Productions	Owner, Oliver Peters Post Productions in Orlando, FL which offers Creative Editorial Services, Color Grading, Interactive Design, Post Production Supervision/Project Management and Workflow Consultation.
Mike	Phillips	Principal Product Designer, Avid Technology Inc	Principal Product Designer, Avid Technology Inc
Dennis	Radeke	Business Development Manager, Adobe Systems, Inc.	Business Development Manager, Adobe Systems, Inc.
Mark	Raudonis	VP Post Production, Bunim-Murray Productions	Vice President of Post Production for Bunim-Murray Productions, Mark Raudonis oversees the editing and final finishing of all BMP shows. Mark began his career as a documentary film cameraman for PBS-TV station WMPB in Baltimore. As a freelance editor, Mark worked on many network shows, receiving an Emmy nomination for "The Laugh-In 20th Anniversary Special."
Jeff	Ravitz	Principal Lighting Director, Visual Terrain	Jeff Ravitz was awarded a Primetime Emmy for the Bruce Springsteen and the E Street Band special on HBO, and the 2005 and 2006 Los Angeles Emmys for El Grito de Mexico for Univision. He was previously nominated for Cher…Live At The Mirage.
Debbie	Rein	Osceola Fundamental High School, Avid Certified Instructor	Osceola Fundamental High School, Avid Certified Instructor

First	Last	Title	Credits/Bio Info
Ted	Rich	A.C.E.	Ted Rich is a producer and editor who received a lifetime achievement award from the American Cinema Editors (A.C.E.). Rich was one of the first assistants to use work with the Moviola Monster on the I love Lucy show and went on to run all of postproduction for MTM.
Bob	Russo	Applications Specialist, AVID Technology	Applications Specialist, AVID Technology
Maurice	Schechter	Chief Engineer, DuArt Film Labs in NYC	Chief Engineer, DuArt Film Labs in NYC
Peter	Schneider	Partner, Gotham Sound & Communication in NYC	Peter Schneider is an audio mixer and partner, Gotham Sound and Communications, a full service sound resource, housing a rental, sales, and service department stocked with the very latest in audio technology.
Mark	Schubin	Engineer & Technology Consultant	Engineer & Technology Consultant
Bruce	Sharpe	Founder, Singular Software	Bruce Sharpe is Founder of Singular Software located near Vancouver, British Columbia. Well known for such softwares as The Levelator® and PluralEyes which automatically syncs audio and video clips without the need for timecode, clappers or any special preparation.
Mike	Shore		
Scott	Simmons	Editor	Scott Simmons is a Nashville based commercial, television, music video, and multicamera editor.
Tim	Squyres	Editor	Tim Squyres is an American film editor with about 30 film credits. He has had an extended collaboration with the Taiwanese director Ang Lee, having edited all but one of Lee's feature films. Squyres' work on Crouching Tiger, Hidden Dragon (2000) earned nominations for the Academy Award for Best Film Editing, the BAFTA Award for Best Editing, and the American Cinema Editors Eddie Award.
Billy	Steinberg	Video Engineer	Billy Steinberg is an Emmy Award winner for Outstanding Technical Direction/Camera/Video for a Special. He is a renowned engineer.
Alan	Stewart	Freelance Editor	Freelance Editor
Troy	Takaki, A.C.E.	Editor	Troy Takaki, A.C.E. is a Film Editor at Sony Pictures Entertainment
Cheri	Tanimura	Associate Producer, Rules of Engagement	Cheri Tanimura produced TV shows such as Rules of Engagement, Dear John, and Oh Baby.
Tom	Tcimpidis	Technical Director and Cameraman	Three time Emmy Award winning Technical Director and Cameraman
David	Tedeschi	Editor	David Tedeschi is an Emmy nominated editor who curently is a film editor for Sikelia Films. Credits include: Shine A Light, No Direction Home, The Sheild & The Blues.

(*Continued*)

First	Last	Title	Credits/Bio Info
David	Thaler	Founder, Thaler Films	David Thaler is founder of Thaler Films, an Emmy Award winning production company providing video production and distribution services to the broadcast, film, and corporate industries in Hauppauge, NY.
Eli	Tishberg	Director/Editor	Eli Tishberg is a veteran New York director/editor with notable credits that include MTV Music Video Awards, VH1 Storytellers with Bruce Springsteen and Jay-Z, and 70 other artists, and live concerts and documentaries featuring The Ramones, Sheryl Crow, Phish and Bon Jovi.
Richard	Topham, C.A.S.		Richard Topham has experience in just about all aspects of sound and recording in productions and post-productions, Rich has worked with many major films, televisions series, sitcoms, commercials and industrial videos. His clients include Paramount, Universal, Warner Brothers and all major networks, awarding him six Emmy Awards for sound recording. Rich is a member of Cinema Audio Society (CAS), Society of Motion Pictures Technicians and Engineers (SMPTE), Audio Engineering Society (AES) and National Technical Investigators' Association (NATIA).
Bouke	Váhl	Software Developer	Bouke Váhl from VideoToolshed in The Netherlands is one of the developers of Livecut.
Alexis	Van Hurkman	Colorist, Writer, Director	Alexis Van Hurkman is a NYC based Colorist, Writer, and Director. He has color-corrected programs that have aired on Mojo HD, The History Channel, BBC Four, and WNET
Ray	Volkema	Editor, HD Net	Ray Volkema currently of HDNet Concerts, has been a director of live television and post production editor of sports, news, and entertainment, including several olympics and over 50 concerts. He has over 30 years experience.
John	Walker	Executive Producer, Great Performances, PBS	Executive Producer, Great Performances, PBS
Mark	Weingartner	Oscar nominated sound mixer	Oscar nominated sound mixer
Marc	Wielage	Colorist & Owner, Cinesound/LA	Colorist & Owner, Cinesound/LA
Richard	Wirth	Technical Director	Richard Wirth is Technical Director of The Rachael Ray Show
Laura	Young	Editor	Laura Young is an Emmy nominated editor based in NYC.
John	Zale	Director of Educational Development, WEVA	Director of Educational Development, Weddings and Events Videographers Association (WEVA).
Bob	Zelin	Systems Integrator	Bob Zelin is President of Rescue 1, Inc., a systems integration, and video maintenance service based in Orlando, FL
Thom	Zimney	Editor	Thom Zimney is a veteran editor who has won an Emmy award for Bruce Springsteen and the E Street Band: Live in New York City (2001).

COMPANION DVD CONTENTS

Register on-line to subscribe to future downloads of additional multicamera footage, blogs and training updates at: www.MasteringMulticam.com

1. Bonus Chapters:

A) Supporting The Director
B) HDSLR and Multicam
C) On-Set Editing
D) No Such Thing as a Firewire Drive
E) How and When to Use Auxiliary Timecode
F) Genlocking And Tri-Level Sync

2. Multicamera Video Clips

The companion DVD also consists of some very exciting multicamera footage from two of the greatest musical "Sirs" Elton John and Paul McCartney. Both clips are exclusive to this book and have never been released. Band on the Run is a "leftover" track from Paul McCartney: The Space Within US concert film that was edited by myself and Zoran Jevromov. Elton's clip is recorded live from his 2009 tour specifically for this book and as part of a technology test for Telestream's Pipeline products. I captured all the clips live on-location concurrently onto one MacPro tower with an a eSata RAID. My Final Cut Pro multicamera line cut of "Love Lies Bleeding" was edited and finished before the captureing was complete.

A) Paul McCartney Live in Concert

Never before released performance of Band on the Run (2:30). Show 200 has 13 angles in ProRes 422 (Proxy) HD 720/23.98 including: Techno crane, dolly, rail cam, cable cam, jib and handheld. Seven bonus angles are included from Show 100. Master audio track included for layback to show 200.

Paul McCartney footage courtesy MPL Tours, Inc
Executive producer: Sir Paul McCartney
Directed by Mark Haefeli, MHP3
Master audio tracks mixed by David Kahne
For MPL Publishing: Krisstina Hawks
©MPL Tours Inc. All Rights Reserved

Exercises

a) Group individual show 200 angles by source timecode.
b) Group show 200 angles with bonus angles from show 100 with manual sync points. Use Sync Map to find inpoints or use music.
c) Adjust for sync drift. Re group as necessary.
d) Make Syncmap with multiclip from show 100 on track one and individual shots from show 2 in sync on vertical tracks above. Cut in "Magic Momments"
e) ThrashGroup® multi-clips from sync map.
f) Audio Layback-manually. (Show 200)
g) Duplicate group clips for PIP FX.

B) Elton John Live in Concert

© Universal Music - All Rights Reserved.
Love Lies Bleeding (1:00) 5 angles and 1 linecut.
ProRes 422 (LT) NTSC 720x480 29.97
Elton John footage courtesy HST Management, Ltd
Directed by Peter Moll, Gray Matter Entertainment, Inc.
For Elton John: Keith Bradley, Johnny Barbus, Jon Howard, George Kangis, Clive Banks, and Sanctuary Group plc.
Music Publishing courtesy Universal Music Publishing Group, Brian Lambert, Sarah Maniquis, Jim Doyle, Responsive Music
"LOVE LIES BLEEDING" Words and Music by Elton John, Bernie Taupin © UNIVERSAL-SONGS OF POLYGRAM INT., INC. ON BEHALF OF UNIVERSAL/DICK JAMES MUSIC LTD. (BMI) Not for broadcast transmission. All rights reserved. DO NOT DUPLICATE.

Exercises

a) Group line cut with ISOs.
b) Recreate director's line cut and switch out shots.
c) Audio is only on the linecut. Switch video only to maintain soundtrack.
d) Throw out line cut and edit from scratch.
e) Compare your cut to director's line cut.
All video clips that are contained on this DVD are for educational purposes related to training excersises that accompany this book. Please respect the copyrights and do not share these clips electronicaly or otherwise.

For PC and Avid users, please download the ProRes Decoders from the Apple Website before importing these clips. (Please check with your IT departments before loading any software):

http://support.apple.com/downloads/Apple_ProRes_QuickTime_Decoder_1_0_for_Mac

http://support.apple.com/downloads/Apple_ProRes_QuickTime_Decoder_1_0_for_Windows

3. Video Tutorials

The Essentials of Multi-camera Editing: Final Cut Pro Training video clip from RippleTraining.com. Additional video tutorial links are also provided for Avid Media Composer, Sony Vegas and Adobe Premiere Pro

4. Free Applications

AJA DataCalc: AJA DataCalc: The AJA DataCalc application computes storage requirements for professional video and audio media. Designed for video professionals, this application works with all the most popular industry video formats and compression methods, including Apple ProRes, DVCProHD, HDV, XDCAM, DV, CineForm, REDCODE, Avid DNxHD, Apple Intermediate, 16 bit RGB and RGBA, uncompressed, and more. Video standards supported include NTSC, PAL, 1080i, 1080p, 720p, 2K and 4K. (for updates go to www.aja.com)

******AJA DataCalc by AJA Video Systems, Inc. is also available for the iPhone, iTouch and iPad:

http://itunes.apple.com/us/app/aja-datacalc/id343454572?mt=8

SequenceLiner application: full working version free from Spherico.com and Andreas Kiel. (Mac only/FCP)

QT_CHANGE: An application fron Videotoolshed.com that will restripe timecode and add reel names to Quicktime files. This is great for preparing HDSLR footage for editing. Convert H.264 to codec of your choice and set timecode and reels. For Windows version and future updates go online to: http://www.videotoolshed.com/product/42/qtchange

5. Research Links

Weblinks for blogs, research and equipment websites (html)

6. Multicam Madness: Unedited Case Studies:

Chapter 19: Case Study: A Hybrid 10-Camera Red 4k and EFP HD Production—*Journey: Live from Manila*

Chapter 20: Case Study: A Mixed-Platform Workflow—*Paul McCartney: The Space Within Us*

Chapter 21: The Filmed Concert Workflow: The Rolling Stones' *Shine a Light*

Chapter 22: A Thumbnail History of Multicamera Production and Editing

INDEX